500
HEART-HEALTHY
SLOW COOKER
RECIPES

500
HEART-HEALTHY SLOW COOKER RECIPES

COMFORT FOOD FAVORITES THAT BOTH YOUR FAMILY
AND YOUR DOCTOR WILL LOVE

Dick Logue

FAIR WINDS
PRESS
BEVERLY, MASSACHUSETTS

Text © 2010 Dick Logue

First published in the USA in 2010 by
Fair Winds Press, a member of
Quayside Publishing Group
100 Cummings Center
Suite 406-L
Beverly, MA 01915-6101
www.fairwindspress.com

16 15 14 13   4 5 6 7

ISBN-13: 978-1-59233-454-4
ISBN-10: 1-59233-454-7

Library of Congress Cataloging-in-Publication Data available

Printed in the U.S.A.

The information in this book is for educational purposes only. It is not intended to replace the advice of a physician or medical practitioner. Please see your health care provider before beginning any new health program.

Dedication

To all the email correspondents, newsletter subscribers,
and others who encouraged me to continue producing more recipes.
Even though sometimes it seemed like work, their assurances
that it was useful information kept me going.

Contents

Why a Heart-Healthy Slow Cooker Book?

For a number of years, the slow cooker has been one of the most often-used appliances in our kitchen. It can be a real savior for working people, delivering a hot, ready-to-eat meal when you come home from a long day and feel least like cooking. (Not to mention that wonderful aroma that will be filling the house.) It also is good for your food budget, allowing you to use less costly cuts of meat and turn them into fork-tender delicacies. But the sad truth is that a lot of the recipes out there for the slow cooker are not all that great from a health standpoint. Do a quick search online or open a typical slow cooker cookbook and you'll find recipes that are full of more fat, sodium, and calories than are good for you. Of course, most don't include any nutrition analysis, but you can imagine what it would look like for the first slow-cooked dip recipe that comes up on Google, which calls for 2 pounds of Velveeta cheese, plus taco seasoning mix and other high-sodium ingredients.

As someone who's been making recipes more heart-friendly for more than 10 years, that bothered me. It forced people to either eat things that were less healthy than they should or limit their use of the slow cooker. So I decided to take some of the slow cooker recipes that we had used for years, add some new ones, and put together a book that would solve the problem—a book of heart-healthy slow cooker recipes. This is that book.

What Do We Mean By Heart-Healthy?

A fair question is what we really mean by heart-healthy and how these recipes fit that description better than the ones in other slow cooker books. It seems like there is a lot of discussion and some controversy about what really is heart-healthy. But there are a couple of key concepts that I have come to believe in over the years that most mainstream medical people agree with as well. They are as follows:

- Reduced sodium
- Reduced saturated fats and trans fats
- Less dietary cholesterol
- Higher fiber

Let's look at each of these in turn and see why these recipes adhere to these concepts.

Reduced Sodium

As many of you who are familiar with my other books or my website may know, reducing sodium was the first goal of my heart-healthy cooking journey. As a starting point, consider the following facts:

- The United States Food and Drug Administration recommends 2,300 milligrams (mg) of sodium daily for healthy adults.
- The US Department of Agriculture recommends that individuals with hypertension, African Americans, and adults 50 and older should consume no more than 1,500 mg of sodium per day.
- The United Kingdom Recommended Nutritional Intake (RNI) is 1,600 mg daily.
- The National Research Council of the National Academy of Sciences recommends 1,100 to 1,500 mg daily for adults.
- Studies have shown that many people in the United States and Canada routinely consume 2 to 3 times that amount.

Given these figures, it's pretty safe to say that many of us consume more sodium than is good for us. If you already have a history of heart disease or have a family history of it, it's even worse. I know I sound a bit like a zealot in this, but I can honestly say that I felt much better when I first started my low-sodium diet over 10 years ago. And I'm probably in a better position now medically than I was then. All I can say is that it's worked for me and for lots of other people I've talked to.

Reduced Saturated Fats and Trans Fats

These have been shown by a number of studies to be major contributors to high cholesterol. In general, saturated fats are fats that are solid at room temperature. There are several sources of saturated fats. The most common ones are the following:

- Red meats—Beef, pork, and lamb contribute a significant amount of saturated fat to our diets. Many experts recommend reducing the amount of red meat we eat. If you find that difficult, and I admit that I do, the slow cooker can help by allowing you to use leaner cuts of meat.
- Poultry skin—Any slow cooker recipe you look at recommends removing the skin from poultry, thus problem solved.
- Whole fat dairy products—By using other items like cream soups and fat-free evaporated milk in our slow cooker recipes, you won't even notice that you aren't using whole milk or cream for that chowder.
- Tropical oils—We use only healthier oils like olive and canola and don't even miss things like palm and coconut oil.

Trans fats are also called trans-fatty acids. They are produced by adding hydrogen to vegetable oil through a process called hydrogenation. This makes the fat more solid and less likely to spoil. Research has clearly linked trans fats to a number of health problems. The most common sources are margarine and other solid shortenings. In general, I never use them.

Less Dietary Cholesterol

Although there has been some disagreement about how significant the role of eating foods high in cholesterol is in increasing your blood cholesterol, most experts still recommend reducing it. Common sources of dietary cholesterol are the following:

- Egg yolks—I almost never use whole eggs, preferring to use an egg substitute like Egg Beaters that is made from egg whites. I can't tell the difference.
- Organ meats—This is good news for everyone who hates liver. (I happen to like it, but I only eat it once every couple of months.)
- Shellfish—This is another thing I like but try to limit.

Higher Fiber

There have been a number of studies showing the benefits of increasing our fiber intake, not only for heart health, but for many other areas of the body as well. A few key findings are as follows:

- A study published in the May 11, 2000 issue of *The New England Journal of Medicine* reported that diabetic patients who maintained a very high-fiber daily diet lowered their glucose levels by 10 percent.
- A 1976 study by the Veterans Administration Medical Center in Lexington, Kentucky, showed that fiber is useful in treating diabetes, high blood pressure, and obesity and in reducing cholesterol levels.
- Two studies published in *The Lancet* showed that people with high fiber diets suffered from fewer incidents of colon polyps and colon cancer.

So there are a lot of good reasons to add more fiber to your diet, even if you aren't currently being treated for a medical condition that requires it.

In the next section I describe what we've done to bring these recipes in line with these guidelines.

How We Make Recipes Heart-Healthy

Most of the things we've done to make these recipes more heart-friendly involve simple substitutions and changes to the usual ingredients. Some may seem obvious, particularly to anyone who has read any of my other books. Some may be less so. The following are some of the key ones.

Eliminate the Salt

One question that may occur to some people looking over the recipes in this book is, "Why is there no salt in any of the ingredient lists?" That's a fair question and deserves an answer. As I said in the Introduction, I first got involved with heart-healthy cooking because my doctor put me on a low-sodium diet. It took some time and lots of experimentation, but I learned how to cook things that both taste good and are easy to prepare that are still low in sodium. Along the way, we literally threw away our salt shaker. There's one shaker full of light salt (half salt and half salt substitute) on the table. My wife uses that occasionally. Two of my children have given up salt completely, not because they need to for medical reasons, but because they are convinced like I am that it's the healthy thing to do. When I started creating recipes focused on other areas of heart health, going back to using salt wasn't even something I considered. In creating these recipes, I was not as strict about the amount of sodium as I usually am in my own diet. I didn't plan on people buying special sodium-free baking powder that is difficult to find except online. I didn't eliminate most cheeses except Swiss. But I also didn't add any salt. I think if you try the recipes, you'll find that they taste good without it. If you are tempted to add some salt because you think it's needed, I'd suggest that first you try the recipe and see whether you like it without the salt. And if you have trouble with the idea of giving up salt, you might check with your own doctor. I believe that most doctors will agree that in the interest of total health, you are better off without the salt.

Use Lower-Fat Meats and Dairy Products

I already talked about this, but the slow cooker makes it really easy because you can use lean meat, skinned poultry, and fat-free dairy products and no one will even notice.

Use Egg Substitute Instead of Whole Eggs

Again, this is a simple change, and one that won't be noticed. But it can significantly decrease the amount of cholesterol you eat.

Substitute Whole-Grain Products

I've discovered that I like whole-grain products better than the refined ones in most cases. You can use brown rice in place of white, whole-grain pasta, and other whole grains like barley in a number of these recipes. Many of these recipes make stews or other dishes with sauces that are even better over brown rice than white. Give it a try.

Use Healthier Fats

The only fats used in these recipes are healthier oils like olive and canola and unsalted butter. Yes, I know that butter has cholesterol that we are trying to hold down. But it is a lot easier to find than unsalted margarine. And considering the many health problems that may be linked to trans fats in our diet, I've made the personal decision that butter is probably healthier than margarine. Given the choice, I always try to go with the more natural product.

Substitute Healthier Ingredients

In some cases, this is as easy as reading the food labels and picking the healthier option. There are low-fat, low-sodium versions of many soups available. There are no-salt-added tomato products like sauce, paste, chopped and crushed tomatoes, and even ketchup. And they are all available at most large grocery stores. If you go to a store that specializes in organic and gourmet foods like Whole Foods or Trader Joe's, you'll find more options. Seek them out and you'll have more options yourself when looking at recipes.

But this is also where chapter 2 comes in. Many of the items in that chapter are not, in themselves, slow cooker recipes. But they are the building blocks that can allow you to easily create heart-healthy recipes in your slow cooker. For example, the first recipe is for a reduced-sodium soy sauce that contains only 33 mg of sodium per serving, about one-tenth what the lowest commercially available product contains. So now when a recipe calls for ¼ cup (60 ml) of soy sauce, you don't have to immediately discard it as something you are not allowed to have. Other recipes there include low-sodium chili and barbecue sauces, low-fat and low-sodium sausage, no-salt onion soup mix, seasoning blends and dressing mixes, and even a low-fat and low-sodium baking mix to use in place of Bisquick. I usually make these up in large quantities and store them in the refrigerator or freezer to have on hand. I realize that depending on where you live it may not be easy to find heart-healthy options on your grocer's shelves. So my answer is, "If you can't find it, make it."

Why the Slow Cooker Is Good for Heart-Healthy Cooking

Of course, as I said at the beginning of this introduction, there is nothing inherently healthy about slow cooker cooking. But there are a few features that you can take advantage of that make the slow cooker a friend in your quest to eat heart-healthy.

Perhaps the most readily noticeable thing is that it's easier to cook lower-fat recipes in the slow cooker. Not only do leaner cuts of meat cook well in the slow cooker, they actually cook better, ending up more tender and with more flavor than if you cook them by conventional means. Cooking lean meat quickly often toughens it, while boiling it breaks it down to the point where it has no flavor. Long, slow cooking makes it tender and keeps the flavor, the ideal situation. You'll find that the beef recipes in this book usually call for the lean cuts like round steak or roast, which are both lower in fat and cheaper. On the chicken side of the aisle, most recipes recommend that you remove the fat and skin before slow cooking. This also supports our desire to cut back on saturated fats since the skin is where most of the fat in poultry resides.

But perhaps the biggest advantage is one that is not so obvious. One of the most common things I hear from many people that prevents them from cooking heart-healthy meals is that is takes time. If you are serious about reducing your sodium eating less fat, increasing the amount of fiber in your diet, you will almost certainly have to cook more things from scratch. You just aren't going to find that kind of nutrition in the quick and easy prepackaged mixes and frozen dinners. However, the slow cooker can cut your preparation time, particularly in the evening when you are tired and don't feel like cooking. You can throw things in it in the morning, and when you get home, dinner is ready. Or if you want to make something like pasta sauce that benefits from long, slow cooking, the slow cooker can handle that unattended. And that is a real advantage that making things from scratch the conventional way does not offer.

How This Book Came About

If you've seen some of my other books, a lot of this material will be familiar to you. This is just the next step in a journey, one that I've been on and one that I'm trying to help others with. Perhaps the best way to start in telling you who I am is by telling you who I'm not. I'm not a doctor. I'm not a dietician. I'm not a professional chef. What I *am* is an ordinary person just like you who has some special dietary needs. What I am going to do is give you 500 recipes that I have made for myself and my family using the slow cooker. Some of these have been in our recipe file for a long while. Others are relatively new. But they all incorporate what I've learned about heart healthy cooking, as I explained earlier in this chapter. Many of them will seem familiar to you since they are the kind of things people cook in their own kitchens all the time, but they are modified to make them healthier without losing the flavor.

I've enjoyed cooking most of my life. I guess I started in seriously about the time my mother went back to work when I was 12 or so. In those days, it was simple stuff like burgers and hot dogs and spaghetti. But the interest stayed. After I married my wife, we got pretty involved in some food-related stuff, like growing vegetables in our garden, making bread and other baked goods, canning and jelly making, that kind of thing. She always said that my "mad chemist" cooking was an outgrowth of the time I spent in college as a chemistry major, and she might be right.

Some of you may already know me from my website (www.lowsodiumcooking.com) and newsletter or from my other books focused on low-sodium, low-cholesterol, high-fiber, and low-glycemic index recipes. I started thinking about heart-healthy cooking after being diagnosed with congestive heart failure in 1999. One of the first, and biggest, things I had to deal with was the doctor's insistence that I follow a low sodium diet: 1,200 mg a day or less. At first, like many people, I found it easiest to just avoid the things that had a lot of sodium in them. But I was bored. And I was convinced that there had to be a way to create low-sodium versions of the food I missed. So I learned all kinds of *new* cooking things. I researched where to get low-sodium substitutes for the things that I couldn't have any more, bought cookbooks, and basically re-did my whole diet. And I decided to try to share this information with others who may be in the same position I had been in. I started a website to share recipes and information. I sent out an email newsletter with recipes that now has over 18,000 subscribers. And I wrote my first book, *500 Low Sodium Recipes*.

Along the way, I also discovered that there were other areas of the diet besides sodium that were important. When I was told that my blood sugar levels indicated that I was a borderline diabetic, I became interested in the role of carbohydrates in the diet. I became more aware of the work that had been done on the glycemic index and glycemic load and began incorporating these concepts into the food we prepared and ate. Each of these adventures eventually became a new book. And now I've decided to combine all that knowledge into a collection of recipes for the slow cooker.

How Is the Nutritional Information Calculated?

The nutritional information included with these recipes was calculated using the AccuChef program. It calculates the values using the latest US Department of Agriculture Standard reference nutritional database. I've been using this program since I first started trying to figure out how much sodium was in the recipes I've created. It's inexpensive, easy to use, and has a number of really handy features. AccuChef is available online from www.accuchef.com. They offer a free trial version if you want to try it out, and the full version costs less than $20.

Of course, that implies that these figures are estimates. Every brand of tomatoes, or any other product, is a little different in nutritional content. These figures were calculated using products that I buy here in southern Maryland. If you use a different brand, your nutrition figures may be different. Use the nutritional analysis as a guideline in determining whether a recipe is right for your diet.

1

Slow Cooker Tips and Techniques

What Exactly Is a Slow Cooker?

In general terms, a slow cooker is a countertop electric appliance that cooks food at relatively low temperatures, allowing long periods of unattended cooking. It was originally invented by the Naxon Utilities Corporation as a bean cooker. The Rival Company bought Naxon in 1970 and introduced the first Crock-Pot in 1971. The name is often used generically to mean a slow cooker. The brand now belongs to Sunbeam Products, a subsidiary of Jarden Corporation, which has a website at www.crock-pot.com. A number of other companies also make slow cookers.

Slow cookers generally are round or oval and contain a removable stoneware liner where the food is placed. Electric heating elements are in the outer metal part of the cooker, on the bottom, and sometimes up the sides. Some of the earlier cookers did not have removable liners. We've still got one of those buried in a kitchen cabinet, but we don't use it very often because it's a lot more difficult to clean. Most slow cookers have at least two heat settings: low or high. The low setting generally corresponds to a temperature of about 170 to 200 degrees Fahrenheit (77 to 93 degrees Celsius) and the high setting to 250 to 300 degrees Fahrenheit (120 to 150 degrees Celsius) or higher. Temperatures will be higher near the heating elements, on the bottom, and along the sides. Newer cookers may have a lot more options, including more than two temperature settings, automatic timers, "keep warm" options, and the ability to program them for things like cooking on high for an hour, then on low for five hours automatically. Some of those features are nice to have, but they are not essential. Most of the recipes here don't use those features since my cooker is about 15 years old and doesn't have them. Cookers come in a variety of sizes, from less than a quart to seven quarts or more. Cookers usually have a glass lid that helps to hold in heat and keep moisture from escaping.

Tips for Slow Cooker Success

The following tips will help to ensure that you are pleased with the result of your slow cooking. (Yes, I know that some of the recipes in this book don't follow all these rules.)

- Fill the slow cooker one-half to two-thirds full. If you fill it to the top, foods may not cook properly or will take longer to cook. If the level is lower, the foods may cook too quickly. If you cook for different numbers of people at different times, you may want to have several slow cookers of different sizes.
- Don't lift the lid, especially if you are cooking on the low setting. Each time you lift the lid, enough heat will escape that the cooking time should be extended by 20 to 30 minutes.
- For safe cooking, always thaw meat or poultry before putting it into a slow cooker. Frozen food takes too long to thaw and get to a safe cooking temperature.
- Foods cooked on the bottom of the slow cooker cook faster and will be more moist because they are immersed in the simmering liquid.
- Fresh root vegetables, such as potatoes, carrots, and onions should be placed in the bottom of the pot, under the meat, for faster cooking. They tend to cook more slowly than meat. Cut them into bite-sized pieces so they cook faster and more evenly.
- Add softer vegetables like tomatoes, mushrooms, and zucchini during the last 45 minutes of cooking time if you don't want them to be very soft.
- Buy roasts and other large cuts of meat that will fit in your slow cooker or trim them to fit. Trim extra fat from meat. This is not only healthier, but it will allow the meat to cook more evenly.
- Use cheaper cuts of meat. Not only do you save money, but these meats work better in the slow cooker. Cheaper cuts of meat have less fat, which makes them more suited to slow-cooker cooking. Moist, long cooking times result in very tender meats.

- Ground meat should usually be browned before adding it to the slow cooker. Larger pieces of meat can be browned before cooking, but this step isn't necessary. Browning will add color and flavor.
- Remove the skin from poultry. It will end up flabby and rubbery anyway, and it contains the majority of the fat in poultry.
- Seafood should usually be added during the last hour of cooking time, or it will overcook and have a rubbery texture.
- Dairy products should usually be added during the last half hour of cooking time. They tend to break down if cooked too long.
- Long-grain converted rice works best for long cooking times. If using rice, you should not reduce the amount of liquid when converting a recipe for the slow cooker.
- Pasta quickly overcooks in the slow cooker. Cook pasta separately until it is just starting to soften and then add it during the last half hour of cooking.
- You can thicken the juices by removing the lid and cooking on high for the last half hour of cooking time. If there is a lot of liquid to be thickened, dissolve a tablespoon or two of cornstarch in cold water and stir it in when you turn the heat to high.
- Slow cookers sometimes dilute flavors over a long period because of the amount of moisture generated. Taste and add more garlic powder, onion powder, pepper, or herbs and spices as needed near the end of cooking.
- At altitudes above 3,500 feet (1 km), you may need to add 30 minutes or more to the cooking time.

Slow Cooker Safety

There have been questions raised about the safety of cooking at low temperatures. It is true that if food is held at too low a temperature for too long, bacteria that would be a health concern could grow. However, used properly the slow cooker produces a safe cooking environment. Follow these tips to ensure that you don't have any problems.

- Keep food refrigerated before putting it in the slow cooker. Having food at room temperature provides an environment that is conducive to bacteria growth.
- Thaw frozen foods before placing them in the slow cooker to allow it to get to the proper operating temperature.
- To get the food up to temperature faster, heat the liquid before adding it to the cooker.

- If possible, cook on high for the first hour to get the food temperature up, and then reduce to low for the remainder of the time. Some newer cooker models can be programmed to do this automatically.
- Keep the lid on to help maintain the temperature. Resist the temptation to peek; it will be all right on its own.
- If your cooker has a "keep warm" setting, use that to maintain the food temperature once cooking is finished. If not, remove the food when the cooker is finished and refrigerate any leftovers promptly.
- To check that your cooker heats properly, fill it two-thirds full of water, turn it to low, cover, and let it cook for 8 hours without removing the lid. Remove the lid and check the temperature with a cooking thermometer. The water temperature should be at least 170 degrees Fahrenheit (77 degrees Celsius).

Converting Recipes for the Slow Cooker

Many regular recipes can be successfully converted to use the slow cooker. Some types of food fit the slow cooking method better than others. Because you generally need some liquid, foods like soups, stews, and roasts are usually good candidates. The following guidelines will help you in converting your favorite recipes to the slow cooker.

- Many slow cooker recipes recommend cooking for 8 to 10 hours on low, so this is usually a good starting point. Some recipes recommend using the high setting based on the food. For example, beef cuts will be better when cooked on low for 8 to 10 hours to get a more tender texture, while chicken can be cooked on high for 2½ to 3 hours.
- One hour of cooking on the high setting is approximately equal to 2 to 2½ hours on low.
- Reduce the amount of liquid used in most oven recipes when using the slow cooker since it retains moisture that usually evaporates when cooking in the oven. You will normally end up with more liquid at the end of the cooking time, not less. A general rule is to reduce liquids by half, unless rice or pasta is in the dish.
- Herbs and spices may need to be increased. Ground spices tend to lose some flavor during the long cooking. Add ground spices during the last hour of cooking to avoid this.
- Pasta, seafood, and milk do not hold up well during long cooking. Add these about 2 hours before the end when using the low setting or 1 hour on high. Evaporated milk can be added at the beginning of cooking.

- Dry beans can be soaked or cooked overnight on low in the slow cooker. Drain and combine with other ingredients. If your recipe includes tomatoes or other acidic ingredients, make sure the beans are tender before adding the acidic foods.
- Dense vegetables like potatoes, carrots, and other root vegetables should be cut no larger than 1 inch (2.5 cm) thick and placed in the bottom of the pot since they take longer to cook.
- If the conventional cooking time is 15 to 30 minutes, cooking time in a slower cooker on low should be about 4 to 6 hours.
- If the conventional cooking time is 30 to 60 minutes, cooking time in a slow cooker on low should be about 6 to 8 hours.
- If the conventional cooking time is 1 to 3 hours, cooking time in a slow cooker on low should be about 8 to 16 hours.

2

Some Heart-Healthy Basic Ingredients

As I explained in the introduction, these items are building blocks that are used in the rest of the recipes. Most reduce the amount of sodium, but a few target things like fat. They are handy things to have on hand.

Low-Sodium Soy Sauce

Sodium is definitely connected to heart health. Soy sauce, even the reduced-sodium kinds, contains more sodium than many people's diets can stand. A teaspoonful often contains at least a quarter of the amount of sodium that is recommended for a healthy adult per day. If you have heart disease or are African American, the daily amount of sodium recommended is even less. This sauce gives you real soy sauce flavor while holding the sodium to a level that should fit in most people's diets.

4 tablespoons (24 g) sodium-free beef bouillon

¼ cup (60 ml) cider vinegar

2 tablespoons (40 g) molasses

1½ cups (355 ml) water, boiling

⅛ teaspoon black pepper

⅛ teaspoon ginger

¼ teaspoon garlic powder

¼ cup (60 ml) low-sodium soy sauce

Combine ingredients, stirring to blend thoroughly. Pour into jars. Cover and seal tightly. It may be kept refrigerated indefinitely.

Yield: 48 servings

Per serving: 10 g water; 6 calories (13% from fat, 11% from protein, 76% from carb); 0 g protein; 0 g total fat; 0 g saturated fat; 0 g monounsaturated fat; 0 g polyunsaturated fat; 1 g carb; 0 g fiber; 1 g sugar; 3 mg phosphorus; 4 mg calcium; 0 mg iron; 33 mg sodium; 19 mg potassium; 3 IU vitamin A; 0 mg ATE vitamin E; 0 mg vitamin C; 0 mg cholesterol

Low-Sodium Teriyaki Sauce

The story on this recipe is the same as the soy sauce. In this case, you can sometimes find some commercial teriyaki sauces that aren't too high to sodium. But this one is much lower and to my mind tastes as good, if not better.

(continued on page 24)

1 cup (235 ml) low-sodium soy sauce (see recipe page 23)

1 tablespoon (15 ml) sesame oil

2 tablespoons (28 ml) mirin wine

½ cup (100 g) sugar

3 cloves garlic, crushed

Two ½-inch (1.3 cm) slices ginger root

Dash black pepper

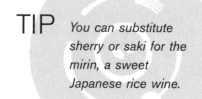

TIP *You can substitute sherry or saki for the mirin, a sweet Japanese rice wine.*

Combine all ingredients in a saucepan and heat until sugar is dissolved. Store in the refrigerator.

Yield: 20 servings

Per serving: 10 g water; 35 calories (18% from fat, 8% from protein, 74% from carb); 1 g protein; 1 g total fat; 0 g saturated fat; 0 g monounsaturated fat; 0 g polyunsaturated fat; 6 g carb; 0 g fiber; 5 g sugar; 14 mg phosphorus; 2 mg calcium; 0 mg iron; 80 mg sodium; 24 mg potassium; 0 IU vitamin A; 0 mg ATE vitamin E; 0 mg vitamin C; 0 mg cholesterol

Chili Sauce

I've got to admit, I've never been a really big fan of the bottled chili sauce. I much prefer the flavor of this chili sauce, which was adapted from a recipe from the American Heart Association, to the kind found in stores. There are enough veggies in it to give it something more than a glorified ketchup taste. It keeps well in the refrigerator for weeks, and you could freeze it if you wanted.

2 cups (360 g) canned diced no-salt-added tomatoes

1 can (8 ounces, or 225 g) no-salt-added tomato sauce

½ cup (80 g) onion, chopped

½ cup (100 g) sugar

½ cup (50 g) celery, chopped

½ cup (75 g) green bell pepper, chopped

1 tablespoon (15 ml) lemon juice

1 tablespoon (15 g) brown sugar

1 tablespoon (20 g) molasses

¼ teaspoon hot pepper sauce

⅛ teaspoon cloves

⅛ teaspoon cinnamon

⅛ teaspoon black pepper

⅛ teaspoon basil

⅛ teaspoon tarragon

½ cup (120 ml) cider vinegar

Combine all ingredients in a large saucepan. Bring to a boil, reduce heat, and simmer uncovered 1½ hours or until mixture is reduced to half its original volume.

Yield: 48 servings

Per serving: 20 g water; 15 calories (2% from fat, 5% from protein, 94% from carb); 0 g protein; 0 g total fat; 0 g saturated fat; 0 g monounsaturated fat; 0 g polyunsaturated fat; 4 g carb; 0 g fiber; 3 g sugar; 5 mg phosphorus; 6 mg calcium; 0 mg iron; 28 mg sodium; 52 mg potassium; 39 IU vitamin A; 0 mg ATE vitamin E; 3 mg vitamin C; 0 mg cholesterol

Barbecue Sauce

This is a quick-to-make barbecue sauce that starts with low-sodium ketchup. It's tomatoey, relatively sweet, with the spices having a basic chili flavor. In other words, not too different than most bottled sauces.

½ cup (120 ml) low-sodium ketchup

½ cup (120 ml) vinegar

½ cup (170 g) honey

¼ cup (85 g) molasses

1 tablespoon (7.5 g) chili powder

1 tablespoon (7 g) onion powder

½ teaspoon garlic powder

1 tablespoon (9 g) dry mustard

¼ teaspoon cayenne

(continued on page 26)

Combine all ingredients and mix well. Store in a covered jar in the refrigerator.

Yield: 10 servings

Per serving: 24 g water; 97 calories (2% from fat, 2% from protein, 96% from carb); 1 g protein; 0 g total fat; 0 g saturated fat; 0 g monounsaturated fat; 0 g polyunsaturated fat; 25 g carb; 0 g fiber; 22 g sugar; 14 mg phosphorus; 27 mg calcium; 1 mg iron; 15 mg sodium; 213 mg potassium; 354 IU vitamin A; 0 mg ATE vitamin E; 3 mg vitamin C; 0 mg cholesterol

Low-Sodium Beef Broth

This recipe produces broth that can be diluted before using. It cooks easily in the slow cooker and gives you a good quantity of broth, plus beef that can be used for soup, barbecued beef sandwiches, or other uses. If you don't need all the broth, package it in 2 cup (475 ml) freezer containers that can be thawed and used in place of a can of beef broth. The nutritional estimates are just that—estimates—since it's hard to know how much of the nutrients from the beef end up in the broth.

1 cup (160 g) sliced onion

1 cup (130 g) sliced carrot

1 cup (100 g) sliced celery

1½ pounds (680 g) beef chuck

1½ (355 ml) cups water

½ teaspoon black pepper

1 teaspoon thyme

Place vegetables in bottom of slow cooker. Cut up beef and place on top. Pour water over. Add spices. Cook on low 8 to 9 hours. Remove meat from pot and let cool until easy to handle. Remove meat from bones and cut up as needed. Strain broth and discard vegetables. Cool broth in refrigerator and remove fat from top. Broth may be mixed with an equal amount of water and used in any recipe calling for beef broth. The meat may be used in another recipe or frozen until needed.

Yield: 8 servings

Per serving: 115 g water; 53 calories (51% from fat, 47% from protein, 1% from carb); 8 g protein; 3 g total fat; 1 g saturated fat; 2 g monounsaturated fat; 0 g polyunsaturated fat; 1 g carb; 0 g fiber; 0 g sugar; 167 mg phosphorus; 26 mg calcium; 2 mg iron; 63 mg sodium; 341 mg potassium; 62 IU vitamin A; 0 mg ATE vitamin E; 0 mg vitamin C; 37 mg cholesterol

Chicken and Broth

This homemade broth is at least as flavorful as the low-sodium canned stuff and a lot lower in sodium. You could also make your own version of the fancier broths now available by adding a couple of cloves of garlic or a tablespoon (6 **g**) of Italian seasoning. This makes a broth that may be diluted by adding an equal amount of water.

1 cup (160 g) sliced onion

1 cup (130 g) sliced carrot

1 cup (100 g) sliced celery

1 chicken

1½ cups (355 ml) water

Place vegetables in bottom of slow cooker. Put chicken on top, breast side up. You can also use leg quarters, necks, and backs or whatever is cheap. Pour water over. Cook on low 8 to 9 hours. Remove chicken from pot and let cool until easy to handle. Remove chicken from bones and cut up as needed. Strain broth and discard veggies. Cool broth in refrigerator and remove fat from top. Broth may mixed with equal amount of water and used in any recipe calling for chicken broth. Use chicken in other recipes or freeze until needed.

Yield: 8 servings

Per serving: 77 g water; 46 calories (17% from fat, 50% from protein, 33% from carb); 4 g protein; 1 g total fat; 0 g saturated fat; 0 g monounsaturated fat; 0 g polyunsaturated fat; 4 g carb; 1 g fiber; 2 g sugar; 57 mg phosphorus; 18 mg calcium; 0 mg iron; 41 mg sodium; 170 mg potassium; 2760 IU vitamin A; 4 mg ATE vitamin E; 3 mg vitamin C; 17 mg cholesterol

Beef Stock

The main difference between broth and stock is that broth is usually just meat simmered with water and vegetables, while stock is made by browning meaty bones and then simmering them. This produces a richer, more flavorful broth. This recipe produces broth that can be diluted before using. It cooks easily in the slow cooker and gives you a good quantity of stock.

1½ pounds (680 g) meaty beef bones

1 cup (160 g) sliced onion

1 cup (130 g) sliced carrot

1 cup (100 g) sliced celery

1½ cups (355 ml) water

½ teaspoon black pepper

1 teaspoon thyme

Place beef bones and vegetables in a single layer in a roasting pan and roast at 350°F (180°C, or gas mark 4) until browned, about an hour. Transfer to slow cooker. Pour water over. Add spices. Cook on low 8 to 9 hours. Remove meat from pot and let cool until easy to handle. Remove meat from bones and save for another use. Strain vegetables from stock and discard. Cool stock in refrigerator and remove fat from top. Stock may mixed with equal amount of water and used in any recipe calling for beef stock or broth. Both beef and stock may be frozen until needed.

Yield: 8 servings

Per serving: 140 g water; 70 calories (66% from fat, 27% from protein, 7% from carb); 4 g protein; 3 g total fat; 2 g saturated fat; 1 g monounsaturated fat; 1 g polyunsaturated fat; 4 g carb; 1 g fiber; 2 g sugar; 153 mg phosphorus; 28 mg calcium; 2 mg iron; 81 mg sodium; 347 mg potassium; 2752 IU vitamin A; 0 mg ATE vitamin E; 3 mg vitamin C; 60 mg cholesterol

Chicken Stock

The main difference between broth and stock is that broth is usually just meat simmered with water and vegetables, while stock is made by browning meaty bones and then simmering them. This produces a richer, more flavorful broth. This recipe produces stock that can be diluted before using. It cooks easily in the slow cooker and gives you a good quantity of stock. You can use any chicken bones that have most of the meat removed. I often buy chicken breasts, remove most of the meat to make a much cheaper boneless, skinless breast piece, and then use the ribs and backs to make stock.

1½ pounds (680 g) meaty chicken bones

1 cup (160 g) sliced onion

1 cup (130 g) sliced carrot

1 cup (100 g) sliced celery

1½ cups (355 ml) water

½ teaspoon black pepper

1 teaspoon thyme

Place bones and vegetables in a single layer in a roasting pan and roast at 350°F (180°C, or gas mark 4) until browned, about an hour. Transfer to slow cooker. Pour water over. Add spices. Cook on low 8 to 9 hours. Remove meat from pot and let cool until easy to handle. Remove meat from bones and save for another use. Strain vegetables from stock and discard. Cool stock in refrigerator and remove fat from top. Stock may mixed with equal amount of water and used in any recipe calling for chicken broth. Both chicken and stock may be frozen until needed.

Yield: 8 servings

Per serving: 123 g water; 134 calories (35% from fat, 53% from protein, 12% from carb); 17 g protein; 5 g total fat; 1 g saturated fat; 2 g monounsaturated fat; 1 g polyunsaturated fat; 4 g carb; 1 g fiber; 2 g sugar; 143 mg phosphorus; 33 mg calcium; 1 mg iron; 92 mg sodium; 290 mg potassium; 2836 IU vitamin A; 26 mg ATE vitamin E; 3 mg vitamin C; 69 mg cholesterol

Fish Stock

Use this stock to make soups or fish sauce. If you don't have fish bones, heads, or tails to put in, use a pound of fish instead.

1 pound (455 g) fish bones, heads, and tails

4 cups (950 ml) low-sodium chicken broth

(continued on page 30)

1 cup (160 g) onion, minced

¼ cup (25 g) scallions, chopped

¼ teaspoon black pepper

2 tablespoons (28 ml) cider vinegar

2 tablespoons (4 g) cilantro, dried

2 tablespoons (12 g) low-sodium chicken bouillon

Combine first 7 ingredients (through cilantro) in a slow cooker. Cook on low for 5 to 6 hours. Stir in bouillon and cook for 1 hour more. Strain.

Yield: 8 servings

Per serving: 156 g water; 50 calories (17% from fat, 50% from protein, 33% from carb); 7 g protein; 1 g total fat; 0 g saturated fat; 0 g monounsaturated fat; 0 g polyunsaturated fat; 4 g carb; 1 g fiber; 1 g sugar; 81 mg phosphorus; 17 mg calcium; 1 mg iron; 116 mg sodium; 239 mg potassium; 122 IU vitamin A; 2 mg ATE vitamin E; 3 mg vitamin C; 10 mg cholesterol

Vegetable Broth

It's fairly easy to make your own low-sodium vegetable broth. Feel free to vary the amount and type of vegetables to get a flavor you like. Potato peels can be included if you have any, as can a sweet potato or mushrooms. I picked the ones I used for a combination of flavor and low cost. Strongly flavored vegetables such as tomatoes and cabbage can overwhelm the others, so use them sparingly unless you are after a broth that is primarily tomato- or cabbage-flavored. You can use a strainer like the ones sold to cook pasta to simplify the straining. The nutritional values are probably a little high since I don't have any way to separate out the discarded vegetable solids.

2 quarts (1.9 L) water

¾ cup (75 g) sliced celery

1½ cups (195 g) sliced carrot

1 onion, quartered

2 turnips, quartered

1 cup (30 g) spinach leaves, tightly packed

2 leeks, sliced

1 tablespoon (5 g) peppercorns

1 bay leaf

½ cups (30 g) fresh parsley

Combine all ingredients in slow cooker and cook on low for 6 to 8 hours. Strain and use as needed. May be frozen.

Yield: 6 servings

Per serving: 509 g water; 73 calories (5% from fat, 12% from protein, 83% from carb); 2 g protein; 0 g total fat; 0 g saturated fat; 0 g monounsaturated fat; 0 g polyunsaturated fat; 16 g carb; 4 g fiber; 7 g sugar; 66 mg phosphorus; 100 mg calcium; 2 mg iron; 131 mg sodium; 526 mg potassium; 7015 IU vitamin A; 0 mg ATE vitamin E; 30 mg vitamin C; 0 mg cholesterol

Onion Soup Mix

Some of these recipes call for onion soup mix. I've used Goodman's Low-Sodium Onion Soup Mix, which I find in the kosher foods section of my local Safeway. However, it can be hard to locate. You can easily make your own mix that is even lower in sodium. You can use this the same as you would a one-serving envelope of one of the commercial brands (some brands make multiple servings per envelope).

1 tablespoon (15 g) dried minced onion

1 teaspoon sodium-free beef bouillon

½ teaspoon onion powder

⅛ teaspoon black pepper

⅛ teaspoon paprika

TIP
Mixed with a pint of sour cream, this makes a good dip.

Combine all ingredients and store in an airtight jar or bag.

Yield: 1 serving

(continued on page 32)

Per serving: 0 g water; 26 calories (3% from fat, 10% from protein, 87% from carb); 1 g protein; 0 g total fat; 0 g saturated fat; 0 g monounsaturated fat; 0 g polyunsaturated fat; 6 g carb; 1 g fiber; 2 g sugar; 21 mg phosphorus; 20 mg calcium; 0 mg iron; 84 mg sodium; 125 mg potassium; 206 IU vitamin A; 0 mg ATE vitamin E; 5 mg vitamin C; 0 mg cholesterol

Condensed Cream of Mushroom Soup

Many slow cooker recipes seem to call for mushroom soup. You can find reduced-sodium ones, but if you are really watching your sodium you might want to try this one instead. It makes an amount that can be substituted for one can of the condensed soup.

1 cup (70 g) sliced mushrooms

½ cup (80 g) chopped onion

½ cup (120 ml) low-sodium chicken broth

1 tablespoon (1 g) dried parsley

¼ teaspoon garlic powder

⅔ cup (160 ml) skim milk

2 tablespoons (16 g) cornstarch

Cook mushrooms, onion, broth, parsley, and garlic powder until vegetables are soft. Process in a blender or food processor until well puréed; set aside. In an airtight container, shake together milk and cornstarch until dissolved. Pour into a saucepan and cook over medium heat, stirring, until thick. Stir in vegetable mixture.

Yield: 6 servings

Per serving: 67 g water; 31 calories (5% from fat, 22% from protein, 73% from carb); 2 g protein; 0 g total fat; 0 g saturated fat; 0 g monounsaturated fat; 0 g polyunsaturated fat; 6 g carb; 0 g fiber; 1 g sugar; 48 mg phosphorus; 44 mg calcium; 0 mg iron; 30 mg sodium; 117 mg potassium; 108 IU vitamin A; 17 mg ATE vitamin E; 2 mg vitamin C; 1 mg cholesterol

Breakfast Sausage

Wassi's Meat Market (www.wassis.com) is my favorite place to buy salt-free sausage seasonings. But if I don't have any of theirs or am looking for something a little different, I make my own. You can buy ground pork in most large supermarkets, but if you have a grinder you can make a much lower-fat version by trimming leaner cuts of pork, like a whole pork loin, and grinding them yourself. You can also use ground turkey for an even leaner sausage.

1 pound (455 g) pork loin, ground

¼ teaspoon black pepper

¼ teaspoon white pepper

¾ teaspoon dried sage

¼ teaspoon mace

½ teaspoon garlic powder

¼ teaspoon onion powder

¼ teaspoon ground allspice

Combine all ingredients, mixing well. Fry, grill, or cook sausage on a greased baking sheet in an oven at 325°F (170°C, or gas mark 3) until done.

Yield: 8 servings

Per serving: 42 g water; 74 calories (31% from fat, 67% from protein, 2% from carb); 12 g protein; 2 g total fat; 1 g saturated fat; 1 g monounsaturated fat; 0 g polyunsaturated fat; 0 g carb; 0 g fiber; 0 g sugar; 125 mg phosphorus; 10 mg calcium; 1 mg iron; 29 mg sodium; 215 mg potassium; 9 IU vitamin A; 1 mg ATE vitamin E; 1 mg vitamin C; 36 mg cholesterol

Italian Sausage

This is a traditional Italian-flavored sausage that can be used in many other recipes. Be aware that the serving size I've listed is 2 ounces (55 g), but you might eat more than that if you use it as the only meat in a meal. Feel free to add more red pepper flakes depending on how hot you like it.

(continued on page 34)

1½ pounds (680 g) pork loin, ground

1 teaspoon black pepper

¼ teaspoon garlic powder

½ teaspoon fennel

½ teaspoon coriander

Dash red pepper flakes

TIP *This is one recipe where adding ¼ teaspoon makes a big difference in the flavor. It adds about 50 mg of sodium per serving.*

Mix spices into meat. Shape into patties if desired and fry, grill, or cook sausage on a greased baking sheet in an oven at 325°F (170°C, or gas mark 3) until done.

Yield: 12 servings

Per serving: 42 g water; 74 calories (31% from fat, 68% from protein, 1% from carb); 12 g protein; 2 g total fat; 1 g saturated fat; 1 g monounsaturated fat; 0 g polyunsaturated fat; 0 g carb; 0 g fiber; 0 g sugar; 125 mg phosphorus; 9 mg calcium; 1 mg iron; 29 mg sodium; 215 mg potassium; 6 IU vitamin A; 1 mg ATE vitamin E; 1 mg vitamin C; 36 mg cholesterol

Cajun Sausage

Andouille is a traditional Cajun smoked sausage. It's stuffed in relatively large casings and then cut into thin slices for cooking. My smoker gets too hot to slow smoke sausage, but I came across a variation of this recipe that used liquid smoke to impart that flavor. This is not a very hot sausage, the flavor relying mostly on the garlic and liquid smoke, but you could add more cayenne if you desire. It does give a nice authentic flavor to recipes when just crumbled and browned.

2½ pounds (1.1 kg) ground pork

2 tablespoons (20 g) minced garlic

½ teaspoon black pepper

½ teaspoon cayenne

⅛ teaspoon thyme

½ tablespoon paprika

⅛ teaspoon bay leaf

⅛ teaspoon sage

2½ teaspoons (13 ml) liquid smoke

In a large bowl, mix together the ground pork with the garlic, pepper, cayenne, thyme, paprika, bay leaf, sage, and liquid smoke. Shape into patties and fry, grill, or cook sausage on a greased baking sheet in an oven at 325°F (170°C, or gas mark 3) until done.

Yield: 10 servings

Per serving: 61 g water; 341 calories (64% from fat, 35% from protein, 1% from carb); 29 g protein; 24 g total fat; 9 g saturated fat; 10 g monounsaturated fat; 2 g polyunsaturated fat; 1 g carb; 0 g fiber; 0 g sugar; 261 mg phosphorus; 30 mg calcium; 2 mg iron; 83 mg sodium; 429 mg potassium; 228 IU vitamin A; 2 mg ATE vitamin E; 2 mg vitamin C; 107 mg cholesterol

Salt-Free Seasoning Blend

This blend comes close to approximating the flavors in the typical seasoned salt blends like Lawry's, but without the sodium. Use it anywhere seasoned salt is called for or when you want to give food a little extra flavor. I like it in soups and egg dishes.

1 teaspoon chili powder

¼ teaspoon celery seed

½ teaspoon nutmeg

½ teaspoon coriander

1 teaspoon onion powder

1 teaspoon paprika

¼ teaspoon garlic powder

1 teaspoon turmeric

Mix together. Store in an airtight container.

Yield: 24 servings

Per serving: 0 g water; 2 calories (28% from fat, 11% from protein, 60% from carb); 0 g protein; 0 g total fat; 0 g saturated fat; 0 g monounsaturated fat; 0 g polyunsaturated fat; 0 g carb; 0 g fiber; 0 g sugar; 2 mg phosphorus; 2 mg calcium; 0 mg iron; 1 mg sodium; 9 mg potassium; 82 IU vitamin A; 0 mg ATE vitamin E; 0 mg vitamin C; 0 mg cholesterol

Salt-Free Cajun Seasoning

Add a little Cajun flavor to your favorite dishes, while leaving out the sodium that almost all commercial Cajun seasonings contain.

1 tablespoon (7 g) paprika

2½ teaspoons (13 g) dried onion flakes

2 teaspoons minced garlic

1½ teaspoons thyme

1 teaspoon marjoram

½ teaspoon fennel

1 teaspoon cumin

½ teaspoon cayenne

Mix well and store in an airtight container.

Yield: 24 servings

Per serving: 0 g water; 3 calories (22% from fat, 13% from protein, 65% from carb); 0 g protein; 0 g total fat; 0 g saturated fat; 0 g monounsaturated fat; 0 g polyunsaturated fat; 1 g carb; 0 g fiber; 0 g sugar; 3 mg phosphorus; 4 mg calcium; 0 mg iron; 0 mg sodium; 14 mg potassium; 172 IU vitamin A; 0 mg ATE vitamin E; 0 mg vitamin C; 0 mg cholesterol

Salt-Free Mexican Seasoning

Add this blend to chili, beans, or other Mexican dishes or sprinkle on grilled vegetables like potatoes or onions.

1 tablespoon (5 g) ground dried chili peppers

2 teaspoons garlic powder

2 teaspoons onion powder

1 teaspoon paprika

1½ teaspoons cumin

1 teaspoon celery seed

1 teaspoon oregano

¼ teaspoon cayenne

¼ teaspoon ground bay leaf

Mix well and store in an airtight container.

Yield: 11 servings

Per serving: 0 g water; 7 calories (20% from fat, 14% from protein, 65% from carb); 0 g protein; 0 g total fat; 0 g saturated fat; 0 g monounsaturated fat; 0 g polyunsaturated fat; 1 g carb; 0 g fiber; 0 g sugar; 7 mg phosphorus; 10 mg calcium; 0 mg iron; 1 mg sodium; 28 mg potassium; 193 IU vitamin A; 0 mg ATE vitamin E; 1 mg vitamin C; 0 mg cholesterol

Salt-Free Seafood Seasoning

Here in Maryland, summer means crabs and other seafood. And seafood means steamed, with Old Bay Seasoning or the locally produced equivalent from the local seafood market. The only trouble is that Old Bay contains 330 mg of sodium per ½ teaspoon. So the next time you want some steamed seafood, try our low-sodium taste alike substitute.

1 tablespoon (6.5 g) celery seed

1 tablespoon (6 g) black pepper

6 bay leaves, ground

½ teaspoon cardamom

½ teaspoon dry mustard

⅛ teaspoon cloves, ground

1 teaspoon paprika

¼ teaspoon mace

Combine all ingredients. Store in an airtight container.

Yield: 16 servings

(continued on page 38)

Per serving: 0 g water; 4 calories (33% from fat, 14% from protein, 53% from carb); 0 g protein; 0 g total fat; 0 g saturated fat; 0 g monounsaturated fat; 0 g polyunsaturated fat; 1 g carb; 0 g fiber; 0 g sugar; 4 mg phosphorus; 10 mg calcium; 0 mg iron; 1 mg sodium; 15 mg potassium; 78 IU vitamin A; 0 mg ATE vitamin E; 0 mg vitamin C; 0 mg cholesterol

Salt-Free Oriental Seasoning

Add this to stir-fries. It's also good in salad dressings and dips.

2 tablespoons (16 g) sesame seeds, roasted

1 tablespoon (15 g) dried onion flakes

1 tablespoon (9 g) garlic powder

1 teaspoon black pepper

1 teaspoon celery seed

1 teaspoon dried lemon peel

1 teaspoon dry mustard

1 tablespoon (3.6 g) red pepper flakes

Mix well and store in an airtight container.

Yield: 38 servings

Per serving: 0 g water; 4 calories (49% from fat, 13% from protein, 38% from carb); 0 g protein; 0 g total fat; 0 g saturated fat; 0 g monounsaturated fat; 0 g polyunsaturated fat; 0 g carb; 0 g fiber; 0 g sugar; 5 mg phosphorus; 7 mg calcium; 0 mg iron; 0 mg sodium; 9 mg potassium; 1 IU vitamin A; 0 mg ATE vitamin E; 0 mg vitamin C; 0 mg cholesterol

Ranch Dressing Mix

Commercial ranch dressing mix is a great ready-to-use ingredient, but it's loaded with sodium. Our version is not.

½ cup (60 g) buttermilk powder

1 tablespoon (1.3 g) dried parsley, crushed

1 teaspoon dried dill weed

1 teaspoon onion powder

1 teaspoon dried minced onion

¼ teaspoon ground pepper

½ teaspoon garlic powder

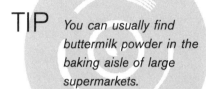

TIP *You can usually find buttermilk powder in the baking aisle of large supermarkets.*

Combine all ingredients in the container of a food processor or blender and process on high speed until well blended and powdery smooth. To make ranch dressing, combine 2 tablespoons (13 g) dry mix with 1 cup (235 ml) milk and 1 cup (225 g) mayonnaise. Mix well.

Yield: 88 servings

Per serving: 0 g water; 3 calories (13% from fat, 33% from protein, 54% from carb); 0 g protein; 0 g total fat; 0 g saturated fat; 0 g monounsaturated fat; 0 g polyunsaturated fat; 0 g carb; 0 g fiber; 0 g sugar; 7 mg phosphorus; 9 mg calcium; 0 mg iron; 4 mg sodium; 12 mg potassium; 5 IU vitamin A; 0 mg ATE vitamin E; 0 mg vitamin C; 0 mg cholesterol

Italian Salad Dressing Mix

Occasionally you'll come across a recipe that calls for a package of Italian dressing mix. Unfortunately, those mixes are high in sodium. The solution is to make your own.

2 teaspoons dried oregano

1 teaspoon onion powder

2 teaspoons dried basil

2 teaspoons paprika

(continued on page 40)

1½ teaspoons black pepper

2 tablespoons (18 g) garlic powder

6 tablespoons (78 g) granulated sugar

Mix and store in an airtight container. To make dressing, use 1½ tablespoons of (11 g) mix with ¾ cup (175 ml) vegetable oil and ¼ cup (60 ml) wine vinegar.

Yield: 32 servings

Per serving: 0 g water; 12 calories (2% from fat, 4% from protein, 93% from carb); 0 g protein; 0 g total fat; 0 g saturated fat; 0 g monounsaturated fat; 0 g polyunsaturated fat; 3 g carb; 0 g fiber; 3 g sugar; 3 mg phosphorus; 3 mg calcium; 0 mg iron; 0 mg sodium; 14 mg potassium; 85 IU vitamin A; 0 mg ATE vitamin E; 0 mg vitamin C; 0 mg cholesterol

Heart-Healthy Baking Mix

This makes a mix similar to Reduced Fat Bisquick but even lower in fat. Use it in any recipes that call for baking mix. You can also reduce the sodium if you buy sodium-free baking powder. For unrefrigerated storage, use trans fat-free shortening.

6 cups (750 g) flour

3 tablespoons (41 g) baking powder

⅓ cup (75 g) unsalted butter

Stir flour and baking powder together. Cut in butter with pastry blender or 2 knives until mixture resembles coarse crumbs. Store in a container with a tight-fitting lid in the refrigerator.

Yield: 12 servings

Per serving: 9 g water; 275 calories (19% from fat, 10% from protein, 71% from carb); 7 g protein; 6 g total fat; 3 g saturated fat; 1 g monounsaturated fat; 0 g polyunsaturated fat; 49 g carb; 2 g fiber; 0 g sugar; 145 mg phosphorus; 214 mg calcium; 3 mg iron; 368 mg sodium; 69 mg potassium; 158 IU vitamin A; 42 mg ATE vitamin E; 0 mg vitamin C; 14 mg cholesterol

Pesto

This makes a fairly typical pesto but without the usual added salt. It's good in recipes or just over warm pasta.

2 cups (80 g) fresh basil, packed

3 tablespoons (27 g) pine nuts

1 teaspoon garlic, finely minced

¼ cup (20 g) Parmesan cheese, screened

½ cup (120 ml) olive oil

Place one-third of the basil leaves in a food processor and pulse until well chopped. Add about one-third of the pine nuts and garlic; blend again. Add about one-third of the Parmesan cheese; blend while slowly adding about one-third of the olive oil, stopping to scrape down sides of container. Process pesto until it forms a thick, smooth paste. Repeat until all ingredients are used and then mix all batches together well. Serve over pasta. Basil pesto keeps in refrigerator for one week or freeze for a few months.

Yield: 12 servings

Per serving: 1 g water; 115 calories (82% from fat, 6% from protein, 13% from carb); 2 g protein; 11 g total fat; 2 g saturated fat; 7 g monounsaturated fat; 2 g polyunsaturated fat; 4 g carb; 2 g fiber; 0 g sugar; 52 mg phosphorus; 140 mg calcium; 3 mg iron; 30 mg sodium; 208 mg potassium; 536 IU vitamin A; 2 mg ATE vitamin E; 4 mg vitamin C; 1 mg cholesterol

Salsa

It took me a while, but I finally came up with a recipe for salsa that satisfies me and that I actually wrote down the ingredients for while I was concocting it. And it passed the taste test, with a whole pint jar disappearing into the young people who attended my daughter's college graduation party, so I guess it's okay to share. This makes a mild version. You could add another chili pepper or two depending on how hot you like it.

(continued on page 42)

3 pounds (1.4 kg) plum tomatoes, peeled and chopped

½ cup (86 g) black beans, cooked

½ cup (82 g) frozen corn

1 can (8 ounces, or 225 g) no-salt-added tomato sauce

1 chili pepper

¼ cup (60 ml) red wine vinegar

½ cup (80 g) chopped onion

1 teaspoon minced garlic

1½ teaspoons cilantro

½ teaspoon oregano

1½ teaspoons cumin

TIP *To peel tomatoes, dip them into boiling water for about 30 seconds. The skins will come right off.*

Combine all ingredients in a large pot. Simmer until desired thickness, about 15 minutes. Pack into jars and store in refrigerator. Makes about 3 pints.

Yield: 48 servings

Per serving: 37 g water; 18 calories (7% from fat, 19% from protein, 74% from carb); 1 g protein; 0 g total fat; 0 g saturated fat; 0 g monounsaturated fat; 0 g polyunsaturated fat; 4 g carb; 1 g fiber; 1 g sugar; 21 mg phosphorus; 8 mg calcium; 0 mg iron; 25 mg sodium; 132 mg potassium; 305 IU vitamin A; 0 mg ATE vitamin E; 7 mg vitamin C; 0 mg cholesterol

3

Let's Have a Party with Easy and Healthy Appetizers and Snacks

The slow cooker is a great choice for appetizers, whether for your family or even more so when you are entertaining. It allows you to mix everything up well ahead of time and have it ready and waiting when guests arrive. The recipes in this chapter are a variety of nibbles, dips, nuts, and other munchies.

Cocktail Meatballs

Grape jelly sweetens the sauce these meatballs cook in, although the flavor is not so distinct that most people will be able to pick it out. They will just know they are good.

1 pound (455 g) lean ground beef

½ cup (60 g) bread crumbs

⅓ cup (55 g) minced onion

¼ cup (60 ml) skim milk

¼ cup (60 ml) egg substitute

1 tablespoon (4 g) fresh parsley, chopped

⅛ teaspoon black pepper

½ teaspoon Worcestershire sauce

2 tablespoons (28 ml) olive oil

1 cup (275 g) chili sauce (see recipe in Chapter 2)

½ cup (170 g) grape jelly

Mix the first 8 ingredients (through Worcestershire sauce) and make into bite-size meatballs. Heat the oil in a skillet and brown meatballs in the oil. Transfer to the slow cooker. Mix the chili sauce and the jelly in a saucepan over low heat until melted. Add to meatballs and stir until coated. Cook on low for 4 to 6 hours.

Yield: 12 servings

Per serving: 60 g water; 181 calories (47% from fat, 20% from protein, 33% from carb); 9 g protein; 9 g total fat; 3 g saturated fat; 5 g monounsaturated fat; 1 g polyunsaturated fat; 15 g carb; 1 g fiber; 8 g sugar; 77 mg phosphorus; 30 mg calcium; 1 mg iron; 60 mg sodium; 163 mg potassium; 390 IU vitamin A; 3 mg ATE vitamin E; 6 mg vitamin C; 26 mg cholesterol

Sweet and Sour Hot Dog Bites

These tasty little hot dog slices are always a hit as an appetizer. Serve directly out of the slow cooker with toothpicks to use for retrieving them.

1 cup (340 g) grape jelly

½ cup (88 g) mustard

1 pound (455 g) hot dogs, sliced

8 ounces (225 g) pineapple tidbits

Microwave jelly until thin, about 30 seconds. Stir in mustard, hot dogs, and pineapple. Transfer to slow cooker and cook on low for 2 hours.

Yield: 16 servings

Per serving: 34 g water; 160 calories (51% from fat, 9% from protein, 40% from carb); 4 g protein; 9 g total fat; 4 g saturated fat; 4 g monounsaturated fat; 0 g polyunsaturated fat; 16 g carb; 0 g fiber; 11 g sugar; 44 mg phosphorus; 14 mg calcium; 1 mg iron; 297 mg sodium; 84 mg potassium; 11 IU vitamin A; 0 mg ATE vitamin E; 3 mg vitamin C; 16 mg cholesterol

Beer Barbecued Meatballs

These tasty meatballs simmer in beer and spicy vegetable juice to take on a great flavor.

3 pounds (1.4 kg) lean ground beef

1 cup (160 g) chopped onion, divided

½ cup (60 g) dry bread crumbs

¾ cup (175 ml) egg substitute

12 ounces (355 ml) beer

6 ounces (175 ml) spicy vegetable juice, such as V-8

1 teaspoon lemon juice

1 teaspoon hot pepper sauce

(continued on page 46)

14 ounces (390 g) no-salt-added ketchup

1 teaspoon horseradish

1 teaspoon Worcestershire sauce

Combine ground beef, ½ cup (80 g) onions, bread crumbs, and egg substitute. Make the mixture into small meatballs. Cook meatballs in a large skillet, turning to brown all sides, or bake in a 375°F (190°C, or gas mark 5) oven until browned, about 30 minutes. Drain meatballs and discard fat. In a saucepan, combine remaining ingredients. Simmer for 15 minutes. Put meatballs and sauce into slow cooker. Cover and cook on low for 3 to 6 hours. Makes about 6 dozen meatballs.

Yield: 36 servings

Per serving: 53 g water; 116 calories (54% from fat, 29% from protein, 17% from carb); 8 g protein; 7 g total fat; 3 g saturated fat; 3 g monounsaturated fat; 0 g polyunsaturated fat; 5 g carb; 0 g fiber; 3 g sugar; 69 mg phosphorus; 12 mg calcium; 1 mg iron; 42 mg sodium; 190 mg potassium; 198 IU vitamin A; 0 mg ATE vitamin E; 4 mg vitamin C; 26 mg cholesterol

Asian Chicken Wings

Asian-flavored wings cook easily in the slow cooker, soaking up lots of flavor in the process.

3 pounds (1.4 kg) chicken wings

1 cup (160 g) chopped onion

1 cup (235 ml) low sodium soy sauce (see recipe in Chapter 2)

1 cup (225 g) brown sugar

2 teaspoons ground ginger

½ teaspoon minced garlic

¼ cup (60 ml) sherry

Rinse chicken wings; pat dry. Cut off and discard wing tips and then cut each wing at the joint to make two sections. Place wings on a lightly oiled broiler pan. Broil about 4 inches from the heat for 10 minutes on each side or until chicken wings are nicely browned. Transfer chicken wings to slow cooker. In a bowl, combine chopped onion, soy sauce, brown sugar, ginger, garlic, and sherry. Pour sauce over chicken wings. Cover and cook on low for 4 to 5 hours or on high for 2 to

2½ hours. Stir wings once about halfway through cooking. Serve directly from slow cooker, keeping temperature on low. Makes about 32 wing pieces.

Yield: 16 servings

Per serving: 87 g water; 178 calories (16% from fat, 46% from protein, 38% from carb); 20 g protein; 3 g total fat; 1 g saturated fat; 1 g monounsaturated fat; 1 g polyunsaturated fat; 16 g carb; 0 g fiber; 14 g sugar; 156 mg phosphorus; 28 mg calcium; 1 mg iron; 125 mg sodium; 263 mg potassium; 51 IU vitamin A; 15 mg ATE vitamin E; 2 mg vitamin C; 48 mg cholesterol

Cranberry Meatballs

Sweet and saucy, these meatballs are a perfect appetizer when you have friends over.

For Meatballs:

2 pounds (910 g) lean ground beef

1 cup (115 g) bread crumbs

½ cup (30 g) fresh parsley, chopped

½ cup (120 ml) egg substitute

⅓ cup (80 g) no-salt-added ketchup

3 tablespoons (30 g) minced onions

2 tablespoons (28 ml) low-sodium soy sauce (see recipe in Chapter 2)

¼ teaspoon garlic powder

¼ teaspoon pepper

For Sauce:

1 can (16 ounces, or 455 g) whole berry cranberry sauce

1½ cups (413 g) chili sauce (see recipe in Chapter 2)

1 tablespoon (15 g) brown sugar

1 tablespoon (15 ml) lemon juice

(continued on page 48)

To make the meatballs: In a large bowl, combine ground beef, bread crumbs, parsley, egg substitute, ketchup, onion, soy sauce, garlic powder, and pepper. Mix well and form into small balls, from ½ inch (1.3 cm) to ¾ inch (2 cm) in diameter. Place in a casserole dish or baking pan. Heat oven to 300°F (150°C, or gas mark 2). Bake meatballs until nearly done, about 20 minutes.

To make the sauce: In a saucepan, combine cranberry sauce, chili sauce, brown sugar, and lemon juice. Cook, stirring, over medium heat until smooth. Transfer meatballs to slow cooker. Pour hot sauce over meatballs. Cook on low for 2 hours.

Yield: 16 servings

Per serving: 88 g water; 229 calories (41% from fat, 23% from protein, 36% from carb); 13 g protein; 10 g total fat; 4 g saturated fat; 4 g monounsaturated fat; 1 g polyunsaturated fat; 20 g carb; 1 g fiber; 15 g sugar; 108 mg phosphorus; 31 mg calcium; 2 mg iron; 85 mg sodium; 248 mg potassium; 587 IU vitamin A; 0 mg ATE vitamin E; 8 mg vitamin C; 39 mg cholesterol

Honey Chicken Wings

Sweet, with a sort of almost barbecue flavor, these wings are always popular, especially with those who don't like the heat of Buffalo wings.

3 pounds (1.4 kg) chicken wings

1 cup (340 g) honey

½ cup (120 ml) low sodium soy sauce

2 tablespoons (28 ml) olive oil

2 tablespoons (30 g) no-salt-added ketchup

½ teaspoon minced garlic

Cut off and discard chicken wing tips. Cut each wing into 2 parts. Combine remaining ingredients and mix well. Place wings in slow cooker and pour sauce over. Cook 6 to 7 hours on low.

Yield: 16 servings

Per serving: 74 g water; 193 calories (22% from fat, 40% from protein, 38% from carb); 19 g protein; 5 g total fat; 1 g saturated fat; 2 g monounsaturated fat; 1 g polyunsaturated fat; 19 g carb; 0 g fiber; 18 g sugar; 142 mg phosphorus; 14 mg calcium; 1 mg iron; 95 mg sodium; 198 mg potassium; 68 IU vitamin A; 15 mg ATE vitamin E; 1 mg vitamin C; 48 mg cholesterol

Sweet and Sour Chicken Wings

These are a nice sweet and hot combination if you use the full teaspoon of hot pepper sauce. If you like them milder, feel free to reduce the amount.

3 pounds (1.4 kg) chicken wings

¼ cup (60 ml) balsamic vinegar

1 cup (330 g) apricot preserves

1 cup (240 g) no-salt-added ketchup

3 tablespoons (45 g) horseradish

1 cup (160 g) finely chopped onion

1 teaspoon hot pepper sauce, or to taste

Pat the chicken wings dry and place them in the slow cooker. In a bowl, mix together remaining ingredients. Taste and adjust seasonings. Pour the sauce over the wings. Cover the slow cooker and cook on low until the chicken is tender, about 4 to 5 hours.

Yield: 16 servings

Per serving: 95 g water; 183 calories (16% from fat, 43% from protein, 42% from carb); 19 g protein; 3 g total fat; 1 g saturated fat; 1 g monounsaturated fat; 1 g polyunsaturated fat; 19 g carb; 1 g fiber; 14 g sugar; 145 mg phosphorus; 22 mg calcium; 1 mg iron; 90 mg sodium; 262 mg potassium; 195 IU vitamin A; 15 mg ATE vitamin E; 6 mg vitamin C; 48 mg cholesterol

Beer Sausages

You can use kielbasa or any other kind of smoked sausage for this recipe. They simmer in a sweet and sour mustard sauce that will have people coming back for more.

2 pounds (910 g) smoked sausage

1 cup (235 ml) beer

¼ cup (60 g) brown sugar

2 tablespoons (16 g) cornstarch

(continued on page 50)

¼ cup (60 ml) vinegar

¼ cup (44 g) mustard

1 tablespoon (15 g) horseradish

Cut sausage into ½-inch (1.3 cm) lengths. Boil them in beer for 10 minutes. Transfer to slow cooker. Mix brown sugar with cornstarch. Add to vinegar, mustard, and horseradish. Stir into slow cooker and cook on high for 2 hours.

Yield: 16 servings

Per serving: 53 g water; 156 calories (60% from fat, 20% from protein, 19% from carb); 8 g protein; 10 g total fat; 4 g saturated fat; 5 g monounsaturated fat; 1 g polyunsaturated fat; 7 g carb; 0 g fiber; 3 g sugar; 4 mg phosphorus; 7 mg calcium; 1 mg iron; 390 mg sodium; 28 mg potassium; 3 IU vitamin A; 0 mg ATE vitamin E; 9 mg vitamin C; 40 mg cholesterol

Sweet and Spicy Bratwurst

I don't eat bratwurst very often because of the amount of sodium in them, but these are excellent and cut in such a way that you can grab a taste without ruining your diet.

2 pounds (910 g) bratwurst, cut in 1-inch (2.5 cm) pieces

2 tablespoons (28 ml) oil

1 cup (160 g) chopped onions

¼ cup (60 g) brown sugar

4 teaspoons (11 g) cornstarch

¼ cup (60 ml) cider vinegar

¼ cup (44 g) mustard

4 teaspoons (20 g) horseradish

In a skillet over medium heat, brown meat in oil and remove, sautéing onions in remaining oil. Drain oil. Transfer to slow cooker. Combine remaining ingredients and add to cooker. Cook on low for 3 hours.

Yield: 16 servings

Per serving: 51 g water; 145 calories (60% from fat, 24% from protein, 17% from carb); 9 g protein; 10 g total fat; 0 g saturated fat; 5 g monounsaturated fat; 1 g polyunsaturated fat; 6 g carb; 0 g fiber; 5 g sugar; 79 mg phosphorus; 17 mg calcium; 1 mg iron; 563 mg sodium; 179 mg potassium; 4 IU vitamin A; 0 mg ATE vitamin E; 1 mg vitamin C; 32 mg cholesterol

Bourbon Hot Dogs

Hot dogs simmered in a bourbon tomato sauce are a real winner the day the big game is on TV. You could also use the little cocktail sausages.

1 cup (240 g) no-salt-added ketchup

1 cup (225 g) brown sugar

½ cup (120 ml) bourbon

2 pounds (910 g) hot dogs, sliced

Mix ketchup, brown sugar, and bourbon in slow cooker. Put hot dogs in and heat until hot dogs are cooked. Turn down to low and let them simmer in the sauce for at least an hour, then serve from the cooker.

Yield: 24 servings

Per serving: 30 g water; 179 calories (61% from fat, 10% from protein, 29% from carb); 4 g protein; 11 g total fat; 5 g saturated fat; 6 g monounsaturated fat; 1 g polyunsaturated fat; 12 g carb; 0 g fiber; 12 g sugar; 58 mg phosphorus; 13 mg calcium; 1 mg iron; 393 mg sodium; 119 mg potassium; 93 IU vitamin A; 0 mg ATE vitamin E; 2 mg vitamin C; 21 mg cholesterol

Pizza Dip

Here's the flavor of pizza in a snackable dip. What's not to like? This is good with vegetables, pita chips, tortilla chips, or just about anything.

1 pound (455 g) extra-lean ground beef

3 cups (750 g) low-sodium spaghetti sauce

(continued on page 52)

4 ounces (115 g) Cheddar, shredded

4 ounces (115 g) mozzarella, shredded

1 teaspoon oregano

1 teaspoon basil

½ teaspoon fennel seed

Brown beef in a skillet over medium heat and crumble fine. Combine beef and remaining ingredients in slow cooker and cook on low for 2 to 3 hours.

Yield: 12 servings

Per serving: 80 g water; 219 calories (58% from fat, 23% from protein, 19% from carb); 13 g protein; 14 g total fat; 6 g saturated fat; 6 g monounsaturated fat; 1 g polyunsaturated fat; 10 g carb; 2 g fiber; 7 g sugar; 169 mg phosphorus; 166 mg calcium; 1 mg iron; 161 mg sodium; 369 mg potassium; 535 IU vitamin A; 36 mg ATE vitamin E; 7 mg vitamin C; 42 mg cholesterol

Salsa Cheese Dip

This is a quick and easy dip using prepared salsa and Cheddar cheese. Adjust the amount of the canned chilies you add to match the heat level desired.

1 pound (455 g) Cheddar cheese, shredded

3 ounces (85 g) cottage cheese

4 ounces (115 g) canned green chilies

1½ cups (390 g) salsa (see recipe in Chapter 2)

Heat all ingredients in slow cooker. Cook on low until cheese melts and flavors are well mixed, about 2 hours.

Yield: 24 servings

Per serving: 27 g water; 84 calories (67% from fat, 26% from protein, 7% from carb); 6 g protein; 6 g total fat; 4 g saturated fat; 2 g monounsaturated fat; 0 g polyunsaturated fat; 1 g carb; 0 g fiber; 1 g sugar; 105 mg phosphorus; 143 mg calcium; 0 mg iron; 169 mg sodium; 67 mg potassium; 238 IU vitamin A; 49 mg ATE vitamin E; 2 mg vitamin C; 20 mg cholesterol

Mexican Dip

This isn't spicy, just tasty. Ground beef cooks with refried beans and a Mexican sauce to make a dip that everyone will like.

2 pounds (910 g) lean ground beef

1 cup (160 g) chopped onion

2 cups (476 g) refried beans (see recipe in Chapter 11)

1½ cups (360 ml) picante sauce

Dash hot pepper sauce

1 teaspoon cumin

¼ teaspoon cayenne

Cook meat and onion in a skillet over medium heat until meat loses pink color. Add other ingredients to the skillet. Transfer to slow cooker and cook on low at least 1 hour to allow flavors to blend. Serve from cooker with corn chips for dipping.

Yield: 32 servings

Per serving: 45 g water; 87 calories (54% from fat, 30% from protein, 16% from carb); 6 g protein; 5 g total fat; 2 g saturated fat; 2 g monounsaturated fat; 0 g polyunsaturated fat; 3 g carb; 1 g fiber; 1 g sugar; 55 mg phosphorus; 11 mg calcium; 1 mg iron; 111 mg sodium; 131 mg potassium; 54 IU vitamin A; 0 mg ATE vitamin E; 2 mg vitamin C; 21 mg cholesterol

Pinto Bean Dip

This dip goes together quickly and only needs to cook in the slow cooker long enough for the cheese to melt and the flavors to mix.

2 pounds (910 g) lean ground beef

1 cup (160 g) chopped onion

2 cups (480 ml) refried beans (see recipe in Chapter 11)

1½ cups (390 g) picante sauce

(continued on page 54)

Dash hot pepper sauce

1 teaspoon cumin

¼ teaspoon cayenne

Combine ingredients in small slow cooker and heat until warm and cheese is melted, about 1 hour. Serve with corn chips.

Yield: 16 servings

Per serving: 17 g water; 115 calories (21% from fat, 24% from protein, 55% from carb); 7 g protein; 3 g total fat; 2 g saturated fat; 1 g monounsaturated fat; 0 g polyunsaturated fat; 16 g carb; 4 g fiber; 1 g sugar; 138 mg phosphorus; 82 mg calcium; 1 mg iron; 75 mg sodium; 363 mg potassium; 119 IU vitamin A; 18 mg ATE vitamin E; 5 mg vitamin C; 7 mg cholesterol

Hot Crab Dip

Pepper jack cheese adds a little zip to this crab dip, which takes only as long to prepare as it takes you to put everything in the slow cooker.

16 ounces (455 g) fat-free cream cheese

4 ounces (115 g) pepper jack cheese, shredded

2 teaspoons Worcestershire sauce

1½ cups (150 g) scallions, chopped

¼ cup (15 g) fresh parsley, chopped

1 pound (455 g) crab meat

½ cup (120 ml) skim milk

Cook together in slow cooker on low heat until dip reaches desired consistency, about 2 hours.

Yield: 16 servings

Per serving: 60 g water; 123 calories (55% from fat, 34% from protein, 11% from carb); 10 g protein; 7 g total fat; 5 g saturated fat; 2 g monounsaturated fat; 0 g polyunsaturated fat; 3 g carb; 0 g fiber; 1 g sugar; 150 mg phosphorus; 127 mg calcium; 1 mg iron; 216 mg sodium; 194 mg potassium; 437 IU vitamin A; 70 mg ATE vitamin E; 5 mg vitamin C; 44 mg cholesterol

Seafood Dip

A great combination of shrimp and crab, this dip is one that I often pull out and make when we are invited somewhere.

2 cans (10.75 ounces, or 300 g) condensed cream of celery soup

2 cups (225 g) grated Cheddar cheese

½ pound (225 g) shrimp, cooked and chopped

1 cup (118 g) cooked crabmeat, chopped

Dash paprika

Dash nutmeg

Dash cayenne pepper

1 loaf French bread, cut into 1-inch (2.5 cm) cubes

Spray bottom and sides of slow cooker with nonstick cooking spray. Combine all ingredients except bread cubes in prepared slow cooker; stir well. Cover and cook on low for about 2 hours or until cheese is melted. Keep slow cooker on low for serving. Serve with bread cubes for dipping.

Yield: 16 servings

Per serving: 92 g water; 123 calories (56% from fat, 31% from protein, 14% from carb); 9 g protein; 8 g total fat; 4 g saturated fat; 2 g monounsaturated fat; 1 g polyunsaturated fat; 4 g carb; 0 g fiber; 0 g sugar; 149 mg phosphorus; 148 mg calcium; 1 mg iron; 453 mg sodium; 114 mg potassium; 285 IU vitamin A; 65 mg ATE vitamin E; 1 mg vitamin C; 51 mg cholesterol

Shrimp Dip

This tasty shrimp dip is perfect for entertaining, but it's also good just for the family.

16 ounces (455 g) fat free cream cheese

16 ounces (455 g) small frozen shrimp

(continued on page 56)

1 cup (160 g) chopped onion

½ cup (90 g) chopped tomato

Combine all ingredients in a slow cooker and cook slowly until cream cheese is melted and everything is cooked, about 2 hours. Keep warm in cooker. Serve with corn chips or toasted pita bread triangles.

Yield: 16 servings

Per serving: 53 g water; 100 calories (50% from fat, 36% from protein, 14% from carb); 9 g protein; 5 g total fat; 3 g saturated fat; 1 g monounsaturated fat; 0 g polyunsaturated fat; 3 g carb; 0 g fiber; 1 g sugar; 104 mg phosphorus; 49 mg calcium; 1 mg iron; 127 mg sodium; 125 mg potassium; 283 IU vitamin A; 67 mg ATE vitamin E; 2 mg vitamin C; 59 mg cholesterol

TIP *Serve with cubes of French bread and some veggies to dip in it and make it a meal.*

Artichoke Dip

There's nothing particularly special about the ingredients in this dip, but it seems to be just the right combination to please people. Serve with cubes of crusty bread or assorted crackers.

16 ounces (455 g) mozzarella, shredded

1 cup (100 g) grated Parmesan cheese

1 cup (225 g) mayonnaise

1 cup (300 g) artichoke hearts, drained and chopped

2 teaspoons grated onion

2 teaspoons grated scallions

Mix all ingredients except scallions together. Spray bottom and sides of a 3½-quart (3.3 L) slow cooker with nonstick cooking spray. Pour artichoke mixture into prepared cooker and bake on high for about 1 hour or low for 2 to 3 hours. Sprinkle with scallions.

Yield: 24 servings

Per serving: 19 g water; 135 calories (76% from fat, 19% from protein, 5% from carb); 7 g protein; 11 g total fat; 4 g saturated fat; 3 g monounsaturated fat; 4 g polyunsaturated fat; 2 g carb; 0 g fiber; 0 g sugar; 125 mg phosphorus; 197 mg calcium; 0 mg iron; 237 mg sodium; 44 mg potassium; 148 IU vitamin A; 36 mg ATE vitamin E; 0 mg vitamin C; 19 mg cholesterol

Broccoli Dip

This is a simple dip with veggies and cream of mushroom soup. It's great to dip fresh broccoli or bread cubes in.

10 ounces (280 g) frozen broccoli, chopped

½ cup (50 g) chopped celery

1 cup (160 g) chopped onion

2 tablespoons (28 g) unsalted butter

4 ounces (115 g) mushroom, sliced

8 ounces (225 g) fat-free cream cheese

10 ounces (280 g) low-sodium cream of mushroom soup (see recipe in Chapter 2)

6 ounces (170 g) water chestnuts, sliced

2 teaspoons Worcestershire sauce

Cook broccoli until tender. In a skillet over medium-high heat, sauté celery and onion in butter until tender. Place broccoli and sautéed vegetables in slow cooker; add mushrooms, cream cheese, and cream of mushroom soup. Stir well and heat on low until cheese is melted. Add water chestnuts and Worcestershire sauce. Serve warm in the slow cooker.

(continued on page 58)

Yield: 20 servings

Per serving: 54 g water; 62 calories (49% from fat, 14% from protein, 38% from carb); 2 g protein; 3 g total fat; 2 g saturated fat; 1 g monounsaturated fat; 0 g polyunsaturated fat; 6 g carb; 1 g fiber; 1 g sugar; 47 mg phosphorus; 26 mg calcium; 0 mg iron; 101 mg sodium; 207 mg potassium; 214 IU vitamin A; 30 mg ATE vitamin E; 15 mg vitamin C; 10 mg cholesterol

Queso Dip

This is a moderately spicy cheese dip, perfect with either vegetables or corn chips.

1 cup (160 g) chopped onion

2 tablespoons (28 g) butter

4 ounces (115 g) jalapeños, chopped

2 cups (360 g) chopped tomatoes, undrained

4 ounces (115 g) pimientos, chopped and drained

¾ cup (90 g) grated Cheddar cheese

Sauté onion in butter in medium saucepan. Combine jalapeños, tomatoes, pimientos, and cheese with onion and heat through; transfer to slow cooker and cook on low for 2 hours.

Yield: 12 servings

Per serving: 56 g water; 65 calories (64% from fat, 15% from protein, 20% from carb); 3 g protein; 5 g total fat; 3 g saturated fat; 1 g monounsaturated fat; 0 g polyunsaturated fat; 3 g carb; 1 g fiber; 1 g sugar; 55 mg phosphorus; 68 mg calcium; 0 mg iron; 106 mg sodium; 109 mg potassium; 560 IU vitamin A; 37 mg ATE vitamin E; 19 mg vitamin C; 14 mg cholesterol

Creamy Mexican Beef and Bean Dip

Sort of like a burrito in a dip, this is great with corn chips.

1 pound (455 g) lean ground beef

½ cup (80 g) chopped onion

¾ cup (175 g) mild picante sauce

2 cups (512 g) cooked kidney beans

1 cup (230 g) sour cream

½ teaspoon chili powder

8 ounces (225 g) Cheddar cheese, shredded

Jalapeños or mild chili peppers, chopped, to taste

Cook ground beef with onion in a skillet over medium-high heat; drain. Mix beef mixture and remaining ingredients together in slow cooker and cook on low about 3 to 4 hours. Serve with your favorite vegetables or chips.

Yield: 32 servings

Per serving: 32 g water; 88 calories (59% from fat, 26% from protein, 15% from carb); 6 g protein; 6 g total fat; 3 g saturated fat; 2 g monounsaturated fat; 0 g polyunsaturated fat; 3 g carb; 1 g fiber; 0 g sugar; 80 mg phosphorus; 66 mg calcium; 1 mg iron; 78 mg sodium; 103 mg potassium; 133 IU vitamin A; 26 mg ATE vitamin E; 1 mg vitamin C; 20 mg cholesterol

Spinach Dip

We sometimes like to make a meal of this tasty spinach dip, serving it fondue-style with bread cubes and vegetables like mushrooms and broccoli.

8 ounces (225 g) cream cheese, cubed

¼ cup (60 ml) whipping cream

1 cup (190 g) frozen chopped spinach, thawed and squeezed dry

(continued on page 60)

2 tablespoons (24 g) pimiento, diced

1 teaspoon Worcestershire sauce

¼ teaspoon garlic powder

2 tablespoons (10 g) grated Parmesan cheese

2 teaspoons finely chopped onion

¼ teaspoon thyme

Combine cream cheese and cream in slow cooker. Cover and heat on low until cheese is melted, about 1 hour. Add remaining ingredients. Cover and heat on low 30 to 45 minutes longer.

Yield: 12 servings

Per serving: 29 g water; 84 calories (80% from fat, 12% from protein, 8% from carb); 3 g protein; 8 g total fat; 5 g saturated fat; 2 g monounsaturated fat; 0 g polyunsaturated fat; 2 g carb; 1 g fiber; 0 g sugar; 38 mg phosphorus; 53 mg calcium; 1 mg iron; 92 mg sodium; 82 mg potassium; 2248 IU vitamin A; 76 mg ATE vitamin E; 3 mg vitamin C; 24 mg cholesterol

Spicy Bean Dip

This dip doesn't have to be that spicy. The taco seasoning gives it a nice flavor but not one that is overpowering. Vary the heat to suit your taste by adding more or fewer chilies.

4 cups (952 g) refried beans

2 tablespoons (14 g) Salt-Free Mexican Seasoning (see recipe in Chapter 2)

½ cup (80 g) chopped onion

2 cups (230 g) shredded Monterey Jack cheese

4 drops hot pepper sauce, or to taste

Chopped jalapeños or mild chilies, to taste

Place refried beans, Mexican seasoning, onion, cheese, and hot pepper sauce in the slow cooker; stir well to blend. Stir in chopped jalapeños or mild chilies. Cover and cook on low until cheese is melted, about 1 to 1½ hours; add a little water if mixture seems too thick. Serve from the slow cooker with French bread cubes, crackers, or chips.

Yield: 32 servings

Per serving: 30 g water; 65 calories (40% from fat, 24% from protein, 36% from carb); 4 g protein; 3 g total fat; 2 g saturated fat; 1 g monounsaturated fat; 0 g polyunsaturated fat; 6 g carb; 2 g fiber; 0 g sugar; 64 mg phosphorus; 73 mg calcium; 1 mg iron; 219 mg sodium; 94 mg potassium; 190 IU vitamin A; 16 mg ATE vitamin E; 2 mg vitamin C; 10 mg cholesterol

Hot Cheesy Crabmeat Dip

This is similar to a baked crab dip that I make sometimes, but so much easier to make. And the dip stays warm in the pot it cooked in.

10 ounces (280 g) sharp Cheddar cheese

8 ounces (225 g) fat-free cream cheese

½ cup (120 ml) skim milk

½ cup (120 ml) dry white wine

8 ounces (225 g) crabmeat

Spray the bottom and sides of slow cooker with nonstick cooking spray. Place the two cheeses and milk in prepared slow cooker. Cook 1 to 2 hours. Add wine and crabmeat and stir to combine; cover and cook for 1 hour longer.

Yield: 8 servings

Per serving: 79 g water; 255 calories (64% from fat, 30% from protein, 6% from carb); 18 g protein; 17 g total fat; 11 g saturated fat; 5 g monounsaturated fat; 1 g polyunsaturated fat; 4 g carb; 0 g fiber; 0 g sugar; 316 mg phosphorus; 339 mg calcium; 1 mg iron; 408 mg sodium; 227 mg potassium; 581 IU vitamin A; 153 mg ATE vitamin E; 1 mg vitamin C; 79 mg cholesterol

Curry Dip

This cheesy dip with curry makes a perfect dip for vegetables.

½ cup (58 g) shredded Cheddar cheese

8 ounces (225 g) fat-free cream cheese

¼ cup (60 ml) skim milk

1 teaspoon curry powder

Mix ingredients together in slow cooker. Cover and cook on high 1 hour or until cheeses are melted. Stir.

Yield: 10 servings

Per serving: 22 g water; 82 calories (68% from fat, 21% from protein, 10% from carb); 4 g protein; 6 g total fat; 4 g saturated fat; 2 g monounsaturated fat; 0 g polyunsaturated fat; 2 g carb; 0 g fiber; 0 g sugar; 75 mg phosphorus; 83 mg calcium; 0 mg iron; 112 mg sodium; 59 mg potassium; 235 IU vitamin A; 62 mg ATE vitamin E; 0 mg vitamin C; 20 mg cholesterol

American Fondue

This is a little different from the traditional fondue with Cheddar cheese, but that seems to increase the appeal for some people.

1 can (10.5 ounces, or 295 g) Cheddar cheese soup

2 cups (225 g) shredded Cheddar cheese

2 cups (220 g) shredded Swiss cheese

12 ounces (355 ml) beer or 1½ cups (355 ml) apple cider

½ teaspoon hot pepper sauce

2 drops liquid smoke

Place all ingredients in slow cooker. Stir to mix. Cover and cook on low for 2 hours. After 1 hour of cooking time, stir. Before serving, whisk to blend. Serve with bread sticks or vegetables for dipping.

Per serving: 63 g water; 215 calories (67% from fat, 25% from protein, 8% from carb); 13 g protein; 15 g total fat; 10 g saturated fat; 4 g monounsaturated fat; 0 g polyunsaturated fat; 4 g carb; 0 g fiber; 1 g sugar; 277 mg phosphorus; 400 mg calcium; 0 mg iron; 336 mg sodium; 85 mg potassium; 481 IU vitamin A; 121 mg ATE vitamin E; 0 mg vitamin C; 49 mg cholesterol

Taco Dip

This creamy Mexican-flavored dip is great with corn chips, but for a treat that is just as tasty and much healthier, try it with broccoli or other vegetables.

16 ounces (455 g) fat-free cream cheese

1 teaspoon low-sodium onion soup mix (see recipe in Chapter 2)

1 pound (455 g) extra-lean ground beef

2 teaspoons salt-free Mexican seasoning (see recipe in Chapter 2)

½ cup (58 g) shredded Cheddar cheese

¼ cup (38 g) finely chopped green bell pepper

Combine cream cheese and onion soup mix and spread in the bottom of slow cooker. In a skillet over medium-high heat, brown beef with Mexican seasoning. Place on top of cheese mixture. Sprinkle with Cheddar cheese, then green pepper. Cover and cook on low 2 to 3 hours.

Yield: 10 servings

Per serving: 63 g water; 238 calories (69% from fat, 25% from protein, 6% from carb); 15 g protein; 18 g total fat; 10 g saturated fat; 6 g monounsaturated fat; 1 g polyunsaturated fat; 3 g carb; 0 g fiber; 0 g sugar; 165 mg phosphorus; 102 mg calcium; 2 mg iron; 205 mg sodium; 218 mg potassium; 388 IU vitamin A; 99 mg ATE vitamin E; 3 mg vitamin C; 64 mg cholesterol

Mexican Dip

Here's a great Mexican layered dip, made easy by the slow cooker. This is especially good with tortilla chips.

1 pound (455 g) extra-lean ground beef

1 cup (160 g) chopped onion

2 cups (476 g) refried beans (see recipe in chapter 16)

1 tablespoon (7 g) Salt-Free Mexican Seasoning (see recipe in chapter 2)

1 cup (230 g) fat-free sour cream

½ cup (58 g) shredded Cheddar cheese

TIP

Sprinkle with jalapeno rings, if desired.

Brown beef and onions in a skillet over medium-high heat and stir in refried beans and Mexican seasoning. Place in bottom of slow cooker. Spread sour cream over and sprinkle with cheese. Cover and cook on low for 1½ to 2 hours.

Yield: 20 servings

Per serving: 52 g water; 110 calories (56% from fat, 25% from protein, 19% from carb); 7 g protein; 7 g total fat; 3 g saturated fat; 3 g monounsaturated fat; 0 g polyunsaturated fat; 5 g carb; 1 g fiber; 0 g sugar; 84 mg phosphorus; 49 mg calcium; 1 mg iron; 46 mg sodium; 162 mg potassium; 78 IU vitamin A; 21 mg ATE vitamin E; 2 mg vitamin C; 26 mg cholesterol

Gourmet Mushrooms

Long, slow cooking gives these mushrooms great flavor. You can serve them as appetizers or as a side dish.

1 pound (455 g) mushrooms

¼ cup (55 g) unsalted butter

1 cup (235 ml) low sodium chicken broth

¼ cup (60 ml) white wine

1 tablespoon (1.7 g) marjoram

1 tablespoon (3 g) chives

Put cleaned mushrooms in slow cooker. Melt butter in a saucepan. Add remaining ingredients. Stir until thoroughly blended and then pour over mushrooms. Cook on high for 4 hours.

Yield: 8 servings

Per serving: 89 g water; 75 calories (73% from fat, 13% from protein, 14% from carb); 2 g protein; 6 g total fat; 4 g saturated fat; 2 g monounsaturated fat; 0 g polyunsaturated fat; 3 g carb; 1 g fiber; 1 g sugar; 62 mg phosphorus; 10 mg calcium; 1 mg iron; 13 mg sodium; 217 mg potassium; 211 IU vitamin A; 48 mg ATE vitamin E; 2 mg vitamin C; 15 mg cholesterol

Butterscotch Dip

This makes a wonderful dip with fruit slices like apples, pears, or bananas.

20 ounces (560 g) butterscotch chips

5 ounces (150 ml) fat-free evaporated milk

1 tablespoon (15 ml) rum extract

Combine all ingredients in slow cooker and cook on low until chips are soft, about 1 hour. Stir.

Yield:16 servings

Per serving: 9 g water; 145 calories (7% from fat, 2% from protein, 91% from carb); 1 g protein; 1 g total fat; 1 g saturated fat; 0 g monounsaturated fat; 0 g polyunsaturated fat; 33 g carb; 0 g fiber; 30 g sugar; 18 mg phosphorus; 27 mg calcium; 0 mg iron; 149 mg sodium; 30 mg potassium; 70 IU vitamin A; 20 mg ATE vitamin E; 0 mg vitamin C; 4 mg cholesterol

Sweet and Spicy Nuts

These spicy little things will be a big hit. They'll keep several weeks at room temperature, but I bet they won't last that long.

1 cup (140 g) unsalted cashews

1 cup (145 g) unsalted almonds, toasted

1 cup (100 g) unsalted pecan halves, toasted

½ cup (100 g) sugar

⅓ cup (75 g) unsalted butter, melted

1 teaspoon ground ginger

½ teaspoon cinnamon

¼ teaspoon cloves

¼ teaspoon cayenne pepper

Place nuts in a slow cooker. In a small bowl, combine sugar, butter, ginger, cinnamon, cloves, and cayenne pepper. Add to cooker, stirring to coat nuts. Cover and cook on low for 2 hours, stirring after 1 hour. Stir nuts again. Spread in a single layer on buttered foil; let cool for at least 1 hour.

Yield: 22 servings

Per serving: 1 g water; 189 calories (75% from fat, 7% from protein, 19% from carb); 3 g protein; 17 g total fat; 3 g saturated fat; 9 g monounsaturated fat; 4 g polyunsaturated fat; 9 g carb; 2 g fiber; 6 g sugar; 92 mg phosphorus; 29 mg calcium; 1 mg iron; 2 mg sodium; 129 mg potassium; 109 IU vitamin A; 23 mg ATE vitamin E; 0 mg vitamin C; 7 mg cholesterol

Spiced Nuts

These nuts have just enough heat to make them interesting. They make a great nibble while watching TV or when you need a little something while you prepare dinner.

½ pound (255 g) pecan halves

½ pound (255 g) unsalted cashews

¼ cup (55 g) unsalted butter, melted

1 tablespoon (7.5 g) chili powder

1 teaspoon dried basil

1 teaspoon dried oregano

1 teaspoon dried thyme

½ teaspoon onion powder

¼ teaspoon garlic powder

¼ teaspoon cayenne

Combine all ingredients in slow cooker. Cover and cook on high for 15 minutes. Turn to low and continue to cook, uncovered, stirring occasionally for 2 hours. Transfer nuts to a baking sheet and cool completely.

Yield: 32 servings

Per serving: 1 g water; 104 calories (81% from fat, 7% from protein, 13% from carb); 2 g protein; 10 g total fat; 2 g saturated fat; 5 g monounsaturated fat; 2 g polyunsaturated fat; 4 g carb; 1 g fiber; 1 g sugar; 56 mg phosphorus; 11 mg calcium; 1 mg iron; 4 mg sodium; 76 mg potassium; 129 IU vitamin A; 12 mg ATE vitamin E; 0 mg vitamin C; 4 mg cholesterol

Sugared Pecans

I have a special fondness for spiced and sugared nuts. This is about the easiest recipe I've found, but it doesn't give up a thing in taste.

1 pound (455 g) pecan halves

¼ cup (55 g) unsalted butter, melted

½ cup (63 g) powdered sugar

¼ teaspoon ground cloves

1½ teaspoons ground cinnamon

¼ teaspoon ground ginger

(continued on page 68)

Turn slow cooker to high for about 15 minutes. In hot slow cooker, stir together the nuts and butter. Add the powdered sugar, stirring to blend and coat evenly. Cover and cook on high for 15 minutes. Reduce the heat to low and remove lid; cook, uncovered, stirring occasionally, for about 2 to 3 hours or until the nuts are coated with a crisp glaze. Transfer the nuts to a bowl. In another small bowl, combine the spices; sift over the nuts, stirring to coat evenly. Let cool before serving.

Yield: 24 servings

Per serving: 1 g water; 158 calories (83% from fat, 4% from protein, 12% from carb); 2 g protein; 16 g total fat; 2 g saturated fat; 8 g monounsaturated fat; 4 g polyunsaturated fat; 5 g carb; 2 g fiber; 3 g sugar; 53 mg phosphorus; 16 mg calcium; 1 mg iron; 0 mg sodium; 79 mg potassium; 70 IU vitamin A; 16 mg ATE vitamin E; 0 mg vitamin C; 5 mg cholesterol

4

Start Your Day Right with a Healthy Slow Cooker Breakfast

We don't use the slow cooker for breakfast all that often, but there are some occasions where we almost always turn to it. If you have guests over or for a holiday where you want to get the family fed something everyone will like without going to a lot of trouble in the morning, it makes perfect sense. We have recipes here for eggs and other savory dishes, breakfast potatoes, and a variety of oatmeal and other cereals.

Mexican Egg Scramble

Mexican-accented eggs and sausage cook overnight while you sleep.

1 pound (455 g) breakfast sausage, cooked and drained

1 cup (160 g) chopped onion

1 cup (150 g) chopped green bell pepper

4 ounces (115 g) canned chopped green chilies, drained

2 cups (230 g) grated Monterey Jack cheese

4 cups (960 ml) egg substitute

TIP

Serve with sour cream or fresh salsa.

Spray the inside of slow cooker with nonstick cooking spray. Layer some of the sausage, onions, peppers, chilies, and cheese in the cooker, repeating the layering process until all ingredients are used. Pour egg substitute over mixture in the slow cooker. Cover and cook on low 7 to 8 hours.

Yield: 12 servings

Per serving: 130 g water; 293 calories (66% from fat, 29% from protein, 4% from carb); 21 g protein; 21 g total fat; 9 g saturated fat; 8 g monounsaturated fat; 3 g polyunsaturated fat; 3 g carb; 1 g fiber; 2 g sugar; 260 mg phosphorus; 223 mg calcium; 3 mg iron; 325 mg sodium; 441 mg potassium; 528 IU vitamin A; 42 mg ATE vitamin E; 15 mg vitamin C; 49 mg cholesterol

Slow Cooker Poached Eggs

It's amazing the things you can do with a slow cooker. Don't have an egg poacher or have trouble getting them cooked just right? Here's the slow cooker to the rescue!

2 eggs

Pour about ½ inch (1.3 cm) of tap water, as hot as possible, into the slow cooker. Cover and cook on high for 20 to 30 minutes. Coat two custard cups, one for each egg, with nonstick cooking spray. Break 1 egg into each cup. Place the cups in the cooker in a single layer. Cover and cook on high for 12 to 15 minutes if you like your yolks runny. You can test them by pressing each egg yolk gently with a spoon. When the white is firm but the yolk is still soft, they are done.

Yield: 2 servings

Per serving: 42 g water; 80 calories (63% from fat, 35% from protein, 2% from carb); 7 g protein; 6 g total fat; 2 g saturated fat; 2 g monounsaturated fat; 1 g polyunsaturated fat; 0 g carb; 0 g fiber; 0 g sugar; 107 mg phosphorus; 30 mg calcium; 1 mg iron; 78 mg sodium; 75 mg potassium; 273 IU vitamin A; 78 mg ATE vitamin E; 0 mg vitamin C; 237 mg cholesterol

Western Omelet

This makes big batch of breakfast. It's great if you have a number of people staying over because you can put it in the night before and have a nice hot breakfast with no work in the morning.

32 ounces (1 kg) frozen hash brown potatoes

½ cup (75 g) chopped ham

¾ cup (120 g) chopped onion

½ cup (75 g) chopped green bell pepper

12 eggs

1 cup (235 ml) skim milk

TIP

To lower cholesterol, use 3 cups (705 ml) of egg substitute.

Layer half the potatoes, ham, onion, and peppers in the slow cooker. Repeat with the other half. Beat together eggs and milk. Pour over potato mixture. Cover and cook on low 8 to 10 hours.

Yield: 10 servings

Per serving: 146 g water; 322 calories (48% from fat, 17% from protein, 35% from carb); 14 g protein; 18 g total fat; 6 g saturated fat; 8 g monounsaturated fat; 2 g polyunsaturated fat; 29 g carb; 2 g fiber; 3 g sugar; 242 mg phosphorus; 88 mg calcium; 3 mg iron; 215 mg sodium; 585 mg potassium; 405 IU vitamin A; 108 mg ATE vitamin E; 13 mg vitamin C; 288 mg cholesterol

Broccoli Egg Casserole

Eggs and veggies are a favorite breakfast combination around our house. So this easy recipe is a big favorite.

24 ounces (680 g) cottage cheese

10 ounces (280 g) frozen broccoli, thawed and drained

1½ cups (355 ml) egg substitute

⅓ cup (40 g) flour

¼ cup (55 g) unsalted butter, melted

3 tablespoons (30 g) finely chopped onion

2½ cups (288 g) shredded Cheddar cheese, divided

In a large bowl, combine the cottage cheese, broccoli, egg substitute, flour, butter, onion, and 2 cups (225 g) Cheddar cheese. Pour into a slow cooker sprayed with nonstick cooking spray. Cover and cook on high for 1 hour. Stir. Reduce heat to low; cover and cook 2½ to 3 hours longer. Sprinkle with remaining ½ cup (58 g) cheese.

Yield: 6 servings

Per serving: 212 g water; 479 calories (54% from fat, 36% from protein, 10% from carb); 43 g protein; 29 g total fat; 17 g saturated fat; 8 g monounsaturated fat; 2 g polyunsaturated fat; 12 g carb; 2 g fiber; 4 g sugar; 510 mg phosphorus; 486 mg calcium; 3 mg iron; 592 mg sodium; 381 mg potassium; 1576 IU vitamin A; 216 mg ATE vitamin E; 19 mg vitamin C; 87 mg cholesterol

Overnight Breakfast Casserole

This is a traditional sort of breakfast casserole, with eggs, ham, hash browns, and cheese. But being traditional doesn't make it any less delicious.

32 ounces (905 g) frozen hash brown potatoes

1 pound (455 g) cooked ham, cubed

1 cup (160 g) diced onion

1 cup (150 g) diced green bell pepper

1½ cups (173 g) shredded Cheddar cheese

3 cups (705 ml) egg substitute

1 cup (235 ml) skim milk

1 teaspoon black pepper

Layer one-third of the hash browns, ham, onions, peppers, and cheese in the slow cooker. Repeat until you have three layers. Beat egg substitute, milk, and pepper and pour over layers in the slow cooker; cover and turn on low. Cook for 10 to 12 hours overnight.

Yield: 8 servings

Per serving: 251 g water; 546 calories (48% from fat, 25% from protein, 27% from carb); 35 g protein; 29 g total fat; 13 g saturated fat; 11 g monounsaturated fat; 4 g polyunsaturated fat; 38 g carb; 3 g fiber; 4 g sugar; 492 mg phosphorus; 301 mg calcium; 5 mg iron; 984 mg sodium; 1149 mg potassium; 719 IU vitamin A; 83 mg ATE vitamin E; 24 mg vitamin C; 51 mg cholesterol

Hash Brown and Bacon Casserole

When you have a crowd to feed for breakfast, this is the recipe you are looking for. Stir it up and put it in the slow cooker the night before, and you're ready to go in the morning.

32 ounces (905 g) frozen hash brown potatoes

½ pound (225 g) low-sodium bacon, fried and drained

½ cup (80 g) diced onion

½ cup (75 g) diced green bell pepper

4 ounces (115 g) Cheddar cheese, shredded

3 cups (705 ml) egg substitute

1 cup (235 ml) skim milk

½ teaspoon dry mustard

Layer the frozen potatoes, bacon, onion, green pepper, and cheese in the slow cooker in two or three layers, ending with cheese. Beat the egg substitute, milk, and mustard together. Pour over the whole mixture. Cook on low for 10 to 12 hours.

(continued on page 74)

Yield: 12 servings

Per serving: 130 g water; 370 calories (53% from fat, 22% from protein, 26% from carb); 20 g protein; 22 g total fat; 8 g saturated fat; 9 g monounsaturated fat; 3 g polyunsaturated fat; 24 g carb; 2 g fiber; 2 g sugar; 306 mg phosphorus; 146 mg calcium; 3 mg iron; 349 mg sodium; 711 mg potassium; 392 IU vitamin A; 39 mg ATE vitamin E; 10 mg vitamin C; 32 mg cholesterol

Breakfast Casserole 2

Another overnight breakfast casserole, this one based on bread and sausage.

½ pound (225 g) breakfast sausage (see recipe in Chapter 2)

2 tablespoons (22 g) mustard

10 slices bread

1½ cups (355 ml) egg substitute

1½ cups (355 ml) skim milk

1 cup (115 g) shredded Cheddar cheese

Brown and crumble the sausage. Drain remaining fat. Spread mustard on one side of each of the bread slices and cut bread into cubes. Beat egg substitute and milk together. Spray inside of slow cooker with nonstick cooking spray. Layer bread, cheese, and sausage in slow cooker. Pour milk and egg mixture over everything. Cook on low 8 to 12 hours.

Yield: 6 servings

Per serving: 154 g water; 436 calories (49% from fat, 24% from protein, 27% from carb); 26 g protein; 24 g total fat; 10 g saturated fat; 9 g monounsaturated fat; 3 g polyunsaturated fat; 29 g carb; 3 g fiber; 6 g sugar; 405 mg phosphorus; 338 mg calcium; 4 mg iron; 564 mg sodium; 554 mg potassium; 575 IU vitamin A; 94 mg ATE vitamin E; 2 mg vitamin C; 54 mg cholesterol

Breakfast Burritos

Here are some breakfast rollups courtesy of the slow cooker.

1 cup (235 ml) egg substitute

⅓ cup (60 g) chopped and seeded tomatoes

¼ cup (25 g) chopped scallions

1 cup (115 g) shredded Monterey Jack cheese

4 flour tortillas

TIP *For even more Mexican flavor, top with salsa and sour cream or add a 4-ounce (115 g) can of chopped green chilies to the mixture.*

Place egg substitute, tomatoes, and scallions in slow cooker. Cook on low for 2 hours. Add cheese and cook for another 30 minutes to 1 hour or until cheese is completely melted and eggs are set. Fill flour tortillas with egg mixture and roll up to serve.

Yield: 4 servings

Per serving: 92 g water; 274 calories (48% from fat, 27% from protein, 25% from carb); 18 g protein; 14 g total fat; 7 g saturated fat; 5 g monounsaturated fat; 2 g polyunsaturated fat; 17 g carb; 1 g fiber; 1 g sugar; 265 mg phosphorus; 323 mg calcium; 3 mg iron; 482 mg sodium; 325 mg potassium; 619 IU vitamin A; 63 mg ATE vitamin E; 4 mg vitamin C; 30 mg cholesterol

Breakfast Potatoes

Here's an easy, cheesy version of home fried potatoes that cook overnight. They are also great as a side dish.

4 large potatoes

1 tablespoon (14 g) unsalted butter, melted

1 cup (160 g) coarsely chopped onion

4 ounces (115 g) Cheddar cheese, shredded

(continued on page 76)

Slice potatoes 1/4-inch (63 mm) thick. Layer potatoes, butter, onion, and cheese, making two layers of each. Cook on high 8 to10 hours.

Yield: 6 servings

Per serving: 230 g water; 276 calories (27% from fat, 14% from protein, 59% from carb); 10 g protein; 9 g total fat; 5 g saturated fat; 2 g monounsaturated fat; 0 g polyunsaturated fat; 42 g carb; 5 g fiber; 4 g sugar; 255 mg phosphorus; 168 mg calcium; 2 mg iron; 133 mg sodium; 1177 mg potassium; 266 IU vitamin A; 65 mg ATE vitamin E; 23 mg vitamin C; 25 mg cholesterol

Spicy Hash Browns

If you're looking for something to wake you up, try these spicy hash browns. They are heated up with pepper jack cheese and canned jalapeños and will definitely help to get you going in the morning.

5 cups (1 kg) frozen hash brown potatoes

1 cup (133 g) shredded pepper jack cheese

½ cup (80 g) chopped onion

½ cup (75 g) chopped red bell pepper

4 ounces (115 g) canned sliced jalapeños

2 cups (475 ml) water

Place hash browns in slow cooker. Combine remaining ingredients and pour over potatoes. Cover and cook on low for 8 to 9 hours or on high for 4 to 5 hours. If desired, top with additional shredded cheese.

Yield: 8 servings

Per serving: 151 g water; 283 calories (50% from fat, 10% from protein, 40% from carb); 7 g protein; 16 g total fat; 8 g saturated fat; 6 g monounsaturated fat; 1 g polyunsaturated fat; 30 g carb; 3 g fiber; 2 g sugar; 150 mg phosphorus; 148 mg calcium; 2 mg iron; 180 mg sodium; 489 mg potassium; 437 IU vitamin A; 32 mg ATE vitamin E; 24 mg vitamin C; 15 mg cholesterol

Breakfast Cobbler

Here's a simple and easy breakfast recipe. Depending on the size of your cooker and the number of people you are feeding, this can easily be doubled.

2 cups (220 g) sliced apple

2 cups (250 g) granola

1 teaspoon cinnamon

¼ cup (85 g) honey

2 tablespoons (28 g) unsalted butter, melted

Mix all ingredients in slow cooker. Cover and cook on low for 8 to 10 hours.

Yield: 4 servings

Per serving: 55 g water; 302 calories (22% from fat, 5% from protein, 73% from carb); 4 g protein; 8 g total fat; 4 g saturated fat; 2 g monounsaturated fat; 1 g polyunsaturated fat; 58 g carb; 3 g fiber; 37 g sugar; 122 mg phosphorus; 28 mg calcium; 1 mg iron; 157 mg sodium; 180 mg potassium; 200 IU vitamin A; 48 mg ATE vitamin E; 2 mg vitamin C; 15 mg cholesterol

TIP

Serve with milk.

Breakfast Grains

This great multigrain hot cereal cooks overnight while you sleep.

¼ cup (46 g) barley

¼ cup (25 g) bulgur

¼ cup (20 g) rolled oats

¼ cup (29 g) wheat germ

¼ cup (25 g) chopped almonds

1 teaspoon cinnamon

1 apple, chopped

TIP

Serve with milk and fruit, if desired. Or, switch grains or change the proportions as long as you have about a cup of grains total.

(continued on page 78)

3 cups (705 ml) apple juice

1 cup (235 ml) water

Combine everything in the slow cooker. Cook on low for 10 to 12 hours.

Yield: 4 servings

Per serving: 248 g water; 274 calories (19% from fat, 11% from protein, 70% from carb); 8 g protein; 6 g total fat; 1 g saturated fat; 3 g monounsaturated fat; 2 g polyunsaturated fat; 50 g carb; 7 g fiber; 24 g sugar; 219 mg phosphorus; 53 mg calcium; 2 mg iron; 20 mg sodium; 476 mg potassium; 25 IU vitamin A; 0 mg ATE vitamin E; 3 mg vitamin C; 0 mg cholesterol

Breakfast Risotto

This is a delightful fruit-flavored rice dish that is perfect for breakfast when you are looking for something a little different.

¼ cup (55 g) unsalted butter, melted

1½ cups (345 g) arborio rice

3 apples, washed, cored, and cubed

1½ teaspoons cinnamon

⅛ teaspoon nutmeg

⅛ teaspoon cloves

⅓ cup (75 g) brown sugar

2 cups (475 ml) apple juice

2 cups (475 ml) skim milk

Spray the inside of slow cooker with nonstick cooking spray. Pour melted butter into slow cooker. Add the rice to the butter and stir it around to coat it. Add the apples, cinnamon, nutmeg, cloves, and brown sugar. Stir in the juice and the milk. Cover and cook on low 6 to 9 hours. Stir before serving.

Yield: 6 servings

Per serving: 228 g water; 269 calories (27% from fat, 7% from protein, 66% from carb); 5 g protein; 8 g total fat; 5 g saturated fat; 2 g monounsaturated fat; 0 g polyunsaturated fat; 45 g carb; 1 g fiber; 27 g sugar; 127 mg phosphorus; 149 mg calcium; 1 mg iron; 60 mg sodium; 369 mg potassium; 429 IU vitamin A; 113 mg ATE vitamin E; 4 mg vitamin C; 22 mg cholesterol

Date Nut Oatmeal

Now this is what oatmeal should taste like. And I guarantee that you won't get it out of some paper pouch that you microwave.

2½ cups (570 ml) skim milk

1 cup (80 g) rolled oats

⅔ cup (119 g) chopped dates

½ cup (55 g) chopped pecans

½ cup (120 ml) half and half

¼ cup (60 g) brown sugar

½ teaspoon cinnamon

TIP

Serve with milk.

Spray the inside of the slow cooker lightly with nonstick cooking spray. Mix together all of the ingredients in a bowl. Pour into slow cooker. Cover and cook on low 8 to 10 hours.

Yield: 4 servings

Per serving: 170 g water; 411 calories (32% from fat, 11% from protein, 57% from carb); 12 g protein; 15 g total fat; 3 g saturated fat; 7 g monounsaturated fat; 4 g polyunsaturated fat; 61 g carb; 6 g fiber; 33 g sugar; 356 mg phosphorus; 298 mg calcium; 2 mg iron; 110 mg sodium; 690 mg potassium; 431 IU vitamin A; 123 mg ATE vitamin E; 2 mg vitamin C; 14 mg cholesterol

Apple Oatmeal Breakfast Pudding

Put this in the slow cooker before you go to bed and have a hot breakfast waiting for you when you get up.

2 cups (160 g) rolled oats

3 cups (705 ml) water

½ cup (115 g) brown sugar

1 teaspoon cinnamon

5 apples, peeled and sliced

2 tablespoons (28 g) butter, melted

Combine all ingredients. Place in slow cooker, cover, and cook on low 8 to 12 hours.

Yield: 6 servings

Per serving: 214 g water; 259 calories (19% from fat, 7% from protein, 74% from carb); 5 g protein; 6 g total fat; 3 g saturated fat; 2 g monounsaturated fat; 1 g polyunsaturated fat; 50 g carb; 4 g fiber; 29 g sugar; 145 mg phosphorus; 44 mg calcium; 2 mg iron; 39 mg sodium; 258 mg potassium; 160 IU vitamin A; 32 mg ATE vitamin E; 4 mg vitamin C; 10 mg cholesterol

Slow Cooker Breakfast Oatmeal

This is simple oatmeal, but it's very tasty. The raisins tend to sweeten it, so it requires less sugar when you eat it.

1 cup (80 g) rolled oats

⅓ cup (50 g) raisins

2¼ cups (535 ml) water

Spray slow cooker with nonstick cooking spray. Combine all ingredients in slow cooker, cover, and cook on low for 8 to 10 hours.

Per serving: 137 g water; 119 calories (10% from fat, 12% from protein, 79% from carb); 4 g protein; 1 g total fat; 0 g saturated fat; 0 g monounsaturated fat; 0 g polyunsaturated fat; 24 g carb; 2 g fiber; 8 g sugar; 110 mg phosphorus; 21 mg calcium; 1 mg iron; 6 mg sodium; 175 mg potassium; 0 IU vitamin A; 0 mg ATE vitamin E; 0 mg vitamin C; 0 mg cholesterol

Apple Oatmeal

Apple-flavored and full of fruit, this breakfast cereal is sure to please.

3 cups (705 ml) water

1¾ cups (420 ml) apple juice

1½ cups (120 g) rolled oats

7 ounces (200 g) dried mixed fruit

⅓ cup (75 g) brown sugar

½ teaspoon cinnamon

12 ounces (340 g) vanilla yogurt

1 cup (125 g) granola

Combine first six ingredients (through cinnamon) in slow cooker. Cover and cook on low for 6 to 8 hours. Top with yogurt and granola to serve.

Yield: 8 servings

Per serving: 178 g water; 254 calories (7% from fat, 9% from protein, 84% from carb); 6 g protein; 2 g total fat; 1 g saturated fat; 1 g monounsaturated fat; 1 g polyunsaturated fat; 55 g carb; 4 g fiber; 24 g sugar; 182 mg phosphorus; 109 mg calcium; 2 mg iron; 82 mg sodium; 472 mg potassium; 624 IU vitamin A; 5 mg ATE vitamin E; 2 mg vitamin C; 2 mg cholesterol

Cranberry Oatmeal

Another easy overnight breakfast, this oatmeal is full of fruit.

4¼ cups (1 L) water

1½ cups (120 g) rolled oats

¼ cup (80 g) maple syrup

⅓ cup (50 g) raisins

⅓ cup (40 g) dried cranberries

1 teaspoon cinnamon

1 teaspoon vanilla

Spray the inside of the slow cooker with nonstick cooking spray. Combine all ingredients in slow cooker, cover, and cook on low for 6 to 8 hours.

Yield: 8 servings

Per serving: 135 g water; 110 calories (8% from fat, 9% from protein, 82% from carb); 3 g protein; 1 g total fat; 0 g saturated fat; 0 g monounsaturated fat; 0 g polyunsaturated fat; 23 g carb; 2 g fiber; 11 g sugar; 80 mg phosphorus; 26 mg calcium; 1 mg iron; 6 mg sodium; 133 mg potassium; 4 IU vitamin A; 0 mg ATE vitamin E; 1 mg vitamin C; 0 mg cholesterol

Apple Butter

This makes quite a lot of apple butter, but it freezes well so you can save it for later. Tart apples like Jonathan or Macintosh are best.

12 apples

1 cup (235 ml) apple cider

1 cup (340 g) honey

1 teaspoon cinnamon

¼ teaspoon cloves

Core and chop apples but do not peel. Combine with cider in slow cooker. Stir in honey and spices. Cover and cook on high for 6 to 8 hours then uncover, stir, and cook for up to 3 hours longer until desired consistency.

Yield: 48 servings

Per serving: 33 g water; 39 calories (1% from fat, 1% from protein, 98% from carb); 0 g protein; 0 g total fat; 0 g saturated fat; 0 g monounsaturated fat; 0 g polyunsaturated fat; 11 g carb; 0 g fiber; 10 g sugar; 4 mg phosphorus; 3 mg calcium; 0 mg iron; 0 mg sodium; 39 mg potassium; 12 IU vitamin A; 0 mg ATE vitamin E; 1 mg vitamin C; 0 mg cholesterol

5

Fill-Up on Low-Calorie, Low-Cholesterol Vegitarian Main Dishes

The slow cooker makes easy work of many meatless dishes. Here you'll find pasta dishes like lasagna that are actually easy to make, as well as sauces for pasta or rice and a number of dishes featuring the protein from beans and legumes.

Pasta and Mushrooms

A quick and very flavorful mushroom sauce cooks in the slow cooker, allowing the flavors to develop fully.

8 ounces (225 g) mushrooms, sliced

½ teaspoon minced garlic

¼ cup (14 g) chopped sun dried tomatoes

½ cup (120 ml) dry white wine

½ cup (120 ml) vegetable broth (see recipe in Chapter 2)

¼ cup (15 g) chopped Italian parsley

1 pound (455 g) pasta

TIP

For a more special sauce, substitute porcini or wild mushrooms.

Combine all ingredients except the pasta in the slow cooker, cover, and cook on low 4 to 6 hours. Cook pasta according to directions on box and serve with sauce.

Yield: 4 servings

Per serving: 126 g water; 487 calories (7% from fat, 15% from protein, 78% from carb); 17 g protein; 4 g total fat; 1 g saturated fat; 1 g monounsaturated fat; 1 g polyunsaturated fat; 91 g carb; 5 g fiber; 4 g sugar; 287 mg phosphorus; 41 mg calcium; 2 mg iron; 49 mg sodium; 596 mg potassium; 405 IU vitamin A; 0 mg ATE vitamin E; 14 mg vitamin C; 0 mg cholesterol

Slow Cooker Lasagna

The slow cooker can make easy work of lasagna, cooking the noodles in the sauce so you avoid all the boiling and sticking to the bottom of the pan that I always end up fighting with. This vegetarian version goes together in a snap and tastes great.

58 ounces (1.6 kg) low-sodium spaghetti sauce

8 ounces (225 g) uncooked lasagna noodles

4 cups (460 g) shredded mozzarella cheese

1¼ cups (280 g) fat-free cottage cheese

(continued on page 86)

Spray the interior of the cooker with nonstick cooking spray. Spread one-fourth of the sauce on the bottom of the slow cooker. Arrange one-third of the uncooked noodles over the sauce. Break to fit if necessary. Combine the cheeses in a bowl. Spoon one-third of the cheeses over the noodles. Repeat these layers twice. Top with remaining sauce. Cover and cook on low 4 hours.

Yield: 8 servings

Per serving: 212 g water; 523 calories (39% from fat, 18% from protein, 42% from carb); 24 g protein; 23 g total fat; 9 g saturated fat; 11 g monounsaturated fat; 2 g polyunsaturated fat; 56 g carb; 7 g fiber; 25 g sugar; 320 mg phosphorus; 367 mg calcium; 3 mg iron; 471 mg sodium; 908 mg potassium; 1655 IU vitamin A; 101 mg ATE vitamin E; 23 mg vitamin C; 46 mg cholesterol

Mushroom Lasagna

This meatless lasagna gets a boost from mushrooms. And like the previous recipe, it is so much easier to prepare than the old way.

6 ounces (170 g) uncooked lasagna noodles

28 ounces (785 g) low-sodium spaghetti sauce

⅓ cup (80 ml) water

8 ounces (225 g) mushrooms, sliced

15 ounces (425 g) ricotta cheese

2 cups (230 g) shredded mozzarella cheese

Break noodles. Place half in bottom of greased slow cooker. Layer half of sauce and water, half of mushrooms, half of ricotta cheese, and half of mozzarella cheese over noodles. Repeat layers. Cover and cook on low 5 hours.

Yield: 8 servings

Per serving: 164 g water; 351 calories (40% from fat, 20% from protein, 40% from carb); 18 g protein; 16 g total fat; 7 g saturated fat; 6 g monounsaturated fat; 1 g polyunsaturated fat; 36 g carb; 4 g fiber; 12 g sugar; 256 mg phosphorus; 319 mg calcium; 2 mg iron; 275 mg sodium; 593 mg potassium; 1003 IU vitamin A; 105 mg ATE vitamin E; 12 mg vitamin C; 39 mg cholesterol

Cannelloni

Cannelloni is one of those things that many people don't make because they think it's difficult. In this case, we make it easier by wrapping lasagna noodles around the filling, rather than trying to stuff it into tubes. Then the slow cooker does the rest.

1 tablespoon (15 ml) olive oil

1 cup (160 g) finely chopped onion

1 cup (180 g) peeled and chopped roma tomatoes

½ teaspoon minced garlic

½ teaspoon Italian seasoning

⅔ cup (160 ml) dry white wine

⅔ cup (160 ml) vegetable broth (see recipe in Chapter 2)

2 tablespoons (32 g) no-salt-added tomato paste

12 lasagna noodles

1 cup (250 g) ricotta

4 ounces (115 g) fresh mozzarella, shredded

⅓ cup (27 g) shredded Parmesan

Sauté the onion in the oil until soft. Transfer to the slow cooker. Stir in the tomatoes, garlic, and seasoning. Cover and cook on high for 1 hour. Reserve about half the sauce. Stir the wine, broth, and tomato paste into the sauce remaining in the cooker. Cook for 1 hour more. Cook the lasagna noodles according to package directions. Drain. Add the ricotta and mozzarella to the reserved tomato mixture. Divide the ricotta mixture between the lasagna sheets, placing near one end. Roll up the sheets to form a tube. Fit the lasagna rolls into the sauce in the cooker, spooning some sauce over each roll. Cover and cook on high for 1 hour and then turn to low and cook for 1 hour longer.

Yield: 6 servings

Per serving: 142 g water; 413 calories (27% from fat, 20% from protein, 53% from carb); 20 g protein; 12 g total fat; 6 g saturated fat; 4 g monounsaturated fat; 1 g polyunsaturated fat; 52 g carb; 2 g fiber; 3 g sugar; 233 mg phosphorus; 350 mg calcium; 3 mg iron; 282 mg sodium; 352 mg potassium; 570 IU vitamin A; 73 mg ATE vitamin E; 7 mg vitamin C; 30 mg cholesterol

Greek Stuffed Peppers

Here's the flavor of the Mediterranean in a stuffed pepper variation.

4 green bell peppers

½ cup (120 ml) vegetable broth, boiling

½ cup (88 g) couscous

2 teaspoons white wine vinegar

3 ounces (85 g) feta cheese, crumbled

3 tablespoons (27 g) pine nuts

1 tablespoon (1.3 g) dried parsley

¼ teaspoon freshly ground black pepper

Halve the peppers and remove the seeds; set aside. Pour the boiling broth over the couscous, cover, and let stand 5 minutes. Fluff with a fork and then stir in the remaining ingredients. Stuff couscous mixture into the peppers and then place peppers in the bottom of the slow cooker. Turn to high, pour ⅔ cup (160 ml) of boiling water around the peppers, cover, and cook until peppers are tender, about 2 hours.

Yield: 4 servings

Per serving: 186 g water; 224 calories (39% from fat, 14% from protein, 47% from carb); 8 g protein; 10 g total fat; 4 g saturated fat; 3 g monounsaturated fat; 3 g polyunsaturated fat; 27 g carb; 4 g fiber; 5 g sugar; 182 mg phosphorus; 132 mg calcium; 1 mg iron; 262 mg sodium; 368 mg potassium; 723 IU vitamin A; 27 mg ATE vitamin E; 122 mg vitamin C; 19 mg cholesterol

Macaroni and Two Cheeses

Everyone likes macaroni and cheese, and the slow cooker does a great job on it. This version gets extra flavor from Parmesan cheese added to the topping.

8 ounces (225 g) elbow macaroni, cooked al dente

13 ounces (365 ml) fat-free evaporated milk

1 cup (235 ml) skim milk

¼ cup (60 ml) egg substitute

4 cups (450 g) shredded Cheddar cheese, divided

½ teaspoon white pepper

¼ cup (25 g) grated Parmesan cheese

Spray inside of cooker with nonstick cooking spray. Then, in cooker, combine cooked macaroni, evaporated milk, milk, egg substitute, 3 cups (345 g) Cheddar cheese, salt, and pepper. Top with remaining Cheddar and Parmesan cheeses. Cover and cook on low 3 hours.

Yield: 8 servings

Per serving: 98 g water; 440 calories (49% from fat, 25% from protein, 27% from carb); 27 g protein; 24 g total fat; 15 g saturated fat; 7 g monounsaturated fat; 1 g polyunsaturated fat; 29 g carb; 1 g fiber; 6 g sugar; 548 mg phosphorus; 699 mg calcium; 2 mg iron; 544 mg sodium; 367 mg potassium; 947 IU vitamin A; 247 mg ATE vitamin E; 1 mg vitamin C; 75 mg cholesterol

Pasta and Red Beans

Pasta and beans cook in a spicy vegetable broth in this dish that is part soup, part chili—and all good.

5 cups (1.2 L) low-sodium vegetable broth

1 teaspoon cumin

1 tablespoon (7.5 g) chili powder

½ teaspoon minced garlic

8 ounces (225 g) uncooked pasta

½ cup (75 g) diced green bell pepper

½ cup (75 g) diced red bell pepper

¾ cup (120 g) diced onion

1 can (15 ounces, or 425 g) no-salt-added kidney beans, rinsed and drained

(continued on page 90)

Combine broth, cumin, chili powder, and garlic in slow cooker. Cover and cook on high until mixture comes to boil. Add pasta, vegetables, and beans. Stir together well. Cover and cook on low 3 to 4 hours.

Yield: 8 servings

Per serving: 216 g water; 206 calories (7% from fat, 24% from protein, 70% from carb); 12 g protein; 2 g total fat; 0 g saturated fat; 0 g monounsaturated fat; 0 g polyunsaturated fat; 36 g carb; 6 g fiber; 2 g sugar; 185 mg phosphorus; 83 mg calcium; 2 mg iron; 94 mg sodium; 458 mg potassium; 337 IU vitamin A; 2 mg ATE vitamin E; 21 mg vitamin C; 0 mg cholesterol

Lentils and Rice

Until a few years ago, I had never had lentils. Then somehow we discovered them, and now we have them all the time. Since an old family phrase is "you can never have too many onions," this dish suits us just fine.

1½ cups (240 g) sliced onions

2 tablespoons (28 ml) olive oil

6 cups (1.4 L) water

1 cup (192 g) lentils, sorted, washed, and drained

2 cups (380 g) brown rice, washed and drained

Place onions in nonstick skillet with olive oil. Sauté over medium heat until onions are golden brown. Remove about ½ cup (80 g) from skillet and place on paper towel to drain. Place remaining onions and drippings in slow cooker. Combine with water, lentils, and brown rice. Cover and cook on low 6 to 8 hours. Garnish with reserved onions.

Yield: 8 servings

Per serving: 257 g water; 125 calories (28% from fat, 12% from protein, 60% from carb); 4 g protein; 4 g total fat; 1 g saturated fat; 3 g monounsaturated fat; 1 g polyunsaturated fat; 19 g carb; 3 g fiber; 2 g sugar; 94 mg phosphorus; 22 mg calcium; 1 mg iron; 10 mg sodium; 158 mg potassium; 3 IU vitamin A; 0 mg ATE vitamin E; 3 mg vitamin C; 0 mg cholesterol

Lentil Meal

This is a meal in a bowl, full of vegetables with lentils providing the base.

8 ounces (225 g) dried lentils, rinsed

2 cups (470 ml) water

1 whole bay leaf

¼ teaspoon pepper

⅛ teaspoon marjoram

⅛ teaspoon sage

⅛ teaspoon thyme

2 cups (320 g) chopped onions

½ teaspoon minced garlic

2 cups (300 g) canned no-salt-added diced tomatoes

½ cup (65 g) carrots, sliced ⅛ inch (32 mm) thick

½ cup (50 g) celery, thinly sliced

3 medium potatoes, diced

½ cup (75 g) chopped green bell pepper

2 tablespoons (8 g) finely chopped fresh parsley

1½ cups (173 g) shredded Cheddar cheese

Mix all ingredients except cheese in slow cooker; cover and cook on high 6 hours. Remove bay leaf and add cheese just before serving.

Yield: 8 servings

Per serving: 315 g water; 263 calories (29% from fat, 18% from protein, 53% from carb); 12 g protein; 9 g total fat; 5 g saturated fat; 2 g monounsaturated fat; 0 g polyunsaturated fat; 36 g carb; 6 g fiber; 6 g sugar; 292 mg phosphorus; 236 mg calcium; 3 mg iron; 185 mg sodium; 995 mg potassium; 1823 IU vitamin A; 64 mg ATE vitamin E; 30 mg vitamin C; 26 mg cholesterol

Barley Vegetable Soup

This a hearty soup is full of barley, mushrooms, and other good things that taste so good you won't miss the meat.

1 cup (160 g) chopped onion

½ cup (65 g) sliced carrots

½ cup (50 g) sliced celery

8 ounces (225 g) mushrooms, sliced

2 cups (512 g) kidney beans, cooked or canned without salt

14 ounces (390 g) no-salt-added stewed tomatoes

10 ounces (280 g) frozen corn

½ cup (100 g) barley, not quick-cooking

2 teaspoons Italian seasoning, crushed

½ teaspoon black pepper

1 teaspoon minced garlic

5 cups (1.2 L) low-sodium vegetable broth (see recipe in Chapter 2)

In a slow cooker, place onion, carrot, and celery. Add mushrooms, beans, undrained tomatoes, frozen corn, barley, Italian seasoning, pepper, and garlic. Pour broth over mushroom mixture in cooker. Cover and cook on low for 8 to 10 hours or on high for 4 to 5 hours.

Yield: 6 servings

Per serving: 410 g water; 246 calories (7% from fat, 23% from protein, 70% from carb); 15 g protein; 2 g total fat; 0 g saturated fat; 0 g monounsaturated fat; 1 g polyunsaturated fat; 45 g carb; 11 g fiber; 7 g sugar; 269 mg phosphorus; 137 mg calcium; 4 mg iron; 146 mg sodium; 876 mg potassium; 1985 IU vitamin A; 2 mg ATE vitamin E; 11 mg vitamin C; 0 mg cholesterol

Vegetables for Pasta

This is just what the name says: mostly vegetables with just enough sauce to hold it together. Spoon some of this over pasta and you won't even worry that it doesn't contain any meat.

2 cups (226 g) sliced zucchini

16 cherry tomatoes, cut in half

½ cup (75 g) sliced green bell pepper

½ cup (75 g) sliced red bell pepper

¾ cup (120 g) sliced onion

4 ounces (115 g) sliced mushrooms

1 teaspoons minced garlic

1 tablespoon (15 ml) olive oil

1 tablespoon (6 g) Italian seasoning

8 ounces (225 g) no-salt-added tomato sauce

Combine all ingredients in slow cooker. Cook on low 6 hours or until vegetables are tender.

Yield: 6 servings

Per serving: 132 g water; 70 calories (32% from fat, 13% from protein, 55% from carb); 2 g protein; 3 g total fat; 0 g saturated fat; 2 g monounsaturated fat; 0 g polyunsaturated fat; 11 g carb; 3 g fiber; 4 g sugar; 57 mg phosphorus; 30 mg calcium; 1 mg iron; 11 mg sodium; 497 mg potassium; 966 IU vitamin A; 0 mg ATE vitamin E; 49 mg vitamin C; 0 mg cholesterol

Mushroom Pasta Sauce

This is a vegetarian pasta sauce full of mushrooms, onions, and other good things.

1 tablespoon (15 ml) olive oil

8 ounces (225 g) mushrooms, sliced

1 cup (160 g) chopped onion

(continued on page 94)

1 teaspoon minced garlic

½ teaspoon oregano

¼ cup (25 g) grated Parmesan cheese

1 can (6 ounces, or 170 g) no-salt-added tomato paste

24 ounces (680 g) no-salt-added tomato sauce

Heat oil in a large skillet and sauté mushrooms, onion, and garlic until onions are transparent. Add to slow cooker. Add remaining ingredients to cooker. Mix well. Cover and cook on low 6 hours.

Yield: 8 servings

Per serving: 136 g water; 92 calories (27% from fat, 18% from protein, 55% from carb); 4 g protein; 3 g total fat; 1 g saturated fat; 2 g monounsaturated fat; 0 g polyunsaturated fat; 13 g carb; 3 g fiber; 8 g sugar; 98 mg phosphorus; 61 mg calcium; 2 mg iron; 80 mg sodium; 657 mg potassium; 638 IU vitamin A; 4 mg ATE vitamin E; 18 mg vitamin C; 3 mg cholesterol

Lentil Sauce

This is a different kind of meatless sauce for pasta, with the fiber and protein boost of lentils. If it sounds strange, give it a try anyway.

½ cup (80 g) chopped onion

¼ cup (33 g) chopped carrots

¼ cup (25 g) chopped celery

2 cups (480 ml) diced tomatoes

1 can (8 ounces, or 225 g) no-salt-added tomato sauce

½ cup (96 g) lentils, rinsed and drained

½ teaspoon oregano

¼ teaspoon basil

¼ teaspoon garlic powder

¼ teaspoon red pepper flakes

Mix all ingredients in slow cooker. Cover and cook on low 8 to 10 hours or on high 3 to 5 hours.

Yield: 6 servings

Per serving: 112 g water; 57 calories (6% from fat, 19% from protein, 75% from carb); 3 g protein; 0 g total fat; 0 g saturated fat; 0 g monounsaturated fat; 0 g polyunsaturated fat; 11 g carb; 4 g fiber; 3 g sugar; 69 mg phosphorus; 53 mg calcium; 2 mg iron; 17 mg sodium; 419 mg potassium; 1547 IU vitamin A; 0 mg ATE vitamin E; 21 mg vitamin C; 0 mg cholesterol

Slow Cooked Marinara Sauce

Everyone knows that the best pasta sauce requires long, slow cooking. So why wouldn't the slow cooker be perfect for that? The answer is that it is. This is a really simple sauce, but it develops great flavor by the time it's done.

1 cup (160 g) finely chopped onion

½ cup (65 g) finely chopped carrots

½ teaspoon chopped garlic

2 tablespoons (28 ml) olive oil

2 cans (28 ounces, or 785 g) no-salt-added crushed tomatoes

1 tablespoon (15 g) brown sugar

In a skillet, sauté onion, carrots, and garlic in oil until tender. Do not brown. Combine onion mixture, tomatoes, and brown sugar in slow cooker. Stir well. Cover and cook on low 6 to 10 hours. Remove cover. Stir well. Cook on high uncovered for 1 hour for a thicker marinara sauce.

Yield: 12 servings

Per serving: 141 g water; 54 calories (37% from fat, 8% from protein, 55% from carb); 1 g protein; 2 g total fat; 0 g saturated fat; 2 g monounsaturated fat; 0 g polyunsaturated fat; 8 g carb; 2 g fiber; 5 g sugar; 31 mg phosphorus; 47 mg calcium; 1 mg iron; 22 mg sodium; 290 mg potassium; 1052 IU vitamin A; 0 mg ATE vitamin E; 14 mg vitamin C; 0 mg cholesterol

Vegetarian Spaghetti Sauce

Chock-full of fresh veggies, this sauce is a real winner.

4 cups (328 g) eggplant, peeled and cut into 1-inch
  (2.5 cm) cubes

1 cup (160 g) chopped onion

2 cups (300 g) chopped red bell pepper

4 teaspoons (12 g) minced garlic

1 can (28 ounces, or 785 g) no-salt-added crushed
  tomatoes, undrained

1 can (28 ounces, or 785 g) no-salt-added diced
  tomatoes, undrained

1 can (6 ounces, or 170 g) no-salt-added tomato paste

2 tablespoons (30 g) brown sugar

2 tablespoons (12 g) Italian seasoning

¼ teaspoon red pepper flakes

TIP *Garnish with fresh oregano sprigs and Parmesan cheese. Store extra in the refrigerator for up to 3 days or freeze for later use.*

In a slow cooker, combine all ingredients. Cover and cook on low for 10 to 12 hours or on high for 5 to 6 hours.

Yield: 6 servings

Per serving: 392 g water; 128 calories (5% from fat, 13% from protein, 82% from carb); 5 g protein; 1 g total fat; 0 g saturated fat; 0 g monounsaturated fat; 0 g polyunsaturated fat; 30 g carb; 8 g fiber; 19 g sugar; 114 mg phosphorus; 130 mg calcium; 4 mg iron; 69 mg sodium; 1096 mg potassium; 2412 IU vitamin A; 0 mg ATE vitamin E; 99 mg vitamin C; 0 mg cholesterol

Easy Pasta Sauce

Quick and easy to make, this pasta sauce has great taste. Make a big batch and freeze the extra for future use.

2 teaspoons olive oil

1 cup (160 g) finely chopped onion

1½ teaspoons minced garlic

2 cans (28 ounces, or 785 g) no-salt-added crushed tomatoes

2 teaspoons basil

1 teaspoon oregano

½ teaspoon black pepper

1 tablespoon (13 g) sugar

1 tablespoon (4 g) fresh parsley

Heat oil in a saucepan over medium heat. Add onion and garlic. Sauté until onion becomes very soft (about 10 minutes). Combine all ingredients except parsley in slow cooker. Cover and cook on low 6 to 8 hours. Add parsley. Cook an additional 30 minutes.

Yield: 8 servings

Per serving: 206 g water; 60 calories (19% from fat, 11% from protein, 70% from carb); 2 g protein; 1 g total fat; 0 g saturated fat; 1 g monounsaturated fat; 0 g polyunsaturated fat; 12 g carb; 3 g fiber; 7 g sugar; 46 mg phosphorus; 74 mg calcium; 2 mg iron; 27 mg sodium; 417 mg potassium; 298 IU vitamin A; 0 mg ATE vitamin E; 21 mg vitamin C; 0 mg cholesterol

6

Low-Fat, Protein-Packed Fish and Seafood Main Dishes

Fish and seafood are a special case with the slow cooker. They can easily become overcooked, so you'll usually want to use a shorter cooking time or add them near the end. But that doesn't mean there aren't some easy and delicious dishes here. And if you are thinking chowder, you should definitely be thinking slow cooker.

Salmon Risotto

Take a shortcut from the usual process of stirring and cooking risotto and let the slow cooker do the work.

2 tablespoons (28 g) unsalted butter

¼ cup (40 g) finely chopped onion

8 ounces (225 g) Arborio rice

3 cups (705 ml) vegetable broth (see recipe in Chapter 2)

½ cup (120 ml) dry white wine

¼ teaspoon freshly ground black pepper

1 pound (455 g) salmon fillet, cut in 1-inch (2.5 cm) cubes

In a small skillet over medium-high heat, melt butter and sauté onion until softened. Transfer to slow cooker. Add remaining ingredients except salmon. Cover and cook on low 3 to 4 hours, stirring once. Stir in salmon, turn to high, and cook until fish is done and rice is tender, about 30 to 60 minutes.

Yield: 4 servings

Per serving: 331 g water; 441 calories (49% from fat, 25% from protein, 26% from carb); 26 g protein; 23 g total fat; 7 g saturated fat; 8 g monounsaturated fat; 6 g polyunsaturated fat; 27 g carb; 1 g fiber; 1 g sugar; 340 mg phosphorus; 50 mg calcium; 1 mg iron; 175 mg sodium; 541 mg potassium; 237 IU vitamin A; 65 mg ATE vitamin E; 8 mg vitamin C; 82 mg cholesterol

Fish Pie

This is a wonderfully creamy fish dish with a bread crumb topping.

1 pound (455 g) haddock, or other firm white fish

10 ounces (280 g) frozen corn

10 ounces (280 g) no-salt-added frozen peas

½ cup (115 g) fat-free cream cheese

(continued on page 100)

⅔ cup (160 ml) skim milk

¼ cup (30 g) bread crumbs

½ cup (58 g) shredded Cheddar cheese

Cut fish into bite-size pieces. Combine with corn and peas and place into slow cooker. Stir cream cheese and milk until well blended and pour over fish mixture. Cover and cook on high until fish is done, about 2 hours. Preheat oven to 400°F (200°C, or gas mark 6). Combine bread crumbs and cheese and sprinkle over fish. Remove liner from slow cooker and bake until cheese melts and topping begins to brown, about 10 minutes.

Yield: 4 servings

Per serving: 263 g water; 394 calories (29% from fat, 37% from protein, 33% from carb); 37 g protein; 13 g total fat; 7 g saturated fat; 4 g monounsaturated fat; 1 g polyunsaturated fat; 33 g carb; 6 g fiber; 6 g sugar; 516 mg phosphorus; 279 mg calcium; 4 mg iron; 354 mg sodium; 776 mg potassium; 2153 IU vitamin A; 141 mg ATE vitamin E; 12 mg vitamin C; 100 mg cholesterol

TIP *To brown the bread crumbs, you'll need a slow cooker with a removable pot.*

Poached Fish

Fish poached in a tomato sauce goes great with rice or pasta.

1 tablespoon (15 ml) olive oil

1 cup (160 g) finely chopped onion

½ cup (120 ml) fish stock (see recipe in Chapter 2)

1 can (8 ounces, or 225 g) no-salt-added tomato sauce

½ teaspoon minced garlic

⅛ teaspoon cumin

2 tablespoons (28 ml) lemon juice

1½ pounds (680 g) haddock, or other firm white fish

Heat oil in a skillet and cook onion until soft. Bring fish stock to boiling. Combine onion, fish stock, and remaining ingredients except fish in slow cooker and cook on high until it begins to simmer around the edge, about 1½ to 2 hours. Add fish to sauce and cook until fish is tender, about 1 to 1½ hours.

Yield: 4 servings

Per serving: 259 g water; 222 calories (21% from fat, 63% from protein, 16% from carb); 34 g protein; 5 g total fat; 1 g saturated fat; 3 g monounsaturated fat; 1 g polyunsaturated fat; 9 g carb; 2 g fiber; 4 g sugar; 360 mg phosphorus; 84 mg calcium; 2 mg iron; 141 mg sodium; 836 mg potassium; 298 IU vitamin A; 29 mg ATE vitamin E; 14 mg vitamin C; 97 mg cholesterol

Seafood Jambalaya

I love jambalaya, and this version is both easy to fix and great-tasting.

4 slices low sodium bacon, chopped

1 cup (160 g) chopped onion

¾ cup (75 g) sliced celery

½ teaspoon minced garlic

½ teaspoon cayenne

1 teaspoon oregano

½ teaspoon thyme

2 cups (360 g) no-salt-added diced tomatoes

3 cups (705 ml) vegetable broth (see recipe in Chapter 2)

1½ cups (278 g) uncooked long-grain rice

8 ounces (225 g) catfish, cut in 1-inch (2.5 cm) cubes

8 ounces (225 g) shrimp, peeled

Cook the bacon, onion, celery, and garlic in a skillet until bacon is crisp and vegetables are softened. Transfer to slow cooker. Add remaining ingredients except fish and shrimp, cover, and cook on low until rice is tender, about 4 hours. Turn to high, add fish and shrimp, cover, and cook until fish flakes easily, about 30 minutes to 1 hour.

(continued on page 102)

Yield: 4 servings

Per serving: 472 g water; 379 calories (32% from fat, 30% from protein, 38% from carb); 28 g protein; 13 g total fat; 3 g saturated fat; 6 g monounsaturated fat; 3 g polyunsaturated fat; 36 g carb; 3 g fiber; 5 g sugar; 381 mg phosphorus; 126 mg calcium; 4 mg iron; 312 mg sodium; 757 mg potassium; 476 IU vitamin A; 40 mg ATE vitamin E; 20 mg vitamin C; 122 mg cholesterol

Shrimp Creole

I've always (well, for a long while anyway) been a fan of Cajun and Creole food. So this is a dish that we end up having regularly.

1½ cups (150 g) sliced celery

1¼ cup (200 g) chopped onion

1 cup (150 g) chopped green bell pepper

1 can (8 ounces, or 225 g) no-salt-added tomato sauce

1 can (28 ounces, or 785 g) no-salt-added whole tomatoes, broken up

½ teaspoons minced garlic

¼ teaspoon pepper

6 drops hot pepper sauce

1 pound (455 g) shrimp, peeled

Combine all ingredients except shrimp. Cook 3 to 4 hours on high or 6 to 8 hours on low. Add shrimp during the last hour of cooking. Serve over hot rice.

Yield: 6 servings

Per serving: 293 g water; 139 calories (11% from fat, 50% from protein, 39% from carb); 18 g protein; 2 g total fat; 0 g saturated fat; 0 g monounsaturated fat; 1 g polyunsaturated fat; 14 g carb; 3 g fiber; 7 g sugar; 213 mg phosphorus; 106 mg calcium; 4 mg iron; 156 mg sodium; 688 mg potassium; 632 IU vitamin A; 41 mg ATE vitamin E; 42 mg vitamin C; 115 mg cholesterol

Curried Fish

This is a nice, mild curried fish. Serve it over rice.

1 cup (160 g) chopped onion

1 tablespoon (9 g) chopped green chilies

1 teaspoon garlic

2 tablespoons (9 g) coconut

⅔ cup (160 ml) water, divided

2 tablespoons (28 ml) olive oil

1 tablespoon (6.3 g) mild curry powder

⅔ cup (160 ml) fat-free evaporated milk

1 pound (455 g) catfish, or other firm white fish

2 tablespoons (28 ml) lime juice

3 tablespoons (6 g) cilantro, dried

Combine the onion, chilies, garlic, coconut and 3 tablespoons (45 ml) of the water. Process in a food processor until it forms a paste. Heat the oil in a skillet. Stir-fry the curry powder in the oil for a few seconds and then add the onion mixture and fry for about 5 minutes more. Stir in the remaining water and bring to a boil. Transfer to the slow cooker and stir in the milk. Cover and cook on high for 1 hour. While the curry cooks, cut the fish into bite-size pieces. Combine the line juice and cilantro and pour over the fish to marinate for 15 minutes. Stir the fish into the sauce in the slow cooker, cover, and cook until fish flakes easily, 30 to 60 minutes.

Yield: 4 servings

Per serving: 206 g water; 282 calories (53% from fat, 31% from protein, 16% from carb); 22 g protein; 16 g total fat; 4 g saturated fat; 9 g monounsaturated fat; 3 g polyunsaturated fat; 12 g carb; 1 g fiber; 7 g sugar; 335 mg phosphorus; 157 mg calcium; 1 mg iron; 123 mg sodium; 597 mg potassium; 380 IU vitamin A; 67 mg ATE vitamin E; 8 mg vitamin C; 55 mg cholesterol

Dijon Fish

Lemon and Dijon mustard give this fish a great flavor boost.

1¼ pounds (570 g) orange roughy fillets

2 tablespoons (22 g) Dijon mustard

3 tablespoons (42 g) unsalted butter, melted

1 teaspoon Worcestershire sauce

1 tablespoon (15 ml) lemon juice

Cut fillets to fit in slow cooker. In a bowl, mix remaining ingredients together. Pour sauce over fish. Cover and cook on low 3 hours or until fish flakes easily but is not dry or overcooked.

Yield: 4 servings

Per serving: 119 g water; 191 calories (47% from fat, 50% from protein, 2% from carb); 24 g protein; 10 g total fat; 6 g saturated fat; 3 g monounsaturated fat; 1 g polyunsaturated fat; 1 g carb; 0 g fiber; 0 g sugar; 164 mg phosphorus; 20 mg calcium; 2 mg iron; 201 mg sodium; 264 mg potassium; 373 IU vitamin A; 101 mg ATE vitamin E; 4 mg vitamin C; 108 mg cholesterol

Lemon Catfish

This lemony flavored fish cooks on its own to a flaky perfection. You can substitute any firm-fleshed white fish.

1½ pounds (680 g) catfish fillets

½ cup (80 g) chopped onion

1 tablespoon (1.3 g) parsley

4 teaspoons (8 g) grated lemon rind

TIP *Serve garnished with lemon slices and sprigs of fresh parsley.*

Spray slow cooker with nonstick cooking spray. Place fish in cooker. Put onion, parsley, and lemon rind over fish. Cover and cook on low for 1½ hours.

Yield: 4 servings

Per serving: 148 g water; 239 calories (50% from fat, 46% from protein, 4% from carb); 27 g protein; 13 g total fat; 3 g saturated fat; 6 g monounsaturated fat; 3 g polyunsaturated fat; 2 g carb; 1 g fiber; 1 g sugar; 350 mg phosphorus; 24 mg calcium; 1 mg iron; 92 mg sodium; 546 mg potassium; 165 IU vitamin A; 26 mg ATE vitamin E; 6 mg vitamin C; 80 mg cholesterol

Salmon Loaf

Salmon loaf is an old favorite for me, going back to the days of my childhood when canned salmon was cheaper than tuna. It still makes a nice treat, especially when it's this easy to fix.

16 ounces (455 g) canned salmon

½ cup (120 ml) egg substitute

1½ cups (175 g) bread crumbs

¼ cup (40 g) finely chopped onion

2 tablespoons (28 g) unsalted butter, melted

1 tablespoon (4 g) fresh parsley

1 tablespoon (15 ml) lemon juice

Dash cayenne

Drain salmon; reserve juices. If necessary, add water to juices to make ¼ cup (60 ml) liquid. Combine liquid with remaining ingredients except the salmon. Flake salmon; stir into mixture. Shape into round loaf slightly smaller in diameter than slow cooker. Line cooker with foil to come up 2 or 3 inches (5 or 7.5 cm) on sides. Place loaf on foil, not touching sides. Cover and cook on low for 5 hours.

Yield: 6 servings

Per serving: 82 g water; 268 calories (35% from fat, 34% from protein, 31% from carb); 22 g protein; 10 g total fat; 4 g saturated fat; 3 g monounsaturated fat; 2 g polyunsaturated fat; 20 g carb; 1 g fiber; 2 g sugar; 341 mg phosphorus; 252 mg calcium; 2 mg iron; 95 mg sodium; 366 mg potassium; 293 IU vitamin A; 45 mg ATE vitamin E; 2 mg vitamin C; 40 mg cholesterol

Tuna Vegetable Casserole

This recipe is a variation of the usual tuna noodle casserole with mixed vegetables and an almond topping.

16 ounces (455 g) water-packed tuna

20 ounces (560 g) low-sodium cream of mushroom soup (see recipe in Chapter 2)

1 cup (235 ml) milk

2 tablespoons (2.6 g) dried parsley

10 ounces (280 g) frozen mixed vegetables, thawed

10 ounces (280 g) egg noodles, cooked and drained

¼ cup (30 g) sliced almonds, toasted

Combine tuna, soup, milk, parsley, and vegetables. Fold in noodles. Spray slow cooker with nonstick cooking spray and pour tuna mixture in. Top with almonds. Cover and cook on low 7 to 9 hours or on high 3 to 4 hours.

Yield: 6 servings

Per serving: 248 g water; 286 calories (23% from fat, 34% from protein, 43% from carb); 24 g protein; 7 g total fat; 1 g saturated fat; 3 g monounsaturated fat; 2 g polyunsaturated fat; 30 g carb; 6 g fiber; 6 g sugar; 343 mg phosphorus; 101 mg calcium; 2 mg iron; 104 mg sodium; 739 mg potassium; 2259 IU vitamin A; 31 mg ATE vitamin E; 3 mg vitamin C; 35 mg cholesterol

Tuna Noodle Casserole

Here is classic American comfort food. This will definitely remind you of the good old days, but it's healthier and easier to fix.

10 ounces (280 g) low-sodium cream of mushroom soup (see recipe in Chapter 2)

⅓ cup (80 ml) low-sodium chicken broth (see recipe in Chapter 2)

⅔ cup (160 ml) skim milk

2 tablespoons (2.6 g) dried parsley

10 ounces (280 g) frozen no-salt-added peas

14 ounces (390 g) tuna, well drained

10 ounces (280 g) egg noodles, cooked until just tender

3 tablespoons (21 g) bread crumbs

Spray slow cooker with nonstick cooking spray. In a large bowl, combine soup, chicken broth, milk, parsley, peas, and tuna. Fold in the cooked noodles. Pour mixture into prepared slow cooker. Top with bread crumbs. Cover and cook on low for 5 to 6 hours.

Yield: 6 servings

Per serving: 199 g water; 231 calories (14% from fat, 38% from protein, 49% from carb); 22 g protein; 4 g total fat; 1 g saturated fat; 1 g monounsaturated fat; 1 g polyunsaturated fat; 28 g carb; 5 g fiber; 3 g sugar; 278 mg phosphorus; 75 mg calcium; 2 mg iron; 273 mg sodium; 467 mg potassium; 1196 IU vitamin A; 22 mg ATE vitamin E; 7 mg vitamin C; 30 mg cholesterol

Tuna Stuffed Peppers

Tuna gives variety to this version of stuffed peppers.

2 cups (475 ml) low-sodium tomato juice

1 can (6 ounces, or 170 g) no-salt-added tomato paste

14 ounces (390 g) tuna, drained and rinsed

2 tablespoons (30 g) dried minced onion

¼ teaspoon garlic powder

4 green bell peppers, tops removed and seeded

TIP

Serve with rice or noodles.

Mix tomato juice and tomato paste, reserving 1 cup (235 ml). Mix remaining tomato mixture with tuna, minced onion, and garlic powder. Fill peppers equally with mixture. Place upright in slow cooker. Pour the reserved 1 cup (235 ml) tomato mixture over peppers. Cover and cook on low 8 to 9 hours or until peppers are done.

Yield: 4 servings

(continued on page 108)

Per serving: 359 g water; 222 calories (14% from fat, 48% from protein, 39% from carb); 28 g protein; 3 g total fat; 1 g saturated fat; 1 g monounsaturated fat; 1 g polyunsaturated fat; 22 g carb; 5 g fiber; 14 g sugar; 311 mg phosphorus; 63 mg calcium; 3 mg iron; 108 mg sodium; 1248 mg potassium; 1766 IU vitamin A; 6 mg ATE vitamin E; 153 mg vitamin C; 42 mg cholesterol

Salmon Casserole

This is a great creamy salmon and potato casserole, made easier with the use of canned salmon and cream of mushroom soup.

4 medium potatoes, peeled and sliced

3 tablespoons (24 g) flour

16 ounces (455 g) salmon, drained and flaked

½ cup (80 g) chopped onion

10 ounces (280 g) low-sodium cream of mushroom soup (see recipe in Chapter 2)

¼ cup (60 ml) water

Dash nutmeg

Spray slow cooker with nonstick cooking spray. Place half of the potatoes in slow cooker. Sprinkle with half of the flour. Cover with half the flaked salmon and then sprinkle with half the onion. Repeat layers. Combine soup and water; pour over top of potato and salmon mixture. Sprinkle with just a dash of nutmeg. Cover and cook on low for 7 to 9 hours or until potatoes are tender.

Yield: 6 servings

Per serving: 316 g water; 323 calories (15% from fat, 27% from protein, 58% from carb); 22 g protein; 5 g total fat; 1 g saturated fat; 2 g monounsaturated fat; 2 g polyunsaturated fat; 47 g carb; 5 g fiber; 4 g sugar; 450 mg phosphorus; 223 mg calcium; 3 mg iron; 253 mg sodium; 1547 mg potassium; 67 IU vitamin A; 15 mg ATE vitamin E; 22 mg vitamin C; 31 mg cholesterol

Tuna Lasagna

The slow cooker and no-boil noodles make this lasagna easier than usual. The tuna and mushroom cream sauce give it a different sort of flavor.

5 tablespoons (70 g) unsalted butter, divided

1 cup (160 g) chopped onion

½ teaspoon minced garlic

4 ounces (115 g) mushrooms, sliced

⅓ cup (42 g) flour

¼ cup (60 ml) dry white wine

3 cups (705 ml) skim milk

1 tablespoon (1.3 g) dried parsley

14 ounces (390 g) tuna, in water

6 ounces (170 g) mozzarella, shredded

9 to 12 no boil lasagna noodles

3 tablespoons (15 g) grated Parmesan

Spray the slow cooker with nonstick cooking spray. Melt 2 tablespoons (28 g) of the butter in a skillet. Sauté the onions until soft. Add the garlic and mushrooms and sauté 3 minutes more. Remove from pan. Melt the remaining butter in the skillet and stir in the flour. Gradually stir in the wine and milk and cook until thickened. Reserve 1½ cups (355 ml) of the sauce. Add the mushroom mixture to the remaining sauce. Drain the tuna and flake and then mix the mozzarella into the tuna. Spoon a layer of the mushroom sauce in the bottom of the cooker. Cover with 3 to 4 of the noodles, breaking if necessary to fit. Cover with half of the tuna mixture, then half of the remaining mushroom sauce. Add another layer of the noodles and then repeat the tuna, mushroom sauce, and noodle layers. Pour the reserved sauce over the top and then sprinkle with the Parmesan cheese. Cover and cook on low for 2 to 3 hours or until noodles are tender.

Yield: 6 servings

Per serving: 228 g water; 512 calories (33% from fat, 29% from protein, 39% from carb); 36 g protein; 18 g total fat; 10 g saturated fat; 5 g monounsaturated fat; 2 g polyunsaturated fat; 48 g carb; 2 g fiber; 2 g sugar; 472 mg phosphorus; 462 mg calcium; 3 mg iron; 336 mg sodium; 598 mg potassium; 761 IU vitamin A; 197 mg ATE vitamin E; 5 mg vitamin C; 77 mg cholesterol

Hot and Sour Soup

This makes a heartier version than some, with shrimp and tofu.

4 cups (950 ml) low-sodium chicken broth

8 ounces (225 g) bamboo shoots, drained

¼ cup (30 g) julienned carrot

8 ounces (225 g) water chestnuts, drained

4 ounces (115 g) mushroom, sliced

1 tablespoon (15 ml) rice wine vinegar

1 tablespoon (15 ml) low-sodium soy sauce (see recipe in Chapter 2)

¼ teaspoon white pepper

¼ teaspoon red pepper flakes

8 ounces (225 g) shrimp, peeled

4 ounces (115 g) tofu, drained and cubed

¼ cup (60 ml) egg substitute

Combine all ingredients except shrimp, tofu, and egg substitute in slow cooker. Cover and cook on low 8 to 10 hours or on high 4 to 5 hours. Add shrimp and tofu. Cover and cook 45 to 60 minutes longer. Drizzle egg substitute into the soup in a thin stream, stirring so it forms shreds.

Yield: 4 servings

Per serving: 443 g water; 222 calories (17% from fat, 51% from protein, 32% from carb); 28 g protein; 4 g total fat; 1 g saturated fat; 1 g monounsaturated fat; 2 g polyunsaturated fat; 18 g carb; 2 g fiber; 4 g sugar; 360 mg phosphorus; 76 mg calcium; 3 mg iron; 320 mg sodium; 884 mg potassium; 1600 IU vitamin A; 46 mg ATE vitamin E; 5 mg vitamin C; 132 mg cholesterol

Tuna Chowder

Similar to Manhattan clam chowder, this tomato-based, spicy tuna chowder is great for a cool evening with some freshly baked bread.

14 ounces (390 ml) low-sodium chicken broth (see recipe in Chapter 2)

2 medium red potatoes, chopped

1 can (14 ounces, or 400 g) no-salt-added diced tomatoes

1 cup (100 g) chopped celery

1 cup (160 g) chopped onion

1 cup (130 g) coarsely shredded carrot

1 teaspoon dried thyme, crushed

1 teaspoon cayenne pepper

1 teaspoon ground black pepper

12 ounces (340 g) water-packed tuna, drained and broken into chunks

In a slow cooker, combine broth, potatoes, undrained tomatoes, celery, onion, carrot, thyme, cayenne pepper, and black pepper. Cover and cook on low for 6 to 7 hours or on high for 3 to 4 hours. Gently stir in tuna. Let stand, covered, for 5 minutes.

Yield: 6 servings

Per serving: 237 g water; 149 calories (12% from fat, 42% from protein, 46% from carb); 16 g protein; 2 g total fat; 1 g saturated fat; 0 g monounsaturated fat; 1 g polyunsaturated fat; 17 g carb; 4 g fiber; 4 g sugar; 183 mg phosphorus; 63 mg calcium; 3 mg iron; 109 mg sodium; 552 mg potassium; 3883 IU vitamin A; 3 mg ATE vitamin E; 13 mg vitamin C; 24 mg cholesterol

Corn Chowder with Crab

Here's an elegant sort of soup that you could serve to company. But why wait? It's easy to make just for the family.

6 slices low-sodium bacon, diced

¼ cup (40 g) chopped onion

2 potatoes, peeled and diced

1 pound (455 g) frozen corn

1 tablespoon (13 g) sugar

1 teaspoon Worcestershire sauce

¼ teaspoon pepper

½ cup (120 ml) water

1 cup (235 ml) skim milk

6 ounces (170 g) crab meat

In skillet, brown bacon until crisp. Remove bacon, reserving drippings. Add onions and potatoes to skillet and sauté for 5 minutes. Drain. Combine all ingredients in slow cooker except milk and crab meat. Mix well. Cover and cook on low 6 to 7 hours. Stir in milk and crab during the last 30 minutes of cooking.

Yield: 4 servings

Per serving: 336 g water; 364 calories (15% from fat, 22% from protein, 62% from carb); 21 g protein; 6 g total fat; 2 g saturated fat; 3 g monounsaturated fat; 1 g polyunsaturated fat; 59 g carb; 6 g fiber; 9 g sugar; 412 mg phosphorus; 152 mg calcium; 2 mg iron; 280 mg sodium; 1351 mg potassium; 155 IU vitamin A; 40 mg ATE vitamin E; 25 mg vitamin C; 48 mg cholesterol

Salmon Chowder

If you are looking for a way to get more fish into your diet, stock up on salmon when you find it on sale and make this chowder often.

2 pounds (900 g) salmon fillets

1 cup (160 g) chopped onion

4 medium potatoes, peeled and cubed

2 cups (475 ml) water

¼ teaspoon pepper

12 ounces (355 ml) fat-free evaporated milk

Cut salmon into bite-size pieces. Place in slow cooker. Add onion, potatoes, water, and pepper. Cover and cook on low for 5 to 8 hours. Add evaporated milk and continue cooking until heated through.

Yield: 6 servings

Per serving: 451 g water; 504 calories (30% from fat, 31% from protein, 38% from carb); 39 g protein; 17 g total fat; 3 g saturated fat; 6 g monounsaturated fat; 6 g polyunsaturated fat; 48 g carb; 5 g fiber; 10 g sugar; 621 mg phosphorus; 216 mg calcium; 3 mg iron; 173 mg sodium; 1895 mg potassium; 321 IU vitamin A; 90 mg ATE vitamin E; 30 mg vitamin C; 91 mg cholesterol

Shrimp Chowder

This rich chowder with bacon and shrimp is sure to become a favorite.

3 slices low-sodium bacon, diced

1 cup (160 g) chopped onion

3 medium red potatoes, diced, unpeeled

1 pound (455 g) frozen corn

1 teaspoon Worcestershire sauce

(continued on page 114)

½ teaspoon paprika

½ teaspoon black pepper

12 ounces (340 g) shrimp

2 cups (475 ml) water

12 ounces (355 ml) fat-free evaporated milk

¼ cup (12 g) chives

Brown bacon in nonstick skillet until lightly crisp. Add onions to drippings and sauté until transparent. Using a slotted spoon, transfer bacon and onions to slow cooker. Add remaining ingredients to cooker except milk and chives. Cover and cook on low 3 to 4 hours, adding milk and chives 30 minutes before the end of cooking time.

Yield: 6 servings

Per serving: 265 g water; 257 calories (11% from fat, 32% from protein, 57% from carb); 21 g protein; 3 g total fat; 1 g saturated fat; 1 g monounsaturated fat; 1 g polyunsaturated fat; 38 g carb; 5 g fiber; 10 g sugar; 331 mg phosphorus; 219 mg calcium; 4 mg iron; 201 mg sodium; 652 mg potassium; 522 IU vitamin A; 98 mg ATE vitamin E; 13 mg vitamin C; 93 mg cholesterol

7

Tender and Tasty Low-Fat Beef Main Dishes

Beef is such a natural for the slow cooker that it's probably the first thing most people think of. The slow cooker makes tender, tasty work of leaner, cheaper cuts of beef like round steak, round roast, and rump roast. Dishes like Swiss steak and other kinds of steak smothered in a sauce are easy and great made this way, as are roasts and cuts that you might usually think about grilling like ribs and briskets. And that's not to mention the sandwich fillings.

Swiss Steak in Wine Sauce

Kind of like a combination of beef Burgundy and Swiss steak, this goes well with mashed potatoes or noodles.

For Steak:

2 pounds (900 g) beef round steak

2 tablespoons (15 g) flour

½ teaspoon black pepper

2 tablespoons (28 ml) olive oil

1 cup (160 g) chopped onion

½ cup (65 g) sliced carrot

1 can (14 ounces, or 400 g) no-salt-added diced tomatoes

¾ cup (175 ml) dry red wine

½ teaspoon minced garlic

For Wine Sauce:

¼ cup (60 ml) water

2 tablespoons (16 g) flour

To make the steak: Trim fat from steak; cut meat into 6 equal pieces. Combine flour and pepper and coat meat with mixture. Pound steak to ½-inch (1.3 cm) thickness using a meat mallet. Heat oil in a large skillet and brown meat; drain. Place onion and carrot in cooker. Place meat on top. Combine undrained tomatoes, wine, and garlic. Pour over meat. Cover and cook on low for 8 to 10 hours. Transfer meat and vegetables to serving platter. Reserve 1½ cups (355 ml) of the cooking liquid for the wine sauce.

To make the wine sauce: Pour reserved liquid into saucepan. Blend cold water slowly into flour; stir into liquid. Cook and stir until thickened and bubbly. Spoon some sauce over meat to serve; pass the remaining sauce at the table.

Yield: 6 servings

Per serving: 239 g water; 303 calories (32% from fat, 52% from protein, 16% from carb); 36 g protein; 10 g total fat; 2 g saturated fat; 5 g monounsaturated fat; 1 g polyunsaturated fat; 11 g carb; 2 g fiber; 3 g sugar; 368 mg phosphorus; 39 mg calcium; 4 mg iron; 97 mg sodium; 823 mg potassium; 1872 IU vitamin A; 0 mg ATE vitamin E; 9 mg vitamin C; 86 mg cholesterol

Easy Pepper Steak

This recipe proves that Asian meals can be prepared in the slow cooker just as easily as the more traditional stir-fry.

1½ pounds (680 g) beef round steak

¼ cup (31 g) plus 1 tablespoon (8 g) flour, divided

¼ teaspoon pepper

1 cup (160 g) chopped or sliced onion

½ teaspoon minced garlic

1½ cups (225 g) green bell pepper, sliced in ½-inch (1.3 cm) strips

1 can (28 ounces, or 785 g) no-salt-added diced tomatoes

1 tablespoon (15 ml) low-sodium soy sauce (see recipe in Chapter 2)

1 teaspoon Worcestershire sauce

3 tablespoons (45 ml) water

Cut beef into strips. Combine ¼ cup (31 g) flour and pepper. Toss with beef until well coated. Place in slow cooker. Add onions, garlic, and green pepper slices. Mix well. Combine tomatoes, soy sauce, and Worcestershire sauce. Pour into slow cooker. Cover and cook on low 8 to 10 hours. One hour before serving, turn to high. Combine remaining 1 tablespoon (8 g) flour and water to make smooth paste. Stir into slow cooker. Cover and cook until thickened. Serve over rice.

Yield: 6 servings

Per serving: 275 g water; 211 calories (17% from fat, 54% from protein, 28% from carb); 28 g protein; 4 g total fat; 1 g saturated fat; 2 g monounsaturated fat; 0 g polyunsaturated fat; 15 g carb; 3 g fiber; 5 g sugar; 300 mg phosphorus; 56 mg calcium; 4 mg iron; 95 mg sodium; 807 mg potassium; 298 IU vitamin A; 0 mg ATE vitamin E; 46 mg vitamin C; 65 mg cholesterol

Fajita Steak

This Mexican-flavored steak can be served as a main dish with rice or used to make fajitas or other favorites.

1 can (14 ounces, or 400 g) no-salt-added diced
  tomatoes

4 ounces (115 g) diced green chilies

¼ cup (65 g) low-sodium salsa (see recipe in Chapter 2)

1 can (8 ounces, or 225 g) no-salt-added tomato sauce

2 pounds (900 g) beef round steak, cut in 2-inch ×
  4-inch (5 cm × 10 cm) strips

2 tablespoons (14 g) Salt-Free Mexican Seasoning (see
  recipe in Chapter 2)

TIP *Serve meat with sautéed onions and green peppers. Offer shredded cheese, avocado chunks, and sour cream as toppings.*

Combine all ingredients in slow cooker. Cover and cook on low 6 to 8 hours or until meat is tender but not overcooked. Check meat occasionally to make sure it isn't cooking dry. If it begins to look dry, stir in up to 1 cup (235 ml) water.

Yield: 6 servings

Per serving: 231 g water; 224 calories (22% from fat, 66% from protein, 13% from carb); 36 g protein; 5 g total fat; 2 g saturated fat; 2 g monounsaturated fat; 0 g polyunsaturated fat; 7 g carb; 2 g fiber; 4 g sugar; 361 mg phosphorus; 40 mg calcium; 4 mg iron; 191 mg sodium; 897 mg potassium; 264 IU vitamin A; 0 mg ATE vitamin E; 18 mg vitamin C; 86 mg cholesterol

Italian Steak

This is a simple recipe for steak slow cooked in spaghetti sauce that is perfect with pasta.

1½ pounds (680 g) beef round steak

½ teaspoon oregano

¼ teaspoon pepper

1 cup (160 g) coarsely chopped onion

15 ounces (425 g) low-sodium spaghetti sauce

Cut steak into 6 pieces. In a bowl, mix together oregano and pepper. Sprinkle over both sides of pieces of meat. Place the meat into the slow cooker. Sprinkle with chopped onion. Spoon spaghetti sauce over top, being careful not to disturb the seasoning and onions. Cover and cook on low 5 to 8 hours or until the meat is tender but not overcooked.

Yield: 6 servings

Per serving: 158 g water; 232 calories (28% from fat, 48% from protein, 24% from carb); 27 g protein; 7 g total fat; 2 g saturated fat; 4 g monounsaturated fat; 1 g polyunsaturated fat; 14 g carb; 3 g fiber; 9 g sugar; 282 mg phosphorus; 31 mg calcium; 3 mg iron; 81 mg sodium; 747 mg potassium; 446 IU vitamin A; 0 mg ATE vitamin E; 10 mg vitamin C; 65 mg cholesterol

Easy Swiss Steak

You could also make this with the traditional cubed steak, but it tends to be more expensive, and the long cooking makes the round steak just as tender.

1 tablespoon (15 ml) vegetable oil

½ cup (60 g) flour

½ teaspoon black pepper

½ teaspoon paprika

2 pounds (900 g) round steak

2 cups (300 g) green bell pepper, sliced into rings

(continued on page 120)

2 cups (300 g) red bell pepper, sliced into rings

4 cups (640 g) onion, sliced into rings

1 can (28 ounces, or 785 g) no-salt-added diced tomatoes

Heat the oil in a skillet over medium heat. In a bowl, mix the flour, pepper, and paprika. Dredge the steaks in the flour mixture and place in the skillet. Brown steaks on both sides and remove from heat. In a slow cooker, alternate layers of steak, green pepper, red pepper, onion, and tomatoes. Cover and cook 6 to 8 hours on low until steaks are very tender.

Yield: 6 servings

Per serving: 414 g water; 392 calories (22% from fat, 49% from protein, 29% from carb); 48 g protein; 9 g total fat; 3 g saturated fat; 3 g monounsaturated fat; 2 g polyunsaturated fat; 29 g carb; 5 g fiber; 11 g sugar; 366 mg phosphorus; 86 mg calcium; 6 mg iron; 83 mg sodium; 971 mg potassium; 1997 IU vitamin A; 0 mg ATE vitamin E; 124 mg vitamin C; 88 mg cholesterol

Creamy Steak

This creamy mushroom-sauced steak and vegetable dish is great over mashed potatoes. It is true comfort food.

1½ pounds (680 g) beef round steak

¼ cup (31 g) flour

2 tablespoons (28 ml) olive oil

1½ cups (240 g) thickly sliced onions

1 cup (150 g) green bell pepper strips

10 ounces (280 g) low-sodium cream of mushroom soup (see recipe in Chapter 2)

Cut steak into serving-size pieces. Dredge in flour. Heat oil in a nonstick skillet and brown the steak on both sides. Place browned steak in slow cooker. Top with onion and pepper slices. Pour soup over all, making sure steak pieces are covered. Cover and cook on low 4 to 5 hours.

Yield: 6 servings

Per serving: 182 g water; 248 calories (34% from fat, 45% from protein, 21% from carb); 28 g protein; 9 g total fat; 2 g saturated fat; 5 g monounsaturated fat; 1 g polyunsaturated fat; 13 g carb; 2 g fiber; 3 g sugar; 295 mg phosphorus; 22 mg calcium; 3 mg iron; 77 mg sodium; 719 mg potassium; 96 IU vitamin A; 1 mg ATE vitamin E; 23 mg vitamin C; 66 mg cholesterol

Italian Swiss Steak

Similar to Swiss steak, but with a definitely Italian flavor, this dish is great with pasta and a salad.

2 tablespoons (16 g) flour

¼ teaspoon black pepper

2 pounds (900 g) beef round steak

2 tablespoons (28 ml) olive oil

1 cup (160 g) sliced onion

1 can (8 ounces, or 225 g) no-salt-added tomato sauce

8 ounces (225 g) low-sodium spaghetti sauce

½ cup (120 ml) water

½ teaspoon basil

½ teaspoon oregano

Combine flour and pepper in a resealable plastic bag. Cut steak into 6 pieces, add to bag, and shake to coat. Heat oil in a large skillet. Brown steak on both sides. Place onions in slow cooker. Place steak on top. Combine remaining ingredients and pour over steak. Cook on low 8 to 10 hours or on high 4 to 5 hours.

Yield: 6 servings

Per serving: 214 g water; 308 calories (34% from fat, 48% from protein, 18% from carb); 36 g protein; 11 g total fat; 3 g saturated fat; 7 g monounsaturated fat; 1 g polyunsaturated fat; 13 g carb; 2 g fiber; 7 g sugar; 368 mg phosphorus; 31 mg calcium; 4 mg iron; 96 mg sodium; 911 mg potassium; 375 IU vitamin A; 0 mg ATE vitamin E; 11 mg vitamin C; 86 mg cholesterol

Mexican Steak

This is kind of like Swiss steak, but with a Mexican flavor. It's good with rice or placed in tortillas.

2 pounds (900 g) flank steak

¼ teaspoon garlic powder

2 cups (520 g) low-sodium salsa (see recipe in Chapter 2)

1 can (8 ounces, or 225 g) no-salt-added tomato sauce

Dash hot pepper sauce

Monterey Jack cheese, shredded

Pound meat on both sides with meat mallet; sprinkle with garlic powder. Place in slow cooker. Combine salsa, tomato sauce, and hot pepper sauce. Pour over meat. Cover; cook on low-heat setting for 8 to 10 hours. Sprinkle with cheese before serving.

Yield: 6 servings

Per serving: 194 g water; 327 calories (36% from fat, 55% from protein, 9% from carb); 44 g protein; 13 g total fat; 5 g saturated fat; 5 g monounsaturated fat; 1 g polyunsaturated fat; 7 g carb; 2 g fiber; 4 g sugar; 354 mg phosphorus; 47 mg calcium; 3 mg iron; 253 mg sodium; 863 mg potassium; 338 IU vitamin A; 0 mg ATE vitamin E; 6 mg vitamin C; 83 mg cholesterol

Hawaiian Steak

This is a delightfully flavored steak that's perfect for a summer evening. Serve it over rice.

1 pound (455 g) flank steak

Dash black pepper

30 ounces (840 g) fruit cocktail, canned in syrup

1 tablespoon (15 ml) olive oil

1 tablespoon (15 ml) lemon juice

¼ cup (60 ml) low-sodium teriyaki sauce (see recipe in Chapter 2)

1 teaspoon red wine vinegar

½ teaspoons minced garlic

Place flank steak in slow cooker. Sprinkle with pepper. Drain fruit cocktail, reserving ¼ cup (60 ml) syrup. Combine reserved syrup with remaining ingredients, except fruit. Pour syrup mixture over steak. Cover and cook on low 7 to 9 hours. Add drained fruit during the last 10 minutes of cooking time. Cut meat into thin slices across the grain to serve.

Yield: 5 servings

Per serving: 220 g water; 296 calories (33% from fat, 35% from protein, 32% from carb); 26 g protein; 11 g total fat; 4 g saturated fat; 5 g monounsaturated fat; 1 g polyunsaturated fat; 24 g carb; 2 g fiber; 21 g sugar; 219 mg phosphorus; 29 mg calcium; 2 mg iron; 90 mg sodium; 480 mg potassium; 519 IU vitamin A; 0 mg ATE vitamin E; 6 mg vitamin C; 50 mg cholesterol

Spanish Steak

Here's another recipe that is sort of like Swiss steak, only with a more southern-European kind of flavor.

1 cup (160 g) sliced onion

½ cup (50 g) chopped celery

¾ cup (113 g) green bell pepper, sliced in rings

1 pound (455 g) beef round steak

2 teaspoons dried parsley

1 tablespoon (15 ml) Worcestershire sauce

1 tablespoon (9 g) dry mustard

1 tablespoon (7.5 g) chili powder

1 cup (180 g) no-salt-added diced tomatoes

2 teaspoons minced garlic

¼ teaspoon pepper

TIP

Serve over noodles or rice.

Put half of onion, celery, and green pepper in slow cooker. Cut steak into serving-size pieces. Place steak pieces in slow cooker. Put remaining onion, celery, and green pepper over steak. Combine remaining ingredients. Pour over meat. Cover and cook on low 8 hours.

Yield: 4 servings

(continued on page 124)

Per serving: 214 g water; 192 calories (21% from fat, 58% from protein, 21% from carb); 28 g protein; 4 g total fat; 1 g saturated fat; 2 g monounsaturated fat; 0 g polyunsaturated fat; 10 g carb; 3 g fiber; 4 g sugar; 292 mg phosphorus; 50 mg calcium; 4 mg iron; 136 mg sodium; 770 mg potassium; 853 IU vitamin A; 0 mg ATE vitamin E; 41 mg vitamin C; 65 mg cholesterol

Pepper Steak

This easy and delicious pepper steak cooks on its own, is tender, and full of flavor.

2 pounds (900 g) beef round steak, cut into 2-inch
(5 cm) strips

½ teaspoon garlic powder

3 tablespoons (45 ml) olive oil

1 tablespoon (8 g) cornstarch

¼ cup (60 ml) low-sodium beef broth
(see recipe in Chapter 2)

1 cup (160 g) chopped onion

2 cups (300 g) roughly chopped green bell peppers

2 cups (510 ml) no-salt-added stewed tomatoes, with
liquid

3 tablespoons (45 ml) low-sodium soy sauce (see recipe in Chapter 2)

1 teaspoon sugar

TIP

Serve over brown rice.

Sprinkle strips of steak with garlic powder. In a large skillet over medium heat, heat the oil and brown the seasoned beef strips. Transfer to a slow cooker. Mix cornstarch into broth until dissolved. Pour into the slow cooker with meat. Stir in onion, green pepper, stewed tomatoes, soy sauce, and sugar. Cover and cook on high for 3 to 4 hours or on low for 6 to 8 hours.

Yield: 6 servings

Per serving: 271 g water; 308 calories (35% from fat, 48% from protein, 17% from carb); 37 g protein; 12 g total fat; 3 g saturated fat; 7 g monounsaturated fat; 1 g polyunsaturated fat; 13 g carb; 2 g fiber; 7 g sugar; 377 mg phosphorus; 47 mg calcium; 5 mg iron; 119 mg sodium; 903 mg potassium; 332 IU vitamin A; 0 mg ATE vitamin E; 49 mg vitamin C; 86 mg cholesterol

Swiss Steak

Swiss steak cooks to a falling-apart-goodness in the slow cooker. Serve it with mashed potatoes.

¼ cup (31 g) flour

2 pounds (900 g) round steak

2 tablespoons (28 ml) olive oil

1 cup (160 g) sliced onion

1 cup (150 g) green bell pepper strips

½ cup (65 g) sliced carrots

½ cup (50 g) chopped celery

1 teaspoon finely minced garlic

1½ cups (355 ml) low-sodium beef broth (see recipe in Chapter 2)

2 cups (360 g) no-salt-added diced tomatoes, drained

1 tablespoon (15 g) brown sugar

Put the flour in a flat dish. Pound the meat using a meat tenderizer for a few minutes and then dredge the meat in the flour and pound it in. Heat oil in a large skillet. Add the meat and brown on both sides. Remove the meat from the skillet and add it to your slow cooker. Add the onions, green pepper, carrots, and celery to the skillet and brown. Put them into your slow cooker. Add the beef broth to the skillet and cook over medium heat, scraping the bottom to get all the browned bits. Add this to your cooker along with the tomatoes and brown sugar. Cook on low for 8 to 10 hours.

Yield: 6 servings

Per serving: 324 g water; 433 calories (35% from fat, 51% from protein, 14% from carb); 54 g protein; 17 g total fat; 5 g saturated fat; 8 g monounsaturated fat; 1 g polyunsaturated fat; 15 g carb; 2 g fiber; 7 g sugar; 377 mg phosphorus; 60 mg calcium; 6 mg iron; 151 mg sodium; 777 mg potassium; 2017 IU vitamin A; 0 mg ATE vitamin E; 30 mg vitamin C; 157 mg cholesterol

Smothered Steak

The slow cooker can turn what is usually a tough cut of beef into something fork-tender. This steak, covered in a mushroom and onion sauce, is excellent with mashed potatoes.

2 pounds (900 g) beef round steak

2 tablespoons (15 g) onion soup mix (see recipe in Chapter 2)

¼ cup (60 ml) water

10 ounces (280 g) cream of mushroom soup (see recipe in Chapter 2)

Cut steak into 5 to 6 serving-size pieces. Place in slow cooker. Add dry onion soup mix, water, and soup. Cover and cook for 6 to 8 hours.

Yield: 6 servings

Per serving: 159 g water; 220 calories (25% from fat, 67% from protein, 9% from carb); 35 g protein; 6 g total fat; 2 g saturated fat; 2 g monounsaturated fat; 0 g polyunsaturated fat; 5 g carb; 0 g fiber; 1 g sugar; 355 mg phosphorus; 13 mg calcium; 3 mg iron; 264 mg sodium; 756 mg potassium; 4 IU vitamin A; 1 mg ATE vitamin E; 0 mg vitamin C; 88 mg cholesterol

Barbecued Short Ribs

Short ribs simmer all day in a fairly traditional barbecue sauce, becoming fork-tender in the process.

⅔ cup (83 g) flour

½ teaspoon pepper

4 pounds (1.8 kg) beef short ribs

¼ cup (60 ml) olive oil

1 cup (160 g) chopped onion

1½ cups (355 ml) low-sodium beef broth (see recipe in Chapter 2)

¾ cup (175 ml) red wine vinegar

¾ cup (170 g) packed brown sugar

½ cup (140 g) chili sauce (see recipe in Chapter 2)

⅓ cup (80 g) low-sodium ketchup

⅓ cup (80 ml) Worcestershire sauce

1½ teaspoons minced garlic

1½ teaspoons chili powder

In a large resealable plastic bag, combine the flour and pepper. Add ribs in batches and shake to coat. In a large skillet, heat the oil over medium-high heat and brown ribs on both sides. Transfer to a slow cooker. In the same skillet, combine the remaining ingredients. Cook and stir until mixture comes to a boil; pour over ribs. Cover and cook on low for 9 to 10 hours or until meat is tender.

Yield: 10 servings

Per serving: 213 g water; 488 calories (45% from fat, 31% from protein, 24% from carb); 37 g protein; 24 g total fat; 9 g saturated fat; 12 g monounsaturated fat; 1 g polyunsaturated fat; 29 g carb; 1 g fiber; 19 g sugar; 381 mg phosphorus; 43 mg calcium; 5 mg iron; 241 mg sodium; 867 mg potassium; 400 IU vitamin A; 0 mg ATE vitamin E; 20 mg vitamin C; 107 mg cholesterol

Short Ribs

I guarantee that this recipe will give you both the most tender and the most flavorful short ribs you've ever had.

⅔ cup (83 g) flour

½ teaspoon pepper

4 pounds (1.8 kg) beef short ribs

¼ cup (60 ml) olive oil

1 cup (160 g) chopped onion

1½ cups (355 ml) low-sodium beef broth (see recipe in Chapter 2)

½ cup (120 ml) dry red wine

¼ cup (60 g) brown sugar

½ cup (140 g) chili sauce (see recipe in Chapter 2)

½ cup (120 g) low-sodium ketchup

(continued on page 128)

¼ cup (60 ml) Worcestershire sauce

1½ teaspoons minced garlic

Combine flour and pepper in a plastic bag. Add ribs and shake to coat. Heat half of the oil in a skillet over medium-high heat. Brown half the short ribs and transfer to slow cooker; repeat with remaining oil and meat. Combine remaining ingredients in skillet. Cook, scraping up browned bits, until mixture comes to boil. Pour over ribs. Cover and cook on low 9 to 10 hours.

Yield: 8 servings

Per serving: 260 g water; 567 calories (50% from fat, 33% from protein, 17% from carb); 46 g protein; 30 g total fat; 11 g saturated fat; 15 g monounsaturated fat; 2 g polyunsaturated fat; 24 g carb; 1 g fiber; 12 g sugar; 473 mg phosphorus; 41 mg calcium; 6 mg iron; 267 mg sodium; 1037 mg potassium; 405 IU vitamin A; 0 mg ATE vitamin E; 20 mg vitamin C; 134 mg cholesterol

Beer-Braised Short Ribs

These ribs are about the most tender and full-flavored that you'll find. The simple seasoning enhances, rather than hides, the flavor of the meat.

3 pounds (1⅓ kg) beef short ribs

2 tablespoons (30 g) packed brown sugar

1 teaspoon minced garlic

¼ cup (31 g) flour

1 cup (160 g) chopped onion

1 cup (235 ml) low-sodium beef broth (see recipe in Chapter 2)

12 ounces (355 ml) beer, preferably ale or dark beer

TIP

Serve with mashed potatoes or noodles.

Place the beef in the slow cooker. Add the brown sugar, garlic, and flour. Toss to coat. Place onions over top. Stir the broth and beer in a small bowl. Pour over the beef. Cover and cook on low for 8 to 9 hours or until the beef is fork-tender.

Yield: 8 servings

Per serving: 205 g water; 350 calories (47% from fat, 41% from protein, 12% from carb); 34 g protein; 17 g total fat; 7 g saturated fat; 7 g monounsaturated fat; 1 g polyunsaturated fat; 10 g carb; 0 g fiber; 4 g sugar; 344 mg phosphorus; 26 mg calcium; 4 mg iron; 132 mg sodium; 682 mg potassium; 0 IU vitamin A; 0 mg ATE vitamin E; 2 mg vitamin C; 100 mg cholesterol

Beef Brisket

This a barbecue-flavored brisket is excellent sliced for sandwiches.

3 pounds (1⅓ kg) beef brisket, trimmed and cut in half

1 cup (240 g) low-sodium ketchup

1 cup (160 g) chopped onion

2 tablespoons (28 ml) cider vinegar

1 tablespoon (15 g) horseradish

1 tablespoon (11 g) mustard

½ teaspoon pepper

Place the brisket in a slow cooker. In a bowl, combine the remaining ingredients. Pour over brisket. Cover and cook on low for 6 hours or until tender. Slice the meat across the grain; serve with sauce.

Yield: 10 servings

Per serving: 135 g water; 205 calories (24% from fat, 60% from protein, 16% from carb); 30 g protein; 5 g total fat; 2 g saturated fat; 2 g monounsaturated fat; 0 g polyunsaturated fat; 8 g carb; 0 g fiber; 6 g sugar; 288 mg phosphorus; 32 mg calcium; 3 mg iron; 111 mg sodium; 581 mg potassium; 230 IU vitamin A; 0 mg ATE vitamin E; 5 mg vitamin C; 56 mg cholesterol

Barbecued Brisket

This makes a great-tasting, falling-apart-tender beef brisket.

4 pounds (1.8 kg) beef brisket

12 ounces (355 ml) beer

1 can (8 ounces, or 225 g) no-salt-added tomato sauce

2 teaspoons prepared mustard

2 tablespoons (28 ml) balsamic vinegar

2 tablespoons (28 ml) Worcestershire sauce

1 teaspoon garlic powder

½ teaspoon ground allspice

1 tablespoon (15 g) brown sugar

1 cup (150 g) chopped red bell pepper

1 cup (160 g) chopped onion

¼ teaspoon pepper

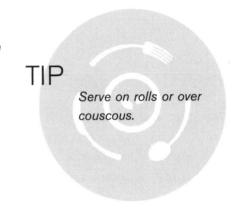

TIP

Serve on rolls or over couscous.

Place brisket in slow cooker. Combine remaining ingredients. Pour over meat. Cover and cook on low 8 to 10 hours. Remove meat from sauce. Slice very thinly.

Yield: 10 servings

Per serving: 217 g water; 274 calories (25% from fat, 63% from protein, 12% from carb); 40 g protein; 7 g total fat; 3 g saturated fat; 3 g monounsaturated fat; 0 g polyunsaturated fat; 8 g carb; 1 g fiber; 4 g sugar; 392 mg phosphorus; 41 mg calcium; 4 mg iron; 170 mg sodium; 795 mg potassium; 552 IU vitamin A; 0 mg ATE vitamin E; 29 mg vitamin C; 74 mg cholesterol

Mexican Brisket

This recipe offers great taste and incredible tenderness.

2 tablespoons (28 ml) olive oil

3 pounds (1⅓ kg) beef brisket, cubed

2 cups (520 g) low-sodium salsa (see recipe in Chapter 2)

2 tablespoons (28 ml) vinegar

1 teaspoon garlic powder

½ teaspoon cinnamon

½ teaspoon oregano

¼ teaspoon cloves

¼ teaspoon pepper

TIP

Serve with potatoes, noodles, or rice.

Heat oil in a skillet over medium-high heat and brown beef. Place in slow cooker. Combine remaining ingredients. Pour over meat. Cover and cook on low 10 to 12 hours. Add water as needed.

Yield: 8 servings

Per serving: 187 g water; 266 calories (35% from fat, 58% from protein, 7% from carb); 38 g protein; 10 g total fat; 3 g saturated fat; 4 g monounsaturated fat; 2 g polyunsaturated fat; 5 g carb; 1 g fiber; 2 g sugar; 366 mg phosphorus; 48 mg calcium; 4 mg iron; 276 mg sodium; 773 mg potassium; 197 IU vitamin A; 0 mg ATE vitamin E; 2 mg vitamin C; 70 mg cholesterol

Brisket with Mixed Potatoes

Beef and both white and sweet potatoes are cooked in salsa for a big flavor boost.

3 large potatoes, peeled and cut into 1-inch (2.5 cm) cubes

3 sweet potatoes, peeled and cut into 1-inch (2.5 cm) cubes

3 pounds (1⅓ kg) beef brisket, fat trimmed

1 cup (260 g) low-sodium salsa (see recipe in Chapter 2)

Place both kinds of potatoes in the slow cooker. Top with the brisket. Pour salsa evenly over the meat. Cover and cook either on low 8 to 10 hours or on high 4 to 5 hours until the meat is tender but not dry. To serve, remove the meat from the cooker, keep warm, and allow to rest for

(continued on page 132)

10 minutes. Then slice the meat across the grain. Place slices on a platter and top with the potatoes and sauce.

Yield: 8 servings

Per serving: 312 g water; 365 calories (17% from fat, 45% from protein, 38% from carb); 41 g protein; 7 g total fat; 2 g saturated fat; 3 g monounsaturated fat; 0 g polyunsaturated fat; 34 g carb; 4 g fiber; 6 g sugar; 456 mg phosphorus; 65 mg calcium; 5 mg iron; 224 mg sodium; 1428 mg potassium; 9017 IU vitamin A; 0 mg ATE vitamin E; 20 mg vitamin C; 70 mg cholesterol

Beef Roast with Apples

Apples are not normally something you think about with beef, but this combination works very well. It's sort of vaguely German in flavor (adding a few tablespoons of vinegar would make it even more so), and it's great over noodles.

3 pounds (1⅓ kg) beef round roast

1 cup (235 ml) water

1 teaspoon Salt-Free Seasoning Blend (see recipe in Chapter 2)

½ teaspoon Worcestershire sauce

¼ teaspoon garlic powder

2 apples, quartered

1 cup (160 g) sliced onion

In a large nonstick skillet coated with nonstick cooking spray, brown roast on all sides. Transfer to slow cooker. Add water to the skillet, stirring to loosen any browned bits; pour over roast. Sprinkle with seasoning blend, Worcestershire sauce, and garlic powder. Top with apple and onion. Cover and cook on low for 5 to 6 hours or until the meat is tender.

Yield: 9 servings

Per serving: 177 g water; 215 calories (24% from fat, 65% from protein, 10% from carb); 34 g protein; 6 g total fat; 2 g saturated fat; 2 g monounsaturated fat; 0 g polyunsaturated fat; 5 g carb; 1 g fiber; 4 g sugar; 337 mg phosphorus; 38 mg calcium; 3 mg iron; 98 mg sodium; 601 mg potassium; 11 IU vitamin A; 0 mg ATE vitamin E; 3 mg vitamin C; 76 mg cholesterol

Pan-Asian Pot Roast

Orange juice spices up this Asian-flavored roast.

3 pounds (1⅓ kg) beef chuck roast

½ cup (120 ml) orange juice

3 tablespoons (45 ml) low-sodium soy sauce (see recipe in Chapter 2)

2 tablespoons (30 g) brown sugar

1 teaspoon Worcestershire sauce

TIP *Shred the meat with two forks. Mix with sauce. Serve over cooked rice, noodles, or mashed potatoes.*

Place meat in slow cooker. In a mixing bowl, combine remaining ingredients and pour over meat. Cover and cook on low for 8 to 10 hours or on high for 5 hours.

Yield: 10 servings

Per serving: 94 g water; 305 calories (32% from fat, 62% from protein, 6% from carb); 45 g protein; 10 g total fat; 4 g saturated fat; 4 g monounsaturated fat; 0 g polyunsaturated fat; 4 g carb; 0 g fiber; 3 g sugar; 372 mg phosphorus; 17 mg calcium; 5 mg iron; 111 mg sodium; 439 mg potassium; 10 IU vitamin A; 0 mg ATE vitamin E; 5 mg vitamin C; 137 mg cholesterol

Barbecued Beef Roast

This makes the most wonderful sandwiches if sliced thinly or shredded. But it's also good with potatoes, rice, or pasta.

4 pounds (1.8 kg) beef round roast

1 cup (240 g) low-sodium ketchup

1 cup (160 g) chopped onion

¾ cup (175 ml) water

¼ cup (60 ml) Worcestershire sauce

¾ cup (170 g) brown sugar

(continued on page 134)

Place roast in slow cooker. Combine remaining ingredients and pour over. Cover and cook on low for 6 to 10 hours.

Yield: 8 servings

Per serving: 229 g water; 411 calories (19% from fat, 51% from protein, 31% from carb); 51 g protein; 8 g total fat; 3 g saturated fat; 4 g monounsaturated fat; 0 g polyunsaturated fat; 31 g carb; 0 g fiber; 28 g sugar; 520 mg phosphorus; 76 mg calcium; 5 mg iron; 230 mg sodium; 1094 mg potassium; 288 IU vitamin A; 0 mg ATE vitamin E; 20 mg vitamin C; 113 mg cholesterol

Chili Beef Roast

Chuck roast is a good choice for the slow cooker. The long, moist cooking makes it fork-tender, and a preparation like this one gives it a lot of flavor.

3 pounds (1⅓ kg) beef chuck roast

2 tablespoons (16 g) flour

1 tablespoon (11 g) prepared mustard

1 tablespoon (20 g) chili sauce (see recipe in Chapter 2)

1 tablespoon (15 ml) Worcestershire sauce

1 teaspoon cider vinegar

1 tablespoon (7.5 g) chili powder

1 teaspoon sugar

4 potatoes, sliced

1 cup (160 g) sliced onions

Place roast in slow cooker. Make a paste with the flour, mustard, chili sauce, Worcestershire sauce, vinegar, chili powder, and sugar. Spread over the roast. Top with potatoes and then the onions. Cover and cook on low 10 to 12 hours.

Yield: 8 servings

Per serving: 270 g water; 511 calories (24% from fat, 48% from protein, 27% from carb); 60 g protein; 13 g total fat; 5 g saturated fat; 5 g monounsaturated fat; 1 g polyunsaturated fat; 34 g carb; 4 g fiber; 3 g sugar; 581 mg phosphorus; 43 mg calcium; 8 mg iron; 154 mg sodium; 1399 mg potassium; 326 IU vitamin A; 0 mg ATE vitamin E; 22 mg vitamin C; 172 mg cholesterol

Mushroom Pot Roast

If the meat were cut up, I'd call this more of a stew than a pot roast. Whatever you call it, the onion flavoring and beer make a great-tasting meal.

1 pound (455 g) mushrooms, sliced

3 pounds (1⅓ kg) beef round roast

2 tablespoons (15 g) onion soup mix (see recipe in
   Chapter 2)

12 ounces (355 ml) beer

½ teaspoon black pepper

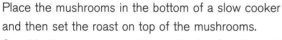

TIP

Serve over mashed potatoes.

Place the mushrooms in the bottom of a slow cooker and then set the roast on top of the mushrooms. Sprinkle the onion soup mix over the beef and pour the beer over everything; season with black pepper. Cover and cook on low 9 to 10 hours or until the meat easily pulls apart with a fork.

Yield: 9 servings

Per serving: 192 g water; 221 calories (25% from fat, 69% from protein, 6% from carb); 35 g protein; 6 g total fat; 2 g saturated fat; 2 g monounsaturated fat; 0 g polyunsaturated fat; 3 g carb; 1 g fiber; 1 g sugar; 377 mg phosphorus; 35 mg calcium; 3 mg iron; 98 mg sodium; 718 mg potassium; 0 IU vitamin A; 0 mg ATE vitamin E; 1 mg vitamin C; 76 mg cholesterol

Beef with Italian Sauce

This Italian beef roast with vegetables and sauce is great with pasta or in sandwiches.

3 pounds (1⅓ kg) beef round roast

¼ teaspoon garlic powder

¼ teaspoon pepper

4 ounces (115 g) mushrooms, sliced

(continued on page 136)

1 cup (160 g) diced onion

14 ounces (390 g) low-sodium spaghetti sauce

½ cup (120 ml) low-sodium beef broth (see recipe in Chapter 2)

Cut roast in half. Combine garlic powder and pepper. Rub over both halves of the roast. Place in slow cooker. Top with mushrooms and onions. Combine spaghetti sauce and broth. Pour over roast. Cover and cook on low 8 to 9 hours. Slice roast. Serve in sauce over pasta.

Yield: 10 servings

Per serving: 166 g water; 227 calories (28% from fat, 57% from protein, 15% from carb); 32 g protein; 7 g total fat; 2 g saturated fat; 3 g monounsaturated fat; 0 g polyunsaturated fat; 8 g carb; 2 g fiber; 5 g sugar; 326 mg phosphorus; 44 mg calcium; 3 mg iron; 105 mg sodium; 710 mg potassium; 246 IU vitamin A; 0 mg ATE vitamin E; 6 mg vitamin C; 68 mg cholesterol

Italian Roast with Vegetables

This is a traditional pot roast, except for the Italian seasonings. It's always good to have something a little different.

4 medium potatoes, cut into quarters

2 cups (260 g) sliced carrots

1 cup (100 g) celery, cut into 1-inch (2.5 cm) pieces

½ cup (90 g) diced roma tomato

2½ pounds (1.1 kg) beef bottom round roast

½ teaspoon black pepper

1 can (8 ounces, or 225 g) no-salt-added tomato sauce

½ cup (120 ml) water

1 tablespoon (10 g) chopped roasted or fresh garlic

1 teaspoon basil

1 teaspoon oregano

1 teaspoon parsley flakes

1 teaspoon vinegar

Place potatoes, carrots, celery, and tomato in slow cooker. Season roast with pepper and place on top. Mix tomato sauce, water, garlic, basil, oregano, parsley, and vinegar. Pour over roast in cooker. Cover and cook on low 10 to 12 hours or until done.

Yield: 8 servings

Per serving: 313 g water; 580 calories (43% from fat, 32% from protein, 25% from carb); 45 g protein; 28 g total fat; 11 g saturated fat; 12 g monounsaturated fat; 1 g polyunsaturated fat; 36 g carb; 5 g fiber; 5 g sugar; 388 mg phosphorus; 69 mg calcium; 5 mg iron; 115 mg sodium; 1443 mg potassium; 5649 IU vitamin A; 0 mg ATE vitamin E; 24 mg vitamin C; 135 mg cholesterol

Italian Beef Roast

This is the easiest way to get Italian beef sandwiches. And the flavor will make you want to come back for more. It's also good over mashed potatoes, noodles, or pasta.

2½ cups (570 ml) water

2 tablespoons (28 g) onion soup mix (see recipe in Chapter 2)

2 tablespoons (28 ml) Worcestershire sauce

1 teaspoon garlic powder

1 teaspoon marjoram

1 teaspoon thyme

1 teaspoon oregano

4 pounds (1.8 kg) beef chuck roast

In a slow cooker, combine the water, soup mix, Worcestershire sauce, garlic powder, marjoram, thyme, and oregano. Add the meat. Cook for either 4 to 6 hours on high or 8 to 10 hours on low until the meat falls apart. Pull the meat apart and use for sandwiches or over pasta.

Yield: 10 servings

Per serving: 166 g water; 385 calories (34% from fat, 65% from protein, 1% from carb); 60 g protein; 14 g total fat; 5 g saturated fat; 6 g monounsaturated fat; 1 g polyunsaturated fat; 1 g carb; 0 g fiber; 0 g sugar; 491 mg phosphorus; 23 mg calcium; 7 mg iron; 151 mg sodium; 555 mg potassium; 18 IU vitamin A; 0 mg ATE vitamin E; 6 mg vitamin C; 183 mg cholesterol

Italian Pot Roast

Round roast is not the most tender cut of beef, but the long, slow, moist cooking here makes it fall-apart tender.

3 pounds (1⅓ kg) beef round roast

2 tablespoons (15 g) Italian dressing mix (see recipe in Chapter 2)

2 onions, cut in wedges

½ teaspoon minced garlic

2 cups (300 g) red bell peppers, cut into 1½-inch (3.8 cm) pieces

½ cup (120 ml) low-sodium beef broth (see recipe in Chapter 2)

1 cup (115 g) zucchini, cut into ¼-inch (66 mm) thick slices

Press dressing mix evenly onto all surfaces of beef roast. Place onions and garlic in slow cooker; top with pot roast. Add red peppers and broth. Cover and cook on high 5 hours or on low 8 hours. Add zucchini. Continue cooking, covered, 30 minutes or until pot roast is tender.

Yield: 9 servings

Per serving: 199 g water; 220 calories (24% from fat, 65% from protein, 11% from carb); 35 g protein; 6 g total fat; 2 g saturated fat; 2 g monounsaturated fat; 0 g polyunsaturated fat; 6 g carb; 1 g fiber; 3 g sugar; 354 mg phosphorus; 45 mg calcium; 3 mg iron; 106 mg sodium; 712 mg potassium; 1065 IU vitamin A; 0 mg ATE vitamin E; 47 mg vitamin C; 76 mg cholesterol

Sour Cream Pot Roast

The sour cream makes the flavor of this roast reminiscent of stroganoff. The gravy is great over mashed potatoes or noodles.

4 pounds (1.8 kg) beef chuck roast

1 garlic clove, cut in half

½ teaspoon pepper

½ cup (65 g) chopped carrot

½ cup (50 g) chopped celery

½ cup (80 g) sliced onion

¾ cup (180 g) sour cream

3 tablespoons (24 g) flour

½ cup (120 ml) dry white wine

Rub roast with garlic. Season with pepper. Place in slow cooker. Add carrots, celery, and onion. Combine sour cream, flour, and wine. Pour into slow cooker. Cover and cook on low 6 to 7 hours.

Yield: 8 servings

Per serving: 186 g water; 538 calories (36% from fat, 60% from protein, 4% from carb); 76 g protein; 20 g total fat; 8 g saturated fat; 8 g monounsaturated fat; 1 g polyunsaturated fat; 5 g carb; 1 g fiber; 1 g sugar; 642 mg phosphorus; 53 mg calcium; 9 mg iron; 171 mg sodium; 755 mg potassium; 1464 IU vitamin A; 23 mg ATE vitamin E; 2 mg vitamin C; 238 mg cholesterol

Oriental Pot Roast

If you are looking for something a little different, this could be it: a traditional pot roast with Asian ingredients and seasonings.

3 pounds (1⅓ kg) beef chuck roast

2 tablespoons (28 ml) olive oil

1 pound (455 g) bean sprouts, rinsed and drained

5 ounces (140 g) water chestnuts, drained and thinly sliced

1 cup (150 g) green bell pepper, cut in 1-inch (2.5 cm) pieces

⅓ cup (107 g) apricot jam

¼ cup (60 ml) cider vinegar

1 tablespoon (15 ml) low-sodium soy sauce (see recipe in Chapter 2)

½ teaspoon minced garlic

½ teaspoon ground ginger

TIP

Serve over rice.

(continued on page 140)

¼ teaspoon pepper

11 ounces (310 g) mandarin oranges, packed in syrup

3 tablespoons (24 g) cornstarch

Trim excess fat from roast; cut in half to fit into slow cooker. Heat the oil in a skillet over medium-high heat; brown meat and drain. Place meat in cooker; add bean sprouts, water chestnuts, and green pepper. Stir together jam, vinegar, soy sauce, garlic, ginger, and pepper. Pour over meat and vegetables. Cover; cook on low for 8 to 10 hours. Remove meat and vegetables. Skim fat from cooking liquid. Measure 2 cups (475 ml) liquid; reserve. Return meat and vegetables to cooker; cover to keep warm. Drain oranges, reserving ¼ cup (60 ml) of the syrup. In a saucepan, blend reserved syrup slowly into cornstarch; stir in reserved cooking liquid. Cook and stir until thickened and bubbly. Stir in orange sections; heat through. Season to taste. Place meat and vegetables on platter. Spoon some sauce over; pass remaining sauce at the table.

Yield: 8 servings

Per serving: 232 g water; 481 calories (32% from fat, 49% from protein, 19% from carb); 58 g protein; 16 g total fat; 5 g saturated fat; 8 g monounsaturated fat; 1 g polyunsaturated fat; 22 g carb; 2 g fiber; 12 g sugar; 499 mg phosphorus; 35 mg calcium; 7 mg iron; 208 mg sodium; 717 mg potassium; 409 IU vitamin A; 0 mg ATE vitamin E; 31 mg vitamin C; 172 mg cholesterol

Marinated Pot Roast

The flavor of this is hard to describe. It's kind of German and kind of sweet and sour, but whatever you call it, it's good.

3 pounds (1⅓ kg) beef chuck roast

1½ cups (355 ml) low-sodium tomato juice

¼ cup (60 ml) red wine vinegar

½ teaspoon minced garlic

2 teaspoons Worcestershire sauce

½ teaspoon basil

½ teaspoon thyme

¼ teaspoon pepper

1 cup (160 g) chopped onion

1 cup (130 g) sliced carrot

½ cup (120 ml) cold water

¼ cup (31 g) flour

Trim excess fat from roast. If necessary, cut roast in halves or thirds to fit in cooker. Place meat in a resealable plastic bag; set in deep bowl. Stir together tomato juice, vinegar, garlic, Worcestershire sauce, basil, thyme, and pepper. Pour marinade over meat; close bag. Marinate overnight in refrigerator, turning twice. Place onions and carrot In slow cooker. Place roast on top of vegetables; add marinade. Cover and cook on low for 8 to 10 hours. Remove roast and vegetables. Skim off excess fat from cooking liquid. Measure 2 cups (475 ml) cooking liquid; pour into saucepan. Return meat and vegetables to cooker; cover to keep warm. Blend cold water slowly into flour; stir into reserved cooking liquid in saucepan. Cook and stir until mixture is thickened and bubbly. Place meat on a warm serving platter; top with vegetables. Pour some of the gravy over; pass the remaining gravy at the table.

Yield: 6 servings

Per serving: 263 g water; 529 calories (31% from fat, 60% from protein, 9% from carb); 76 g protein; 17 g total fat; 6 g saturated fat; 7 g monounsaturated fat; 1 g polyunsaturated fat; 12 g carb; 1 g fiber; 4 g sugar; 643 mg phosphorus; 45 mg calcium; 9 mg iron; 189 mg sodium; 929 mg potassium; 3875 IU vitamin A; 0 mg ATE vitamin E; 18 mg vitamin C; 229 mg cholesterol

German Beef Roast

This German-flavored roast will remind you of sauerbraten but with a lot less work.

4 pounds (1.8 kg) beef chuck roast

⅓ cup (80 ml) cider vinegar

1 cup (160 g) sliced onion

3 bay leaves

¼ teaspoon cloves

¼ teaspoon garlic powder

½ teaspoon ginger

(continued on page 142)

Place roast in slow cooker. Add remaining ingredients. Cover and cook on low 8 to 10 hours. Remove bay leaves before serving.

Yield: 8 servings

Per serving: 160 g water; 487 calories (33% from fat, 65% from protein, 2% from carb); 75 g protein; 17 g total fat; 6 g saturated fat; 7 g monounsaturated fat; 1 g polyunsaturated fat; 2 g carb; 0 g fiber; 1 g sugar; 615 mg phosphorus; 26 mg calcium; 9 mg iron; 151 mg sodium; 695 mg potassium; 1 IU vitamin A; 0 mg ATE vitamin E; 2 mg vitamin C; 229 mg cholesterol

Smoky Beef Roast

Liquid smoke is one of the secret ingredients that give this roast its unique flavor. What's the other? Coffee!

2 pounds (900 g) beef round roast

8 ounces (255 g) mushrooms, sliced

½ cup (80 g) sliced onion

½ teaspoon minced garlic

1½ cups (355 ml) coffee

1 teaspoon liquid smoke

½ teaspoon chili powder

½ teaspoon black pepper

Place roast in slow cooker. Combine remaining ingredients and pour over roast. Cover and cook on low for 9 to 10 hours.

Yield: 8 servings

Per serving: 162 g water; 157 calories (25% from fat, 69% from protein, 6% from carb); 26 g protein; 4 g total fat; 1 g saturated fat; 2 g monounsaturated fat; 0 g polyunsaturated fat; 2 g carb; 1 g fiber; 1 g sugar; 275 mg phosphorus; 29 mg calcium; 2 mg iron; 74 mg sodium; 550 mg potassium; 47 IU vitamin A; 0 mg ATE vitamin E; 2 mg vitamin C; 57 mg cholesterol

Mexican Beef Roast

Beef and vegetables cooked in a Mexican sauce can be served over rice or used for fajitas.

4 pounds (1.8 kg) beef round roast

1 can (28 ounces, or 785 g) no-salt-added stewed tomatoes

2 cups (520 g) low-sodium salsa, your choice of heat (see recipe in Chapter 2)

4 ounces (115 g) diced green chilies

2 small onions, cut in chunks

1½ cups (225 g) sliced green bell peppers

Brown the roast on top and bottom in a nonstick skillet and place in slow cooker. In a bowl, combine stewed tomatoes, salsa, and green chilies. Spoon over meat. Cover and cook on low 8 to 10 hours or until the meat is tender but not dry. Add onions halfway through cooking time in order to keep fairly crisp. Push down into the sauce. One hour before serving, add pepper slices. Push down into the sauce. Remove meat from cooker and allow to rest 10 minutes before slicing.

Yield: 10 servings

Per serving: 306 g water; 285 calories (22% from fat, 60% from protein, 18% from carb); 42 g protein; 7 g total fat; 2 g saturated fat; 3 g monounsaturated fat; 0 g polyunsaturated fat; 12 g carb; 3 g fiber; 7 g sugar; 439 mg phosphorus; 91 mg calcium; 5 mg iron; 271 mg sodium; 1053 mg potassium; 368 IU vitamin A; 0 mg ATE vitamin E; 31 mg vitamin C; 91 mg cholesterol

Asian Pot Roast

A delicious beef roast flavored with soy sauce and ginger makes a great starting point for an Asian meal.

3 pounds (1⅓ kg) beef chuck roast

2 tablespoons (16 g) flour

1 tablespoon (15 ml) olive oil

1 cup (160 g) chopped onion

(continued on page 144)

¼ teaspoon pepper

½ cup (120 ml) low-sodium soy sauce (see recipe in Chapter 2)

1 cup (235 ml) water

½ teaspoon ground ginger

Dredge roast in flour. Heat oil in a skillet over medium-high heat and brown roast on both sides. Place in slow cooker. Top with onions and pepper. Combine soy sauce, water, and ginger. Pour over meat. Cover and cook on high 30 minutes. Reduce heat to low and cook 8 to 10 hours. Slice and serve with rice.

Yield: 8 servings

Per serving: 159 g water; 396 calories (35% from fat, 60% from protein, 5% from carb); 57 g protein; 15 g total fat; 5 g saturated fat; 7 g monounsaturated fat; 1 g polyunsaturated fat; 5 g carb; 1 g fiber; 1 g sugar; 482 mg phosphorus; 24 mg calcium; 7 mg iron; 164 mg sodium; 554 mg potassium; 4 IU vitamin A; 0 mg ATE vitamin E; 2 mg vitamin C; 172 mg cholesterol

Beef with Horseradish Sauce

Tangy horseradish makes this beef roast a real favorite. It's great for sandwiches or with mashed potatoes.

2 tablespoons (28 ml) olive oil

3 pounds (1⅓ kg) beef chuck roast

½ teaspoon black pepper

1 cup (160 g) chopped onion

1 can (6 ounces, or 170 g) no-salt-added tomato paste

⅓ cup (85 g) horseradish sauce

Heat oil in a skillet over medium-high heat; brown roast on all sides. Place in slow cooker. Combine remaining ingredients and pour over roast. Cover and cook on low 8 to 10 hours.

Yield: 8 servings

Per serving: 141 g water; 418 calories (37% from fat, 57% from protein, 7% from carb); 57 g protein; 16 g total fat; 5 g saturated fat; 8 g monounsaturated fat; 1 g polyunsaturated fat; 7 g carb; 2 g fiber; 4 g sugar; 483 mg phosphorus; 34 mg calcium; 7 mg iron; 165 mg sodium; 763 mg potassium; 325 IU vitamin A; 0 mg ATE vitamin E; 9 mg vitamin C; 172 mg cholesterol

Beef Paprikash

Paprika is the primary flavoring of this dish, which originated in Hungary.

2 pounds (900 g) beef round steak, cubed

1 cup (160 g) sliced onion

½ teaspoon garlic powder

½ cup (120 g) low-sodium ketchup

2 tablespoons (28 ml) Worcestershire sauce

2 tablespoons (30 g) brown sugar

2 teaspoons paprika

½ teaspoon dry mustard

TIP

Serve over noodles.

Place beef in slow cooker. Cover with onion. Combine remaining ingredients and pour over meat. Cover and cook on low for 8 hours.

Yield: 8 servings

Per serving: 110 g water; 185 calories (19% from fat, 58% from protein, 22% from carb); 27 g protein; 4 g total fat; 1 g saturated fat; 1 g monounsaturated fat; 0 g polyunsaturated fat; 10 g carb; 1 g fiber; 8 g sugar; 267 mg phosphorus; 15 mg calcium; 3 mg iron; 101 mg sodium; 579 mg potassium; 448 IU vitamin A; 0 mg ATE vitamin E; 11 mg vitamin C; 65 mg cholesterol

Beef with Gravy

This is a very quick meat course for a comfort food kind of meal.

10 ounces (280 g) low-sodium cream of mushroom soup
(see recipe in Chapter 2)

2 tablespoons (28 g) low-sodium onion soup mix (see
recipe in Chapter 2)

1 pound (455 g) beef round steak, cut into 1-inch
(2.5 cm) cubes

TIP *Serve over cooked
noodles or mashed
potatoes.*

Spray the interior of the cooker with nonstick cooking
spray. In the slow cooker, combine soup and soup mix.
Stir in beef. Cover and cook on low 6 to 8 hours or until
meat is tender but not dry.

Yield: 3 servings

Per serving: 190 g water; 241 calories (26% from fat, 61% from protein, 13% from carb); 36 g protein; 7 g
total fat; 2 g saturated fat; 2 g monounsaturated fat; 1 g polyunsaturated fat; 8 g carb; 1 g fiber; 2 g sugar;
379 mg phosphorus; 17 mg calcium; 4 mg iron; 109 mg sodium; 933 mg potassium; 8 IU vitamin A; 2 mg
ATE vitamin E; 0 mg vitamin C; 89 mg cholesterol

Salsa Beef

Serve this Mexican-flavored beef over rice or wrap it up in tortillas.

1 tablespoon (15 ml) olive oil

2 pounds (900 g) beef round steak, cut in bite-size cubes

2 cups (520 g) low-sodium salsa (see recipe in Chapter 2)

1 can (8 ounces, or 225 g) no-salt-added tomato sauce

½ teaspoon minced garlic

2 tablespoons (30 g) brown sugar

1 cup (180 g) no-salt-added diced tomatoes

Heat oil in a large skillet over medium-high heat; brown beef cubes. Place in slow cooker. Combine remaining ingredients and add to cooker. Cover and cook on low 6 to 8 hours.

Yield: 6 servings

Per serving: 247 g water; 271 calories (25% from fat, 54% from protein, 20% from carb); 36 g protein; 7 g total fat; 2 g saturated fat; 4 g monounsaturated fat; 1 g polyunsaturated fat; 14 g carb; 2 g fiber; 9 g sugar; 376 mg phosphorus; 47 mg calcium; 4 mg iron; 265 mg sodium; 1036 mg potassium; 399 IU vitamin A; 0 mg ATE vitamin E; 10 mg vitamin C; 86 mg cholesterol

Beef Roll-Ups

These beef roll-ups are fancy enough for company but easy enough to make that you can have them for everyday.

4 pounds (1.8 kg) beef round steak

4 cups (800 g) stuffing, prepared according to package directions

20 ounces (560 g) low-sodium cream of mushroom soup (see recipe in Chapter 2)

2 cups (475 ml) water

Cut steak into 12 long pieces. Pound each piece until thin and flattened. Place ⅓ cup (65 g) prepared stuffing on each slice of meat. Roll up and fasten with toothpick. Place in slow cooker. In a bowl, mix soup and water together and then pour over steak. Cover and cook on high 4 to 6 hours or until meat is tender but not overcooked.

Yield: 12 servings

Per serving: 231 g water; 335 calories (32% from fat, 46% from protein, 22% from carb); 37 g protein; 12 g total fat; 3 g saturated fat; 5 g monounsaturated fat; 2 g polyunsaturated fat; 18 g carb; 2 g fiber; 2 g sugar; 383 mg phosphorus; 33 mg calcium; 4 mg iron; 212 mg sodium; 806 mg potassium; 212 IU vitamin A; 75 mg ATE vitamin E; 0 mg vitamin C; 88 mg cholesterol

Mexican Steak Stew

This simple Mexican stew is good served over rice.

2½ pounds (1.1 kg) beef round steak

1 cup (160 g) chopped onion

2 tablespoons (15 g) Salt-Free Mexican Seasoning (see recipe in Chapter 2)

1 can (14 ounces, or 400 g) no-salt-added diced tomatoes, undrained

1 cup (150 g) red bell pepper, cut into 1-inch (2.5 cm) pieces

Trim excess fat from beef and cut into 2-inch (5 cm) pieces. Combine with onion in slow cooker. Mix together seasoning and undrained tomatoes. Pour over beef. Place red pepper on top. Cover. Cook on low 6 to 8 hours or until beef is tender.

Yield: 8 servings

Per serving: 183 g water; 201 calories (22% from fat, 68% from protein, 10% from carb); 33 g protein; 5 g total fat; 2 g saturated fat; 2 g monounsaturated fat; 0 g polyunsaturated fat; 5 g carb; 1 g fiber; 3 g sugar; 331 mg phosphorus; 26 mg calcium; 4 mg iron; 82 mg sodium; 705 mg potassium; 642 IU vitamin A; 0 mg ATE vitamin E; 30 mg vitamin C; 81 mg cholesterol

Beef with Wild Rice

This delicious beef and rice meal cooks while you are gone, providing a great dinner with the addition of a salad and bread.

1 cup (160 g) wild rice, rinsed and drained

1 cup (100 g) chopped celery

1 cup (130 g) chopped carrots

4 ounces (115 g) mushrooms, sliced

1 cup (160 g) chopped onion

½ cup (55 g) slivered almonds

2 pounds (900 g) beef round steak, cut in bite-size pieces

2 cups (475 ml) low-sodium beef broth (see recipe in Chapter 2)

Layer ingredients in slow cooker in order listed. Do not stir. Cover and cook on low 6 to 8 hours. Stir before serving.

Yield: 8 servings

Per serving: 198 g water; 291 calories (27% from fat, 44% from protein, 29% from carb); 32 g protein; 9 g total fat; 2 g saturated fat; 4 g monounsaturated fat; 1 g polyunsaturated fat; 21 g carb; 3 g fiber; 3 g sugar; 412 mg phosphorus; 50 mg calcium; 3 mg iron; 118 mg sodium; 775 mg potassium; 2751 IU vitamin A; 0 mg ATE vitamin E; 3 mg vitamin C; 65 mg cholesterol

Quick Stroganoff

Meals don't get any easier than this tasty three-ingredient recipe.

1 pound (455 g) beef round steak, cubed

1 can (10 ounces, or 280 g) low-sodium cream of
    mushroom soup (see recipe in Chapter 2)

1 cup (230 g) fat-free sour cream

TIP

Serve over cooked rice, pasta, or baked potatoes.

Place beef in slow cooker. Cover with mushroom soup. Cover and cook on low 8 hours or on high 4 to 5 hours. Before serving, stir in sour cream.

Yield: 4 servings

Per serving: 191 g water; 263 calories (43% from fat, 44% from protein, 13% from carb); 28 g protein; 12 g total fat; 6 g saturated fat; 4 g monounsaturated fat; 1 g polyunsaturated fat; 8 g carb; 0 g fiber; 2 g sugar; 342 mg phosphorus; 76 mg calcium; 3 mg iron; 355 mg sodium; 777 mg potassium; 231 IU vitamin A; 62 mg ATE vitamin E; 1 mg vitamin C; 90 mg cholesterol

Beef Stroganoff

Traditional beef stroganoff—another classic comfort food—is made easier using the slow cooker.

1½ pounds (680 g) beef round steak, cut into strips

½ cup (80 g) chopped onion

10 ounces (280 g) low-sodium cream of mushroom soup
(see recipe in Chapter 2)

8 ounces (225 g) mushrooms, sliced

¼ cup (60 ml) water

1 tablespoon (3 g) chives

½ teaspoon minced garlic

1 teaspoon Worcestershire sauce

¼ cup (60 ml) white wine

1 tablespoon (8 g) flour

16 ounces (460 g) fat-free sour cream

TIP *Serve over noodles, garnished with chopped fresh parsley.*

Place the beef in the bottom of slow cooker. Place onion on top of beef and then add mushroom soup, mushrooms, and water. Season with chives, garlic, and Worcestershire sauce. In a small bowl, mix together the wine with the flour. Pour over the beef. Cover and cook on low for 6 to 7 hours. Stir in the sour cream and continue cooking for 1 hour.

Yield: 4 servings

Per serving: 373 g water; 448 calories (43% from fat, 42% from protein, 15% from carb); 45 g protein; 21 g total fat; 11 g saturated fat; 6 g monounsaturated fat; 1 g polyunsaturated fat; 17 g carb; 1 g fiber; 4 g sugar; 578 mg phosphorus; 142 mg calcium; 5 mg iron; 424 mg sodium; 1299 mg potassium; 462 IU vitamin A; 115 mg ATE vitamin E; 6 mg vitamin C; 143 mg cholesterol

Beef and Beans

A chili flavored dish, this is sure to please.

1½ pounds (680 g) beef round steak

1 tablespoon (11 g) mustard

1 tablespoon (7.5 g) chili powder

¼ teaspoon black pepper

½ teaspoon minced garlic

1 can (14 ounces, or 400 g) no-salt-added diced tomatoes

1 cup (160 g) chopped onion

2 cups (512 g) kidney beans

TIP

Serve over rice.

Cut steak into thin strips. Combine mustard, chili powder, pepper, and garlic in a bowl. Add steak and toss to coat. Transfer to slow cooker. Add tomatoes and onion. Cover and cook on low 5 to 7 hours. Stir in beans. Cook 30 minutes longer.

Yield: 8 servings

Per serving: 155 g water; 184 calories (16% from fat, 53% from protein, 31% from carb); 24 g protein; 3 g total fat; 1 g saturated fat; 1 g monounsaturated fat; 0 g polyunsaturated fat; 14 g carb; 5 g fiber; 2 g sugar; 268 mg phosphorus; 46 mg calcium; 4 mg iron; 63 mg sodium; 639 mg potassium; 339 IU vitamin A; 0 mg ATE vitamin E; 7 mg vitamin C; 48 mg cholesterol

Beef and Eggplant

Sweet spices give this a Middle Eastern flavor. It's great over rice or couscous.

2 cups (164 g) eggplant, peeled and cubed

1 can (8 ounces, or 225 g) no-salt-added tomato sauce

½ cup (50 g) chopped celery

½ cup (80 g) chopped onion

¼ cup (38 g) chopped green pepper

(continued on page 152)

½ teaspoon marjoram, crushed

¼ teaspoon cinnamon

¼ teaspoon nutmeg

1½ pounds (680 g) beef round steak, cut in 1-inch (2.5 cm) cubes

In slow cooker, stir together the eggplant, tomato sauce, celery, onion, green pepper, marjoram, cinnamon, and nutmeg. Place meat on top. Cover and cook on low for 8 to 10 hours.

Yield: 6 servings

Per serving: 165 g water; 173 calories (21% from fat, 64% from protein, 15% from carb); 27 g protein; 4 g total fat; 1 g saturated fat; 1 g monounsaturated fat; 0 g polyunsaturated fat; 6 g carb; 2 g fiber; 3 g sugar; 275 mg phosphorus; 20 mg calcium; 3 mg iron; 71 mg sodium; 691 mg potassium; 204 IU vitamin A; 0 mg ATE vitamin E; 12 mg vitamin C; 65 mg cholesterol

Creamy Beef Burgundy

This beef roast only has a few ingredients, but it still has a lot of flavor. The slow cooker is ideal for turning bargain cuts of meat like round roast into tender, juicy meals.

4 pounds (1.8 g) beef round roast

1 can (10 ounces, or 280 g) low-sodium cream of mushroom soup (see recipe in Chapter 2)

1 cup (235 ml) burgundy wine

1 cup (160 g) finely chopped onion

1 tablespoon (1.3 g) dried parsley

Place meat in slow cooker. Blend soup and wine together in a mixing bowl. Pour over meat. Top with onion and parsley. Cover and cook on low 5 hours or until meat is tender but not dry. Serve the sauce as gravy over the sliced or cubed meat.

Yield: 8 servings

Per serving: 241 g water; 342 calories (26% from fat, 67% from protein, 7% from carb); 51 g protein; 9 g total fat; 3 g saturated fat; 4 g monounsaturated fat; 1 g polyunsaturated fat; 6 g carb; 1 g fiber; 2 g sugar; 523 mg phosphorus; 60 mg calcium; 5 mg iron; 279 mg sodium; 1020 mg potassium; 43 IU vitamin A; 1 mg ATE vitamin E; 2 mg vitamin C; 114 mg cholesterol

Beef and Bacon in Beer

A tasty English meal to make in the slow cooker. Serve with baked potatoes or mashed potatoes and vegetables.

1½ pounds (680 g) beef stew meat, cubed

3 tablespoons (24 g) flour

4 tablespoons (60 ml) oil, divided

4 slices low-sodium bacon

1 cup (160 g) finely chopped onion

1 teaspoon minced garlic

1 teaspoon mustard

2 teaspoons no-salt-added tomato paste

2 cups (475 ml) beer, preferably dark

1 teaspoon low-sodium beef bouillon

1 teaspoon Worcestershire sauce

½ teaspoon sugar

Toss the beef in the flour until covered. Heat 2 tablespoons (28 ml) of oil in a large frying pan or wok and fry the beef until brown. Remove the meat. In the remaining oil, gently fry the onion and the garlic until soft and transparent. Return the meat to the pan with the onion and garlic. Add the remaining ingredients and cook until the sauce thickens. Put in the slow cooker and cook for approximately 7 hours or until tender.

Yield: 6 servings

Per serving: 100 g water; 173 calories (67% from fat, 8% from protein, 25% from carb); 3 g protein; 11 g total fat; 2 g saturated fat; 3 g monounsaturated fat; 5 g polyunsaturated fat; 9 g carb; 1 g fiber; 2 g sugar; 55 mg phosphorus; 13 mg calcium; 0 mg iron; 138 mg sodium; 123 mg potassium; 32 IU vitamin A; 1 mg ATE vitamin E; 4 mg vitamin C; 6 mg cholesterol

Fajitas

Get away from the frying and make fajitas the easy way with the slow cooker. The long cooking makes the meat both more tender and more flavorful.

1½ pounds (680 g) flank steak

1 can (14 ounces, or 400 g) no-salt-added diced tomatoes, undrained

1 jalapeño, seeded and chopped

½ teaspoon minced garlic

1 teaspoon coriander

1 teaspoon cumin

1 teaspoon chili powder

2 cups (320 g) sliced onion

2 cups (300 g) sliced green bell pepper

2 cups (300 g) sliced red bell pepper

1 tablespoon (1 g) fresh cilantro

TIP *Serve on flour tortillas with sour cream and salsa.*

Thinly slice steak across the grain into strips; place in slow cooker. Add tomatoes, jalapeño, garlic, coriander, cumin, and chili powder. Cover and cook on low for 7 hours. Add onion, peppers, and cilantro. Cover and cook 1 to 2 hours longer or until meat is tender.

Yield: 6 servings

Per serving: 278 g water; 279 calories (32% from fat, 48% from protein, 19% from carb); 34 g protein; 10 g total fat; 4 g saturated fat; 4 g monounsaturated fat; 1 g polyunsaturated fat; 14 g carb; 4 g fiber; 7 g sugar; 295 mg phosphorus; 65 mg calcium; 4 mg iron; 83 mg sodium; 804 mg potassium; 1999 IU vitamin A; 0 mg ATE vitamin E; 116 mg vitamin C; 62 mg cholesterol

French Dip

We like these sandwiches a lot, so this recipe makes quite a bit. We often have them a couple of days in a week, but you could also freeze extras (or serve this when you are entertaining and impress everyone).

3 pounds (1⅓ kg) beef round roast

2 cups (475 ml) low-sodium beef broth (see recipe in Chapter 2)

2 tablespoons (15 g) onion soup mix (see recipe in Chapter 2)

12 ounces (355 ml) beer

Place roast in a slow cooker. Add the beef broth, onion soup, and beer. Cook on low for 7 hours. Slice the meat on the diagonal to serve.

Yield: 12 servings

TIP *Serve on French rolls, accompanied by the sauce for dipping. We like this with steak fries, which can also be dipped.*

Per serving: 148 g water; 160 calories (26% from fat, 71% from protein, 3% from carb); 26 g protein; 4 g total fat; 1 g saturated fat; 2 g monounsaturated fat; 0 g polyunsaturated fat; 1 g carb; 0 g fiber; 0 g sugar; 255 mg phosphorus; 27 mg calcium; 2 mg iron; 95 mg sodium; 439 mg potassium; 0 IU vitamin A; 0 mg ATE vitamin E; 0 mg vitamin C; 57 mg cholesterol

Greek Sandwich Filling

Similar in flavor to a number of Greek and Middle Eastern dishes like gyros, this is always popular. This recipe makes a large batch that is perfect when entertaining.

4 tablespoons (60 ml) olive oil, divided

4 pounds (1.8 kg) beef round steak, cut in ½-inch (1.3 cm) cubes, divided

2 cups (320 g) chopped onions

(continued on page 156)

½ teaspoon minced garlic

1 cup (235 ml) dry red wine

1 can (6 ounces, or 170 g) no-salt-added tomato paste

1 teaspoon oregano

1 teaspoon basil

½ teaspoon rosemary

Dash black pepper

1 tablespoon (8 g) cornstarch

2 tablespoons (28 ml) water

TIP *Serve in pita bread pockets, topped with shredded lettuce, tomato, cucumber, and plain yogurt.*

Heat 1 tablespoon (15 ml) oil in a skillet and then add 1 pound (455 g) meat and brown. Repeat with remaining oil and meat. Reserve drippings and transfer meat to slow cooker. Sauté onion and garlic in drippings until tender. Add to meat. Add wine, tomato paste, oregano, basil, rosemary, salt, and pepper. Cover and cook on low 6 to 8 hours. Turn cooker to high. Combine cornstarch and water in small bowl until smooth. Stir into meat mixture. Cook until bubbly and thickened, stirring occasionally.

Yield: 16 servings

Per serving: 119 g water; 204 calories (34% from fat, 56% from protein, 9% from carb); 27 g protein; 7 g total fat; 2 g saturated fat; 4 g monounsaturated fat; 1 g polyunsaturated fat; 4 g carb; 1 g fiber; 2 g sugar; 267 mg phosphorus; 15 mg calcium; 3 mg iron; 71 mg sodium; 593 mg potassium; 171 IU vitamin A; 0 mg ATE vitamin E; 4 mg vitamin C; 65 mg cholesterol

Shredded Beef

Use this versatile beef to make sandwiches, stir-fries, soups, and other great meals.

3 pounds (1⅓ kg) boneless beef chuck

2 small onions, cut into thin wedges

1 teaspoon minced garlic

1¾ cups (410 ml) low-sodium beef broth (see recipe in Chapter 2)

1 tablespoon (15 ml) Worcestershire sauce

2 teaspoons dry mustard

1 teaspoon dried thyme, crushed

¼ teaspoon cayenne

Trim fat from beef. If necessary, cut beef to fit slow cooker. Place onion and garlic in the cooker. Top with beef. In a medium bowl, combine broth, Worcestershire sauce, dry mustard, thyme, and cayenne. Pour over beef in cooker. Cover and cook on low for 11 to 12 hours or on high for 5 to 6 hours. Remove beef and onion from cooker, reserving juices. Using two forks, shred beef, discarding any fat. Skim fat from juices. Add onion to beef; add enough juices to beef to moisten.

Yield: 12 servings

TIP *To save beef for later, place desired portions of beef in airtight containers and refrigerate for up to 3 days or freeze for up to 3 months.*

Per serving: 115 g water; 352 calories (57% from fat, 39% from protein, 3% from carb); 34 g protein; 22 g total fat; 9 g saturated fat; 9 g monounsaturated fat; 1 g polyunsaturated fat; 3 g carb; 0 g fiber; 1 g sugar; 211 mg phosphorus; 29 mg calcium; 3 mg iron; 86 mg sodium; 332 mg potassium; 6 IU vitamin A; 0 mg ATE vitamin E; 4 mg vitamin C; 108 mg cholesterol

8

Easy and Lean Pork and Lamb Main Dishes

Like beef, pork cooks very well in the slow cooker. And like beef, you can use the leaner cuts that are better for you. Chops, roasts, and sandwiches are the stars here. I also included a few recipes for lamb, which we don't eat very often, but also lends itself to long, moist cooking.

Southern Stuffed Pork Chops

Slow-cooked stuffed pork chops go great with greens and cornbread.

4 pork loin chops, 1-inch (2.5 cm) thick

2 cups (150 g) dry corn bread stuffing mix

2 tablespoons (28 ml) low-sodium chicken broth (see recipe in Chapter 2)

⅓ cup (80 ml) orange juice

1 tablespoon (7 g) finely chopped pecans

¼ cup (60 ml) light corn syrup

½ teaspoon grated orange peel

With a sharp knife cut a horizontal slit in side of each chop, forming a pocket for stuffing. Combine stuffing with remaining ingredients. Fill pockets with stuffing. Place on metal rack in slow cooker. Cover and cook on low for 6 to 8 hours. Uncover and brush with sauce. Cook on high for 15 to 20 minutes.

Yield: 4 servings

Per serving: 106 g water; 295 calories (20% from fat, 32% from protein, 48% from carb); 24 g protein; 7 g total fat; 2 g saturated fat; 3 g monounsaturated fat; 1 g polyunsaturated fat; 35 g carb; 3 g fiber; 7 g sugar; 254 mg phosphorus; 36 mg calcium; 2 mg iron; 340 mg sodium; 471 mg potassium; 59 IU vitamin A; 2 mg ATE vitamin E; 9 mg vitamin C; 64 mg cholesterol

Pork Chops with Sweet Potatoes

Pork chops and sweet potatoes just seem to go together, so this recipe is a natural. If you like it sweeter, add a couple of tablespoons of honey or brown sugar.

4 pork loin chops

1 tablespoon (15 ml) olive oil

1 cup (160 g) sliced onions

(continued on page 160)

2 sweet potatoes, peeled and cut into large chunks

1 cup (235 ml) low-sodium chicken broth (see recipe in Chapter 2)

In a large skillet, heat oil over medium-high heat. Brown pork chops on both sides. Spray the inside surface of a slow cooker with nonstick cooking spray. Arrange sliced onions in the bottom and place pork chops on top of onions. Place sweet potatoes on top. Pour broth over everything. Cover and cook on low for 5 to 6 hours

Yield: 4 servings

Per serving: 229 g water; 235 calories (31% from fat, 40% from protein, 30% from carb); 23 g protein; 8 g total fat; 2 g saturated fat; 4 g monounsaturated fat; 1 g polyunsaturated fat; 17 g carb; 3 g fiber; 6 g sugar; 263 mg phosphorus; 45 mg calcium; 2 mg iron; 109 mg sodium; 624 mg potassium; 11892 IU vitamin A; 2 mg ATE vitamin E; 14 mg vitamin C; 64 mg cholesterol

TIP *If you want firmer sweet potatoes, add them about halfway through the cooking time.*

Pork Chops in Beer

Lightly seasoned, tender pork chops are great with mashed potatoes or noodles.

1 tablespoon (15 ml) olive oil

6 pork loin chops

2 cups (320 g) chopped onion

12 ounces (355 ml) beer

1 teaspoon thyme

Heat oil in a large skillet over medium-high heat and brown chops on both sides. Place onions in slow cooker and then place chops over top. Combine beer and thyme and pour over chops. Cover and cook on low for 8 to 10 hours or on high for 4 to 5 hours.

Yield: 6 servings

Per serving: 174 g water; 195 calories (34% from fat, 50% from protein, 16% from carb); 22 g protein; 7 g total fat; 2 g saturated fat; 4 g monounsaturated fat; 1 g polyunsaturated fat; 7 g carb; 1 g fiber; 2 g sugar; 244 mg phosphorus; 31 mg calcium; 1 mg iron; 56 mg sodium; 468 mg potassium; 14 IU vitamin A; 2 mg ATE vitamin E; 5 mg vitamin C; 64 mg cholesterol

Pork Chops with Apples

Pork loin chops, which are great because they are low in fat, can be tough if you aren't careful cooking them. This slow cooker recipe solves that issue, making sure they are always fork-tender.

4 pork loin chops

1 cup (160 g) sliced onion

2 apples, peeled, cored and sliced

1 tablespoon (15 g) brown sugar

½ teaspoon nutmeg

¼ teaspoon freshly ground black pepper

Heat a skillet over medium-high heat and coat with cooking spray. Quickly brown the pork chops on each side. Set aside. Arrange onion slices, then the apple slices in slow cooker. Sprinkle brown sugar, nutmeg, and pepper over the apples. Place the pork chops on top. Cover and cook on low for 5 to 6 hours.

Yield: 4 servings

Per serving: 165 g water; 191 calories (21% from fat, 46% from protein, 33% from carb); 22 g protein; 4 g total fat; 2 g saturated fat; 2 g monounsaturated fat; 0 g polyunsaturated fat; 15 g carb; 2 g fiber; 12 g sugar; 240 mg phosphorus; 30 mg calcium; 1 mg iron; 55 mg sodium; 504 mg potassium; 33 IU vitamin A; 2 mg ATE vitamin E; 6 mg vitamin C; 64 mg cholesterol

Italian Pork Chops

Slightly spicy Italian-flavored chops are great with pasta since there will be enough sauce to use over it.

4 boneless pork loin chops

1 can (8 ounces, or 225 g) no-salt-added tomato sauce

2 tablespoons (15 g) Italian dressing mix (see recipe in Chapter 2)

¼ cup (60 g) brown sugar

¼ cup (44 g) Dijon mustard

Place pork chops in slow cooker. Mix remaining ingredients together in a bowl. Pour over chops. Cover and cook on low 6 to 8 hours or until meat is tender but not dry.

Yield: 4 servings

Per serving: 137 g water; 212 calories (21% from fat, 43% from protein, 35% from carb); 23 g protein; 5 g total fat; 2 g saturated fat; 2 g monounsaturated fat; 1 g polyunsaturated fat; 18 g carb; 1 g fiber; 16 g sugar; 257 mg phosphorus; 41 mg calcium; 2 mg iron; 233 mg sodium; 652 mg potassium; 214 IU vitamin A; 2 mg ATE vitamin E; 9 mg vitamin C; 64 mg cholesterol

Pork Chops with Mushrooms

These pork chops cook in a creamy mushroom sauce that is perfect over noodles or mashed potatoes.

10 ounces (280 g) low-sodium cream of mushroom soup (see recipe in Chapter 2)

1 cup (160 g) chopped onion

8 ounces (225 g) mushrooms, sliced

1 teaspoon Worcestershire sauce

6 boneless pork loin chops

Mix soup, onions, and mushrooms. Stir in Worcestershire sauce. Pour half of mixture into slow cooker. Place pork chops in slow cooker. Cover with the remaining sauce. Cover and cook on low 4 to 5 hours or until meat is tender but not dry.

Yield: 6 servings

Per serving: 174 g water; 173 calories (27% from fat, 55% from protein, 18% from carb); 23 g protein; 5 g total fat; 2 g saturated fat; 2 g monounsaturated fat; 1 g polyunsaturated fat; 8 g carb; 1 g fiber; 3 g sugar; 285 mg phosphorus; 27 mg calcium; 1 mg iron; 78 mg sodium; 716 mg potassium; 12 IU vitamin A; 3 mg ATE vitamin E; 5 mg vitamin C; 65 mg cholesterol

Honey Barbecue Chops

These are super-easy, super-tasty barbecued pork chops. Serve with potato salad and green beans.

8 pork chops

1 cup (160 g) sliced onion

1 cup (235 ml) low-sodium barbecue sauce

¼ cup (85 g) honey

Place one layer of pork chops in slow cooker. Arrange a proportionate amount of sliced onions over top. Mix barbecue sauce and honey together in a small bowl. Spoon a proportionate amount of sauce over the chops. Repeat the layers with remaining chops, onions, and sauce. Cover and cook on low 6 to 8 hours.

Yield: 8 servings

Per serving: 39 g water; 335 cal (40% from fat, 29% from protein, 31% from carb); 24 g protein; 15 g total fat; 5 g saturated fat; 7 g monounsaturated fat; 2 g polyunsaturated fat; 26 g carb; 0 g fiber; 21 g sugar; 6 mg phosphorus; 26 mg calcium; 1 mg iron; 31 mg sodium; 451 mg potassium; 9 IU vitamin A; 0 mg ATE vitamin E; 2 mg vitamin C; 74 mg cholesterol

Hawaiian Pork Roast

Pork loin roast cooks to tender perfection with island flavors.

1½ pounds (680 g) pork loin roast

1 cup (235 ml) pineapple juice

¼ cup (60 ml) sherry

2 tablespoons (28 ml) low-sodium soy sauce
(see recipe in Chapter 2)

1 teaspoon ground ginger

1 tablespoon (13 g) sugar

Place pork in slow cooker. Combine remaining
ingredients and pour over pork. Cover and cook on low
until done, but not dry, 4 to 5 hours.

Yield: 4 servings

TIP

Serve with rice.

Per serving: 195 g water; 292 calories (24% from fat, 54% from protein, 21% from carb); 37 g protein; 7 g total fat; 2 g saturated fat; 3 g monounsaturated fat; 1 g polyunsaturated fat; 14 g carb; 0 g fiber; 11 g sugar; 387 mg phosphorus; 33 mg calcium; 2 mg iron; 114 mg sodium; 745 mg potassium; 16 IU vitamin A; 3 mg ATE vitamin E; 8 mg vitamin C; 107 mg cholesterol

Cranberry Pork Roast

This great-tasting roast can be the centerpiece of any meal, proving again that the slow cooker is not just for everyday family meals.

3 pounds (1⅓ kg) pork loin roast

¼ teaspoon black pepper

1 pound (455 g) whole berry cranberry sauce

¼ cup (85 g) honey

1 teaspoon grated orange peel

⅛ teaspoon cloves

⅛ teaspoon nutmeg

Cut roast in half and place in a slow cooker; sprinkle with pepper. Combine the remaining ingredients; pour over roast. Cover and cook on low for 4 to 5 hours or until a meat thermometer reads 160°F (71°C). Let stand 10 minutes before slicing.

Yield: 9 servings

Per serving: 144 g water; 299 calories (20% from fat, 43% from protein, 37% from carb); 32 g protein; 6 g total fat; 2 g saturated fat; 3 g monounsaturated fat; 1 g polyunsaturated fat; 27 g carb; 1 g fiber; 27 g sugar; 333 mg phosphorus; 23 mg calcium; 1 mg iron; 92 mg sodium; 579 mg potassium; 33 IU vitamin A; 3 mg ATE vitamin E; 3 mg vitamin C; 95 mg cholesterol

Apple Cranberry Pork Roast

This flavor of this roast really says fall, with its apple and cranberry combination. We like this with sweet potatoes. (You can even put them in the cooker to cook with the roast if you like.)

1 tablespoon (15 ml) canola oil

3 pounds (1⅓ kg) pork loin roast

2 cups (475 ml) apple juice

3 cups (330 g) sliced apples

1 cup (100 g) cranberries

¼ teaspoon black pepper

Heat oil in a skillet over medium-high heat. Brown roast on all sides. Place in slow cooker. Add remaining ingredients. Cover and cook on low 6 to 8 hours.

Yield: 8 servings

Per serving: 225 g water; 288 calories (29% from fat, 51% from protein, 20% from carb); 36 g protein; 9 g total fat; 3 g saturated fat; 4 g monounsaturated fat; 1 g polyunsaturated fat; 14 g carb; 1 g fiber; 11 g sugar; 381 mg phosphorus; 29 mg calcium; 2 mg iron; 91 mg sodium; 754 mg potassium; 36 IU vitamin A; 3 mg ATE vitamin E; 5 mg vitamin C; 107 mg cholesterol

Asian Pork Roast

This tender and tasty pork roast is perfect with stir-fried vegetables and rice.

3 pounds (1⅓ kg) pork loin roast

½ cup (120 ml) low-sodium soy sauce (see recipe in Chapter 2)

½ cup (120 ml) sherry

½ teaspoon minced garlic

1 tablespoon (9 g) dry mustard

1 teaspoon ground ginger

1 teaspoon thyme

Place the pork roast in a resealable plastic bag; set in a deep bowl. Thoroughly blend together the soy sauce, sherry, garlic, mustard, ginger, and thyme. Pour marinade over meat in bag; close bag. Place the roast in the refrigerator and marinate for 2 to 3 hours or overnight. Transfer the pork roast and marinade to a slow cooker. Cover and cook on high for 3½ to 4 hours. Lift roast out onto a cutting board; let stand for 10 minutes before slicing.

Yield: 8 servings

Per serving: 147 g water; 253 calories (29% from fat, 65% from protein, 7% from carb); 37 g protein; 7 g total fat; 2 g saturated fat; 3 g monounsaturated fat; 1 g polyunsaturated fat; 4 g carb; 0 g fiber; 1 g sugar; 391 mg phosphorus; 30 mg calcium; 2 mg iron; 138 mg sodium; 680 mg potassium; 18 IU vitamin A; 3 mg ATE vitamin E; 2 mg vitamin C; 107 mg cholesterol

Glazed Pork Roast

A sweet apricot glaze makes this pork roast special.

2 cups (475 ml) low-sodium chicken broth (see recipe in Chapter 2)

1 cup (320 g) apricot preserves

1 cup (160 g) chopped onion

2 tablespoons (22 g) Dijon mustard

4 pounds (1.8 kg) boneless pork loin roast

Mix broth, preserves, onion, and mustard in slow cooker. Cut pork to fit. Add to cooker. Cover and cook on low for 8 to 9 hours or high for 4 to 5 hours until done.

Yield: 12 servings

Per serving: 170 g water; 313 calories (30% from fat, 44% from protein, 26% from carb); 34 g protein; 10 g total fat; 3 g saturated fat; 5 g monounsaturated fat; 1 g polyunsaturated fat; 20 g carb; 1 g fiber; 14 g sugar; 329 mg phosphorus; 19 mg calcium; 1 mg iron; 129 mg sodium; 692 mg potassium; 13 IU vitamin A; 3 mg ATE vitamin E; 4 mg vitamin C; 83 mg cholesterol

Pork and Sweet Potato Dinner

This meal in a pot has just enough sweetener and spice added to give it great flavor without overpowering it.

3 pounds (1⅓ kg) boneless pork loin roast

4 sweet potatoes, peeled

2 medium apples, sliced

¼ cup (60 ml) apple juice or white wine

2 tablespoons (30 g) brown sugar

½ teaspoon apple pie spice

Cube the pork and the sweet potatoes into bite-size pieces. In a skillet, brown the pork cubes. In the bottom of the slow cooker place apple slices, then sweet potatoes, then browned pork cubes. Combine juice, brown sugar, and apple pie spice and pour over the pork. Cook on low for 8 to 12 hours.

Yield: 6 servings

Per serving: 290 g water; 464 calories (30% from fat, 45% from protein, 25% from carb); 51 g protein; 15 g total fat; 5 g saturated fat; 7 g monounsaturated fat; 2 g polyunsaturated fat; 29 g carb; 3 g fiber; 16 g sugar; 508 mg phosphorus; 45 mg calcium; 3 mg iron; 132 mg sodium; 1253 mg potassium; 15877 IU vitamin A; 5 mg ATE vitamin E; 15 mg vitamin C; 125 mg cholesterol

Barbecue Pork Roast

This makes a great-tasting roast that can be the centerpiece of a meal or sliced thinly for sandwiches. Or you can do what we usually do: make a meal of it then slice the rest when it's cold.

3 pounds (1⅓ kg) boneless pork loin roast, cut in half

1 can (8 ounces, or 225 g) no-salt-added tomato sauce

¼ cup (60 ml) low-sodium soy sauce (see recipe in Chapter 2)

½ cup (100 g) sugar

2 teaspoons dry mustard

Place roast in slow cooker. Combine remaining ingredients in a bowl. Pour over roast. Cover and cook on low 6 to 8 hours or on high 3 to 4 hours until meat is tender but not dry.

Yield: 8 servings

Per serving: 153 g water; 323 calories (32% from fat, 48% from protein, 20% from carb); 38 g protein; 11 g total fat; 4 g saturated fat; 5 g monounsaturated fat; 1 g polyunsaturated fat; 15 g carb; 0 g fiber; 14 g sugar; 370 mg phosphorus; 15 mg calcium; 2 mg iron; 105 mg sodium; 838 mg potassium; 111 IU vitamin A; 3 mg ATE vitamin E; 4 mg vitamin C; 94 mg cholesterol

Asian Ribs

Country-style ribs marinate in an Asian sauce and then dry cook in the slow cooker for a marvelous flavor and tenderness.

¼ cup (60 g) brown sugar

1 cup (235 ml) low-sodium soy sauce (see recipe in Chapter 2)

¼ cup (60 ml) sesame oil

2 tablespoons (28 ml) olive oil

2 tablespoons (28 ml) rice vinegar

2 tablespoons (28 ml) lime juice

2 tablespoons (20 g) minced garlic

2 tablespoons (12 g) minced fresh ginger

½ teaspoon hot pepper sauce

3 pounds (1⅓ kg) country-style pork ribs

Stir together the brown sugar, soy sauce, sesame oil, olive oil, rice vinegar, lime juice, garlic, ginger, and hot pepper sauce in the slow cooker. Add the ribs; cover and refrigerate for 8 hours or overnight. Before cooking, drain marinade and discard. Cook on low for 9 hours.

Yield: 9 servings

Per serving: 28 g water; 104 calories (78% from fat, 6% from protein, 16% from carb); 2 g protein; 9 g total fat; 1 g saturated fat; 5 g monounsaturated fat; 3 g polyunsaturated fat; 4 g carb; 0 g fiber; 1 g sugar; 37 mg phosphorus; 10 mg calcium; 1 mg iron; 92 mg sodium; 81 mg potassium; 8 IU vitamin A; 0 mg ATE vitamin E; 2 mg vitamin C; 0 mg cholesterol

Barbecued Ribs

You can spend all day cooking and smoking and grilling ribs. Or you can let the slow cooker work on them all day and have falling-off-the-bone meat.

4 pounds (1.8 kg) pork back ribs

2 cups (480 g) low-sodium ketchup

1 cup (275 g) chili sauce (see recipe in Chapter 2)

½ cup (115 g) packed brown sugar

¼ cup (60 ml) cider vinegar

2 teaspoons oregano

2 teaspoons Worcestershire sauce

1 dash hot pepper sauce

(continued on page 170)

Preheat oven to 400°F (200°C, or gas mark 6). Place ribs in a shallow baking pan. Brown in oven 15 minutes. Turn over and brown another 15 minutes; drain fat. In a medium bowl, mix together the ketchup, chili sauce, brown sugar, vinegar, oregano, Worcestershire sauce, and hot pepper sauce. Place ribs in slow cooker. Pour sauce over ribs and turn to coat. Cover and cook on low 6 to 8 hours or until ribs are tender.

Yield: 8 servings

Per serving: 211 g water; 766 calories (64% from fat, 20% from protein, 17% from carb); 38 g protein; 54 g total fat; 20 g saturated fat; 24 g monounsaturated fat; 5 g polyunsaturated fat; 32 g carb; 0 g fiber; 29 g sugar; 350 mg phosphorus; 106 mg calcium; 3 mg iron; 224 mg sodium; 825 mg potassium; 1103 IU vitamin A; 7 mg ATE vitamin E; 18 mg vitamin C; 184 mg cholesterol

Honey Mustard Ribs

The simple pleasure of eating fall-off-the-bone ribs starts with your favorite barbecue sauce. Spice it up with an herb blend and a jar of honey mustard. To make it really low sodium, use our recipes in Chapter 2.

3½ pounds (1.6 kg) country style pork ribs

1 cup (250 g) barbecue sauce (see recipe in Chapter 2)

½ cup (88 g) honey mustard

2 teaspoons Salt-Free Seasoning Blend (see recipe in Chapter 2)

Place ribs in a slow cooker. In a small bowl, stir together barbecue sauce, honey mustard, and seasoning blend. Pour over ribs in cooker; stir to coat. Cover and cook on low for 8 to 10 hours or on high for 4 to 5 hours. Transfer ribs to a serving platter. Strain sauce into a bowl; skim fat from sauce. Drizzle some of the sauce over the ribs and pass the remaining sauce at the table.

Yield: 8 servings

Per serving: 174 g water; 385 calories (41% from fat, 42% from protein, 17% from carb); 39 g protein; 17 g total fat; 6 g saturated fat; 8 g monounsaturated fat; 2 g polyunsaturated fat; 16 g carb; 0 g fiber; 12 g sugar; 395 mg phosphorus; 54 mg calcium; 2 mg iron; 333 mg sodium; 695 mg potassium; 25 IU vitamin A; 4 mg ATE vitamin E; 2 mg vitamin C; 127 mg cholesterol

Slow Cooker Shredded Pork

Shredded pork requires slow cooking. If you have a smoker, you can use that. If not, the slow cooker does a great job of producing a flavorful roast that can be easily shredded.

4 pounds (1.8 kg) pork shoulder roast

1½ teaspoons minced garlic

1 cup (160 g) finely chopped onion

4 ounces (115 g) diced green chilies

1 cup (235 ml) cider vinegar

Place roast in slow cooker. Combine remaining ingredients and pour over roast. Cover and cook on low 8 to 10 hours. Remove to a cutting board and shred with two forks, discarding fat and bones.

Yield: 8 servings

Per serving: 206 g water; 550 calories (69% from fat, 29% from protein, 2% from carb); 39 g protein; 41 g total fat; 14 g saturated fat; 18 g monounsaturated fat; 4 g polyunsaturated fat; 2 g carb; 0 g fiber; 1 g sugar; 422 mg phosphorus; 42 mg calcium; 2 mg iron; 150 mg sodium; 738 mg potassium; 16 IU vitamin A; 5 mg ATE vitamin E; 3 mg vitamin C; 161 mg cholesterol

North Carolina Pork

This is not quite as spicy as some "native" North Carolina recipes, so feel free to add more hot pepper sauce or some red pepper flakes if you want.

5 pounds (2.3 kg) pork shoulder roast

1 teaspoon black pepper

1½ cups (355 ml) cider vinegar

2 tablespoons (30 g) brown sugar

1½ tablespoons (23 ml) hot pepper sauce

1 teaspoon cayenne

TIP

Serve on plain hamburger buns with coleslaw.

(continued on page 172)

Place the pork shoulder into a slow cooker and season with pepper. Pour the vinegar around the pork. Cover and cook on low for 12 hours. Pork should easily pull apart into strands. Remove the pork from the slow cooker and discard any bones. Strain out the liquid and save 2 cups (475 ml). Discard any extra. Shred the pork using tongs or two forks and return to the slow cooker. Stir the brown sugar, hot pepper sauce, and cayenne into the reserved liquid. Mix into the pork in the slow cooker. Cover and cook on low for 1 hour more.

Yield: 15 servings

Per serving: 121 g water; 370 calories (68% from fat, 29% from protein, 2% from carb); 26 g protein; 27 g total fat; 9 g saturated fat; 12 g monounsaturated fat; 3 g polyunsaturated fat; 2 g carb; 0 g fiber; 2 g sugar; 278 mg phosphorus; 27 mg calcium; 2 mg iron; 109 mg sodium; 486 mg potassium; 83 IU vitamin A; 3 mg ATE vitamin E; 1 mg vitamin C; 107 mg cholesterol

Pork for Sandwiches

You can use this pork for any number of recipes. Add a little barbecue sauce and use it for sandwiches or use it in stir-fries or soups.

3 pounds (1⅓ kg) boneless pork shoulder

1 large sweet onion, chopped

1 tablespoon (10 g) minced garlic

1½ cups (413 g) chili sauce (see recipe in Chapter 2)

2 tablespoons (26 g) sugar

2 tablespoons (28 ml) cider vinegar

1 tablespoon (15 ml) Worcestershire sauce

1 tablespoon (7.5 g) chili powder

½ teaspoon black pepper

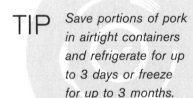

TIP *Save portions of pork in airtight containers and refrigerate for up to 3 days or freeze for up to 3 months.*

Trim fat from pork. If necessary, cut pork to fit slow cooker. Place pork, onion, and garlic in slow cooker. In a medium bowl, combine chili sauce, brown sugar, cider vinegar, Worcestershire sauce, chili powder, and pepper. Pour over pork in cooker. Cover and cook on low for 10 to 11 hours or on high for 5 to 6 hours. Remove park from cooker, reserving juices. Using two forks, shred pork, discarding any fat. Skim fat from juices. Add enough juices to the pork to moisten.

Yield: 12 servings

Per serving: 123 g water; 189 calories (35% from fat, 50% from protein, 14% from carb); 23 g protein; 7 g total fat; 2 g saturated fat; 3 g monounsaturated fat; 1 g polyunsaturated fat; 7 g carb; 1 g fiber; 4 g sugar; 256 mg phosphorus; 19 mg calcium; 2 mg iron; 134 mg sodium; 434 mg potassium; 649 IU vitamin A; 2 mg ATE vitamin E; 10 mg vitamin C; 74 mg cholesterol

Pizza Casserole

I suppose you could also call this a variation of lasagna, but either way, if you like Italian food you'll love this both for the flavor and the ease of preparation.

1 pound (455 g) sausage (see recipe in Chapter 2)

1 cup (160 g) chopped onion

1 pound (455 g) uncooked pasta

28 ounces (785 g) low-sodium spaghetti sauce

2 cups (490 g) no-salt-added tomato sauce

¾ cup (175 ml) water

4 ounces (115 g) mushrooms, sliced

4 ounces (115 g) pepperoni

2 cups (230 g) shredded mozzarella

Brown sausage and onion in skillet. Drain. Place half of mixture in slow cooker. Spread half the pasta over the sausage mixture. Combine sauces, water, and mushrooms. Ladle half over pasta. Repeat layers. Top with pepperoni, then cheese. Cover and cook on low 6 to 8 hours.

Yield: 6 servings

Per serving: 289 g water; 815 calories (42% from fat, 15% from protein, 43% from carb); 30 g protein; 38 g total fat; 12 g saturated fat; 19 g monounsaturated fat; 4 g polyunsaturated fat; 88 g carb; 8 g fiber; 23 g sugar; 391 mg phosphorus; 87 mg calcium; 4 mg iron; 1025 mg sodium; 1296 mg potassium; 1075 IU vitamin A; 0 mg ATE vitamin E; 27 mg vitamin C; 81 mg cholesterol

Sausage Stew

A nice, hearty stew of smoked sausage and beans, this will both fill and warm you. I like it with a slice of freshly baked dark bread.

2 tablespoons (28 ml) olive oil

1 cup (160 g) chopped onion

1 pound (455 g) turkey kielbasa, thinly sliced

2 cans (15 ounces, or 425 g) no-salt-added great northern beans, undrained

2 cups (490 g) no-salt-added tomato sauce

4 ounces (115 g) diced green chilies

1 cup (130 g) thinly sliced carrots

½ cup (75 g) chopped green bell pepper

¼ teaspoon Italian seasoning

½ teaspoon thyme

¼ teaspoon black pepper

Heat in oil in a large skillet over medium-high heat. Sauté onions and kielbasa until onions are soft. Transfer onions and kielbasa to slow cooker. Add all remaining ingredients to cooker and stir together well. Cover and cook on low 8 to 10 hours or until vegetables are tender.

Yield: 8 servings

Per serving: 214 g water; 320 calories (39% from fat, 20% from protein, 41% from carb); 17 g protein; 14 g total fat; 4 g saturated fat; 7 g monounsaturated fat; 2 g polyunsaturated fat; 33 g carb; 7 g fiber; 4 g sugar; 178 mg phosphorus; 82 mg calcium; 3 mg iron; 464 mg sodium; 698 mg potassium; 2944 IU vitamin A; 0 mg ATE vitamin E; 32 mg vitamin C; 40 mg cholesterol

Green Beans with Smoked Sausage

These Southern-style green beans, cooked until *very* done, are flavored with smoked meat. They go great with boiled potatoes.

1 pound (455 g) turkey smoked sausage, sliced ½–inch (1.3 cm) thick

1 pound (455 g) frozen green beans

½ cup (80 g) chopped onion

¼ cup (60 g) brown sugar

Place sausage in slow cooker. Top with beans and then onion. Sprinkle with sugar. Cover and cook on low 4 to 5 hours.

Yield: 5 servings

Per serving: 153 g water; 281 calories (50% from fat, 19% from protein, 31% from carb); 14 g protein; 16 g total fat; 6 g saturated fat; 8 g monounsaturated fat; 2 g polyunsaturated fat; 22 g carb; 3 g fiber; 13 g sugar; 42 mg phosphorus; 47 mg calcium; 2 mg iron; 626 mg sodium; 251 mg potassium; 626 IU vitamin A; 0 mg ATE vitamin E; 29 mg vitamin C; 64 mg cholesterol

Barbecued Ham

This recipe is higher in sodium than I usually recommend. It is the sort of thing that you ought to serve in small quantities along with other dishes, as reflected by the portion size of just 2 ounces (55 g).

2 cups (360 g) sliced onions

6 whole cloves

3 pounds (1⅓ kg) reduced-sodium boneless ham

2 cups (475 ml) water

2 cups (500 g) barbecue sauce

(continued on page 176)

Place half of the onions in bottom of slow cooker. Stick cloves in ham and place it on top of onions in slow cooker. Put the rest of the onions on top. Add water. Cook on low 10 to 12 hours. Shred or cut up meat and onion. Put back into slow cooker. Add barbecue sauce. Cook 4 to 6 hours more.

Yield: 24 servings

Per serving: 83 g water; 101 calories (15% from fat, 41% from protein, 43% from carb); 10 g protein; 2 g total fat; 1 g saturated fat; 1 g monounsaturated fat; 0 g polyunsaturated fat; 11 g carb; 0 g fiber; 7 g sugar; 127 mg phosphorus; 9 mg calcium; 0 mg iron; 587 mg sodium; 218 mg potassium; 0 IU vitamin A; 0 mg ATE vitamin E; 1 mg vitamin C; 27 mg cholesterol

Red Beans

These are not quite traditional New Orleans red beans, but very good nonetheless.

1 pound (455 g) dried kidney beans

½ teaspoon chopped garlic

1 cup (160 g) finely chopped onion

½ cup (50 g) chopped celery

1 pound (455 g) smoked sausage, browned and cut in
    thin slices

3 bay leaves

6 cups (1.4 L) water

TIP

Serve over rice.

Wash beans and cover with water, boil until done (about 1 hour) and then drain. In a skillet, sauté garlic, onion, and celery. Add to beans after beans are cooked. Add browned sausage and bay leaves. Put all ingredients in slow cooker with 6 cups (1.4 L) water; cover and cook on low for 2 to 2½ hours. Remove bay leaves before serving.

Yield: 6 servings

Per serving: 366 g water; 276 calories (43% from fat, 25% from protein, 32% from carb); 17 g protein; 13 g total fat; 5 g saturated fat; 6 g monounsaturated fat; 2 g polyunsaturated fat; 22 g carb; 8 g fiber; 1 g sugar; 117 mg phosphorus; 50 mg calcium; 3 mg iron; 532 mg sodium; 350 mg potassium; 41 IU vitamin A; 0 mg ATE vitamin E; 14 mg vitamin C; 53 mg cholesterol

Ham and Scalloped Potatoes

This makes a big pot of potatoes and ham, but I'm willing to bet that you won't have any trouble getting rid of it.

8 medium potatoes, peeled and thinly sliced

½ teaspoon cream of tartar

1 cup (235 ml) water

1 pound (455 g) ham, sliced

2 cups (320 g) thinly sliced onions

1 cup (120 g) grated Cheddar cheese

10 ounces (280 g) low-sodium cream of mushroom soup (see recipe in Chapter 2)

Paprika

Toss sliced potatoes in cream of tartar and water. Drain. Put half of ham, potatoes, and onions in slow cooker. Sprinkle with grated cheese. Repeat with remaining half of ham, potatoes, and onions. Spoon undiluted soup over top. Sprinkle with paprika. Cover and cook on low 8 to 10 hours or on high 4 hours.

Yield: 8 servings

Per serving: 378 g water; 435 calories (22% from fat, 21% from protein, 57% from carb); 23 g protein; 11 g total fat; 5 g saturated fat; 4 g monounsaturated fat; 1 g polyunsaturated fat; 63 g carb; 7 g fiber; 5 g sugar; 446 mg phosphorus; 169 mg calcium; 3 mg iron; 732 mg sodium; 1953 mg potassium; 192 IU vitamin A; 43 mg ATE vitamin E; 35 mg vitamin C; 41 mg cholesterol

Lamb Stew

This is a creamy stew made with lamb, similar to a stroganoff.

2 pounds (900 g) lean lamb

2 tablespoons (28 ml) olive oil

1 onion, cut in wedges

(continued on page 178)

½ teaspoon minced garlic

10 ounces (280 g) low-sodium cream of mushroom soup (see recipe in Chapter 2)

½ cup (120 ml) water

½ teaspoon thyme

8 ounces (225 g) fat-free sour cream

2 tablespoons (16 g) flour

Cut lamb in 1-inch (2.5 cm) cubes. Heat oil in a large skillet over medium-high heat and brown meat. Transfer to a slow cooker. Add onion and garlic to skillet; cook until onion is tender but not brown. Stir in soup, water, and thyme, scraping browned bits from bottom of skillet. Pour over lamb in slow cooker. Cover and cook on low for 8 to 10 hours. Turn cooker to high. Thoroughly blend sour cream and flour. Slowly stir 1 cup (235 ml) hot liquid from the slow cooker into the sour cream mixture; return mixture to hot stew. Cover and cook until thickened, 15 minutes.

Yield: 6 servings

Per serving: 211 g water; 417 calories (46% from fat, 44% from protein, 10% from carb); 45 g protein; 21 g total fat; 8 g saturated fat; 9 g monounsaturated fat; 2 g polyunsaturated fat; 10 g carb; 1 g fiber; 2 g sugar; 410 mg phosphorus; 74 mg calcium; 4 mg iron; 313 mg sodium; 776 mg potassium; 148 IU vitamin A; 39 mg ATE vitamin E; 2 mg vitamin C; 152 mg cholesterol

Lamb Paprikash

Here's a wonderful lamb stew with great gravy.

2 pounds (900 g) lamb, cut in 1-inch (2.5 cm) pieces

1 can (14 ounces, or 400 g) no-salt-added diced tomatoes

1 cup (160 g) chopped onion

½ teaspoon minced garlic

1 teaspoon paprika

½ cup (120 ml) cold water

¼ cup (31 g) flour

½ cup (115 g) fat-free sour cream

TIP

Serve over noodles and garnish with parsley.

In slow cooker, combine lamb, undrained tomatoes, onion, garlic, and paprika. Cover and cook on low for 8 to 10 hours. Turn cooker to high; spoon off any excess fat. Blend cold water slowly into flour; stir into the meat mixture. Cover and cook until thickened and bubbly, 20 to 30 minutes. Blend about ½ cup (120 ml) of the hot liquid from the slow cooker into the sour cream; stir sour cream mixture into cooker. Heat through.

Yield: 6 servings

Per serving: 219 g water; 351 calories (36% from fat, 52% from protein, 12% from carb); 44 g protein; 14 g total fat; 6 g saturated fat; 5 g monounsaturated fat; 1 g polyunsaturated fat; 10 g carb; 1 g fiber; 3 g sugar; 385 mg phosphorus; 70 mg calcium; 5 mg iron; 134 mg sodium; 712 mg potassium; 355 IU vitamin A; 20 mg ATE vitamin E; 9 mg vitamin C; 144 mg cholesterol

Lamb Cassoulet

A different variation on the cassoulet theme, this time with lamb in place of the sausage or chicken.

2 cups (364 g) great northern beans, cooked or canned without salt

1 cup (235 ml) dry white wine

1 cup (245 g) no-salt-added tomato sauce

2 bay leaves

½ teaspoon minced garlic

1 tablespoon (4 g) fresh parsley

½ teaspoon thyme, crushed

2 tablespoons (28 ml) olive oil

8 ounces (225 g) lean lamb, cut in ½-inch (1.3 cm) pieces

¾ cup (120 g) chopped onion

¼ cup (60 ml) cold water

2 tablespoons (16 g) flour

In a slow cooker combine beans, wine, tomato sauce, bay leaves, garlic, parsley, and thyme. Heat oil in a saucepan over medium-high heat and cook lamb and onion until lamb is well browned on

(continued on page 180)

all sides; drain. Stir lamb and onion into bean mixture in slow cooker. Cover and cook on low for 5 to 6 hours. Turn to high. Heat until bubbly (do not lift cover). Slowly blend the cold water into flour; stir into meat-bean mixture. Cover and cook until slightly thickened. Before serving, remove bay leaves and discard.

Yield: 6 servings

Per serving: 181 g water; 274 calories (28% from fat, 29% from protein, 42% from carb); 18 g protein; 8 g total fat; 2 g saturated fat; 4 g monounsaturated fat; 1 g polyunsaturated fat; 26 g carb; 5 g fiber; 3 g sugar; 232 mg phosphorus; 68 mg calcium; 3 mg iron; 40 mg sodium; 638 mg potassium; 187 IU vitamin A; 0 mg ATE vitamin E; 9 mg vitamin C; 34 mg cholesterol

9

Family-Pleasing and Healthful Ground Meat Dishes

As I was collecting recipes for this book, ground meats demanded a chapter of their own. So here it is. Whether it's beef, turkey, or pork, you can't go wrong. There are casseroles and stews, meat loaves, and all kinds of sandwiches and dishes with international flavors like Mexican or Italian. There is also a whole section of meatball recipes. I've provided two basic recipes for beef and turkey meatballs and then a variety of dishes where you can use either.

Italian Rice Casserole

Here's the flavor of pizza in a one-dish meal made in your slow cooker. That offers a lot for everyone to like.

1 pound (455 g) ground beef

1 cup (160 g) chopped onion

3 cups (555 g) uncooked long-grain rice

3 cups (735 g) no-salt-added tomato sauce

1 teaspoon Italian seasoning

½ teaspoon minced garlic

6 ounces (170 g) mozzarella, shredded

1 cup (225 g) low-fat cottage cheese

4 cups (950 ml) water

Place ground beef and chopped onion in a nonstick skillet. Brown over medium-high heat and then drain. Combine beef mixture and remaining ingredients in slow cooker. Cover and cook on high for 6 hours or until the rice is tender.

Yield: 8 servings

Per serving: 295 g water; 508 calories (26% from fat, 21% from protein, 53% from carb); 26 g protein; 14 g total fat; 7 g saturated fat; 5 g monounsaturated fat; 1 g polyunsaturated fat; 66 g carb; 3 g fiber; 5 g sugar; 336 mg phosphorus; 232 mg calcium; 5 mg iron; 302 mg sodium; 658 mg potassium; 451 IU vitamin A; 32 mg ATE vitamin E; 14 mg vitamin C; 55 mg cholesterol

Stuffed Peppers

This is a traditional stuffed pepper, with beef, rice, and tomato sauce. Preparation is simplified by using the slow cooker.

6 green bell peppers

1 pound (455 g) extra-lean ground beef

½ cup (80 g) chopped onions

¼ teaspoon black pepper

1½ cups (250 g) cooked rice

2 tablespoons (28 ml) Worcestershire sauce

1 cup (245 g) no-salt-added tomato sauce

Cut tops from peppers. Carefully remove seeds and membrane. Brown ground beef and onions in skillet over medium-high heat. Drain. Place meat and onions in mixing bowl. Add pepper, rice, and Worcestershire sauce to meat and combine well. Stuff green peppers with mixture. Stand stuffed peppers upright in slow cooker. Pour tomato sauce over peppers. Cover and cook on low 5 to 7 hours.

Yield: 6 servings

Per serving: 262 g water; 282 calories (43% from fat, 24% from protein, 33% from carb); 17 g protein; 13 g total fat; 5 g saturated fat; 6 g monounsaturated fat; 1 g polyunsaturated fat; 23 g carb; 4 g fiber; 6 g sugar; 175 mg phosphorus; 33 mg calcium; 3 mg iron; 108 mg sodium; 690 mg potassium; 688 IU vitamin A; 0 mg ATE vitamin E; 135 mg vitamin C; 52 mg cholesterol

TIP

Top with a little shredded cheese for even more flavor.

Stuffed Peppers with Beef and Corn

Stuffed peppers are incredibly easy to make in the slow cooker, and they are a family favorite.

6 green bell peppers

1 pound (455 g) extra-lean ground beef, browned

½ cup (80 g) chopped onion

¼ teaspoon black pepper

12 ounces (340 g) frozen corn

1 tablespoon (15 ml) Worcestershire sauce

1 teaspoon mustard

1 can (10 ounces, or 280 g) reduced-sodium condensed tomato soup

(continued on page 184)

Cut off the top of each pepper. Remove core, seeds, and white membrane from each. In a small bowl, combine beef, onions, pepper, and corn. Divide evenly among peppers. Stand peppers up in slow cooker. Combine Worcestershire sauce, mustard, and tomato soup. Pour over peppers. Cover and cook on low 5 to 6 hours.

Yield: 6 servings

Per serving: 286 g water; 280 calories (44% from fat, 25% from protein, 31% from carb); 18 g protein; 14 g total fat; 5 g saturated fat; 6 g monounsaturated fat; 1 g polyunsaturated fat; 23 g carb; 4 g fiber; 7 g sugar; 200 mg phosphorus; 28 mg calcium; 3 mg iron; 97 mg sodium; 722 mg potassium; 797 IU vitamin A; 3 mg ATE vitamin E; 142 mg vitamin C; 52 mg cholesterol

Beef and Cabbage Casserole

This is sort of like stuffed cabbage but a lot easier to fix.

1 tablespoon (15 ml) olive oil

1 cup (160 g) chopped onion

1 pound (455 g) extra-lean ground beef

¼ teaspoon pepper

3 cups (210 g) shredded cabbage

1 can (10 ounces, or 280 g) reduced-sodium condensed tomato soup

TIP

Serve with garlic bread.

Heat oil in a skillet over medium-high heat. Sauté onion and then add ground beef and brown. Season with pepper. Layer half of cabbage in slow cooker, followed by half of meat mixture. Repeat layers. Pour soup over top. Cover and cook on low 3 to 4 hours.

Yield: 4 servings

Per serving: 233 g water; 353 calories (60% from fat, 26% from protein, 14% from carb); 23 g protein; 23 g total fat; 8 g saturated fat; 11 g monounsaturated fat; 1 g polyunsaturated fat; 12 g carb; 2 g fiber; 6 g sugar; 199 mg phosphorus; 47 mg calcium; 3 mg iron; 103 mg sodium; 571 mg potassium; 259 IU vitamin A; 4 mg ATE vitamin E; 47 mg vitamin C; 78 mg cholesterol

Beef and Zucchini

This creamy beef and zucchini dish is a great way to use up some of that extra zucchini that the garden always seems to produce.

1 pound (455 g) extra-lean ground beef

½ cup (80 g) chopped onion

¼ teaspoon black pepper

4 cups (480 g) zucchini, sliced

10 ounces (280 g) low-sodium cream of mushroom soup (see recipe in Chapter 2)

1 cup (110 g) shredded Swiss cheese

In a skillet over medium-high heat, brown ground beef with onions and pepper until no longer pink. Drain. Layer zucchini and beef mixture alternately in slow cooker. Top with soup. Sprinkle with cheese. Cover and cook on low 2 to 3 hours or until the zucchini is done.

Yield: 4 servings

Per serving: 281 g water; 454 calories (59% from fat, 29% from protein, 11% from carb); 33 g protein; 30 g total fat; 14 g saturated fat; 11 g monounsaturated fat; 2 g polyunsaturated fat; 13 g carb; 2 g fiber; 5 g sugar; 449 mg phosphorus; 358 mg calcium; 3 mg iron; 364 mg sodium; 980 mg potassium; 524 IU vitamin A; 71 mg ATE vitamin E; 23 mg vitamin C; 111 mg cholesterol

Chili Verde

This is a little different version of chili verde, with potatoes taking the place of the more common beans.

2 tablespoons (28 ml) olive oil

1 cup (160 g) diced onion

1 teaspoon minced garlic

1 pound (455 g) extra-lean ground beef

½ pound (225 g) ground pork

3 cups (700 ml) low-sodium chicken broth

2 cups (475 ml) water

8 ounces (225 g) diced green chilies

4 large potatoes, diced

10 ounces (280 g) frozen corn

1 teaspoon black pepper

½ teaspoon oregano

1 teaspoon cumin

Heat oil in a skillet over medium-high heat and then brown onion, garlic, beef, and pork. Cook until meat is no longer pink. Combine meat mixture and remaining ingredients in slow cooker. Cover and cook on low 4 to 6 hours or until potatoes are soft.

Yield: 8 servings

Per serving: 422 g water; 414 calories (42% from fat, 20% from protein, 38% from carb); 21 g protein; 20 g total fat; 7 g saturated fat; 9 g monounsaturated fat; 2 g polyunsaturated fat; 40 g carb; 5 g fiber; 4 g sugar; 283 mg phosphorus; 53 mg calcium; 4 mg iron; 234 mg sodium; 1233 mg potassium; 60 IU vitamin A; 1 mg ATE vitamin E; 29 mg vitamin C; 60 mg cholesterol

Cowboy Meal

Here's an uptown version of beef and beans. Use either no-salt-added canned beans or pre-cooked dried beans.

1 pound (455 g) extra-lean ground beef, browned

15 ounces (425 g) frozen corn

2 cups (512 g) no-salt-added kidney beans

1 can (10 ounces, or 280 g) reduced-sodium condensed tomato soup

1 cup (115 g) shredded Cheddar cheese

¼ cup (60 ml) milk

1 teaspoon onion flakes

½ teaspoon chili powder

Combine all ingredients in slow cooker. Cover and cook on low for 1 hour.

Yield: 5 servings

Per serving: 241 g water; 506 calories (45% from fat, 26% from protein, 29% from carb); 34 g protein; 26 g total fat; 12 g saturated fat; 10 g monounsaturated fat; 2 g polyunsaturated fat; 37 g carb; 9 g fiber; 5 g sugar; 458 mg phosphorus; 265 mg calcium; 5 mg iron; 258 mg sodium; 900 mg potassium; 692 IU vitamin A; 79 mg ATE vitamin E; 22 mg vitamin C; 91 mg cholesterol

Hamburger Stew

My mother used to make a traditional hamburger soup just like this, and I bet a lot of other mothers did too.

2 pounds (900 g) extra-lean ground beef

1 cup (160 g) chopped onion

½ teaspoon minced garlic

2 cups (475 ml) low-sodium tomato juice

(continued on page 188)

1 cup (130 g) sliced carrots

½ cup (50 g) sliced celery

½ cup (75 g) chopped green bell pepper

2 cups (248 g) frozen green beans

2 medium potatoes, cubed

2 cups (475 ml) water

1 tablespoon (15 ml) Worcestershire sauce

¼ teaspoon oregano

½ teaspoon basil

¼ teaspoon thyme

1 tablespoon (7 g) low-sodium onion soup mix (see recipe in Chapter 2)

¼ teaspoon pepper

Brown meat and onion in saucepan over medium-high heat. Drain. Stir in garlic and tomato juice. Heat to boiling. Combine meat mixture and remaining ingredients in slow cooker. Cover and cook on low 8 to 10 hours.

Yield: 8 servings

Per serving: 335 g water; 368 calories (48% from fat, 26% from protein, 26% from carb); 24 g protein; 20 g total fat; 8 g saturated fat; 8 g monounsaturated fat; 1 g polyunsaturated fat; 24 g carb; 4 g fiber; 5 g sugar; 255 mg phosphorus; 51 mg calcium; 4 mg iron; 126 mg sodium; 1070 mg potassium; 3235 IU vitamin A; 0 mg ATE vitamin E; 37 mg vitamin C; 78 mg cholesterol

Creamy Ground Beef and Vegetables

This hearty casserole is perfect for a winter meal with some freshly baked bread.

1 pound (455 g) ground beef

1 cup (160 g) sliced onions

1 cup (130 g) thinly sliced carrots

⅛ teaspoon pepper

10 ounces (280 g) low-sodium cream of mushroom soup (see recipe in Chapter 2)

¼ cup (60 ml) milk

4 potatoes, thinly sliced

Spray slow cooker with nonstick cooking spray. Layer ground beef, onions, carrots, and pepper in prepared slow cooker. Combine soup and milk. Toss with potatoes. Arrange potato mixture in slow cooker. Cover and cook on low 7 to 9 hours.

Yield: 8 servings

Per serving: 255 g water; 297 calories (32% from fat, 20% from protein, 48% from carb); 15 g protein; 11 g total fat; 4 g saturated fat; 4 g monounsaturated fat; 1 g polyunsaturated fat; 36 g carb; 4 g fiber; 5 g sugar; 230 mg phosphorus; 46 mg calcium; 3 mg iron; 199 mg sodium; 1225 mg potassium; 2723 IU vitamin A; 5 mg ATE vitamin E; 18 mg vitamin C; 40 mg cholesterol

Hamburger Casserole

This is a simple casserole of hamburger and potatoes, but one that has been popular with our family for a long time.

3 potatoes, sliced

1 cup (130 g) sliced carrots

1 cup (160 g) sliced onion

½ teaspoon pepper

1 pound (455 g) ground beef, browned and drained

2 cups (475 ml) low-sodium tomato juice

TIP *Add a 1 pound (455 g) bag of frozen green beans and make it a whole meal.*

Combine all ingredients in slow cooker. Cover and cook on low 6 to 8 hours.

Yield: 4 servings

Per serving: 474 g water; 509 calories (35% from fat, 22% from protein, 43% from carb); 28 g protein; 20 g total fat; 8 g saturated fat; 8 g monounsaturated fat; 1 g polyunsaturated fat; 56 g carb; 7 g fiber; 10 g sugar; 373 mg phosphorus; 68 mg calcium; 5 mg iron; 127 mg sodium; 2021 mg potassium; 5959 IU vitamin A; 0 mg ATE vitamin E; 51 mg vitamin C; 78 mg cholesterol

Stuffed Peppers with Turkey

Here's a healthy version of stuffed peppers using ground turkey instead of the more common beef. The slow cooker makes this an easy meal to assemble ahead of time and then cook while you are gone for the day.

5 green bell peppers, washed and cored

1 pound (455 g) ground turkey

¼ cup (65 g) barbecue sauce

1 cup (165 g) cooked rice

¼ cup (60 ml) egg substitute

½ teaspoon Italian seasoning

1 cup (245 g) no-salt-added tomato sauce

Place peppers into slow cooker. Mix ground turkey, barbecue sauce, rice, egg substitute, and Italian seasoning together. Spoon mixture carefully into peppers, taking care not to tear the peppers. Pour tomato sauce into slow cooker on and around peppers. Cook on low for 6 to 8 hours.

Yield: 5 servings

Per serving: 282 g water; 279 calories (18% from fat, 45% from protein, 37% from carb); 31 g protein; 5 g total fat; 2 g saturated fat; 1 g monounsaturated fat; 2 g polyunsaturated fat; 26 g carb; 3 g fiber; 10 g sugar; 268 mg phosphorus; 56 mg calcium; 3 mg iron; 217 mg sodium; 766 mg potassium; 773 IU vitamin A; 0 mg ATE vitamin E; 126 mg vitamin C; 69 mg cholesterol

Basic Turkey Meatballs

These can be used in place of the beef meatballs in any of the meatball recipes here for a different flavor and lower fat and calories.

2 pounds (900 g) ground turkey

½ cup (120 ml) egg substitute

¾ cup (90 g) bread crumbs

½ cup (80 g) finely chopped onion

1 teaspoon parsley

¼ teaspoon black pepper

¼ teaspoon garlic powder

Combine all ingredients. Shape into walnut-sized balls. Place on waxed paper-lined cookie sheets. Freeze. When fully frozen, place in a resealable plastic bag and store in freezer until needed. When ready to use, place frozen meatballs in slow cooker. Cover and cook on high as you mix up the sauce or whatever accompaniment you are using.

Yield: 8 servings

Per serving: 96 g water; 250 calories (25% from fat, 61% from protein, 14% from carb); 37 g protein; 7 g total fat; 2 g saturated fat; 1 g monounsaturated fat; 2 g polyunsaturated fat; 8 g carb; 1 g fiber; 1 g sugar; 281 mg phosphorus; 58 mg calcium; 3 mg iron; 108 mg sodium; 427 mg potassium; 70 IU vitamin A; 0 mg ATE vitamin E; 1 mg vitamin C; 86 mg cholesterol

Basic Meatballs

These meatballs can be used for a number of different recipes. I give you some slow cooker ones here, but you could also use them in any recipe that calls for frozen or fresh meatballs.

3 pounds (1⅓ kg) extra-lean ground beef

5 ounces (150 ml) fat-free evaporated milk

1 cup (80 g) rolled or quick cooking oats

1 cup (100 g) cracker crumbs

½ cup (120 ml) egg substitute

½ cup (80 g) chopped onion

½ teaspoon garlic powder

½ teaspoon black pepper

(continued on page 192)

Combine all ingredients. Shape into walnut-sized balls. Place on waxed paper-lined cookie sheets. Freeze. When fully frozen, place in a resealable plastic bag and store in freezer until needed. When ready to use, place frozen meatballs in slow cooker. Cover and cook on high as you mix up the sauce or whatever accompaniment you are using.

Yield: 12 servings

Per serving: 96 g water; 322 calories (58% from fat, 31% from protein, 11% from carb); 25 g protein; 20 g total fat; 8 g saturated fat; 9 g monounsaturated fat; 1 g polyunsaturated fat; 9 g carb; 1 g fiber; 2 g sugar; 213 mg phosphorus; 66 mg calcium; 3 mg iron; 107 mg sodium; 426 mg potassium; 85 IU vitamin A; 14 mg ATE vitamin E; 1 mg vitamin C; 79 mg cholesterol

Cranberry Salsa Meatballs

This unusual combination of tastes has proven to be very popular.

2 cups (520 g) low-sodium salsa (see recipe in Chapter 2)

1 pound (455 g) jellied cranberry sauce

2 pounds (900 g) meatballs, basic or turkey (see recipes on pages 190 and 191)

Melt cranberry sauce in saucepan. Stir in salsa and meatballs. Bring to boil. Stir. Pour into slow cooker. Cover and cook on low 6 to 8 hours.

Yield: 6 servings

Per serving: 205 g water; 459 calories (40% from fat, 23% from protein, 37% from carb); 27 g protein; 20 g total fat; 8 g saturated fat; 9 g monounsaturated fat; 1 g polyunsaturated fat; 43 g carb; 3 g fiber; 33 g sugar; 243 mg phosphorus; 84 mg calcium; 4 mg iron; 305 mg sodium; 674 mg potassium; 338 IU vitamin A; 14 mg ATE vitamin E; 3 mg vitamin C; 80 mg cholesterol

Swedish Meatballs

This easy slow cooker version of Swedish meatballs is great for appetizers or for a potluck or buffet supper.

1 pound (455 g) meatballs, basic or turkey (see recipes on pages 190 and 191)

1 cup (160 g) chopped onion

½ teaspoon minced garlic

10 ounces (280 g) low-sodium cream of mushroom soup (see recipe in Chapter 2)

½ cup (120 ml) water

1 cup (230 g) fat-free sour cream

2 tablespoons (16 g) flour

¼ teaspoon pepper

TIP

As a main dish, serve over hot rice or mashed potatoes.

Place all ingredients except sour cream, flour, and pepper in slow cooker. Cover and cook on low for 6 to 8 hours. At the end of cooking time, combine sour cream, flour, and pepper in a small bowl and blend well. Add a spoonful of the hot liquid from the cooker and blend with a whisk. Add sour cream mixture to cooker, stir well, cover, and cook on low 30 to 40 minutes until thickened and blended.

Yield: 4 servings

Per serving: 244 g water; 393 calories (55% from fat, 23% from protein, 23% from carb); 22 g protein; 24 g total fat; 11 g saturated fat; 9 g monounsaturated fat; 1 g polyunsaturated fat; 22 g carb; 2 g fiber; 5 g sugar; 271 mg phosphorus; 129 mg calcium; 3 mg iron; 380 mg sodium; 730 mg potassium; 302 IU vitamin A; 73 mg ATE vitamin E; 4 mg vitamin C; 85 mg cholesterol

Cranberry Orange Meatballs

This recipe is particularly good with the turkey meatballs, but don't be afraid to try it with the beef ones too.

2 tablespoons (28 ml) olive oil

1 cup (160 g) finely chopped onion

1 pound (455 g) jellied cranberry sauce

1 pound (455 g) meatballs, basic or turkey (see recipes on pages 190 and 191)

1 teaspoon orange peel

In small saucepan, heat oil over medium-high heat and sauté onion. Stir cranberry sauce into saucepan. Heat on low until melted. Combine cranberry mixture and remaining ingredients in slow cooker. Cover and cook on low 2 to 4 hours.

Yield: 4 servings

Per serving: 173 g water; 491 calories (40% from fat, 16% from protein, 44% from carb); 20 g protein; 22 g total fat; 7 g saturated fat; 12 g monounsaturated fat; 2 g polyunsaturated fat; 55 g carb; 3 g fiber; 46 g sugar; 180 mg phosphorus; 60 mg calcium; 3 mg iron; 116 mg sodium; 411 mg potassium; 115 IU vitamin A; 11 mg ATE vitamin E; 6 mg vitamin C; 60 mg cholesterol

Meatball Stew

This stew is a complete meal in a bowl. Using previously frozen meatballs makes preparation a snap.

2 pounds (900 g) meatballs, basic or turkey (see recipes on pages 190 and 191)

6 medium potatoes, cubed

1 cup (160 g) sliced onion

1½ cups (195 g) sliced carrots

1 cup (240 g) low-sodium ketchup

1 cup (235 ml) water

2 tablespoons (28 ml) vinegar

1 teaspoon basil

1 teaspoon oregano

¼ teaspoon pepper

Brown meatballs in skillet over medium heat. Drain. Place potatoes, onion, and carrots in slow cooker. Top with meatballs. Combine ketchup, water, vinegar, basil, oregano, and pepper. Pour over meatballs. Cover and cook on high 4 to 5 hours or until vegetables are tender.

Yield: 8 servings

Per serving: 381 g water; 485 calories (29% from fat, 20% from protein, 51% from carb); 25 g protein; 16 g total fat; 6 g saturated fat; 7 g monounsaturated fat; 1 g polyunsaturated fat; 63 g carb; 7 g fiber; 13 g sugar; 355 mg phosphorus; 96 mg calcium; 5 mg iron; 122 mg sodium; 1807 mg potassium; 4418 IU vitamin A; 11 mg ATE vitamin E; 31 mg vitamin C; 60 mg cholesterol

Sour Cream Meatballs

This has sort of a stroganoff kind of flavor. You could add mushrooms, if you like, to make it even more so.

2 pounds (900 g) meatballs, basic or turkey (see recipes
on pages 190 and 191)

¼ cup (31 g) flour

¼ teaspoon garlic powder

¼ teaspoon pepper

1 teaspoon paprika

2 cups (475 ml) boiling water

¾ cup (180 g) fat-free sour cream

TIP

Serve over rice or noodles.

Brown meatballs in skillet. Reserve drippings and place meatballs in slow cooker. Cover and cook on high 10 to 15 minutes. Stir flour, garlic powder, pepper, and paprika into hot drippings in skillet. Stir in water and sour cream. Pour sour cream mixture over meatballs in slow cooker. Cover, reduce heat to low, and cook 4 to 5 hours.

(continued on page 196)

Yield: 6 servings

Per serving: 195 g water; 386 calories (57% from fat, 28% from protein, 15% from carb); 27 g protein; 24 g total fat; 10 g saturated fat; 10 g monounsaturated fat; 1 g polyunsaturated fat; 15 g carb; 1 g fiber; 2 g sugar; 251 mg phosphorus; 96 mg calcium; 3 mg iron; 123 mg sodium; 485 mg potassium; 404 IU vitamin A; 44 mg ATE vitamin E; 1 mg vitamin C; 91 mg cholesterol

Asian Meatballs

I used to work near a little grocery store that had great Chinese meatballs. These aren't as good, but I do make them pretty often.

2 pounds (900 g) meatballs, basic or turkey
   (see recipes on pages 190 and 191)

¼ cup (30 g) cornstarch

2 cups (475 ml) pineapple juice

2 tablespoons (28 ml) reduced-sodium soy sauce
   (see recipe in Chapter 2)

½ cup (120 ml) red wine vinegar

¾ cup (175 ml) water

½ cup (100 g) sugar

1 cup (150 g) green bell pepper strips

6 ounces (170 g) water chestnuts, drained

TIP *Serve over rice or chow mein noodles and garnish with pineapple slices.*

Preheat broiler. Brown meatballs on all sides under broiler. Mix cornstarch with pineapple juice in a medium saucepan. When smooth, mix in soy sauce, vinegar, water, and sugar. Bring to boil. Simmer, stirring until thickened. Combine meatballs and sauce in slow cooker. Cover and cook on low 2 hours. Add green pepper and water chestnuts. Cover and cook 1 hour.

Yield: 6 servings

Per serving: 259 g water; 493 calories (37% from fat, 22% from protein, 41% from carb); 26 g protein; 20 g total fat; 8 g saturated fat; 9 g monounsaturated fat; 1 g polyunsaturated fat; 50 g carb; 3 g fiber; 29 g sugar; 252 mg phosphorus; 80 mg calcium; 4 mg iron; 134 mg sodium; 765 mg potassium; 182 IU vitamin A; 14 mg ATE vitamin E; 30 mg vitamin C; 80 mg cholesterol

Sweet and Sour Meatballs

These Hawaiian-flavored meatballs are great over plain brown rice.

2 pounds (900 g) meatballs, basic or turkey (see recipes on pages 190 and 191)

1 cup (165 g) pineapple chunks, juice reserved

3 tablespoons (24 g) cornstarch

¼ cup (60 ml) cold water

1 cup (240 g) low-sodium ketchup

¼ cup (60 ml) Worcestershire sauce

¼ teaspoon pepper

¼ teaspoon garlic powder

½ cup (75 g) chopped green bell pepper

Brown meatballs in a skillet over medium-high heat, rolling so all sides are browned. Place meatballs in slow cooker. Pour juice from pineapple chunks into skillet. Stir into drippings. Combine cornstarch and cold water. Add to skillet and stir until thickened. Stir in ketchup and Worcestershire sauce and then add pepper and garlic powder. Add green pepper and pineapple chunks. Pour pineapple mixture over meatballs. Cover and cook on low 6 hours.

Yield: 6 servings

Per serving: 180 g water; 403 calories (45% from fat, 26% from protein, 28% from carb); 26 g protein; 20 g total fat; 8 g saturated fat; 9 g monounsaturated fat; 1 g polyunsaturated fat; 29 g carb; 2 g fiber; 15 g sugar; 244 mg phosphorus; 76 mg calcium; 4 mg iron; 215 mg sodium; 738 mg potassium; 535 IU vitamin A; 14 mg ATE vitamin E; 37 mg vitamin C; 80 mg cholesterol

Meatball Nibblers

Use these tasty meatballs over rice for a main dish or serve them as appetizers.

2 pounds (900 g) meatballs, basic or turkey (see recipes on pages 190 and 191)

1 cup (240 g) low-sodium ketchup

1 cup (225 g) packed brown sugar

1 can (6 ounces, or 170 g) no-salt-added tomato paste

¼ cup (60 ml) reduced-sodium soy sauce (see recipe in Chapter 2)

¼ cup (60 ml) cider vinegar

½ teaspoon hot pepper sauce

Preheat oven to 350°F (180°C, or gas mark 4). Place frozen meatballs on baking sheet. Bake for 18 minutes or until brown. Place meatballs in slow cooker. Combine remaining ingredients and pour over meatballs. Cover and cook on low 4 hours.

Yield: 6 servings

Per serving: 157 g water; 533 calories (34% from fat, 21% from protein, 45% from carb); 28 g protein; 20 g total fat; 8 g saturated fat; 9 g monounsaturated fat; 1 g polyunsaturated fat; 61 g carb; 2 g fiber; 50 g sugar; 272 mg phosphorus; 112 mg calcium; 5 mg iron; 194 mg sodium; 1023 mg potassium; 898 IU vitamin A; 14 mg ATE vitamin E; 12 mg vitamin C; 80 mg cholesterol

Barbecued Meatballs

With the sweet, smoky flavor of Midwestern-style barbecue, these meatballs are great over rice or in a sandwich.

2 pounds (900 g) meatballs, basic or turkey (see recipes on pages 190 and 191)

1 cup (240 g) low-sodium ketchup

½ cup (115 g) brown sugar

½ teaspoon liquid smoke

½ teaspoon garlic powder

½ cup (80 g) chopped onion

Place frozen meatballs in slow cooker. Cover and cook on high as you mix the remaining ingredients. Pour ketchup mixture over meatballs. Stir, cover, and continue cooking on high for 1 hour. Stir, turn to low, and cook 6 to 9 hours.

Yield: 6 servings

Per serving: 131 g water; 439 calories (41% from fat, 24% from protein, 35% from carb); 26 g protein; 20 g total fat; 8 g saturated fat; 9 g monounsaturated fat; 1 g polyunsaturated fat; 38 g carb; 1 g fiber; 29 g sugar; 237 mg phosphorus; 87 mg calcium; 4 mg iron; 124 mg sodium; 668 mg potassium; 459 IU vitamin A; 14 mg ATE vitamin E; 7 mg vitamin C; 80 mg cholesterol

Turkey Meat Loaf

Lower in fat and calories than beef meat loaf, this turkey loaf will still please you with its great taste.

1½ pounds (680 g) ground turkey

1 cup (160 g) chopped onion

½ cup (120 ml) egg substitute

⅔ cup (53 g) quick-cooking oats

2 tablespoons (15 g) onion soup mix (see recipe in Chapter 2)

¼ teaspoon liquid smoke

1 teaspoon dry mustard

1 cup (240 g) low-sodium ketchup, divided

Mix turkey and chopped onion thoroughly. Combine with egg substitute, oats, dry soup mix, liquid smoke, mustard, and all but 2 tablespoons (30 g) of ketchup. Shape into loaf and place in slow cooker sprayed with nonstick cooking spray. Top meat loaf with remaining ketchup. Cover and cook on low 8 to 10 hours or on high 4 to 6 hours.

Yield: 8 servings

Per serving: 107 g water; 221 calories (22% from fat, 52% from protein, 26% from carb); 29 g protein; 5 g total fat; 2 g saturated fat; 1 g monounsaturated fat; 2 g polyunsaturated fat; 14 g carb; 1 g fiber; 8 g sugar; 248 mg phosphorus; 43 mg calcium; 2 mg iron; 94 mg sodium; 474 mg potassium; 337 IU vitamin A; 0 mg ATE vitamin E; 6 mg vitamin C; 65 mg cholesterol

Meat Loaf Meal

This great-tasting meat loaf cooks on top of the vegetables, giving them even more flavor than they would usually have.

6 medium potatoes, cubed

1 cup (130 g) thinly sliced carrots

¼ cup (60 ml) egg substitute

¼ cup (25 g) cracker crumbs

¼ cup (70 g) chili sauce (see recipe in Chapter 2)

¼ cup (40 g) finely chopped onion

¼ teaspoon marjoram

1 teaspoon pepper

1 pound (455 g) extra-lean ground beef

Place potatoes and carrots in slow cooker. Combine egg substitute, cracker crumbs, chili sauce, onion, marjoram, and pepper. Add ground beef and mix well. Shape into a loaf slightly smaller in diameter than the cooker. Place on top of vegetables, not touching sides of cooker. Cover and cook on low 9 to 10 hours.

Yield: 6 servings

Per serving: 390 g water; 478 calories (26% from fat, 19% from protein, 54% from carb); 23 g protein; 14 g total fat; 5 g saturated fat; 6 g monounsaturated fat; 1 g polyunsaturated fat; 66 g carb; 7 g fiber; 6 g sugar; 361 mg phosphorus; 67 mg calcium; 5 mg iron; 114 mg sodium; 2016 mg potassium; 3835 IU vitamin A; 0 mg ATE vitamin E; 36 mg vitamin C; 52 mg cholesterol

Mexican Meat Loaf

Since we love Mexican food, this meat loaf is one of our favorites. The leftovers make great sandwiches.

2½ pounds (1.1 kg) extra-lean ground beef

½ cup (130 g) low-sodium salsa (see recipe in Chapter 2)

2 tablespoons (15 g) Salt-Free Mexican Seasoning (see recipe in Chapter 2), divided

¼ cup (60 ml) egg substitute

1 cup (115 g) bread crumbs

8 ounces (225 g) shredded Colby jack cheese

¼ teaspoon pepper

Combine beef, salsa, 1 tablespoon (7.5 g) Mexican seasoning, egg substitute, bread crumbs, cheese, and pepper. Mix well. Shape into loaf and place in slow cooker. Sprinkle with remaining 1 tablespoon (7.5 g) Mexican seasoning. Cover and cook on low 8 to 10 hours.

Yield: 8 servings

Per serving: 127 g water; 509 calories (62% from fat, 29% from protein, 9% from carb); 36 g protein; 34 g total fat; 16 g saturated fat; 13 g monounsaturated fat; 2 g polyunsaturated fat; 12 g carb; 1 g fiber; 2 g sugar; 368 mg phosphorus; 238 mg calcium; 4 mg iron; 316 mg sodium; 550 mg potassium; 527 IU vitamin A; 73 mg ATE vitamin E; 7 mg vitamin C; 125 mg cholesterol

Italian Meat Loaf

This Italian-flavored meat loaf is a nice change of pace with pasta.

2 pounds (900 g) extra-lean ground beef

2 cups (230 g) bread crumbs

½ cup (123 g) low-sodium spaghetti sauce

¼ cup (60 ml) egg substitute

1 tablespoon (15 g) onion flakes

¼ teaspoon pepper

1 teaspoon garlic powder

1 teaspoon Italian seasoning

Fold a 30-inch (75 cm) long piece of foil in half lengthwise. Place in bottom of slow cooker with both ends hanging over the edge of cooker. Spray foil with nonstick cooking spray. Combine all ingredients and shape into a loaf. Place on top of foil in slow cooker. Cover and cook on high for 2½ to 3 hours or on low for 5 to 6 hours.

Yield: 8 servings

Per serving: 92 g water; 399 calories (50% from fat, 27% from protein, 23% from carb); 26 g protein; 22 g total fat; 8 g saturated fat; 9 g monounsaturated fat; 2 g polyunsaturated fat; 23 g carb; 2 g fiber; 4 g sugar; 223 mg phosphorus; 70 mg calcium; 4 mg iron; 94 mg sodium; 477 mg potassium; 136 IU vitamin A; 0 mg ATE vitamin E; 2 mg vitamin C; 78 mg cholesterol

Meat Loaf

This simple meat loaf has unbelievable flavor considering how few ingredients it has and how easy it is to make.

2 pounds (900 g) extra-lean ground beef

½ cup (120 ml) egg substitute

⅔ cup (53 g) quick-cooking or rolled oats

2 tablespoons (15 g) low-sodium onion soup mix (see recipe in Chapter 2)

½ cup (120 g) low-sodium ketchup, divided

Combine ground beef, egg substitute, oats, soup mix, and all but 2 tablespoons (30 g) ketchup. Shape into loaf and place in slow cooker. Top with remaining 2 tablespoons (30 g) ketchup. Cover and cook on low for 6 to 8 hours or on high for 2 to 4 hours.

Yield: 8 servings

Per serving: 96 g water; 318 calories (58% from fat, 31% from protein, 11% from carb); 24 g protein; 20 g total fat; 8 g saturated fat; 9 g monounsaturated fat; 1 g polyunsaturated fat; 8 g carb; 1 g fiber; 4 g sugar; 214 mg phosphorus; 22 mg calcium; 3 mg iron; 106 mg sodium; 455 mg potassium; 196 IU vitamin A; 0 mg ATE vitamin E; 2 mg vitamin C; 78 mg cholesterol

Cornbread Casserole

This mildly Mexican flavored casserole bakes its own crust while it slow cooks.

1 pound (455 g) frozen corn

1 cup (140 g) cornmeal

½ teaspoon baking soda

¼ cup (60 ml) canola oil

1 cup (235 ml) skim milk

½ cup (120 ml) egg substitute

¼ cup (65 g) low-sodium salsa (see recipe in Chapter 2)

1 cup (115 g) shredded Cheddar cheese

1 cup (160 g) chopped onion

½ teaspoon minced garlic

4 ounces (115 g) diced green chilies

1 pound (455 g) extra-lean ground beef, lightly cooked and drained

Combine corn, cornmeal, baking soda, oil, milk, egg substitute, and salsa. Pour half of mixture into slow cooker. Layer cheese, onion, garlic, green chilies, and ground beef on top of cornmeal mixture. Cover with remaining cornmeal mixture. Cover and cook on high 1 hour and then on low for 3 to 4 hours or only on low for 6 hours.

Yield: 6 servings

Per serving: 222 g water; 559 calories (50% from fat, 20% from protein, 30% from carb); 28 g protein; 31 g total fat; 11 g saturated fat; 14 g monounsaturated fat; 4 g polyunsaturated fat; 43 g carb; 4 g fiber; 5 g sugar; 375 mg phosphorus; 254 mg calcium; 4 mg iron; 354 mg sodium; 625 mg potassium; 494 IU vitamin A; 82 mg ATE vitamin E; 12 mg vitamin C; 76 mg cholesterol

Goulash

Goulash is originally of Hungarian origin, although there are now a number of dishes quite unlike the original using the name. This one is made with ground beef.

1 pound (455 g) extra-lean ground beef, browned

1 cup (160 g) chopped onion

½ teaspoon minced garlic

½ cup (120 g) low-sodium ketchup

2 tablespoons (28 ml) Worcestershire sauce

1 tablespoon (15 g) brown sugar

2 teaspoons paprika

½ teaspoon dry mustard

1 cup (235 ml) water

TIP

Serve over noodles or rice.

Place meat in slow cooker. Cover with onions. Combine remaining ingredients and pour over meat. Cook on low for 5 to 6 hours.

Yield: 8 servings

Per serving: 95 g water; 167 calories (53% from fat, 27% from protein, 20% from carb); 11 g protein; 10 g total fat; 4 g saturated fat; 4 g monounsaturated fat; 0 g polyunsaturated fat; 8 g carb; 1 g fiber; 6 g sugar; 97 mg phosphorus; 15 mg calcium; 2 mg iron; 80 mg sodium; 299 mg potassium; 448 IU vitamin A; 0 mg ATE vitamin E; 11 mg vitamin C; 39 mg cholesterol

Creamy Hamburger Sauce

Mushroom soup gives this pasta sauce an unusual creamy flavor and texture.

1 pound (455 g) extra-lean ground beef

2 cups (220 g) shredded Swiss cheese

1 cup (160 g) diced onion

(continued on page 206)

1 can (10 ounces, or 280 g) low-sodium cream of mushroom soup (see recipe in Chapter 2)

1 can (12 ounces, or 340 g) no-salt-added diced tomatoes, undrained

TIP

Serve over cooked pasta or noodles.

Brown ground beef in a nonstick skillet over medium-high heat. Drain. Combine beef and remaining ingredients in slow cooker. Cook on low 3 to 5 hours or until heated through.

Yield: 8 servings

Per serving: 137 g water; 290 calories (60% from fat, 29% from protein, 10% from carb); 21 g protein; 19 g total fat; 10 g saturated fat; 7 g monounsaturated fat; 1 g polyunsaturated fat; 8 g carb; 1 g fiber; 3 g sugar; 312 mg phosphorus; 343 mg calcium; 2 mg iron; 184 mg sodium; 439 mg potassium; 323 IU vitamin A; 70 mg ATE vitamin E; 5 mg vitamin C; 71 mg cholesterol

Cincinnati Spaghetti Casserole

Modeled after Cincinnati chili, which is traditionally served over spaghetti, this dish will be a hit with adults, teens, and younger children.

½ cup (80 g) chopped onions

2 cups (475 ml) low-sodium tomato juice

2 teaspoons chili powder

½ cup (58 g) shredded Cheddar cheese

1½ pounds (680 g) extra-lean ground beef, browned

12 ounces (340 g) spaghetti, cooked

Combine all ingredients in slow cooker. Cover and cook on low 4 hours. Check mixture about halfway through the cooking time. If it's becoming dry, stir in an additional 1 cup (235 ml) of tomato juice.

Yield: 8 servings

Per serving: 151 g water; 301 calories (52% from fat, 28% from protein, 20% from carb); 21 g protein; 18 g total fat; 8 g saturated fat; 7 g monounsaturated fat; 1 g polyunsaturated fat; 15 g carb; 3 g fiber; 3 g sugar; 216 mg phosphorus; 82 mg calcium; 3 mg iron; 121 mg sodium; 434 mg potassium; 543 IU vitamin A; 21 mg ATE vitamin E; 12 mg vitamin C; 67 mg cholesterol

Hamburger Noodle Casserole

This is classic comfort food, updated with tomatoes and the easy prep that the slow cooker affords.

1½ pounds (680 g) extra-lean ground beef, browned and drained

1 cup (150 g) diced green bell pepper

4 cups (720 g) no-salt-added diced tomatoes

10 ounces (280 g) low-sodium cream of mushroom soup (see recipe in Chapter 2)

1 cup (160 g) diced onion

8 ounces (225 g) uncooked egg noodles

¼ teaspoon black pepper

1 cup (110 g) shredded Swiss cheese

Combine all ingredients except cheese in slow cooker. Cover and cook on high 3 to 4 hours. Sprinkle with cheese before serving.

Yield: 8 servings

Per serving: 259 g water; 348 calories (52% from fat, 26% from protein, 22% from carb); 23 g protein; 20 g total fat; 9 g saturated fat; 8 g monounsaturated fat; 1 g polyunsaturated fat; 19 g carb; 3 g fiber; 5 g sugar; 292 mg phosphorus; 213 mg calcium; 3 mg iron; 211 mg sodium; 689 mg potassium; 364 IU vitamin A; 36 mg ATE vitamin E; 28 mg vitamin C; 75 mg cholesterol

Spanish Rice Meal

This is your slow cooker version of a "skillet meal." I think you'll find it easier and better-tasting than similar packaged versions.

2 pounds (900 g) lean ground beef, browned

1 cup (150 g) chopped green bell pepper

1 cup (160 g) chopped onion

2 teaspoons Worcestershire sauce

2 teaspoons chili powder

1 can (6 ounces, or 170 g) tomato paste

1 can (28 ounces, or 785 g) crushed tomatoes

1 cup (185 g) uncooked long-grain rice

1 cup (235 ml) water

Combine all ingredients in slow cooker and cook on low 6 to 8 hours or until rice is done.

Yield: 6 servings

Per serving: 331 g water; 537 calories (45% from fat, 25% from protein, 30% from carb); 33 g protein; 27 g total fat; 10 g saturated fat; 11 g monounsaturated fat; 1 g polyunsaturated fat; 41 g carb; 4 g fiber; 5 g sugar; 321 mg phosphorus; 48 mg calcium; 6 mg iron; 365 mg sodium; 1158 mg potassium; 1598 IU vitamin A; 0 mg ATE vitamin E; 66 mg vitamin C; 104 mg cholesterol

Beef and Potato Casserole

This is kind of a shepherd's pie in the slow cooker. What could be easier or better?

1 pound (455 g) lean ground beef

1 cup (160 g) chopped onion

1 cup (245 g) no-salt-added tomato sauce

12 ounces (340 g) frozen corn

1½ cups (90 g) potato flakes

1½ cups (345 g) fat-free sour cream

⅓ cup (80 ml) water

1½ cups (173 g) grated Cheddar cheese

Brown beef and onion in a skillet over medium-high heat. Drain well. Place in slow cooker and add tomato sauce and corn and mix well. In bowl, mix potato flakes with sour cream and water. Spread mixture over beef. Top with grated cheese. Cover and cook on low for 7 to 10 hours.

Yield: 4 servings

Per serving: 335 g water; 772 calories (54% from fat, 21% from protein, 24% from carb); 42 g protein; 47 g total fat; 25 g saturated fat; 16 g monounsaturated fat; 2 g polyunsaturated fat; 47 g carb; 5 g fiber; 8 g sugar; 613 mg phosphorus; 486 mg calcium; 4 mg iron; 456 mg sodium; 1129 mg potassium; 1036 IU vitamin A; 219 mg ATE vitamin E; 32 mg vitamin C; 166 mg cholesterol

Chili Beans

Baked beans with a mild chili flavor and ground beef are sort of half way to chili.

1 pound (455 g) pinto beans

1 cup (160 g) sliced onion

1 tablespoon (13 g) sugar

1 teaspoon garlic powder

1 teaspoon chili powder

2 cups (360 g) no-salt-added diced tomatoes, smashed

4 ounces (115 g) green chilies

5 slices low-sodium bacon

1 pound (455 g) lean ground beef

TIP

Serve over rice or with corn bread.

Wash beans. Put beans in large pan and cover with water. Bring to a boil and boil for 10 minutes. Cover and simmer for 30 minutes. Turn off heat and let set for 1½ hours. In slow cooker, mix onion, sugar, garlic powder, chili powder, tomatoes, green chilies, and bacon. Drain beans and add to tomato mixture in slow cooker. Cook on high 5 to 6 hours or until beans are done. Before serving, brown ground beef and add to beans.

(continued on page 210)

Yield: 8 servings

Per serving: 131 g water; 386 calories (30% from fat, 26% from protein, 44% from carb); 25 g protein; 13 g total fat; 5 g saturated fat; 5 g monounsaturated fat; 1 g polyunsaturated fat; 42 g carb; 10 g fiber; 5 g sugar; 361 mg phosphorus; 98 mg calcium; 5 mg iron; 150 mg sodium; 1147 mg potassium; 183 IU vitamin A; 1 mg ATE vitamin E; 16 mg vitamin C; 45 mg cholesterol

Ground Beef Curry

A rather mild curry, this is the kind of dish that will appeal even to people who don't normally like curries.

1 pound (455 g) extra-lean ground beef, browned

1 cup (160 g) thinly sliced onion

1 cup (150 g) diced green bell pepper

1 large tomato, peeled and diced

1 apple, peeled, cored, and diced

2 teaspoons curry powder

TIP

Serve over hot rice.

Add all ingredients to slow cooker and mix well. Cover and cook on high 6 to 8 hours.

Yield: 6 servings

Per serving: 137 g water; 210 calories (57% from fat, 29% from protein, 15% from carb); 15 g protein; 13 g total fat; 5 g saturated fat; 6 g monounsaturated fat; 1 g polyunsaturated fat; 8 g carb; 2 g fiber; 5 g sugar; 130 mg phosphorus; 21 mg calcium; 2 mg iron; 53 mg sodium; 386 mg potassium; 314 IU vitamin A; 0 mg ATE vitamin E; 26 mg vitamin C; 52 mg cholesterol

Rice with Beef and Peppers

A kind of one-dish slow cooker version of pepper steak, this doesn't have overwhelming Asian flavor, just enough to be interesting.

1 pound (455 g) ground beef

1 cup (150 g) coarsely chopped green bell pepper

1 cup (150 g) coarsely chopped red bell pepper

1 cup (160 g) chopped onion

1 cup (190 g) brown rice

3 cups (700 ml) low-sodium beef broth (see recipe in Chapter 2)

1 tablespoon (15 ml) reduced-sodium soy sauce (see recipe in Chapter 2)

Brown beef in skillet over medium-high heat. Drain. Combine beef and remaining ingredients in slow cooker and mix well. Cover and cook on low 5 to 6 hours or on high 3 hours until liquid is absorbed.

Yield: 6 servings

Per serving: 260 g water; 245 calories (50% from fat, 28% from protein, 21% from carb); 17 g protein; 14 g total fat; 5 g saturated fat; 6 g monounsaturated fat; 1 g polyunsaturated fat; 13 g carb; 2 g fiber; 3 g sugar; 171 mg phosphorus; 27 mg calcium; 2 mg iron; 133 mg sodium; 433 mg potassium; 870 IU vitamin A; 0 mg ATE vitamin E; 54 mg vitamin C; 52 mg cholesterol

Spanish Rice with Beef

Here's a Spanish dish that is perfect with just a salad for a really quick meal when you come home from work.

2 pounds (900 g) extra-lean ground beef, browned

1½ cups (240 g) chopped onions

1½ cups (225 g) chopped green bell pepper

1 can (28 ounces, or 785 g) no-salt-added diced tomatoes

(continued on page 212)

1 cup (245 g) no-salt-added tomato sauce

1½ cups (355 ml) water

2 teaspoons Worcestershire sauce

1½ cups (278 g) uncooked long-grain rice

Combine all ingredients in slow cooker. Cover and cook on low 8 to 10 hours or on high 6 hours.

Yield: 8 servings

Per serving: 410 g water; 438 calories (41% from fat, 23% from protein, 35% from carb); 25 g protein; 20 g total fat; 8 g saturated fat; 9 g monounsaturated fat; 1 g polyunsaturated fat; 38 g carb; 3 g fiber; 6 g sugar; 243 mg phosphorus; 67 mg calcium; 5 mg iron; 112 mg sodium; 758 mg potassium; 320 IU vitamin A; 0 mg ATE vitamin E; 40 mg vitamin C; 78 mg cholesterol

Meaty Spaghetti Sauce

This spaghetti sauce has a little bit of everything. Sauces like this are better if simmered for a long time, so why not let the slow cooker do it for you?

1 pound (455 g) lean ground beef

½ pound (225 g) Italian sausage (see recipe in Chapter 2)

1 can (28 ounces, or 785 g) no-salt-added diced tomatoes, undrained

1 can (6 ounces, or 170 g) no-salt-added tomato paste

8 ounces (225 g) mushrooms, sliced

1 cup (160 g) chopped onion

¾ cup (113 g) chopped green bell pepper

½ cup (120 ml) dry red wine

⅓ cup (80 ml) water

2¼ ounces (64 g) ripe olives, drained and sliced

2 teaspoons sugar

½ teaspoon Worcestershire sauce

½ teaspoon chili powder

¼ teaspoon black pepper

½ teaspoon minced garlic

TIP *Serve meat mixture over hot cooked spaghetti. If desired, sprinkle each serving with Parmesan cheese.*

In a large skillet, cook ground beef and sausage over medium heat until brown. Drain off fat. Transfer meat mixture to a slow cooker. Stir in remaining ingredients. Cover and cook on low for 9 to 10 hours or on high for 4½ to 5 hours.

Yield: 8 servings

Per serving: 246 g water; 309 calories (59% from fat, 23% from protein, 18% from carb); 18 g protein; 20 g total fat; 7 g saturated fat; 9 g monounsaturated fat; 2 g polyunsaturated fat; 14 g carb; 3 g fiber; 8 g sugar; 194 mg phosphorus; 64 mg calcium; 4 mg iron; 164 mg sodium; 805 mg potassium; 571 IU vitamin A; 0 mg ATE vitamin E; 29 mg vitamin C; 61 mg cholesterol

Taco Bake

The corn tortillas give this slow cooker casserole the flavor of tacos.

1½ pounds (680 g) extra-lean ground beef, browned

1 can (14 ounces, or 400 g) no-salt-added diced tomatoes

4 ounces (115 g) diced green chilies

2 tablespoons (15 g) Salt-Free Mexican Seasoning (see recipe in Chapter 2)

¼ cup (60 ml) water

6 corn tortillas, cut in ½-inch (1.3 cm) strips

½ cup (115 g) fat-free sour cream

1 cup (115 g) shredded Cheddar cheese

TIP

Garnish with lettuce and tomato if desired.

Combine beef, tomatoes, chilies, Mexican seasoning, and water in slow cooker. Stir in tortilla strips. Cover and cook on low 7 to 8 hours. Spread sour cream over casserole. Sprinkle with cheese. Cover and let stand 5 minutes until cheese melts.

Yield: 6 servings

Per serving: 194 g water; 437 calories (61% from fat, 27% from protein, 12% from carb); 29 g protein; 30 g total fat; 14 g saturated fat; 11 g monounsaturated fat; 1 g polyunsaturated fat; 13 g carb; 2 g fiber; 2 g sugar; 365 mg phosphorus; 230 mg calcium; 3 mg iron; 312 mg sodium; 550 mg potassium; 397 IU vitamin A; 77 mg ATE vitamin E; 13 mg vitamin C; 109 mg cholesterol

Enchilada Casserole

This easy-to-fix enchilada-flavored casserole cooks in the slow cooker and leaves you with a house full of delicious aroma and a plate full of delicious food.

1 pound (455 g) extra-lean ground beef

1 cup (160 g) chopped onion

¾ cup (113 g) chopped green bell pepper

2 cups (342 g) no-salt-added cooked pinto beans

2 cups (344 g) no-salt-added cooked black beans

2 cups (360 g) no-salt-added diced tomatoes

4 ounces (115 g) diced green chilies

1 teaspoon chili powder

1 teaspoon ground cumin

½ teaspoon black pepper

4 ounces (115 g) Cheddar cheese, shredded

4 ounces (115 g) Monterey Jack cheese, shredded

6 flour tortillas

In a nonstick skillet, brown beef, onions, and green pepper. Add remaining ingredients except cheese and tortillas to skillet and bring to a boil. Reduce heat. Cover and simmer for 10 minutes. Combine cheeses in a bowl. In slow cooker, layer about ¾ cup (150 g) beef mixture, 1 tortilla, and about ¼ cup (30 g) cheese. Repeat layers until all ingredients are used. Cover and cook on low 5 to 7 hours.

Yield: 8 servings

Per serving: 188 g water; 564 calories (34% from fat, 25% from protein, 41% from carb); 35 g protein; 22 g total fat; 10 g saturated fat; 8 g monounsaturated fat; 1 g polyunsaturated fat; 58 g carb; 14 g fiber; 4 g sugar; 526 mg phosphorus; 341 mg calcium; 7 mg iron; 420 mg sodium; 1241 mg potassium; 490 IU vitamin A; 64 mg ATE vitamin E; 26 mg vitamin C; 67 mg cholesterol

Burrito Bake

These are like burritos, only a lot easier to make.

1 tablespoon (15 ml) olive oil

1 cup (160 g) chopped onion

1 cup (150 g) chopped green bell pepper

¾ teaspoon minced garlic

2 cups (342 g) no-salt-added cooked pinto beans

2 cups (512 g) no-salt-added cooked kidney beans

2 cups (344 g) no-salt-added cooked black beans

4 ounces (115 g) black olives, drained and sliced

4 ounces (115 g) diced green chilies

2 cups (360 g) no-salt-added diced tomatoes

1 teaspoon chili powder

1 teaspoon cumin

6 flour tortillas

1 cup (115 g) shredded Cheddar cheese

TIP
Serve with dollops of sour cream on individual servings.

Heat oil in a large skillet and sauté onions, green pepper, and garlic. Add beans, olives, chilies, tomatoes, chili powder, and cumin. Spray slow cooker with nonstick cooking spray and then layer ¾ cup (170 g) vegetable mixture, a tortilla, and ⅓ cup (40 g) cheese. Repeat layers until all ingredients are used, ending with vegetables. Cover and cook on low 8 to 10 hours.

Yield: 6 servings

Per serving: 249 g water; 543 calories (13% from fat, 21% from protein, 66% from carb); 29 g protein; 8 g total fat; 1 g saturated fat; 5 g monounsaturated fat; 1 g polyunsaturated fat; 92 g carb; 24 g fiber; 6 g sugar; 500 mg phosphorus; 215 mg calcium; 9 mg iron; 460 mg sodium; 1640 mg potassium; 419 IU vitamin A; 0 mg ATE vitamin E; 41 mg vitamin C; 0 mg cholesterol

Taco Filling

This chili-spiced beef mixture can be used for tacos, burritos, or anywhere you want a little Mexican flavor.

3 tablespoons (45 ml) olive oil

2 pounds (900 g) extra-lean ground beef

1 cup (160 g) chopped onion

8 ounces (225 g) diced green chilies

1 teaspoon chili powder

1 teaspoon minced garlic

1 cup (235 ml) water

TIP

Mixed with a pint of sour cream, this makes a good dip.

Heat oil in a large skillet over medium-high heat; brown meat and onion. Transfer to slow cooker. Add chilies, chili powder, garlic, and water. Cover and cook on high 6 to 8 hours.

Yield: 8 servings

Per serving: 146 g water; 326 calories (69% from fat, 27% from protein, 4% from carb); 22 g protein; 25 g total fat; 8 g saturated fat; 12 g monounsaturated fat; 1 g polyunsaturated fat; 3 g carb; 1 g fiber; 1 g sugar; 170 mg phosphorus; 25 mg calcium; 3 mg iron; 192 mg sodium; 391 mg potassium; 129 IU vitamin A; 0 mg ATE vitamin E; 11 mg vitamin C; 78 mg cholesterol

Pizza Burgers

This cheesy Italian meat mixture can be served on hamburger buns or over pasta.

1 pound (455 g) extra-lean ground beef

½ cup (80 g) chopped onions

¼ teaspoon pepper

1 cup (245 g) low-sodium spaghetti sauce

1 cup (115 g) shredded mozzarella cheese

Brown ground beef and onion in a skillet over medium-high heat. Drain. Add remaining ingredients to skillet and mix well. Pour into slow cooker. Cover and cook on low 1 to 2 hours.

Yield: 4 servings

Per serving: 146 g water; 419 calories (61% from fat, 28% from protein, 11% from carb); 29 g protein; 28 g total fat; 12 g saturated fat; 12 g monounsaturated fat; 1 g polyunsaturated fat; 12 g carb; 2 g fiber; 8 g sugar; 285 mg phosphorus; 170 mg calcium; 3 mg iron; 268 mg sodium; 591 mg potassium; 544 IU vitamin A; 49 mg ATE vitamin E; 8 mg vitamin C; 100 mg cholesterol

Italian Beef

Nothing could be easier than these sandwiches, which only have three ingredients. But the flavor is big.

1 pound (455 g) extra-lean ground beef

1 cup (245 g) no-salt-added tomato sauce

2 tablespoons (12 g) Italian seasoning

In a nonstick skillet over medium-high heat, brown ground beef. Drain. Place meat in slow cooker. Stir in tomato sauce and Italian seasoning. Cover and cook on low 2 to 6 hours.

Yield: 4 servings

Per serving: 126 g water; 293 calories (62% from fat, 31% from protein, 8% from carb); 22 g protein; 20 g total fat; 8 g saturated fat; 8 g monounsaturated fat; 1 g polyunsaturated fat; 5 g carb; 2 g fiber; 3 g sugar; 182 mg phosphorus; 40 mg calcium; 3 mg iron; 82 mg sodium; 573 mg potassium; 315 IU vitamin A; 0 mg ATE vitamin E; 9 mg vitamin C; 78 mg cholesterol

Sloppy Joes

These sloppy Joes are easy to put together and have a great flavor. Double or triple the recipe if needed to feed a crowd.

1 pound (455 g) extra-lean ground beef

1 cup (160 g) chopped onion

¾ cup (180 g) low-sodium ketchup

2 tablespoons (40 g) chili sauce (see recipe in Chapter 2)

1 tablespoon (15 ml) Worcestershire sauce

1 tablespoon (11 g) mustard

1 tablespoon (15 ml) vinegar

Brown beef and onion in saucepan over medium-high heat. Drain. Combine beef mixture and remaining ingredients in slow cooker. Cover and cook on low 4 to 5 hours. Serve on buns.

Yield: 4 servings

Per serving: 150 g water; 335 calories (53% from fat, 27% from protein, 20% from carb); 23 g protein; 20 g total fat; 8 g saturated fat; 8 g monounsaturated fat; 1 g polyunsaturated fat; 17 g carb; 1 g fiber; 12 g sugar; 191 mg phosphorus; 30 mg calcium; 3 mg iron; 128 mg sodium; 592 mg potassium; 553 IU vitamin A; 0 mg ATE vitamin E; 18 mg vitamin C; 78 mg cholesterol

Barbecue Burgers

This great tasting beef barbecue can be served on buns or over mashed potatoes, pasta, or rice.

2 tablespoons (28 ml) olive oil

1½ pounds (680 g) extra-lean ground beef

½ cup (80 g) chopped onions

½ cup (50 g) diced celery

½ cup (75 g) chopped green bell pepper

1 tablespoon (15 ml) Worcestershire sauce

½ cup (120 g) low-sodium ketchup

½ teaspoon minced garlic

¼ teaspoon pepper

½ teaspoon paprika

1 can (6 ounces, or 170 g) no-salt-added tomato paste

2 tablespoons (28 ml) vinegar

2 teaspoons brown sugar

1 teaspoon dry mustard

Heat oil in a saucepan over medium-high heat and brown beef. Drain. Combine beef and remaining ingredients in slow cooker. Cover and cook on low 6 to 8 hours or on high 3 to 4 hours.

Yield: 8 servings

Per serving: 108 g water; 276 calories (59% from fat, 25% from protein, 16% from carb); 17 g protein; 18 g total fat; 6 g saturated fat; 9 g monounsaturated fat; 1 g polyunsaturated fat; 11 g carb; 1 g fiber; 8 g sugar; 152 mg phosphorus; 24 mg calcium; 3 mg iron; 105 mg sodium; 589 mg potassium; 609 IU vitamin A; 0 mg ATE vitamin E; 19 mg vitamin C; 59 mg cholesterol

Saucy Beef

This mushroom and tomato beef mixture is equally good on rolls or over noodles or pasta.

3 pounds (1⅓ kg) extra-lean ground beef

1 cup (160 g) thinly sliced onions

10 ounces (280 g) low-sodium cream of mushroom soup (see recipe in Chapter 2)

4 ounces (115 g) mushrooms, sliced

1½ cups (355 ml) beer

½ cup (120 g) low-sodium ketchup

1 bay leaf

¼ teaspoon black pepper

(continued on page 220)

Place meat in slow cooker. Combine remaining ingredients. Pour over meat. Cover and cook on low 7 to 9 hours or on high 4 to 6 hours. Remove bay leaf before serving.

Yield: 12 servings

Per serving: 146 g water; 307 calories (60% from fat, 30% from protein, 9% from carb); 22 g protein; 20 g total fat; 8 g saturated fat; 9 g monounsaturated fat; 1 g polyunsaturated fat; 7 g carb; 1 g fiber; 4 g sugar; 191 mg phosphorus; 17 mg calcium; 2 mg iron; 169 mg sodium; 506 mg potassium; 96 IU vitamin A; 1 mg ATE vitamin E; 3 mg vitamin C; 79 mg cholesterol

Barbecued Beef

Here's a quick and easy but great-flavored recipe for barbecued beef.

3 pounds (1 ⅓ kg) extra-lean ground beef

1 cup (250 g) barbecue sauce

½ cup (160 g) apricot preserves

½ cup (75 g) finely chopped green bell pepper

½ cup (80 g) finely chopped onion

1 tablespoon (11 g) Dijon mustard

1 tablespoon (15 g) brown sugar

TIP

Serve beef and sauce on rolls.

Spray slow cooker with nonstick cooking spray. Place meat in prepared slow cooker. Combine barbecue sauce, preserves, green pepper, onion, mustard, and brown sugar. Pour over meat. Cover and cook on low 6 to 8 hours.

Yield: 12 servings

Per serving: 101 g water; 353 calories (50% from fat, 25% from protein, 25% from carb); 22 g protein; 19 g total fat; 8 g saturated fat; 8 g monounsaturated fat; 1 g polyunsaturated fat; 21 g carb; 0 g fiber; 16 g sugar; 167 mg phosphorus; 14 mg calcium; 2 mg iron; 114 mg sodium; 359 mg potassium; 24 IU vitamin A; 0 mg ATE vitamin E; 7 mg vitamin C; 78 mg cholesterol

10

Great Tasting Low-Calorie and Low-Fat Chicken and Turkey Main Dishes

Chicken and turkey also are popular slow cooker meals, as you can tell by the number of recipes in this chapter. Whether you are considering "roasting" a turkey breast, creating a casserole, or just cooking flavorful poultry to serve with other dishes, you'll find something to please you here.

Slow Cooker Roast Chicken

Let the slow cooker handle the task of roasting your chicken to a tender turn.

1 whole chicken

½ teaspoon pepper

1 teaspoon paprika

Crumple three pieces of aluminum foil into 3- to 4-inch (7.5 to 10 cm) balls and place them in the bottom of the slow cooker. Rinse the chicken, inside and out, under cold running water. Pat dry with paper towels. Season the chicken with the pepper and paprika and place in the slow cooker on top of the crumpled aluminum foil. Cover and cook on high for 1 hour and then turn down to low for about 8 to 10 hours or until the chicken is no longer pink and the juices run clear.

Yield: 8 servings

Per serving: 37 g water; 59 calories (25% from fat, 74% from protein, 1% from carb); 11 g protein; 2 g total fat; 0 g saturated fat; 0 g monounsaturated fat; 0 g polyunsaturated fat; 0 g carb; 0 g fiber; 0 g sugar; 86 mg phosphorus; 6 mg calcium; 1 mg iron; 38 mg sodium; 120 mg potassium; 183 IU vitamin A; 8 mg ATE vitamin E; 2 mg vitamin C; 34 mg cholesterol

Chicken and Dumplings

This recipe requires you to take the soup out of the slow cooker and finish cooking it on the stove so the broth can simmer enough to cook the dumplings. If you don't want to go to that trouble, you can just eat the soup without the dumplings and it will still be good.

For the Soup:

4 cups (560 g) cubed cooked chicken

6 cups (1.4 L) low-sodium chicken broth (see recipe in Chapter 2)

1 tablespoon (4 g) fresh parsley

1 cup (160 g) chopped onion

1 cup (100 g) chopped celery

6 potatoes, diced

12 ounces (340 g) frozen green beans

1 cup (130 g) sliced carrots

For the Dumplings:

2 cups (250 g) flour

4 teaspoons (18 g) baking powder

¼ cup (60 ml) egg substitute

1 tablespoon (15 ml) olive oil

½ cup (120 ml) skim milk

To make the soup: Combine all soup ingredients in slow cooker. Cover and cook on low 4 to 6 hours. Transfer to a large soup kettle with lid. Bring to a boil and then reduce heat to simmer.

To make the dumplings: Combine flour and baking powder in a large bowl. In a separate bowl, combine egg substitute, olive oil, and milk until smooth. Add to flour mixture and stir until combined. Drop by large tablespoons on top of simmering broth. Cover and simmer without lifting the lid for 18 minutes.

Yield: 8 servings

Per serving: 550 g water; 441 calories (10% from fat, 22% from protein, 68% from carb); 24 g protein; 5 g total fat; 1 g saturated fat; 2 g monounsaturated fat; 1 g polyunsaturated fat; 76 g carb; 8 g fiber; 6 g sugar; 428 mg phosphorus; 239 mg calcium; 5 mg iron; 457 mg sodium; 1736 mg potassium; 3188 IU vitamin A; 18 mg ATE vitamin E; 36 mg vitamin C; 40 mg cholesterol

Sweet and Sour Chicken

This isn't, perhaps, what you typically think of when you say sweet and sour chicken, but these tasty breasts will be a hit with all.

3 pounds (1⅓ kg) chicken breast halves, skinned

¾ cup (213 g) frozen lemonade concentrate, thawed

(continued on page 224)

3 tablespoons (45 g) packed brown sugar

3 tablespoons (45 g) low-sodium ketchup

1 tablespoon (15 ml) vinegar

2 tablespoons (16 g) cornstarch

2 tablespoons (15 ml) cold water

TIP

Serve with hot cooked rice.

Place chicken in slow cooker. In a medium bowl combine lemonade, brown sugar, ketchup, and vinegar. Pour over chicken. Cover and cook on low for 6 to 7 hours or on high for 3 to 3½ hours. Transfer chicken to a serving platter; cover and keep warm. Pour cooking liquid into a medium saucepan. Skim off fat. Combine cornstarch and the water; stir into liquid in saucepan. Cook and stir over medium heat until thickened and bubbly. Cook and stir for 2 minutes more. Spoon sauce over chicken.

Yield: 6 servings

Per serving: 180 g water; 484 calories (16% from fat, 60% from protein, 24% from carb); 71 g protein; 8 g total fat; 2 g saturated fat; 3 g monounsaturated fat; 2 g polyunsaturated fat; 28 g carb; 0 g fiber; 25 g sugar; 525 mg phosphorus; 44 mg calcium; 3 mg iron; 174 mg sodium; 659 mg potassium; 118 IU vitamin A; 14 mg ATE vitamin E; 8 mg vitamin C; 193 mg cholesterol

Cassoulet

A traditional French country dish, cassoulet sometimes contains sausage as well as chicken. You can add some if you like, but we like it just like this.

1¼ cups (228 g) dried navy beans

4 cups (950 ml) water

2 tablespoons (28 ml) olive oil

3 pounds (1⅓ kg) chicken, cut up

½ cup (65 g) finely chopped carrot

½ cup (50 g) chopped celery

½ cup (80 g) chopped onion

1½ cups (355 ml) low-sodium tomato juice

1 tablespoon (15 ml) Worcestershire sauce

½ teaspoon basil

½ teaspoon oregano

½ teaspoon paprika

In large saucepan, bring beans and 4 cups (950 ml) water to boiling. Reduce heat and simmer, covered, for 1½ hours. Pour beans and liquid into bowl. Heat oil in a large skillet over medium-high heat and brown the chicken. In slow cooker, place chicken, carrot, celery, and onion. Drain beans; mix with tomato juice, Worcestershire sauce, basil, oregano, and paprika. Pour over meat mixture. Cover and cook on low for 8 hours. Remove chicken and mash bean mixture slightly, if desired.

Yield: 6 servings

Per serving: 282 g water; 347 calories (20% from fat, 62% from protein, 18% from carb); 52 g protein; 7 g total fat; 2 g saturated fat; 2 g monounsaturated fat; 2 g polyunsaturated fat; 16 g carb; 5 g fiber; 4 g sugar; 471 mg phosphorus; 72 mg calcium; 4 mg iron; 220 mg sodium; 909 mg potassium; 2338 IU vitamin A; 36 mg ATE vitamin E; 23 mg vitamin C; 159 mg cholesterol

Arroz Con Pollo

This is a slow cooker version of the classic Spanish chicken and rice dish. Serve with a green salad and hot crusty bread and pass the hot pepper sauce for those who like heat. Turmeric can be used to convey the saffron color in a dish, but it will not provide the same flavor as the original.

1 tablespoon (15 ml) olive oil

3 pounds (1⅓ kg) chicken pieces

1 cup (160 g) finely chopped onion

1 teaspoon minced garlic

(continued on page 226)

¼ teaspoon black pepper

1½ cups (278 g) uncooked long-grain rice

¼ teaspoon saffron, or 1 teaspoon turmeric

2 cups (360 g) no-salt-added diced tomatoes

1½ cups (355 ml) low-sodium chicken broth (see recipe in Chapter 2)

½ cup (120 ml) white wine

¾ cup (115 g) finely chopped green bell pepper

1 cup (130 g) frozen no-salt-added peas, thawed

In a nonstick skillet, heat oil over medium-high heat. Add chicken, in batches, and brown lightly on all sides. Transfer to slow cooker. Reduce heat to medium. Add onions and cook, stirring, until softened. Add garlic and pepper and cook, stirring, for 1 minute. Add rice and stir until grains are well coated with mixture. Stir in saffron, tomatoes, and chicken broth. Transfer to slow cooker and stir to combine with chicken. Cover and cook on low for 6 to 8 hours or on high for 3 to 4 hours until juices run clear when chicken is pierced with a fork. Stir in green pepper and peas; cover and cook on high for 20 minutes or until vegetables are heated through.

Yield: 6 servings

Per serving: 218 g water; 599 calories (41% from fat, 25% from protein, 34% from carb); 36 g protein; 26 g total fat; 7 g saturated fat; 11 g monounsaturated fat; 5 g polyunsaturated fat; 49 g carb; 4 g fiber; 5 g sugar; 123 mg phosphorus; 75 mg calcium; 6 mg iron; 163 mg sodium; 670 mg potassium; 1933 IU vitamin A; 0 mg ATE vitamin E; 31 mg vitamin C; 141 mg cholesterol

Italian Chicken

Italian-flavored chicken is great with pasta or just plain veggies or a salad.

3 pounds (1⅓ kg) chicken, cut-up

¼ cup (55 g) unsalted butter, melted

2 tablespoons (15 g) Italian dressing mix (see recipe in Chapter 2)

1 tablespoon (15 ml) lemon juice

1 tablespoon (3 g) oregano

Place chicken in bottom of slow cooker. Mix melted butter, dressing mix, and lemon juice together and pour over top of chicken. Cover and cook on high for 4 to 6 hours or until chicken is tender but not dry. Baste occasionally with sauce mixture and sprinkle with oregano 1 hour before done.

Yield: 6 servings

Per serving: 175 g water; 340 calories (40% from fat, 59% from protein, 1% from carb); 49 g protein; 15 g total fat; 7 g saturated fat; 4 g monounsaturated fat; 2 g polyunsaturated fat; 1 g carb; 0 g fiber; 0 g sugar; 396 mg phosphorus; 38 mg calcium; 2 mg iron; 176 mg sodium; 533 mg potassium; 389 IU vitamin A; 100 mg ATE vitamin E; 7 mg vitamin C; 179 mg cholesterol

Orange Chicken

Serve this zesty orange chicken with garlic and thyme over rice or noodles.

1½ teaspoons thyme

1½ teaspoons minced garlic

6 chicken breasts

1 cup (284 g) orange juice concentrate

2 tablespoons (28 ml) balsamic vinegar

Rub thyme and garlic over chicken. Reserve any leftover thyme and garlic. Place chicken in slow cooker. Mix orange juice concentrate and vinegar together in a small bowl. Stir in reserved thyme and garlic. Spoon over chicken. Cover and cook on low 5 to 6 hours or on high 2½ to 3 hours until chicken is tender but not dry.

Yield: 6 servings

Per serving: 71 g water; 164 calories (10% from fat, 44% from protein, 46% from carb); 18 g protein; 2 g total fat; 1 g saturated fat; 1 g monounsaturated fat; 0 g polyunsaturated fat; 19 g carb; 0 g fiber; 18 g sugar; 123 mg phosphorus; 29 mg calcium; 1 mg iron; 38 mg sodium; 434 mg potassium; 200 IU vitamin A; 3 mg ATE vitamin E; 66 mg vitamin C; 44 mg cholesterol

Honey Mustard Chicken

If you are as big a fan of the combination of honey and mustard as I am, this will be as big a hit with you as it is with me.

4 chicken breasts

2 tablespoons (28 g) unsalted butter, melted

2 tablespoons (40 g) honey

2 teaspoons prepared mustard

Spray slow cooker with nonstick cooking spray and add chicken. Mix butter, honey, and mustard together in a small bowl. Pour sauce over chicken. Cover and cook on high 3 hours or on low 5 to 6 hours.

Yield: 4 servings

Per serving: 42 g water; 171 calories (40% from fat, 39% from protein, 21% from carb); 17 g protein; 8 g total fat; 4 g saturated fat; 2 g monounsaturated fat; 1 g polyunsaturated fat; 9 g carb; 0 g fiber; 9 g sugar; 96 mg phosphorus; 11 mg calcium; 1 mg iron; 37 mg sodium; 119 mg potassium; 190 IU vitamin A; 51 mg ATE vitamin E; 0 mg vitamin C; 59 mg cholesterol

Chicken in Wine Sauce

This is a French-style chicken dish with an onion-flavored wine sauce.

2 pounds (900 g) chicken breasts

10 ounces (280 g) low-sodium cream of mushroom soup (see recipe in Chapter 2)

2 tablespoons (15 g) low-sodium onion soup mix (see recipe in Chapter 2)

1 cup (235 ml) dry white wine

TIP

Serve over rice, pasta, or potatoes.

Put chicken in slow cooker. Combine remaining ingredients and pour over chicken. Cover and cook on low 6 to 8 hours.

Yield: 8 servings

Per serving: 134 g water; 214 calories (20% from fat, 72% from protein, 8% from carb); 33 g protein; 4 g total fat; 1 g saturated fat; 1 g monounsaturated fat; 1 g polyunsaturated fat; 4 g carb; 0 g fiber; 1 g sugar; 210 mg phosphorus; 22 mg calcium; 1 mg iron; 84 mg sodium; 365 mg potassium; 24 IU vitamin A; 8 mg ATE vitamin E; 0 mg vitamin C; 88 mg cholesterol

Herbed Chicken

These chicken breasts in an Asian-flavored sauce make a great meal with steamed broccoli and rice.

4 whole chicken breasts, halved

10 ounces (280 g) low-sodium cream of mushroom soup (see recipe in Chapter 2)

¼ cup (60 ml) low-sodium soy sauce (see recipe in Chapter 2)

¼ cup (60 ml) white wine vinegar

¼ cup (60 ml) water

¼ teaspoon minced garlic

1 teaspoon ginger

½ teaspoon oregano

1 tablespoon (15 g) brown sugar

Place chicken in slow cooker. Combine remaining ingredients and pour over chicken. Cover and cook on low 2 to 2½ hours. Uncover and cook 15 minutes more.

(continued on page 230)

Yield: 8 servings

Per serving: 71 g water; 75 calories (19% from fat, 51% from protein, 30% from carb); 9 g protein; 1 g total fat; 0 g saturated fat; 0 g monounsaturated fat; 0 g polyunsaturated fat; 5 g carb; 0 g fiber; 3 g sugar; 75 mg phosphorus; 13 mg calcium; 1 mg iron; 56 mg sodium; 214 mg potassium; 13 IU vitamin A; 2 mg ATE vitamin E; 0 mg vitamin C; 23 mg cholesterol

Chicken with Mushrooms

This chicken dish cooks up juicy and delicious in the slow cooker. And it makes its own sauce in the process.

4 boneless skinless chicken breasts

10 ounces (280 g) low-sodium cream of mushroom soup (see recipe in Chapter 2)

1 cup (230 g) sour cream

8 ounces (225 g) mushrooms, sliced

4 slices low-sodium bacon, cooked and crumbled

TIP

Serve over cooked rice or pasta.

Place chicken in slow cooker. In a mixing bowl, combine soup, sour cream, and mushrooms. Pour over chicken. Cover and cook on low 4 to 5 hours or until chicken is tender but not dry. Sprinkle with bacon before serving.

Yield: 4 servings

Per serving: 217 g water; 252 calories (46% from fat, 38% from protein, 16% from carb); 24 g protein; 13 g total fat; 6 g saturated fat; 4 g monounsaturated fat; 1 g polyunsaturated fat; 10 g carb; 1 g fiber; 3 g sugar; 324 mg phosphorus; 83 mg calcium; 1 mg iron; 156 mg sodium; 750 mg potassium; 249 IU vitamin A; 67 mg ATE vitamin E; 3 mg vitamin C; 76 mg cholesterol

Thai Chicken

If you like the flavors of Thai cooking, you'll love this. Ginger, peanut, cilantro, and lime juice provide lots of good flavor. Serve over rice.

6 chicken thighs, skin removed

¾ cup (195 g) low-sodium salsa (see recipe in Chapter 2)

½ cup (130 g) chunky peanut butter

1 tablespoon (15 ml) low-sodium soy sauce (see recipe in Chapter 2)

2 tablespoons (28 ml) lime juice

1 teaspoon grated fresh ginger

1 tablespoon (1 g) chopped cilantro

Put chicken in slow cooker. In a bowl, mix together remaining ingredients except cilantro. Cover and cook on low 8 to 9 hours or until chicken is cooked through but not dry. Skim off any fat. Remove chicken to a platter and serve topped with sauce. Sprinkle with cilantro.

Yield: 6 servings

Per serving: 67 g water; 195 calories (57% from fat, 28% from protein, 15% from carb); 14 g protein; 12 g total fat; 2 g saturated fat; 6 g monounsaturated fat; 3 g polyunsaturated fat; 7 g carb; 2 g fiber; 3 g sugar; 150 mg phosphorus; 23 mg calcium; 1 mg iron; 162 mg sodium; 363 mg potassium; 153 IU vitamin A; 8 mg ATE vitamin E; 2 mg vitamin C; 34 mg cholesterol

Polynesian Chicken

This is a slow cooker version of sweet and sour chicken. Serve over rice.

6 boneless chicken breasts

2 tablespoons (28 ml) oil

2 cups (475 ml) low-sodium chicken broth (see recipe in Chapter 2)

20 ounces (560 g) pineapple chunks

¼ cup (60 ml) cider vinegar

(continued on page 232)

2 tablespoons (30 g) brown sugar

2 teaspoons low-sodium soy sauce (see recipe in Chapter 2)

½ teaspoon minced garlic

1 cup (150 g) sliced green bell peppers

Heat oil in a large skillet over medium-high heat and brown chicken. Transfer chicken to slow cooker. Combine remaining ingredients and pour over chicken. Cover and cook on high 4 to 6 hours.

Yield: 6 servings

Per serving: 252 g water; 177 calories (29% from fat, 40% from protein, 31% from carb); 18 g protein; 6 g total fat; 1 g saturated fat; 1 g monounsaturated fat; 3 g polyunsaturated fat; 14 g carb; 1 g fiber; 12 g sugar; 161 mg phosphorus; 33 mg calcium; 1 mg iron; 102 mg sodium; 396 mg potassium; 143 IU vitamin A; 4 mg ATE vitamin E; 28 mg vitamin C; 41 mg cholesterol

Mandarin Chicken

This is a delightfully orange-flavored chicken.

4 boneless skinless chicken breasts

1 cup (160 g) thinly sliced onion

¼ cup (71 g) orange juice concentrate

1 teaspoon poultry seasoning

9 ounces (255 g) mandarin oranges, drained

TIP

Serve with rice or pasta.

Place chicken in slow cooker. Combine onion, orange juice concentrate, and poultry seasoning. Pour over chicken. Cover and cook on low 4 to 5 hours. Stir in mandarin oranges.

Yield: 4 servings

Per serving: 156 g water; 147 calories (6% from fat, 48% from protein, 46% from carb); 18 g protein; 1 g total fat; 0 g saturated fat; 0 g monounsaturated fat; 0 g polyunsaturated fat; 17 g carb; 1 g fiber; 14 g sugar; 168 mg phosphorus; 33 mg calcium; 1 mg iron; 52 mg sodium; 446 mg potassium; 636 IU vitamin A; 4 mg ATE vitamin E; 50 mg vitamin C; 41 mg cholesterol

Curried Chicken with Sweet Potatoes

The sweet potatoes make this more of an island curry than an Indian curry, but either way it's a great combination.

4 boneless skinless chicken breasts

¾ cup (120 g) chopped onion

2 sweet potatoes, cubed

¼ cup (60 ml) orange juice

½ teaspoon minced garlic

½ teaspoon pepper

4 teaspoons (8 g) curry powder

TIP *Serve over rice and top with your choice of condiments: sliced green onions, shredded coconut, peanuts, or raisins.*

Place chicken in slow cooker. Cover with onions and sweet potatoes. Combine orange juice, garlic, pepper, and curry powder. Pour over vegetables and chicken in slow cooker. Cover and cook on low 5 to 6 hours.

Yield: 4 servings

Per serving: 155 g water; 162 calories (8% from fat, 45% from protein, 47% from carb); 18 g protein; 1 g total fat; 0 g saturated fat; 0 g monounsaturated fat; 0 g polyunsaturated fat; 19 g carb; 3 g fiber; 6 g sugar; 182 mg phosphorus; 47 mg calcium; 2 mg iron; 69 mg sodium; 463 mg potassium; 11944 IU vitamin A; 4 mg ATE vitamin E; 19 mg vitamin C; 41 mg cholesterol

Curried Chicken with Tomatoes

I usually use mild curry powder, so this isn't as hot as you might think from the quantity. You can vary the amount and heat of the spices to suit your own taste.

1 can (28 ounces, or 785 g) no-salt-added diced tomatoes

4 boneless skinless chicken breasts, cut in half

1 cup (160 g) coarsely chopped onion

½ cup (75 g) chopped green bell pepper

(continued on page 234)

½ cup (65 g) chopped carrots

½ cup (50 g) chopped celery

2 tablespoons (12 g) curry powder

1 teaspoon turmeric

¼ teaspoon black pepper

1 tablespoon (13 g) sugar

Combine all ingredients in slow cooker. Cover and cook on high 2 to 3 hours or on low 5 to 6 hours.

Yield: 6 servings

Per serving: 213 g water; 110 calories (9% from fat, 45% from protein, 46% from carb); 13 g protein; 1 g total fat; 0 g saturated fat; 0 g monounsaturated fat; 0 g polyunsaturated fat; 13 g carb; 3 g fiber; 7 g sugar; 142 mg phosphorus; 72 mg calcium; 3 mg iron; 65 mg sodium; 529 mg potassium; 2063 IU vitamin A; 3 mg ATE vitamin E; 26 mg vitamin C; 27 mg cholesterol

TIP

Serve over couscous.

Mexican-Flavored Chicken and Vegetables

Chicken and vegetables are cooked in a tomato sauce with a Mexican flavor.

4 boneless skinless chicken breasts

1 cup (130 g) sliced carrots

2 cups (340 g) frozen lima beans

1 can (14 ounces, or 400 g) no-salt-added diced tomatoes

4 ounces (115 g) diced green chilies

1 teaspoon cumin

½ teaspoon garlic powder

TIP

This is good served with Spanish rice.

Place chicken in slow cooker. Place carrots and lima beans on top of chicken. Combine remaining ingredients and pour over vegetables. Cover and cook on low 3 to 4 hours or until chicken and vegetables are tender but not dry or mushy.

Yield: 4 servings

Per serving: 266 g water; 212 calories (6% from fat, 44% from protein, 49% from carb); 24 g protein; 2 g total fat; 0 g saturated fat; 0 g monounsaturated fat; 0 g polyunsaturated fat; 26 g carb; 8 g fiber; 5 g sugar; 277 mg phosphorus; 89 mg calcium; 4 mg iron; 221 mg sodium; 885 mg potassium; 5703 IU vitamin A; 4 mg ATE vitamin E; 27 mg vitamin C; 41 mg cholesterol

Asian Chicken

This gingery chicken and vegetable combination will spice up any meal.

6 boneless skinless chicken breasts, cubed

1 cup (130 g) diced carrots

¼ cup (40 g) chopped onion

½ cup (120 ml) low-sodium soy sauce (see recipe in Chapter 2)

¼ cup (60 ml) rice vinegar

¼ cup (30 g) sesame seeds

1 tablespoon (5.5 g) ground ginger

1 teaspoon sesame oil

1 cup (71 g) broccoli

1 cup (100 g) cauliflower

TIP

Serve over brown rice.

Combine all ingredients except broccoli and cauliflower in slow cooker. Cover and cook on low 3 to 5 hours. Stir in broccoli and cauliflower and cook 1 hour more.

Yield: 6 servings

Per serving: 135 g water; 157 calories (28% from fat, 50% from protein, 22% from carb); 20 g protein; 5 g total fat; 1 g saturated fat; 2 g monounsaturated fat; 2 g polyunsaturated fat; 8 g carb; 3 g fiber; 2 g sugar; 228 mg phosphorus; 91 mg calcium; 2 mg iron; 137 mg sodium; 422 mg potassium; 3700 IU vitamin A; 4 mg ATE vitamin E; 25 mg vitamin C; 41 mg cholesterol

French Chicken

This French country-style chicken, cooked in a tomato wine sauce with herbs, is a great weeknight meal. Serve with potatoes or rice and green beans.

2½ pounds (1.1 kg) chicken pieces, skinned

2 cups (360 g) chopped tomatoes

2 tablespoons (28 ml) white wine

1 bay leaf

¼ teaspoon pepper

½ teaspoon minced garlic

1 cup (160 g) chopped onion

½ cup (120 ml) low-sodium chicken broth (see recipe in Chapter 2)

1 teaspoon thyme

Combine all ingredients in slow cooker. Cover and cook on low 8 to 10 hours. Remove bay leaf before serving.

Yield: 4 servings

Per serving: 142 g water; 458 calories (59% from fat, 33% from protein, 7% from carb); 37 g protein; 29 g total fat; 8 g saturated fat; 12 g monounsaturated fat; 6 g polyunsaturated fat; 8 g carb; 2 g fiber; 2 g sugar; 35 mg phosphorus; 42 mg calcium; 3 mg iron; 164 mg sodium; 613 mg potassium; 1993 IU vitamin A; 0 mg ATE vitamin E; 28 mg vitamin C; 177 mg cholesterol

Chicken and Vegetable Casserole

Chicken, rice, and veggies cook in the slow cooker while you do something else.

4 chicken breast halves, skin removed

1 can (14 ounces, or 400 g) no-salt-added diced tomatoes

10 ounces (280 g) frozen green beans

2 cups (475 ml) low-sodium chicken broth (see recipe in Chapter 2)

1 cup (190 g) brown rice

1 cup (70 g) sliced mushrooms

½ cup (65 g) chopped carrots

1 cup (160 g) chopped onion

¼ teaspoon minced garlic

½ teaspoon poultry seasoning

Combine all ingredients in slow cooker. Cover and cook on high 2 hours, and then on low 3 to 5 hours.

Yield: 4 servings

Per serving: 411 g water; 211 calories (12% from fat, 39% from protein, 49% from carb); 21 g protein; 3 g total fat; 1 g saturated fat; 1 g monounsaturated fat; 1 g polyunsaturated fat; 26 g carb; 6 g fiber; 6 g sugar; 251 mg phosphorus; 92 mg calcium; 3 mg iron; 142 mg sodium; 692 mg potassium; 3311 IU vitamin A; 3 mg ATE vitamin E; 25 mg vitamin C; 44 mg cholesterol

Chicken and Broccoli Casserole

A simple casserole of chicken, broccoli, and rice, but the kind of thing that is great to come home to and not have to worry about cooking.

1 cup (185 g) uncooked long-grain rice

3 cups (700 ml) low-sodium chicken broth (see recipe in Chapter 2)

10 ounces (280 g) low-sodium cream of chicken soup

2 cups (280 g) chopped cooked chicken breast

¼ teaspoon garlic powder

1 teaspoon onion powder

1 cup (115 g) shredded Cheddar cheese

1 pound (455 g) frozen broccoli, thawed

Combine all ingredients except broccoli in slow cooker. Cook on high for 3 to 4 hours or on low 6 to 7 hours. One hour before end of cooking time, stir in broccoli.

(continued on page 238)

Yield: 8 servings

Per serving: 201 g water; 251 calories (28% from fat, 31% from protein, 41% from carb); 19 g protein; 8 g total fat; 4 g saturated fat; 2 g monounsaturated fat; 1 g polyunsaturated fat; 26 g carb; 2 g fiber; 2 g sugar; 258 mg phosphorus; 167 mg calcium; 2 mg iron; 212 mg sodium; 475 mg potassium; 528 IU vitamin A; 45 mg ATE vitamin E; 51 mg vitamin C; 48 mg cholesterol

Curried Chicken

Here's curried chicken in a tomatoey sauce. Use salsa as a shortcut and to kick up the flavor.

5 boneless skinless chicken breasts, cubed

1 cup (260 g) low-sodium salsa (see recipe in
   Chapter 2)

1 cup (160 g) chopped onion

1 tablespoon (6.3 g) curry powder

1 cup (230 g) sour cream

TIP

*Serve with brown rice
or couscous.*

Place the chicken in the slow cooker. In a medium bowl, combine salsa, onion, and curry powder. Pour the sauce over the meat in the cooker. Cover and cook on high for 3 hours or cook on low for 5 to 6 hours. Remove chicken to serving platter and cover to keep warm. Add sour cream to slow cooker and stir into salsa until well blended. Serve over the chicken.

Yield: 5 servings

Per serving: 161 g water; 173 calories (36% from fat, 44% from protein, 20% from carb); 19 g protein; 7 g total fat; 4 g saturated fat; 2 g monounsaturated fat; 1 g polyunsaturated fat; 9 g carb; 2 g fiber; 3 g sugar; 213 mg phosphorus; 84 mg calcium; 1 mg iron; 173 mg sodium; 444 mg potassium; 340 IU vitamin A; 53 mg ATE vitamin E; 5 mg vitamin C; 60 mg cholesterol

Chicken Rice Casserole

You can use any chicken pieces for this comfort food casserole—just be sure to remove the skin.

10 ounces (280 g) low-sodium cream of mushroom soup (see recipe in Chapter 2)

2 tablespoons (15 g) low-sodium onion soup mix (see recipe in Chapter 2)

2¼ cups (535 ml) water

1 cup (185 g) uncooked long-grain rice

6 boneless skinless chicken breasts

¼ teaspoon black pepper

Combine all ingredients in slow cooker. Cook on low 5 to 6 hours. Stir occasionally.

Yield: 6 servings

Per serving: 187 g water; 215 calories (8% from fat, 37% from protein, 55% from carb); 19 g protein; 2 g total fat; 1 g saturated fat; 0 g monounsaturated fat; 1 g polyunsaturated fat; 29 g carb; 1 g fiber; 1 g sugar; 199 mg phosphorus; 26 mg calcium; 2 mg iron; 65 mg sodium; 395 mg potassium; 19 IU vitamin A; 5 mg ATE vitamin E; 1 mg vitamin C; 43 mg cholesterol

Stuffed Chicken Breast

These chicken breasts, stuffed with cheese and wrapped in bacon, look and taste elegant. But they are really easy to make in the slow cooker.

3 boneless skinless chicken breasts

6 slices Swiss cheese

¼ teaspoon black pepper, or to taste

6 slices low-sodium bacon

¼ cup (60 ml) low-sodium chicken broth (see recipe in Chapter 2)

½ cup (120 ml) white cooking wine

(continued on page 240)

Cut each breast in half lengthwise. Flatten chicken to ½-inch (1.3 cm) thickness. Place a slice of cheese on top of each flattened breast. Sprinkle with pepper. Roll up and wrap with strip of bacon. Secure with toothpick. Place in slow cooker. Combine broth and wine. Pour into slow cooker. Cover. Cook on high 4 hours.

Yield: 6 servings

Per serving: 37 g water; 83 calories (43% from fat, 56% from protein, 1% from carb); 11 g protein; 4 g total fat; 1 g saturated fat; 2 g monounsaturated fat; 0 g polyunsaturated fat; 0 g carb; 0 g fiber; 0 g sugar; 114 mg phosphorus; 6 mg calcium; 0 mg iron; 89 mg sodium; 140 mg potassium; 11 IU vitamin A; 3 mg ATE vitamin E; 0 mg vitamin C; 29 mg cholesterol

Chicken and Stuffing

This is a great use for leftover chicken. It makes a big batch, so you can freeze some for later or if you prefer, cut all the quantities in half.

2½ cups (570 ml) low-sodium chicken broth (see recipe in Chapter 2)

1 cup (225 g) unsalted butter, melted

¼ cup (40 g) chopped onions

½ cup (50 g) celery, chopped

4 ounces (115 g) mushrooms, sliced

1 tablespoon (1.3 g) parsley

1¼ teaspoons sage

1 teaspoon poultry seasoning

½ teaspoon pepper

12 cups (600 g) bread cubes

½ cup (120 ml) egg substitute

10 ounces (280 g) low-sodium cream of chicken soup

6 cups (840 g) cubed cooked chicken breast

Combine all ingredients except bread, egg substitute, soup, and chicken in saucepan. Simmer for 10 minutes. Place bread cubes in large bowl. Combine egg substitute and soup. Stir into broth mixture until smooth. Pour over bread and toss well. Layer half of stuffing and then half of chicken into slow cooker. Repeat layers. Cover and cook on low 4½ to 5 hours.

Yield: 12 servings

Per serving: 270 g water; 422 calories (45% from fat, 27% from protein, 28% from carb); 29 g protein; 21 g total fat; 11 g saturated fat; 6 g monounsaturated fat; 2 g polyunsaturated fat; 29 g carb; 4 g fiber; 3 g sugar; 271 mg phosphorus; 106 mg calcium; 3 mg iron; 238 mg sodium; 749 mg potassium; 1171 IU vitamin A; 132 mg ATE vitamin E; 5 mg vitamin C; 101 mg cholesterol

Shredded Chicken

Like the shredded beef and pork recipes in Chapters 7 and 8, this one can be used in a number of dishes. It makes great sandwiches or Mexican chicken soup.

4 pounds (1.8 kg) chicken thighs, skinned

4 thyme sprigs

4 parsley stems

2 bay leaves

½ teaspoon garlic

½ teaspoon black peppercorns

4 cups (950 ml) low-sodium chicken broth (see recipe in Chapter 2)

Place chicken thighs in slow cooker. Make a bouquet garni by cutting an 8-inch (20 cm) square from a double thickness of 100-percent-cotton cheesecloth. Place thyme sprigs, parsley stems, bay leaves, garlic, and peppercorns in the center of the cheesecloth square. Bring up corners of the cheesecloth and tie with 100-percent-cotton kitchen string. Add bouquet garni to slow cooker. Pour broth over all. Cover and cook on low for 7 to 8 hours or on high for 3½ to 4 hours. Remove bouquet garni and discard. Using a slotted spoon, transfer chicken to a large bowl. When chicken is cool enough to handle, remove meat from bones. Using two forks, shred meat. Add enough of the cooking juices to moisten meat. Strain and reserve cooking juices to use for chicken stock. Place chicken and chicken stock in separate airtight containers and refrigerate for up to 3 days or freeze for up to 3 months.

(continued on page 242)

Yield: 12 servings

Per serving: 189 g water; 183 calories (31% from fat, 69% from protein, 0% from carb); 30 g protein; 6 g total fat; 2 g saturated fat; 2 g monounsaturated fat; 1 g polyunsaturated fat; 0 g carb; 0 g fiber; 0 g sugar; 263 mg phosphorus; 19 mg calcium; 2 mg iron; 174 mg sodium; 374 mg potassium; 99 IU vitamin A; 30 mg ATE vitamin E; 0 mg vitamin C; 125 mg cholesterol

Chicken Gumbo

A quick and easy gumbo that still has that traditional flavor. The long, slow cooking allows the spices to penetrate the chicken. If you like your gumbo hotter, add a little hot pepper sauce.

1 cup (160 g) chopped onion

1½ teaspoons minced garlic

1 cup (150 g) diced green bell pepper

1 cup (100 g) sliced okra

2 cups (360 g) chopped tomatoes

4 cups (950 ml) low-sodium chicken broth (see recipe in Chapter 2)

1 pound (455 g) boneless skinless chicken breast, cut into 1-inch (2.5 cm) pieces

2 teaspoons Cajun seasoning

Combine all ingredients in slow cooker. Cover and cook on low 8 to 10 hours or on high 3 to 4 hours. Serve over rice.

Yield: 6 servings

Per serving: 323 g water; 122 calories (11% from fat, 64% from protein, 25% from carb); 20 g protein; 1 g total fat; 0 g saturated fat; 0 g monounsaturated fat; 0 g polyunsaturated fat; 8 g carb; 2 g fiber; 2 g sugar; 202 mg phosphorus; 41 mg calcium; 1 mg iron; 150 mg sodium; 487 mg potassium; 480 IU vitamin A; 5 mg ATE vitamin E; 39 mg vitamin C; 44 mg cholesterol

Italian Chicken and Bean Stew

I suppose you could call this a kind of chicken minestrone, but whatever you call it, it has great Italian flavor and fills the house with a wonderful aroma while it's cooking.

2 boneless skinless chicken breasts, cut in 1½-inch (3.8 cm) pieces

19 ounces (530 g) no-salt-added cannellini beans, drained and rinsed

15 ounces (425 g) no-salt-added kidney beans, drained and rinsed

1 can (14 ounces, or 400 g) no-salt-added diced tomatoes, undrained

1 cup (100 g) chopped celery

1 cup (130 g) sliced carrots

1 teaspoon minced garlic

1 cup (235 ml) water

½ cup (120 ml) dry red wine

3 tablespoons (48 g) no-salt-added tomato paste

1 tablespoon (13 g) sugar

1¼ teaspoons Italian seasoning

Combine chicken, cannellini beans, kidney beans, tomatoes, celery, carrots, and garlic in slow cooker. Mix well. In medium bowl, thoroughly combine all remaining ingredients. Pour over chicken and vegetables and mix well. Cover and cook on low 5 to 6 hours or on high 3 hours.

Yield: 4 servings

Per serving: 431 g water; 412 calories (3% from fat, 31% from protein, 65% from carb); 31 g protein; 2 g total fat; 0 g saturated fat; 0 g monounsaturated fat; 1 g polyunsaturated fat; 66 g carb; 22 g fiber; 9 g sugar; 498 mg phosphorus; 208 mg calcium; 8 mg iron; 101 mg sodium; 1544 mg potassium; 5830 IU vitamin A; 2 mg ATE vitamin E; 18 mg vitamin C; 21 mg cholesterol

Sesame Chicken Thighs

This will remind you of the sesame chicken that is common at Chinese buffets. To make it even closer, bone the thighs and cut the meat into bite-size pieces.

3 pounds (1⅓ kg) chicken thighs, skin removed

1¼ cups (425 g) honey

1 cup (235 ml) low-sodium soy sauce (see recipe in Chapter 2)

½ cup (120 g) low-sodium ketchup

1 tablespoon (15 ml) canola oil

2 tablespoons (28 ml) sesame oil

1 teaspoon minced garlic

¼ cup (36 g) sesame seeds, toasted

Place chicken in slow cooker. Combine remaining ingredients except sesame seeds. Pour over chicken. Cover and cook on low 5 hours or on high 2½ hours. Sprinkle sesame seeds over top just before serving.

Yield: 8 servings

Per serving: 171 g water; 467 calories (27% from fat, 30% from protein, 43% from carb); 36 g protein; 14 g total fat; 3 g saturated fat; 5 g monounsaturated fat; 5 g polyunsaturated fat; 51 g carb; 1 g fiber; 47 g sugar; 357 mg phosphorus; 73 mg calcium; 3 mg iron; 252 mg sodium; 558 mg potassium; 251 IU vitamin A; 34 mg ATE vitamin E; 3 mg vitamin C; 141 mg cholesterol

North African Chicken

We like this dish relatively mild, so I tend to go easy on the red pepper flakes. For a hotter and more authentic dish, add more.

1½ cups (355 ml) low-sodium chicken broth (see recipe in Chapter 2)

½ cup (50 g) thinly sliced celery

1 cup (160 g) thinly sliced onions

½ cup (75 g) sliced red bell pepper

½ cup (75 g) sliced green bell pepper

½ cup (130 g) chunky peanut butter

8 chicken thighs, skinned

¼ teaspoon red pepper flakes

Combine broth, celery, onions, and peppers in slow cooker. Spread peanut butter over both sides of chicken pieces. Sprinkle with red pepper flakes. Place on top of vegetables in slow cooker. Cover and cook on low 5 to 6 hours.

Yield: 4 servings

Per serving: 233 g water; 331 calories (53% from fat, 31% from protein, 16% from carb); 25 g protein; 19 g total fat; 4 g saturated fat; 9 g monounsaturated fat; 5 g polyunsaturated fat; 13 g carb; 4 g fiber; 6 g sugar; 273 mg phosphorus; 43 mg calcium; 2 mg iron; 201 mg sodium; 621 mg potassium; 809 IU vitamin A; 16 mg ATE vitamin E; 42 mg vitamin C; 68 mg cholesterol

Chicken and Sun-Dried Tomatoes

I love the flavor of sun-dried tomatoes, so this is a favorite of mine. You could add some Italian spices if you like, but it's great even without them.

1 tablespoon (15 ml) olive oil

3 pounds (1⅓ kg) boneless skinless chicken breasts, cut into serving-size pieces

1 teaspoon minced garlic

¼ cup (60 ml) white wine

1¼ cups (295 ml) low-sodium chicken broth (see recipe in Chapter 2)

1 teaspoon basil

½ cup (55 g) oil-packed sun-dried tomatoes, cut into silvers

Heat oil in skillet over medium-high heat. Cook several pieces of chicken at a time but make sure not to crowd the skillet so the chicken can brown evenly. Transfer chicken to slow cooker as it finishes browning. Add garlic, wine, chicken broth, and basil to skillet. Bring to a boil. Scrape up

(continued on page 246)

any bits from the bottom of the pan. Pour over chicken. Scatter tomatoes over the top. Cover and cook on low 4 to 6 hours.

Yield: 8 servings

Per serving: 302 g water; 288 calories (21% from fat, 75% from protein, 4% from carb); 40 g protein; 5 g total fat; 1 g saturated fat; 2 g monounsaturated fat; 1 g polyunsaturated fat; 7 g carb; 0 g fiber; 5 g sugar; 350 mg phosphorus; 27 mg calcium; 6 mg iron; 141 mg sodium; 584 mg potassium; 132 IU vitamin A; 10 mg ATE vitamin E; 9 mg vitamin C; 99 mg cholesterol

Texas Chicken

I suppose you might say it's more Tex-Mex than Texas, but whatever you call it, it's definitely tasty.

1 cup (185 g) uncooked long-grain rice

1 can (28 ounces, or 785 g) no-salt-added diced tomatoes

1 can (6 ounces, or 170 g) no-salt-added tomato paste

3 cups (700 ml) water

2 tablespoons (15 g) Salt-Free Mexican Seasoning (see recipe in Chapter 2)

4 boneless skinless chicken breasts, cut into 1-inch (2.5 cm) cubes

1½ cups (240 g) chopped onions

1 cup (150 g) chopped green bell pepper

4 ounces (115 g) diced green chilies

1 teaspoon garlic powder

¼ teaspoon pepper

Combine all ingredients in large slow cooker. Cover and cook on low 4 to 4½ hours or until rice is tender and chicken is cooked.

Yield: 8 servings

Per serving: 285 g water; 178 calories (5% from fat, 27% from protein, 69% from carb); 12 g protein; 1 g total fat; 0 g saturated fat; 0 g monounsaturated fat; 0 g polyunsaturated fat; 31 g carb; 3 g fiber; 7 g sugar; 148 mg phosphorus; 66 mg calcium; 3 mg iron; 119 mg sodium; 617 mg potassium; 538 IU vitamin A; 2 mg ATE vitamin E; 37 mg vitamin C; 21 mg cholesterol

Barbecued Chicken Thighs

Here's an easy barbecued chicken for those days when you just don't have the time to stand over the grill.

3 pounds (1⅓ kg) chicken thighs, skin removed

½ cup (120 g) low-sodium ketchup

¼ cup (60 ml) water

½ cup (115 g) brown sugar

2 tablespoons (15 g) low-sodium onion soup mix (see recipe in Chapter 2)

Arrange chicken in slow cooker. Combine remaining ingredients and pour over chicken. Cover and cook on high 4 to 5 hours or on low 7 to 8 hours.

Yield: 6 servings

Per serving: 738 g water; 358 calories (23% from fat, 51% from protein, 26% from carb); 45 g protein; 9 g total fat; 2 g saturated fat; 3 g monounsaturated fat; 2 g polyunsaturated fat; 23 g carb; 0 g fiber; 22 g sugar; 392 mg phosphorus; 58 mg calcium; 3 mg iron; 223 mg sodium; 669 mg potassium; 334 IU vitamin A; 45 mg ATE vitamin E; 3 mg vitamin C; 188 mg cholesterol

Mexican Chicken

A creamy Mexican sauce makes this chicken special. To serve, spoon chicken and sauce over cooked rice. Top with shredded Cheddar cheese.

1 can (15 ounces, or 420 g) no-salt-added black beans, drained

2 cups (328 g) frozen corn

1 teaspoon minced garlic

¼ teaspoon cumin

1 cup (260 g) low-sodium salsa (see recipe in Chapter 2), divided

5 boneless skinless chicken breasts

8 ounces (225 g) fat-free cream cheese, cubed

(continued on page 248)

Combine beans, corn, garlic, cumin, and half of salsa in slow cooker. Arrange chicken breasts over top. Pour remaining salsa over top. Cover and cook on high 2 to 3 hours or on low 4 to 6 hours. Remove chicken and cut into bite-size pieces. Return to cooker. Stir in cream cheese. Cook on high until cream cheese melts.

Yield: 5 servings

Per serving: 235 g water; 363 calories (24% from fat, 34% from protein, 43% from carb); 31 g protein; 10 g total fat; 5 g saturated fat; 3 g monounsaturated fat; 1 g polyunsaturated fat; 40 g carb; 10 g fiber; 4 g sugar; 379 mg phosphorus; 100 mg calcium; 4 mg iron; 305 mg sodium; 813 mg potassium; 483 IU vitamin A; 86 mg ATE vitamin E; 4 mg vitamin C; 67 mg cholesterol

Chicken Creole

Cajun and Creole cooking can require a lot of preparation. This easy dish using leftover chicken is very easy to make, but it still has that great Creole taste.

2 tablespoons (28 g) unsalted butter

½ cup (75 g) chopped green bell pepper

¾ cup (120 g) chopped onions

½ cup (50 g) chopped celery

1 can (14 ounces, or 400 g) no-salt-added diced tomatoes

¼ teaspoon pepper

¼ teaspoon cayenne

1 cup (235 ml) water

2 cups (280 g) cubed cooked chicken breast

4 ounces (115 g) mushrooms, sliced

Melt butter in slow cooker set on high. Add green pepper, onions, celery, tomatoes, pepper, cayenne, and water. Cover and cook on high, about a half hour, while preparing remaining ingredients. Add chicken and mushrooms. Cover and cook on low 2 to 3 hours.

Yield: 6 servings

Per serving: 188 g water; 138 calories (37% from fat, 46% from protein, 17% from carb); 16 g protein; 6 g total fat; 3 g saturated fat; 2 g monounsaturated fat; 1 g polyunsaturated fat; 6 g carb; 2 g fiber; 3 g sugar; 147 mg phosphorus; 40 mg calcium; 1 mg iron; 54 mg sodium; 379 mg potassium; 297 IU vitamin A; 35 mg ATE vitamin E; 19 mg vitamin C; 50 mg cholesterol

Chicken Cacciatore

Here's a traditional Italian chicken dish made easy with the slow cooker. Serve with pasta.

1½ cups (240 g) sliced onions

3 pounds (1⅓ kg) chicken thighs, skin removed

½ teaspoon minced garlic

1 can (14 ounces, or 400 g) no-salt-added stewed tomatoes

1 cup (245 g) no-salt-added tomato sauce

½ teaspoon pepper

½ teaspoon oregano

½ teaspoon basil

1 bay leaf

½ cup (120 ml) dry white wine

Place onions in bottom of slow cooker. Lay chicken over onions. Combine remaining ingredients and pour over chicken. Cover and cook on low 6 to 6½ hours. Remove bay leaf before serving.

Yield: 5 servings

Per serving: 383 g water; 401 calories (26% from fat, 59% from protein, 15% from carb); 55 g protein; 11 g total fat; 3 g saturated fat; 3 g monounsaturated fat; 3 g polyunsaturated fat; 14 g carb; 2 g fiber; 8 g sugar; 507 mg phosphorus; 77 mg calcium; 4 mg iron; 248 mg sodium; 1054 mg potassium; 497 IU vitamin A; 54 mg ATE vitamin E; 16 mg vitamin C; 226 mg cholesterol

Slow Cooker Roast Turkey Breast

Turkey breasts can be dry, particularly if you are being careful about your sodium and buy one that doesn't have added broth. The slow cooker avoids that problem, given you a juicy breast every time.

1 turkey breast
2 tablespoons (15 g) low-sodium onion soup mix (see recipe in Chapter 2)

Rinse the turkey breast and pat dry. Cut off any excess skin but leave the skin covering the breast. Rub onion soup mix all over outside of the turkey and under the skin. Place in a slow cooker. Cover and cook on high for 1 hour and then set to low and cook for 7 hours.

Yield: 6 servings

Per serving: 111 g water; 173 calories (13% from fat, 87% from protein, 0% from carb); 35 g protein; 2 g total fat; 1 g saturated fat; 0 g monounsaturated fat; 1 g polyunsaturated fat; 0 g carb; 0 g fiber; 0 g sugar; 306 mg phosphorus; 18 mg calcium; 2 mg iron; 95 mg sodium; 458 mg potassium; 0 IU vitamin A; 0 mg ATE vitamin E; 0 mg vitamin C; 90 mg cholesterol

Asian Turkey

This is a modification of a recipe I found at Food.com (formerly Recipezaar.com) while looking for uses for leftover turkey. The original recipe called for turkey tenderloins, and it also could be made with boneless chicken breasts. The flavor is vaguely Thai.

3 cups (420 g) cooked turkey, cut into ¾-inch (1.9 cm) pieces
1 cup (150 g) red bell pepper, cut into short, thin strips
1¼ cups (295 ml) low-sodium chicken broth (see recipe in Chapter 2), divided
¼ cup (60 ml) low-sodium soy sauce (see recipe in Chapter 2)
¾ teaspoon minced garlic
½ teaspoon red pepper flakes
2 tablespoons (16 g) cornstarch
¼ cup (25 g) scallions, cut in ½-inch (1.3 cm) pieces

⅓ cup (87 g) peanut butter

½ cup (73 g) chopped unsalted dry roasted peanuts

½ cup (8 g) chopped fresh cilantro

Place turkey, bell pepper, 1 cup (235 ml) broth, soy sauce, garlic, and red pepper flakes in slow cooker. Cover and cook on low 3 hours. Mix cornstarch with remaining ¼ cup (60 ml) of broth in small bowl until smooth. Turn slow cooker to high. Stir in scallions, peanut butter, and cornstarch mixture. Cover and cook 30 minutes on high or until sauce is thickened. Serve over rice or angel hair pasta. Sprinkle with chopped nuts and cilantro.

Yield: 6 servings

Per serving: 132 g water; 307 calories (48% from fat, 37% from protein, 15% from carb); 29 g protein; 17 g total fat; 3 g saturated fat; 7 g monounsaturated fat; 5 g polyunsaturated fat; 12 g carb; 3 g fiber; 3 g sugar; 277 mg phosphorus; 43 mg calcium; 2 mg iron; 141 mg sodium; 548 mg potassium; 1115 IU vitamin A; 0 mg ATE vitamin E; 34 mg vitamin C; 54 mg cholesterol

Turkey Breast with Mushrooms

Turkey breast always ends up juicy and flavorful when you cook it in the slow cooker. If you want, you can thicken the sauce here with cornstarch to make gravy.

3 pounds (1⅓ kg) turkey breast, halved

1 tablespoon (14 g) unsalted butter, melted

2 tablespoons (2.6 g) parsley

¼ teaspoon oregano

¼ teaspoon black pepper

¼ cup (60 ml) dry white wine

8 ounces (225 g) mushrooms, sliced

Place turkey in slow cooker. Brush with butter. Mix together parsley, oregano, pepper, and wine. Pour over turkey. Top with mushrooms. Cover and cook on low 7 to 8 hours.

(continued on page 252)

Yield: 9 servings

Per serving: 142 g water; 197 calories (18% from fat, 79% from protein, 2% from carb); 36 g protein; 4 g total fat; 2 g saturated fat; 1 g monounsaturated fat; 1 g polyunsaturated fat; 1 g carb; 0 g fiber; 0 g sugar; 332 mg phosphorus; 22 mg calcium; 2 mg iron; 98 mg sodium; 552 mg potassium; 112 IU vitamin A; 11 mg ATE vitamin E; 2 mg vitamin C; 94 mg cholesterol

Cranberry-Orange Turkey Breast

This is a delightfully sweet and flavorful way to cook a turkey breast. Serve with brown or wild rice.

¼ cup (80 g) orange marmalade

1 pound (455 g) whole berry cranberry sauce

2 teaspoons (8 g) orange peel, grated

3 pounds (1⅓ kg) turkey breast

Combine marmalade, cranberries, and peel in a bowl. Place the turkey breast in the slow cooker and pour half the orange-cranberry mixture over the turkey. Cover and cook on low 7 to 8 hours or on high 3½ to 4 hours until turkey juices run clear. Add remaining half of orange-cranberry mixture for the last half hour of cooking. Remove turkey to warm platter and allow to rest for 15 minutes before slicing. Serve with orange-cranberry sauce.

Yield: 9 servings

Per serving: 145 g water; 272 calories (8% from fat, 53% from protein, 38% from carb); 36 g protein; 2 g total fat; 1 g saturated fat; 0 g monounsaturated fat; 1 g polyunsaturated fat; 26 g carb; 1 g fiber; 24 g sugar; 312 mg phosphorus; 24 mg calcium; 2 mg iron; 115 mg sodium; 478 mg potassium; 29 IU vitamin A; 0 mg ATE vitamin E; 2 mg vitamin C; 91 mg cholesterol

Cranberry Barbecued Turkey

Not your typical cranberry and turkey recipe, this one adds a barbecue flavor to turkey legs for a sweet and spicy treat.

3 pounds (1⅓ kg) turkey legs

1 pound (455 g) jellied cranberry sauce

½ cup (140 g) chili sauce (see recipe in Chapter 2)

2 tablespoons (28 ml) cider vinegar

½ teaspoon cinnamon

Place turkey in slow cooker. Combine remaining ingredients and pour over turkey. Cover and cook on low for 8 to 9 hours or on high for 4 to 5 hours.

Yield: 6 servings

Per serving: 143 g water; 242 calories (22% from fat, 47% from protein, 32% from carb); 28 g protein; 6 g total fat; 2 g saturated fat; 1 g monounsaturated fat; 2 g polyunsaturated fat; 19 g carb; 1 g fiber; 18 g sugar; 255 mg phosphorus; 29 mg calcium; 2 mg iron; 132 mg sodium; 409 mg potassium; 220 IU vitamin A; 0 mg ATE vitamin E; 3 mg vitamin C; 102 mg cholesterol

Barbecued Turkey Thighs

You can serve this as part of a main course or shred the meat and use it for sandwiches. Either way, you won't be disappointed.

3 pounds (1⅓ kg) turkey thighs, skin removed

¼ teaspoon black pepper

⅓ cup (113 g) molasses

⅓ cup (80 ml) cider vinegar

½ cup (120 g) low-sodium ketchup

3 tablespoons (45 ml) Worcestershire sauce

(continued on page 254)

½ teaspoon liquid smoke

2 tablespoons (20 g) minced onion

Place turkey in slow cooker. Combine remaining ingredients and pour over turkey. Cover and cook on low for 5 to 7 hours.

Yield: 6 servings

Per serving: 202 g water; 368 calories (24% from fat, 52% from protein, 25% from carb); 46 g protein; 9 g total fat; 3 g saturated fat; 2 g monounsaturated fat; 3 g polyunsaturated fat; 22 g carb; 0 g fiber; 16 g sugar; 446 mg phosphorus; 86 mg calcium; 5 mg iron; 267 mg sodium; 1106 mg potassium; 195 IU vitamin A; 0 mg ATE vitamin E; 18 mg vitamin C; 170 mg cholesterol

11

Healthy Beef Soups, Stews, and Chilis That Are Slow-Cooker Simple

I was originally going to have just one chapter for soups and stews. But there were so many great recipes that it became obvious it needed to be split up. And with good reason, because this is the kind of dish where the slow cooker really shines. From vegetable soup to chili, this beef soup chapter contains many of my favorites.

Two-Day Vegetable Soup

Don't let the name of this one discourage you. It does take two days to complete but probably less than 15 minutes of your actual time. The result is an old-fashioned soup that no one will even realize is salt-free. The broth has a great flavor, and the vegetables soak this up during the slow cooking.

1 pound (455 g) beef chuck

2 cups (475 ml) low-sodium beef broth (see recipe in Chapter 2)

½ cup (50 g) chopped celery

½ cup (80 g) chopped onion

½ teaspoon garlic powder

4 potatoes, diced

12 ounces (340 g) frozen mixed vegetables

4 ounces (115 g) mushrooms, sliced

1 cup (70 g) shredded cabbage

2 teaspoons (5 g) Salt-Free Seasoning Blend (see recipe in Chapter 2)

1 tablespoon (1.3 g) parsley

Day one: Place beef, broth, celery, and onion in slow cooker and cook on low for 8 to 10 hours. Cool. Remove meat from bones and chop. Skim fat from broth. Day two: Place meat and broth back in slow cooker. Add remaining ingredients and cook on low for 8 to 10 hours.

Yield: 8 servings

Per serving: 283 g water; 313 calories (33% from fat, 19% from protein, 48% from carb); 15 g protein; 11 g total fat; 5 g saturated fat; 5 g monounsaturated fat; 1 g polyunsaturated fat; 38 g carb; 5 g fiber; 4 g sugar; 202 mg phosphorus; 42 mg calcium; 2 mg iron; 104 mg sodium; 849 mg potassium; 1902 IU vitamin A; 0 mg ATE vitamin E; 18 mg vitamin C; 40 mg cholesterol

Easy Hamburger Soup

This soup is easy to prepare and uses simple ingredients, but it makes that kind of old-fashioned soup that takes you back in time.

3 cups (700 ml) low-sodium beef broth (see recipe in Chapter 2)

1 cup (100 g) chopped celery

2 cups (360 g) no-salt-added diced tomatoes

10 ounces (280 g) frozen mixed vegetables

1 cup (160 g) chopped onion

1 cup (130 g) sliced carrots

1 teaspoon pepper

1½ pounds (680 g) lean ground beef

½ cup (63 g) flour

½ cup (60 ml) water

Combine all ingredients except flour and water in slow cooker. Cover and cook on low for 8 hours. One hour before serving time, turn to high. Add flour to water and stir until smooth. Pour into pot and stir. Cook until thickened, about 1 hour.

Yield: 6 servings

Per serving: 384 g water; 378 calories (48% from fat, 28% from protein, 24% from carb); 26 g protein; 20 g total fat; 8 g saturated fat; 9 g monounsaturated fat; 1 g polyunsaturated fat; 22 g carb; 4 g fiber; 6 g sugar; 245 mg phosphorus; 74 mg calcium; 4 mg iron; 202 mg sodium; 781 mg potassium; 5793 IU vitamin A; 0 mg ATE vitamin E; 13 mg vitamin C; 78 mg cholesterol

Beef Stew with Dumplings

This is a simple stew with few ingredients, but the addition of parsley dumplings makes it special.

1 pound (455 g) beef round roast, cubed

2 tablespoons (15 g) low-sodium onion soup mix (see recipe in Chapter 2)

(continued on page 258)

6 cups (1.4 L) low-sodium beef broth (see recipe in Chapter 2)

1 cup (130 g) sliced carrot

2 potatoes, diced

1 cup (120 g) Heart-Healthy Baking Mix (see recipe in Chapter 2)

1 tablespoon (1.3 g) parsley

6 tablespoons (90 ml) skim milk

Place meat in cooker. Sprinkle with soup mix and then add broth and vegetables. Cover and cook on low for 6 to 8 hours. Combine baking mix, parsley, and milk. Drop by teaspoonfuls onto stew. Cover and cook on high until dumplings are done, 30 minutes to 1 hour.

Yield: 6 servings

Per serving: 425 g water; 287 calories (11% from fat, 35% from protein, 54% from carb); 25 g protein; 4 g total fat; 2 g saturated fat; 2 g monounsaturated fat; 0 g polyunsaturated fat; 39 g carb; 3 g fiber; 2 g sugar; 344 mg phosphorus; 144 mg calcium; 4 mg iron; 341 mg sodium; 1085 mg potassium; 3731 IU vitamin A; 23 mg ATE vitamin E; 13 mg vitamin C; 43 mg cholesterol

Cold Weather Beef Stew

This is a hearty stew, warming and filling. Just the sort of thing for a winter's evening with a loaf of freshly baked bread.

2 tablespoons (28 ml) olive oil

1½ pounds (680 g) beef round roast, cut in 1" cubes

1 can (28 ounces, or 785 g) no-salt-added diced tomatoes

1 cup (130 g) sliced carrots

1 cup (100 g) sliced celery

4 cups (950 ml) low-sodium beef broth (see recipe in Chapter 2)

½ cup (120 ml) red wine

1 cup (160 g) coarsely chopped onion

½ teaspoon black pepper

1 teaspoon oregano

½ teaspoon thyme

½ cup (75 g) pasta, small shape like orzo

Heat oil in a large skillet over medium-high heat. Brown beef and drain. Combine beef and remaining ingredients in slow cooker. Cover and cook on low 8 to 10 hours.

Yield: 8 servings

Per serving: 330 g water; 218 calories (31% from fat, 43% from protein, 26% from carb); 22 g protein; 7 g total fat; 2 g saturated fat; 4 g monounsaturated fat; 1 g polyunsaturated fat; 13 g carb; 2 g fiber; 4 g sugar; 250 mg phosphorus; 77 mg calcium; 3 mg iron; 159 mg sodium; 709 mg potassium; 2875 IU vitamin A; 0 mg ATE vitamin E; 12 mg vitamin C; 43 mg cholesterol

Pizza Soup

Here's another soup with the flavor of an old favorite—in this case, pizza.

1 pound (455 g) extra-lean ground beef

26 ounces (725 g) low-sodium spaghetti sauce

1 can (14 ounces, or 400 g) no-salt-added diced tomatoes

1½ cups (115 g) sliced mushrooms

¾ cup (113 g) diced green bell pepper

1 cup (160 g) chopped onion

1 cup (235 ml) water

1 tablespoon (6 g) Italian seasoning

4 ounces (115 g) part-skim mozzarella, shredded

Brown meat in a skillet over medium-high heat. Drain. Combine meat and remaining ingredients except cheese in slow cooker. Cover and cook on low 8 to 10 hours. Ladle into bowls and sprinkle with cheese.

Yield: 6 servings

(continued on page 260)

Per serving: 310 g water; 390 calories (50% from fat, 23% from protein, 27% from carb); 22 g protein; 22 g total fat; 8 g saturated fat; 11 g monounsaturated fat; 1 g polyunsaturated fat; 27 g carb; 6 g fiber; 18 g sugar; 278 mg phosphorus; 226 mg calcium; 3 mg iron; 216 mg sodium; 963 mg potassium; 1027 IU vitamin A; 24 mg ATE vitamin E; 37 mg vitamin C; 64 mg cholesterol

Taco Soup

Tacos in a bowl are sure to be a hit with young and old alike.

1 pound (455 g) extra-lean ground beef

1 cup (160 g) chopped onion

1 cup (150 g) chopped green bell pepper

2 tablespoons (15 g) Salt-Free Mexican Seasoning (see recipe in Chapter 2)

4 cups (950 ml) low-sodium vegetable juice

1 cup (260 g) low-sodium salsa (see recipe in Chapter 2)

TIP *Serve with your choice of traditional taco toppings, such as lettuce, tomato, shredded cheese, sour cream, etc.*

Brown meat in skillet over medium-high heat. Drain. Combine meat and remaining ingredients in slow cooker. Cover and cook on low 8-10 hours.

Yield: 6 servings

Per serving: 285 g water; 235 calories (50% from fat, 27% from protein, 23% from carb); 16 g protein; 13 g total fat; 5 g saturated fat; 6 g monounsaturated fat; 1 g polyunsaturated fat; 14 g carb; 3 g fiber; 8 g sugar; 160 mg phosphorus; 43 mg calcium; 2 mg iron; 245 mg sodium; 737 mg potassium; 2732 IU vitamin A; 0 mg ATE vitamin E; 67 mg vitamin C; 52 mg cholesterol

Old-Fashioned Vegetable Soup

Maybe it's not *just* like Grandma made, but it's close enough to make you remember.

1½ pounds (680 g) beef round steak, cut in ½-inch (1.3 cm) cubes

7 cups (1.6 L) low-sodium beef broth (see recipe in Chapter 2)

1 cup (130 g) thinly sliced carrots

1 pound (455 g) frozen peas

1 pound (455 g) frozen corn

1 pound (455 g) frozen lima beans

1 bay leaf

½ teaspoon dill weed

1 can (28 ounces, or 785 g) no-salt-added diced tomatoes

1 potato, diced

1 cup (160 g) chopped onion

½ teaspoon basil

¼ teaspoon pepper

Combine all ingredients in slow cooker. Cover and cook on high 4 hours or until vegetables are tender. Remove bay leaf before serving.

Yield: 10 servings

Per serving: 446 g water; 269 calories (11% from fat, 37% from protein, 52% from carb); 26 g protein; 3 g total fat; 1 g saturated fat; 1 g monounsaturated fat; 0 g polyunsaturated fat; 36 g carb; 8 g fiber; 8 g sugar; 336 mg phosphorus; 76 mg calcium; 5 mg iron; 317 mg sodium; 1065 mg potassium; 3283 IU vitamin A; 0 mg ATE vitamin E; 21 mg vitamin C; 39 mg cholesterol

Minestrone

This is the traditional Italian soup, with beef added to make it even more of a meal in a bowl.

2 pounds (900 g) extra-lean ground beef

1 cup (160 g) chopped onion

½ teaspoon minced garlic

1 can (28 ounces, or 785 g) no-salt-added diced tomatoes

2 cups (512 g) kidney beans, cooked or canned without salt

½ cup (50 g) sliced celery

1½ cups (180 g) diced zucchini

2 cups (475 ml) low-sodium beef broth (see recipe in Chapter 2)

2 teaspoons Italian seasoning

Brown meat in skillet over medium-high heat. Drain. Combine meat and remaining ingredients in slow cooker. Cover and cook on low 8 to 10 hours.

Yield: 10 servings

Per serving: 239 g water; 284 calories (50% from fat, 31% from protein, 19% from carb); 22 g protein; 16 g total fat; 6 g saturated fat; 7 g monounsaturated fat; 1 g polyunsaturated fat; 13 g carb; 5 g fiber; 3 g sugar; 213 mg phosphorus; 61 mg calcium; 4 mg iron; 107 mg sodium; 656 mg potassium; 168 IU vitamin A; 0 mg ATE vitamin E; 12 mg vitamin C; 63 mg cholesterol

Alphabet Soup

This is just like when you were a child, only better!

1 pound (455 g) beef round roast, cubed

1 can (14 ounces, or 400 g) no-salt-added diced tomatoes

1 cup (245 g) no-salt-added tomato sauce

1 cup (235 ml) water

2 tablespoons (15 g) low-sodium onion soup mix (see recipe in Chapter 2)

1 pound (455 g) frozen mixed vegetables

½ cup (75 g) alphabet pasta

Brown meat in skillet over medium-high heat. Drain. Combine meat and remaining ingredients except pasta in slow cooker. Cover and cook on low 6 to 8 hours. Turn to high, add pasta, and cook until pasta is done, 30 minutes to 1 hour.

Yield: 5 servings

Per serving: 307 g water; 290 calories (13% from fat, 38% from protein, 50% from carb); 27 g protein; 4 g total fat; 1 g saturated fat; 1 g monounsaturated fat; 0 g polyunsaturated fat; 35 g carb; 6 g fiber; 7 g sugar; 316 mg phosphorus; 79 mg calcium; 4 mg iron; 106 mg sodium; 849 mg potassium; 4130 IU vitamin A; 0 mg ATE vitamin E; 16 mg vitamin C; 45 mg cholesterol

Beef Borscht

Borscht is a traditional soup from the Ukraine and many Eastern European countries. More often a vegetarian soup, this version contains beef and other vegetables in addition to the usual beets, making it a hearty main dish.

2 tablespoons (28 ml) olive oil

1 pound (455 g) beef round roast, cut in 1-inch (2.5 cm) cubes

4 potatoes, cubed

1 cup (130 g) sliced carrot

1 cup (225 g) diced beets

1 can (14 ounces, or 400 g) no-salt-added diced tomatoes

1½ cups (240 g) chopped onion

2 cups (180 g) coarsely chopped cabbage

1 teaspoon garlic powder

2 cups (475 ml) low-sodium beef broth (see recipe in Chapter 2)

TIP

Serve topped with a dollop of sour cream.

(continued on page 264)

Heat oil in a large skillet over medium-high heat. Brown meat and drain. Combine meat and remaining ingredients in slow cooker. Cover and cook on low 8 to 10 hours.

Yield: 8 servings

Per serving: 375 g water; 276 calories (19% from fat, 26% from protein, 55% from carb); 18 g protein; 6 g total fat; 1 g saturated fat; 3 g monounsaturated fat; 1 g polyunsaturated fat; 39 g carb; 6 g fiber; 7 g sugar; 278 mg phosphorus; 74 mg calcium; 4 mg iron; 142 mg sodium; 1336 mg potassium; 2788 IU vitamin A; 0 mg ATE vitamin E; 33 mg vitamin C; 28 mg cholesterol

Chili Con Carne

This makes a moderately spicy chili with fairly traditional flavors and ingredients.

2 pounds (900 g) extra lean ground beef

1 cup (160 g) chopped onion

1 cup (150 g) chopped red bell pepper

½ teaspoon minced garlic

½ teaspoon black pepper

1 teaspoon cumin

1 teaspoon cayenne

1 tablespoon (7.5 g) chili powder

3 cups (700 ml) water

1 can (6 ounces, or 170 g) no-salt-added tomato paste

4 cups (720 g) no-salt-added diced tomatoes

4 cups (1 kg) kidney beans, cooked or canned without salt

Brown beef in skillet over medium-high heat. Drain. Combine beef and remaining ingredients in slow cooker. Cover and cook on low 8 to 10 hours.

Yield: 8 servings

Per serving: 377 g water; 455 calories (38% from fat, 34% from protein, 28% from carb); 39 g protein; 19 g total fat; 7 g saturated fat; 8 g monounsaturated fat; 1 g polyunsaturated fat; 33 g carb; 11 g fiber; 7 g sugar; 359 mg phosphorus; 126 mg calcium; 8 mg iron; 134 mg sodium; 1264 mg potassium; 1424 IU vitamin A; 0 mg ATE vitamin E; 43 mg vitamin C; 92 mg cholesterol

Multi-Bean Chili

This hearty chili goes together quickly using mostly canned ingredients. And it makes a crowd-size batch. Just make sure to get the salt-free varieties of these canned goods, or your sodium content will go right through the roof.

½ pound (225 g) extra-lean ground beef

½ pound (225 g) sausage (see recipe in Chapter 2)

1 cup (160 g) chopped onion

1 can (15 ounces, or 420 g) kidney beans, no-salt-added, undrained

1 can (15 ounces, or 420 g) black beans, no-salt-added, undrained

1 can (15 ounces, or 420 g) pinto beans, no-salt-added, undrained

1 can (14 ounces, or 400 g) no-salt-added stewed tomatoes, undrained

1 can (15 ounces, or 420 g) no-salt-added tomato sauce

2 tablespoons (15 g) Salt-Free Mexican Seasoning (see recipe in Chapter 2)

3 tablespoons (45 g) brown sugar

3 tablespoons (23 g) chili powder

Brown beef, sausage, and onion together in a nonstick skillet over medium-high heat. Combine meat mixture and remaining ingredients in large slow cooker. Mix well. Cook on low 8 to 10 hours.

Yield: 12 servings

Per serving: 146 g water; 368 calories (24% from fat, 23% from protein, 52% from carb); 22 g protein; 10 g total fat; 4 g saturated fat; 4 g monounsaturated fat; 1 g polyunsaturated fat; 49 g carb; 14 g fiber; 8 g sugar; 330 mg phosphorus; 97 mg calcium; 5 mg iron; 204 mg sodium; 1119 mg potassium; 740 IU vitamin A; 0 mg ATE vitamin E; 12 mg vitamin C; 28 mg cholesterol

Beef and Lentil Soup

For some reason, we only began eating lentils recently. They just weren't something that we had ever used. Now we like them a variety of ways, this being one of the more popular ones.

1 pound (455 g) extra-lean ground beef

1 cup (160 g) chopped onion

2 potatoes, cubed

1 cup (130 g) sliced carrot

1 cup (100 g) sliced celery

1 cup (192 g) dry lentils

6 cups (1.4 L) low-sodium beef broth (see recipe in Chapter 2)

1 can (14 ounces, or 400 g) no-salt-added diced tomatoes

½ teaspoon black pepper

Brown meat in a nonstick skillet over medium-high heat. Drain. Combine meat and remaining ingredients in slow cooker. Cover and cook on low 8 to 10 hours.

Yield: 8 servings

Per serving: 394 g water; 264 calories (35% from fat, 26% from protein, 38% from carb); 17 g protein; 10 g total fat; 4 g saturated fat; 4 g monounsaturated fat; 1 g polyunsaturated fat; 26 g carb; 5 g fiber; 4 g sugar; 228 mg phosphorus; 60 mg calcium; 4 mg iron; 177 mg sodium; 978 mg potassium; 2814 IU vitamin A; 0 mg ATE vitamin E; 16 mg vitamin C; 39 mg cholesterol

Beef and Black-Eyed Pea Soup

This is a simple meal but one that has become a favorite with our family.

1 pound (455 g) dry black-eyed peas

4 cups (950 ml) low-sodium beef broth (see recipe in Chapter 2)

1 cup (130 g) sliced carrots

1 cup (160 g) chopped onion

2 pounds (900 g) beef round roast, cut into 1" cubes

½ teaspoon black pepper

Combine all ingredients in slow cooker. Cover and cook on low 8 to 10 hours.

Yield: 6 servings

Per serving: 359 g water; 324 calories (18% from fat, 53% from protein, 29% from carb); 42 g protein; 6 g total fat; 2 g saturated fat; 3 g monounsaturated fat; 0 g polyunsaturated fat; 23 g carb; 6 g fiber; 6 g sugar; 457 mg phosphorus; 73 mg calcium; 5 mg iron; 207 mg sodium; 1025 mg potassium; 3644 IU vitamin A; 0 mg ATE vitamin E; 5 mg vitamin C; 76 mg cholesterol

Southwestern Stew

Here's a great stew of beef and vegetables with just enough cumin to give it a Southwestern flavor.

2 tablespoons (28 ml) olive oil

2 pounds (900 g) beef round steak, cubed

1 cup (160 g) diced onion

½ teaspoon minced garlic

1½ cups (355 ml) water

1 tablespoon (1.3 g) parsley

1 teaspoon cumin

½ cup (65 g) sliced carrots

1 can (14 ounces, or 400 g) no-salt-added diced tomatoes

1 pound (455 g) frozen green beans

1 pound (455 g) frozen corn

4 ounces (115 g) diced green chilies

2 cups (240 g) diced zucchini

Heat oil in a large skillet over medium-high heat. Brown meat, onion, and garlic until meat is no longer pink. Place in slow cooker. Stir in remaining ingredients. Cover and cook on high 30 minutes. Reduce heat to low and cook 4 to 6 hours.

(continued on page 268)

Yield: 6 servings

Per serving: 605 g water; 350 calories (25% from fat, 44% from protein, 31% from carb); 39 g protein; 10 g total fat; 2 g saturated fat; 5 g monounsaturated fat; 1 g polyunsaturated fat; 28 g carb; 6 g fiber; 7 g sugar; 445 mg phosphorus; 83 mg calcium; 5 mg iron; 116 mg sodium; 1167 mg potassium; 2535 IU vitamin A; 0 mg ATE vitamin E; 31 mg vitamin C; 86 mg cholesterol

Beef Barley Stew

This stew is full of beef and vegetables and flavor. It's a favorite around our house.

2 tablespoons (28 ml) olive oil

1½ pounds (680 g) beef round steak, cubed

1½ cups (240 g) diced onion

½ cup (75 g) chopped green bell pepper

1 can (28 ounces, or 785 g) no-salt-added diced tomatoes

½ cup (120 g) low-sodium ketchup

⅔ cup (133 g) pearl barley

½ teaspoon pepper

1 tablespoon (7 g) paprika

10 ounces (280 g) frozen lima beans

3 cups (700 ml) water

1 cup (230 g) sour cream

Heat oil in a skillet over medium-high heat. Brown beef cubes and then add onion and green pepper. Sauté until vegetable begin to soften. Pour into slow cooker. Add remaining ingredients except sour cream. Cover and cook on high 5 hours. Stir in sour cream before serving.

Yield: 8 servings

Per serving: 340 g water; 318 calories (29% from fat, 32% from protein, 38% from carb); 26 g protein; 11 g total fat; 4 g saturated fat; 5 g monounsaturated fat; 1 g polyunsaturated fat; 31 g carb; 7 g fiber; 8 g sugar; 333 mg phosphorus; 95 mg calcium; 4 mg iron; 89 mg sodium; 905 mg potassium; 927 IU vitamin A; 30 mg ATE vitamin E; 24 mg vitamin C; 60 mg cholesterol

Beef and Rice Stew

This is a hearty stew containing rice, potatoes, and beans—the kind of thing a guy really likes.

½ cup (80 g) sliced onion

1 pound (455 g) extra-lean ground beef

½ cup (93 g) uncooked long-grain rice

3 potatoes, diced

1 cup (100 g) diced celery

2 cups (508 g) no-salt-added kidney beans, drained

¼ teaspoon pepper

½ teaspoon chili powder

1 teaspoon Worcestershire sauce

1 cup (245 g) no-salt-added tomato sauce

Brown onions and ground beef in skillet over medium-high heat. Drain. Layer beef mixture and remaining ingredients in slow cooker in order given. Cover and cook on low 6 hours or until potatoes and rice are cooked.

Yield: 6 servings

Per serving: 301 g water; 458 calories (26% from fat, 22% from protein, 52% from carb); 25 g protein; 14 g total fat; 5 g saturated fat; 6 g monounsaturated fat; 1 g polyunsaturated fat; 59 g carb; 10 g fiber; 4 g sugar; 342 mg phosphorus; 70 mg calcium; 6 mg iron; 93 mg sodium; 1509 mg potassium; 289 IU vitamin A; 0 mg ATE vitamin E; 25 mg vitamin C; 52 mg cholesterol

Vegetable Beef Soup

This is a quick and easy soup with great flavor. This is the kind of meal that is great to come home to after a winter's day.

2 pounds (900 g) beef round roast, cut into bite-size pieces

15 ounces (425 g) frozen corn

(continued on page 270)

15 ounces (425 g) frozen green beans

32 ounces (905 g) no-salt-added stewed tomatoes

½ cup (80 g) chopped onion

1 potato, diced

2 cups (475 ml) low-sodium beef broth (see recipe in Chapter 2)

Combine all ingredients in slow cooker. Cover and cook on low for 8 to 10 hours until meat is tender and vegetables soft.

Yield: 6 servings

Per serving: 495 g water; 371 calories (17% from fat, 43% from protein, 41% from carb); 41 g protein; 7 g total fat; 2 g saturated fat; 3 g monounsaturated fat; 1 g polyunsaturated fat; 39 g carb; 7 g fiber; 11 g sugar; 498 mg phosphorus; 123 mg calcium; 7 mg iron; 174 mg sodium; 1532 mg potassium; 905 IU vitamin A; 0 mg ATE vitamin E; 36 mg vitamin C; 76 mg cholesterol

Hamburger and Bean Stew

This hearty bean soup with ground beef is definitely a meal in a bowl.

1 pound (455 g) extra-lean ground beef, cooked and drained

2 cups (508 g) kidney beans, cooked or canned without salt

2 cups (480 g) chickpeas, cooked or canned without salt

10 ounces (280 g) yellow beans

10 ounces (280 g) frozen lima beans

1 cup (240 g) low-sodium ketchup

1 cup (225 g) brown sugar

1 tablespoon (11 g) prepared mustard

Combine all ingredients in slow cooker. Cover and simmer on high 2 to 3 hours.

Yield: 8 servings

Per serving: 186 g water; 441 calories (22% from fat, 19% from protein, 59% from carb); 21 g protein; 11 g total fat; 4 g saturated fat; 4 g monounsaturated fat; 1 g polyunsaturated fat; 67 g carb; 10 g fiber; 34 g sugar; 266 mg phosphorus; 96 mg calcium; 5 mg iron; 248 mg sodium; 864 mg potassium; 395 IU vitamin A; 0 mg ATE vitamin E; 15 mg vitamin C; 39 mg cholesterol

Borscht Stew

Full of meaty short ribs and the usual borscht ingredients like beets and cabbage, this stew would warm even a Ukrainian night.

2 pounds (900 g) beef short ribs

2 cups (260 g) sliced carrots

1½ cups (225 g) turnips, peeled, sliced, and cut in strips

2 cups (450 g) beets, peeled, sliced, and cut in strips

1 medium onion, sliced

1 cup (100 g) sliced celery

3 cups (700 ml) water

1 can (6 ounces, or 170 g) no-salt-added tomato paste

1 tablespoon (13 g) sugar

1 tablespoon (15 ml) vinegar

¼ teaspoon pepper

4 cups (360 g) cabbage, cut in wedges

TIP

Pass sour cream to top each serving.

In a large skillet over medium heat, slowly brown the short ribs on all sides. Drain off the excess fat. Place the sliced carrots, turnips, beets, onion, and celery in slow cooker. Place short ribs on top of the vegetables. Stir together the water, tomato paste, sugar, vinegar, and pepper; mix well. Pour the mixture over the ribs. Cover and cook on low for 10 to 12 hours. Just before serving, skim the excess fat from stew. Fifteen minutes before serving, cook cabbage wedges in a 3-quart (2.8 L) saucepan in a large amount of boiling salted water until tender, 10 to 12 minutes. Drain cabbage well. Transfer ribs, vegetables, and cabbage to individual soup bowls.

(continued on page 272)

Yield: 6 servings

Per serving: 463 g water; 364 calories (39% from fat, 35% from protein, 26% from carb); 32 g protein; 16 g total fat; 7 g saturated fat; 7 g monounsaturated fat; 1 g polyunsaturated fat; 24 g carb; 6 g fiber; 15 g sugar; 372 mg phosphorus; 97 mg calcium; 6 mg iron; 292 mg sodium; 1297 mg potassium; 7756 IU vitamin A; 0 mg ATE vitamin E; 40 mg vitamin C; 89 mg cholesterol

12

Low-Fat and Great Tasting Chicken and Turkey Soups, Stews, and Chilis

We probably make soups and stews more than any other kind of recipe in the slow cooker. This chapter contains a variety of chicken and turkey recipes, from the traditional things like chicken rice soup (including a couple of interesting variations) to several chicken and turkey chilis.

Chicken Corn Soup

When I was growing up in north central Maryland, Amish chicken corn soup was served at all the volunteer fire company carnivals and fund raisers. This easy version reminds me of that, but it includes potatoes to make it a more hearty full meal.

1 pound (455 g) boneless skinless chicken breast, cubed

1 cup (160 g) chopped onion

½ teaspoon minced garlic

¾ cup (98 g) sliced carrots

½ cup (50 g) chopped celery

2 medium potatoes, cubed

12 ounces (340 g) cream-style corn

12 ounces (340 g) frozen corn

2 cups (475 ml) low-sodium chicken broth (see recipe in Chapter 2)

¼ teaspoon pepper

Combine all ingredients in slow cooker. Cover and cook on low 8 to 9 hours or until chicken is tender.

Yield: 6 servings

Per serving: 369 g water; 278 calories (6% from fat, 32% from protein, 62% from carb); 23 g protein; 2 g total fat; 0 g saturated fat; 0 g monounsaturated fat; 1 g polyunsaturated fat; 45 g carb; 5 g fiber; 7 g sugar; 309 mg phosphorus; 43 mg calcium; 2 mg iron; 127 mg sodium; 1049 mg potassium; 2800 IU vitamin A; 5 mg ATE vitamin E; 19 mg vitamin C; 44 mg cholesterol

Chicken Rice Soup

This is classic comfort food: chicken and rice in a nice broth. It's sure to warm you and make you feel like everything is all right.

1 pound (455 g) boneless skinless chicken breast, cut into 1-inch (2.5 cm) pieces

5 cups (1.2 L) low-sodium chicken broth (see recipe in Chapter 2)

8 ounces (225 g) mushrooms, sliced

¾ cup (75 g) sliced celery

½ cup (65 g) sliced carrots

½ cup (93 g) uncooked long-grain rice

¼ cup (25 g) chopped scallions

½ teaspoon ground sage

¼ teaspoon black pepper

Combine all ingredients in slow cooker. Cover and cook on low for 7 to 9 hours.

Yield: 6 servings

Per serving: 318 g water; 149 calories (14% from fat, 62% from protein, 24% from carb); 23 g protein; 2 g total fat; 1 g saturated fat; 1 g monounsaturated fat; 1 g polyunsaturated fat; 9 g carb; 1 g fiber; 2 g sugar; 255 mg phosphorus; 31 mg calcium; 1 mg iron; 129 mg sodium; 569 mg potassium; 1908 IU vitamin A; 5 mg ATE vitamin E; 4 mg vitamin C; 44 mg cholesterol

Chicken and Wild Rice Soup

This is a hearty winter soup that will warm you on a cold day.

2 tablespoons (28 g) unsalted butter

½ cup (80 g) wild rice

6 cups (1.4 L) low-sodium chicken broth (see recipe in Chapter 2)

½ cup (80 g) minced onions

½ cup (50 g) minced celery

½ pound (225 g) butternut squash, peeled, seeded, and cut in ½-inch (1.3 cm) cubes

3 cups (420 g) chopped cooked chicken

Melt butter in small skillet. Add rice and sauté for 10 minutes over low heat. Transfer to slow cooker. Add all remaining ingredients except chicken to cooker. Cover and cook on low 4 to 6 hours. One hour before serving, stir in chicken.

(continued on page 276)

Yield: 8 servings

Per serving: 260 g water; 154 calories (30% from fat, 39% from protein, 32% from carb); 15 g protein; 5 g total fat; 2 g saturated fat; 1 g monounsaturated fat; 1 g polyunsaturated fat; 12 g carb; 1 g fiber; 2 g sugar; 176 mg phosphorus; 35 mg calcium; 1 mg iron; 156 mg sodium; 358 mg potassium; 3162 IU vitamin A; 33 mg ATE vitamin E; 8 mg vitamin C; 47 mg cholesterol

Mexican Chicken Soup

This soup is Mexican in flavor, even though it's probably not anywhere near anything you'd actually find in Mexico. Still, we like it.

1 cup (160 g) chopped onion

1 cup (100 g) thinly sliced celery

½ teaspoon minced garlic

1 tablespoon (15 ml) oil

1½ pounds (680 g) boneless, skinless chicken breasts, cubed

3 cups (700 ml) low-sodium chicken broth (see recipe in Chapter 2)

2 cups (520 g) low-sodium salsa (see recipe in Chapter 2)

2 large potatoes, cubed

4 ounces (115 g) diced green chilies

4 ounces (115 g) Cheddar cheese, shredded

Combine onions, celery, garlic, oil, chicken, and broth in slow cooker. Cover and cook on low 2½ hours until chicken is no longer pink. Add salsa, potatoes, chilies, and cheese and combine well. Cook on low 2 to 4 hours or until potatoes are fully cooked.

Yield: 8 servings

Per serving: 326 g water; 262 calories (27% from fat, 40% from protein, 33% from carb); 27 g protein; 8 g total fat; 4 g saturated fat; 2 g monounsaturated fat; 1 g polyunsaturated fat; 21 g carb; 3 g fiber; 4 g sugar; 334 mg phosphorus; 155 mg calcium; 2 mg iron; 400 mg sodium; 925 mg potassium; 407 IU vitamin A; 42 mg ATE vitamin E; 17 mg vitamin C; 64 mg cholesterol

Chicken Vegetable Soup

This is a quick and easy soup that's very low in fat and very high in flavor.

1 can (28 ounces, or 785 g) no-salt-added diced tomatoes, undrained

2 cups (475 ml) low-sodium chicken broth (see recipe in Chapter 2)

12 ounces (340 g) frozen corn

½ cup (50 g) chopped celery

1 can (6 ounces, or 170 g) no-salt-added tomato paste

¼ cup (48 g) lentils, rinsed

1 tablespoon (15 ml) Worcestershire sauce

1 teaspoon parsley flakes

1 teaspoon marjoram

1 cup (140 g) cubed cooked chicken breast

Combine all ingredients in slow cooker except chicken. Cover and cook on low 6 to 8 hours. Stir in chicken 1 hour before the end of the cooking time.

Yield: 6 servings

Per serving: 297 g water; 146 calories (9% from fat, 31% from protein, 60% from carb); 12 g protein; 2 g total fat; 0 g saturated fat; 0 g monounsaturated fat; 0 g polyunsaturated fat; 24 g carb; 5 g fiber; 9 g sugar; 163 mg phosphorus; 68 mg calcium; 3 mg iron; 144 mg sodium; 780 mg potassium; 651 IU vitamin A; 1 mg ATE vitamin E; 25 mg vitamin C; 20 mg cholesterol

Chicken Vegetable Soup with Noodles

The addition of egg noodles makes this chicken vegetable soup even more filling. And the taste is excellent.

2 cups (320 g) chopped onion
2 cups (260 g) sliced carrots

(continued on page 278)

2 cups (200 g) sliced celery

10 ounces (280 g) frozen peas

¼ teaspoon black pepper

½ teaspoon basil

¼ teaspoon thyme

2 tablespoons (2.6 g) parsley

2 cups (475 ml) water

3 pounds (1⅓ kg) chicken, cut-up

1 cup (160 g) uncooked egg noodles

Place all ingredients in slow cooker except chicken and noodles. Remove skin and any fat from chicken pieces. Then place chicken in cooker on top of the rest of the ingredients. Cover and cook on high 4 to 6 hours. One hour before serving, remove chicken. Cool slightly. Cut meat from bones. Return meat to cooker and add noodles. Cover and cook on high 1 hour.

Yield: 6 servings

Per serving: 421 g water; 382 calories (18% from fat, 57% from protein, 25% from carb); 53 g protein; 8 g total fat; 2 g saturated fat; 2 g monounsaturated fat; 2 g polyunsaturated fat; 24 g carb; 7 g fiber; 7 g sugar; 493 mg phosphorus; 90 mg calcium; 4 mg iron; 390 mg sodium; 931 mg potassium; 8505 IU vitamin A; 36 mg ATE vitamin E; 18 mg vitamin C; 159 mg cholesterol

Italian Chili

It's kind of chili, but the spices and the pesto give it a definite Italian flavor. Whatever you call it, I think you'll like it.

1 tablespoon (15 ml) olive oil

½ pound (225 g) boneless skinless chicken breast, cut into bite-size pieces

½ cup (80 g) finely chopped onion

1½ cups (195 g) finely chopped carrots

½ cup (75 g) finely chopped red bell pepper

½ cup (50 g) thinly sliced celery

4 ounces (115 g) diced green chilies

½ teaspoon oregano

½ teaspoon basil

¼ teaspoon black pepper

1 pound (455 g) canned cannellini beans or other white beans, rinsed and drained

1¾ cups (410 ml) low-sodium chicken broth (see recipe in Chapter 2)

¼ cup (65 g) pesto

Heat oil in a skillet over medium-high heat and sauté chicken. Combine chicken and remaining ingredients except pesto in slow cooker. Cook on low 6 to 8 hours. Stir in pesto just before serving.

Yield: 4 servings

Per serving: 334 g water; 347 calories (31% from fat, 30% from protein, 39% from carb); 27 g protein; 12 g total fat; 3 g saturated fat; 7 g monounsaturated fat; 1 g polyunsaturated fat; 35 g carb; 11 g fiber; 4 g sugar; 344 mg phosphorus; 231 mg calcium; 4 mg iron; 267 mg sodium; 962 mg potassium; 8930 IU vitamin A; 3 mg ATE vitamin E; 42 mg vitamin C; 37 mg cholesterol

Italian Chicken Stew

Here's a chicken stew with an Italian accent. This one is very popular at our house.

1 pound (455 g) boneless skinless chicken breast, cubed

1 can (14 ounces, or 400 g) no-salt-added diced tomatoes, undrained

2 potatoes, peeled and cubed

1 cup (130 g) chopped carrots

¾ cup (75 g) chopped celery

1 cup (160 g) chopped onion

4 ounces (115 g) mushrooms, sliced

½ teaspoon basil

½ teaspoon dill weed

1 teaspoon Italian seasoning

½ teaspoon black pepper

TIP

Sprinkle Parmesan cheese on individual servings.

(continued on page 280)

Combine all ingredients in slow cooker. Cover and cook on low 8 to 10 hours until vegetables are tender.

Yield: 5 servings

Per serving: 349 g water; 249 calories (6% from fat, 41% from protein, 53% from carb); 26 g protein; 2 g total fat; 0 g saturated fat; 0 g monounsaturated fat; 0 g polyunsaturated fat; 34 g carb; 5 g fiber; 7 g sugar; 326 mg phosphorus; 79 mg calcium; 3 mg iron; 111 mg sodium; 1304 mg potassium; 4522 IU vitamin A; 5 mg ATE vitamin E; 26 mg vitamin C; 53 mg cholesterol

Brunswick Stew

This is a traditional southern United Stated comfort food (you could tell by the okra, right?). We did decide to go with leftover chicken instead of the original game like squirrels or rabbits.

3 potatoes, peeled and cut in ½-inch (1.3 cm) pieces

10 ounces (280 g) frozen lima beans

10 ounces (280 g) frozen okra

10 ounces (280 g) frozen corn

3 cups (420 g) diced cooked chicken breast

1 tablespoon (13 g) sugar

½ teaspoon rosemary

¼ teaspoon black pepper

¼ teaspoon cloves

1 bay leaf

4 cups (950 ml) low-sodium chicken broth (see recipe in Chapter 2)

1 can (14 ounces, or 400 g) no-salt-added whole peeled tomatoes, cut up

Place potatoes and frozen vegetables in slow cooker. Add chicken, sugar, rosemary, pepper, cloves, and bay leaf. Pour chicken broth and undrained tomatoes over mixture. Cover and cook on low for 8 to 10 hours. Remove bay leaf and stir well before serving.

Yield: 10 servings

Turkey Stew

A hearty stew great for cool weather, this meal contains ground turkey and root vegetables in a flavorful broth.

1 pound (455 g) ground turkey

1 cup (160 g) chopped onion

¾ teaspoon minced garlic

1 cup (130 g) sliced carrots

½ cup (50 g) sliced celery

1 fennel bulb, chopped

2 cups (475 ml) low-sodium chicken broth (see recipe in Chapter 2)

1 cup (180 g) no-salt-added diced tomatoes

1 teaspoon basil

1 teaspoon oregano

1 cup (115 g) pasta, such as shells or elbows, uncooked

2 cups (364 g) navy beans, cooked or canned without salt

Brown turkey in skillet. Drain. Combine turkey and remaining ingredients in slow cooker. Cover and cook on low 8 to 10 hours.

Yield: 6 servings

Turkey Mushroom Soup

Turkey meatballs and mushrooms combine to make this soup a real pleaser.

½ pound (225 g) ground turkey

½ teaspoon garlic powder

½ teaspoon onion powder

½ teaspoon black pepper

¼ cup (60 ml) egg substitute

1 tablespoon (15 ml) olive oil

1 cup (130 g) sliced carrots

½ teaspoon crushed garlic

2 cups (140 g) sliced mushrooms

2 cups (475 ml) low-sodium beef broth (see recipe in Chapter 2)

10 ounces (280 g) low-sodium cream of mushroom soup (see recipe in Chapter 2)

2 tablespoons (32 g) no-salt-added tomato paste

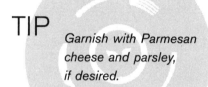

TIP *Garnish with Parmesan cheese and parsley, if desired.*

In a small bowl, mix together ground turkey, garlic powder, onion powder, and pepper. Add egg substitute, stirring until well blended. Form into small meatballs. Heat olive oil in skillet. Brown meatballs and drain well. Transfer meatballs to slow cooker. Add remaining ingredients. Cover and cook on low 6 to 8 hours or on high 3 to 4 hours.

Yield: 8 servings

Per serving: 148 g water; 108 calories (35% from fat, 42% from protein, 23% from carb); 11 g protein; 4 g total fat; 1 g saturated fat; 2 g monounsaturated fat; 1 g polyunsaturated fat; 6 g carb; 1 g fiber; 2 g sugar; 122 mg phosphorus; 28 mg calcium; 1 mg iron; 96 mg sodium; 429 mg potassium; 2784 IU vitamin A; 1 mg ATE vitamin E; 2 mg vitamin C; 23 mg cholesterol

Turkey Bean Soup

Bean soup for a crowd or for lunches the next few days. This one is low-fat thanks to the ground turkey and vaguely Southwestern in flavor with the cumin, which I just happen to like the taste of.

1 pound (455 g) ground turkey

1 cup (160 g) chopped onion

1 cup (100 g) sliced celery

2 cups (260 g) sliced carrot

4 cups (1 kg) kidney beans, cooked or canned without salt

4 cups (684 g) pinto beans, cooked or canned without salt

1 can (28 ounces, or 785 g) no-salt-added diced tomatoes

2 cups (475 ml) water

1 tablespoon (1.3 g) parsley

1 tablespoon (4 g) oregano

1 tablespoon (7 g) cumin

TIP *For an even more filling meal, serve over brown rice.*

Brown turkey and onions in skillet over medium-high heat. Combine turkey mixture and remaining ingredients in slow cooker. Cover and cook on low 8 to 10 hours.

Yield: 12 servings

Per serving: 212 g water; 389 calories (7% from fat, 32% from protein, 61% from carb); 32 g protein; 3 g total fat; 1 g saturated fat; 1 g monounsaturated fat; 1 g polyunsaturated fat; 60 g carb; 17 g fiber; 5 g sugar; 458 mg phosphorus; 152 mg calcium; 7 mg iron; 70 mg sodium; 1481 mg potassium; 3754 IU vitamin A; 0 mg ATE vitamin E; 14 mg vitamin C; 29 mg cholesterol

Asian Turkey and Rice Soup

Chow mein noodles give this richly flavored soup a little bit of a crunch.

3½ cups (820 ml) low-sodium chicken broth (see recipe in Chapter 2)

2 cups (280 g) chopped cooked turkey

2 cups (140 g) sliced mushrooms

1½ cups (355 ml) water

1 cup (130 g) julienned carrots

½ cup (80 g) chopped onion

2 tablespoons (28 ml) low-sodium soy sauce (see recipe in Chapter 2)

2 teaspoons grated fresh ginger

1 teaspoon minced garlic

1½ cups (105 g) sliced bok choy

1 cup (185 g) instant brown rice

1 cup (45 g) chow mein noodles

In a slow cooker, stir together broth, turkey, mushrooms, water, carrots, onion, soy sauce, ginger, and garlic. Cover and cook on high for 3½ to 4 hours. Stir in bok choy and rice. Cover and cook for 10 to 15 minutes more or until rice is tender. Top with chow mein noodles.

Yield: 6 servings

Per serving: 349 g water; 197 calories (18% from fat, 43% from protein, 39% from carb); 21 g protein; 4 g total fat; 1 g saturated fat; 1 g monounsaturated fat; 2 g polyunsaturated fat; 19 g carb; 2 g fiber; 2 g sugar; 245 mg phosphorus; 41 mg calcium; 2 mg iron; 260 mg sodium; 460 mg potassium; 3615 IU vitamin A; 5 mg ATE vitamin E; 5 mg vitamin C; 44 mg cholesterol

Turkey Zucchini Soup

Here's a simple but very tasty soup. This is an excellent use for leftover turkey.

8 ounces (225 g) frozen green beans

2 cups (240 g) thinly sliced zucchini

2 cups (280 g) chopped cooked turkey

1 cup (245 g) no-salt-added tomato sauce

½ cup (80 g) finely chopped onion

1 teaspoon Worcestershire sauce

½ teaspoon ground savory

¼ teaspoon black pepper

4 cups (950 ml) water

3 ounces (85 g) fat-free cream cheese, softened

Thaw green beans by placing in strainer; run hot water over beans. In slow cooker, stir together beans, zucchini, turkey, tomato sauce, onion, Worcestershire sauce, savory, pepper, and water. Cover and cook on high for 2 to 3 hours. Blend about 1 cup (235 ml) hot soup liquid into cream cheese; return to cooker, stirring well. Heat through.

Yield: 8 servings

Per serving: 238 g water; 106 calories (25% from fat, 49% from protein, 26% from carb); 13 g protein; 3 g total fat; 2 g saturated fat; 1 g monounsaturated fat; 0 g polyunsaturated fat; 7 g carb; 2 g fiber; 3 g sugar; 123 mg phosphorus; 44 mg calcium; 2 mg iron; 73 mg sodium; 377 mg potassium; 429 IU vitamin A; 19 mg ATE vitamin E; 15 mg vitamin C; 40 mg cholesterol

Turkey Cheeseburger Soup

Cheeseburgers in a bowl — now that's something everyone can agree on.

1 pound (455 g) ground turkey

1 cup (160 g) chopped onion

½ cup (75 g) chopped green bell pepper

½ cup (50 g) chopped celery

3 cups (700 ml) low-sodium beef broth (see recipe in Chapter 2)

1 cup (235 ml) skim milk

2 cups (475 ml) water

(continued on page 286)

2 tablespoons (15 g) flour

8 ounces (225 g) Cheddar cheese, shredded

Brown turkey in nonstick skillet. Spoon into slow cooker. Add onion, green pepper, and celery to slow cooker. Heat broth, milk, and water in skillet, scraping up browned bits. Sprinkle flour over liquid. Stir until smooth and let boil for 3 minutes. Pour into slow cooker. Cover and cook on low 6 hours. Then add cheese and cook another 2 to 3 hours.

Yield: 6 servings

Per serving: 339 g water; 330 calories (46% from fat, 44% from protein, 10% from carb); 35 g protein; 17 g total fat; 9 g saturated fat; 4 g monounsaturated fat; 1 g polyunsaturated fat; 8 g carb; 1 g fiber; 2 g sugar; 431 mg phosphorus; 371 mg calcium; 2 mg iron; 392 mg sodium; 488 mg potassium; 546 IU vitamin A; 123 mg ATE vitamin E; 13 mg vitamin C; 98 mg cholesterol

Black Bean Turkey Chili

This recipe originally came from a newsletter subscriber. I've made a few changes, including modifying it for the slow cooker. You can also use browned ground turkey.

2 tablespoons (28 ml) oil

1 cup (160 g) chopped onion

1 cup (150 g) cubed red bell pepper

1 teaspoon minced garlic

2 jalapeño peppers, seeded and chopped

2 cups (360 g) no-salt-added diced tomatoes

2 tablespoons (15 g) chili powder

1 teaspoon cumin

1 teaspoon coriander

1 teaspoon marjoram

¼ teaspoon red pepper flakes

¼ teaspoon cinnamon

1 cup (172 g) black beans, cooked or canned without salt

2 cups (240 g) cubed cooked turkey

⅓ cup (5 g) coarsely chopped fresh cilantro

4 teaspoons (19 g) shredded Cheddar

Heat oil in a 3-quart (2.8 L) saucepan over medium-high heat and sauté onion, red bell pepper, garlic, and jalapeños until tender-crisp. Combine sautéed vegetables and all other ingredients except turkey, cilantro, and cheese in a slow cooker. Cook on low heat for 3 to 4 hours and then add turkey and cilantro and cook for another 1 to 2 hours. To serve, ladle into bowls and top with cheese.

Yield: 4 servings

Per serving: 269 g water; 311 calories (35% from fat, 35% from protein, 31% from carb); 28 g protein; 12 g total fat; 3 g saturated fat; 3 g monounsaturated fat; 5 g polyunsaturated fat; 24 g carb; 8 g fiber; 7 g sugar; 289 mg phosphorus; 124 mg calcium; 5 mg iron; 129 mg sodium; 859 mg potassium; 2813 IU vitamin A; 7 mg ATE vitamin E; 70 mg vitamin C; 57 mg cholesterol

White Chili

Sometimes I think I like white chili better than traditional red. This version has no tomatoes, although you could add a can of drained no-salt-added diced tomatoes if you want to.

6 cups (1.1 kg) great northern beans, cooked or canned
   without salt, drained

8 ounces (225 g) shredded cooked chicken breasts

1 cup (160 g) chopped onion

1½ cups (225 g) chopped green bell pepper

4 ounces (115 g) diced green chilies

¾ teaspoon minced garlic

2 teaspoons cumin

½ teaspoon oregano

3½ cups (820 ml) low-sodium chicken broth (see recipe
   in Chapter 2)

TIP *To serve, ladle into bowls and top each serving with sour cream, Cheddar cheese, and tortilla chips.*

(continued on page 288)

Combine all ingredients in slow cooker. Cover and cook on low 8 to 10 hours or on high 4 to 5 hours.

Yield: 8 servings

Per serving: 317 g water; 290 calories (6% from fat, 32% from protein, 62% from carb); 24 g protein; 2 g total fat; 1 g saturated fat; 0 g monounsaturated fat; 1 g polyunsaturated fat; 46 g carb; 11 g fiber; 2 g sugar; 342 mg phosphorus; 131 mg calcium; 4 mg iron; 146 mg sodium; 879 mg potassium; 138 IU vitamin A; 2 mg ATE vitamin E; 31 mg vitamin C; 22 mg cholesterol

13

Maintain Your Healthy Diet with Pork and Lamb Soups, Stews, and Chilis

Pork, including sausage, and lamb make great soups and even greater stews. This chapter contains a variety of everything from curry to chili.

Creamy Potato Soup

A delicious creamy potato soup, flavored with onion and bacon, this soup is hearty enough for a whole meal.

6 slices low-sodium bacon, cut into ½-inch (1.3 cm) pieces

1 cup (160 g) finely chopped onion

3 cups (700 ml) low-sodium chicken broth (see recipe in Chapter 2)

5 large potatoes, diced

½ teaspoon dill weed

½ teaspoon white pepper

½ cup (63 g) flour

3 cups (700 ml) fat-free evaporated milk

Place bacon and onion in a large, deep skillet. Cook over medium-high heat until bacon is evenly brown and onions are soft. Drain off excess grease. Transfer the bacon and onion to a slow cooker and stir in chicken broth, potatoes, dill weed, and white pepper. Cover and cook on low 6 to 7 hours, stirring occasionally. In a small bowl, whisk together the flour and milk. Stir into the soup. Cover and cook another 30 minutes before serving.

Yield: 6 servings

Per serving: 483 g water; 401 calories (10% from fat, 19% from protein, 71% from carb); 19 g protein; 4 g total fat; 1 g saturated fat; 2 g monounsaturated fat; 1 g polyunsaturated fat; 73 g carb; 6 g fiber; 17 g sugar; 484 mg phosphorus; 375 mg calcium; 3 mg iron; 280 mg sodium; 1910 mg potassium; 477 IU vitamin A; 135 mg ATE vitamin E; 30 mg vitamin C; 13 mg cholesterol

Sausage and Bean Stew

After tasting this hearty stew with the flavors of Italy, you'll come back for more.

1¼ cups (269 g) dried navy beans

1 pound (455 g) Italian sausage (see recipe in Chapter 2)

1 cup (160 g) chopped onion

½ cup (50 g) sliced celery

1 cup (235 ml) dry red wine

1 teaspoon rosemary

1½ cups (355 ml) low-sodium vegetable broth (see recipe in Chapter 2)

1 cup (180 g) chopped tomatoes

Soak beans in water overnight. Drain, place in a pot, cover with water and simmer for 20 minutes. Drain. Place in slow cooker. Brown the sausage in a skillet over medium-high heat, stir in the onion and celery, and continue cooking until vegetables are soft. Place over the beans in the cooker. Combine remaining ingredients and pour over sausage-bean mixture. Cover and cook on high for 5 to 6 hours or low 8 to 10 hours.

Yield: 4 servings

Per serving: 317 g water; 588 calories (63% from fat, 17% from protein, 20% from carb); 22 g protein; 38 g total fat; 13 g saturated fat; 17 g monounsaturated fat; 5 g polyunsaturated fat; 28 g carb; 7 g fiber; 3 g sugar; 301 mg phosphorus; 93 mg calcium; 3 mg iron; 130 mg sodium; 794 mg potassium; 295 IU vitamin A; 0 mg ATE vitamin E; 17 mg vitamin C; 86 mg cholesterol

Sausage Soup

You could make this with ground beef also if you wanted to. It would be a little lower in sodium that way, but we like this as a special treat with the sausage, which we don't eat very often.

1 pound (455 g) kielbasa, sliced

6 cups (1.4 L) water

1 can (14 ounces, or 400 g) no-salt-added diced tomatoes

½ cup (50 g) sliced celery

1 cup (130 g) sliced carrots

1 cup (105 g) uncooked macaroni

½ teaspoon Salt-Free Seasoning Blend (see recipe in Chapter 2)

½ teaspoon basil

(continued on page 292)

½ teaspoon oregano

2 tablespoons (15 g) low-sodium onion soup mix (see recipe in Chapter 2)

Combine all ingredients in slow cooker. Cover and cook on low 8 to 10 hours.

Yield: 6 servings

Per serving: 360 g water; 176 calories (54% from fat, 16% from protein, 30% from carb); 7 g protein; 11 g total fat; 4 g saturated fat; 5 g monounsaturated fat; 1 g polyunsaturated fat; 13 g carb; 2 g fiber; 3 g sugar; 92 mg phosphorus; 59 mg calcium; 2 mg iron; 444 mg sodium; 333 mg potassium; 3713 IU vitamin A; 0 mg ATE vitamin E; 8 mg vitamin C; 25 mg cholesterol

Chinese Pork Soup

If you like Chinese food, you'll love this soup. And if you use soy sauce recipe in Chapter 2, it doesn't have the alarmingly high sodium content that most Asian food does.

1 pound (455 g) boneless pork loin roast, cut in ½-inch (1.3 cm) cubes

1 cup (130 g) julienned carrots

½ cup (50 g) chopped scallions

½ teaspoon finely chopped garlic

¼ cup (60 ml) low-sodium soy sauce (see recipe in Chapter 2)

½ teaspoon finely chopped fresh ginger

¼ teaspoon black pepper

2 cups (475 ml) low-sodium beef broth (see recipe in Chapter 2)

4 ounces (115 g) mushrooms, sliced

1 cup (50 g) bean sprouts

Cook pork in large nonstick skillet over medium heat for 8 to 10 minutes. Stir occasionally. Mix pork and remaining ingredients except mushrooms and bean sprouts in slow cooker. Cover and cook on low 7 to 9 hours or on high 3 to 4 hours. Stir in mushrooms and bean sprouts. Cover and cook on low 1 hour.

Yield: 6 servings

Per serving: 204 g water; 145 calories (33% from fat, 54% from protein, 13% from carb); 19 g protein; 5 g total fat; 2 g saturated fat; 2 g monounsaturated fat; 1 g polyunsaturated fat; 5 g carb; 1 g fiber; 2 g sugar; 213 mg phosphorus; 28 mg calcium; 1 mg iron; 160 mg sodium; 540 mg potassium; 3677 IU vitamin A; 2 mg ATE vitamin E; 4 mg vitamin C; 42 mg cholesterol

Curried Pork and Split Pea Soup

Here's a little different version of split pea soup, with curry powder kicking up the flavor.

1½ pounds (680 g) boneless pork loin roast

1 cup (225 g) green split peas, rinsed and drained

½ cup (65 g) finely chopped carrots

½ cup (50 g) finely chopped celery

½ cup (80 g) finely chopped onions

6 cups (1.4 L) low-sodium chicken broth (see recipe in Chapter 2)

2 teaspoons curry powder

½ teaspoon paprika

½ teaspoon ground cumin

¼ teaspoon pepper

2 cups (60 g) fresh spinach, torn

Trim fat from pork and cut pork into 2-inch (5 cm) pieces. Combine split peas, carrots, celery, and onions in slow cooker. Stir in broth, curry powder, paprika, cumin, and pepper. Stir in pork. Cover and cook on low 10 to 12 hours or on high 4 hours. Stir in spinach. Serve immediately.

Yield: 6 servings

Per serving: 407 g water; 329 calories (23% from fat, 45% from protein, 32% from carb); 37 g protein; 9 g total fat; 3 g saturated fat; 3 g monounsaturated fat; 1 g polyunsaturated fat; 27 g carb; 12 g fiber; 5 g sugar; 427 mg phosphorus; 145 mg calcium; 4 mg iron; 273 mg sodium; 1157 mg potassium; 9641 IU vitamin A; 2 mg ATE vitamin E; 5 mg vitamin C; 62 mg cholesterol

Split Pea Soup with Pork

You can minimize the usual sodium of ham or sausage but still have a meaty split pea soup. Ground pork gives this dish just that meaty kick you want.

1 pound (455 g) ground pork

6 cups (1.4 L) water

1 pound (455 g) split peas

2 medium potatoes, peeled and diced

¾ cup (120 g) chopped onion

½ cup (50 g) chopped celery

½ teaspoon marjoram

¼ teaspoon pepper

In a skillet over medium-high heat, brown ground pork; drain off fat. Transfer pork to slow cooker. Stir in water, peas, potatoes, onion, celery, marjoram, and pepper. Cover and cook on low for 10 to 12 hours. Before serving, stir soup; adjust seasonings to taste.

Yield: 8 servings

Per serving: 345 g water; 288 calories (39% from fat, 22% from protein, 39% from carb); 16 g protein; 12 g total fat; 5 g saturated fat; 5 g monounsaturated fat; 1 g polyunsaturated fat; 28 g carb; 7 g fiber; 3 g sugar; 218 mg phosphorus; 37 mg calcium; 2 mg iron; 49 mg sodium; 829 mg potassium; 49 IU vitamin A; 1 mg ATE vitamin E; 10 mg vitamin C; 41 mg cholesterol

Pork Stew

A simple, hearty stew of pork and vegetables, this is just the kind of thing I like to come home to find ready to eat on a cold day.

2 pounds (900 g) ground pork

20 ounces (560 g) low-sodium cream of mushroom soup (see recipe in Chapter 2)

1 pound (455 g) frozen green beans

4 potatoes, diced

1 cup (130 g) chopped carrots

1 cup (160 g) diced onions

3 cups (700 ml) water

½ cup (50 g) chopped celery

¼ teaspoon black pepper

¼ teaspoon garlic powder

Brown ground pork in a nonstick skillet over medium-high heat. Combine pork and remaining ingredients in slow cooker. Cook on low 8 to 10 hours.

Yield: 8 servings

Per serving: 458 g water; 498 calories (46% from fat, 20% from protein, 34% from carb); 25 g protein; 26 g total fat; 9 g saturated fat; 11 g monounsaturated fat; 3 g polyunsaturated fat; 43 g carb; 6 g fiber; 6 g sugar; 382 mg phosphorus; 80 mg calcium; 3 mg iron; 120 mg sodium; 1648 mg potassium; 3137 IU vitamin A; 4 mg ATE vitamin E; 29 mg vitamin C; 84 mg cholesterol

Pork and Sweet Potato Soup

This is a simple soup, really more of a stew, with only a few ingredients. But it has a flavor and a heartiness that definitely pleases.

1 pound (455 g) ground pork

½ cup (80 g) chopped onion

1 sweet potato, cubed and peeled

½ teaspoon rosemary

1 cup (235 ml) low-sodium beef broth (see recipe in Chapter 2)

Brown meat and onion in nonstick skillet over medium-high heat. Drain and place in slow cooker. Add remaining ingredients. Cover and cook on low for 4 hours.

Yield: 4 servings

(continued on page 296)

Per serving: 176 g water; 339 calories (65% from fat, 25% from protein, 10% from carb); 21 g protein; 24 g total fat; 9 g saturated fat; 11 g monounsaturated fat; 2 g polyunsaturated fat; 9 g carb; 1 g fiber; 3 g sugar; 224 mg phosphorus; 34 mg calcium; 1 mg iron; 110 mg sodium; 474 mg potassium; 5952 IU vitamin A; 2 mg ATE vitamin E; 7 mg vitamin C; 82 mg cholesterol

Black Bean Chili

This is a slightly different kind of chili, with black beans and pork, but it's one that we really like at our house.

1 pound (455 g) pork loin, cut in 1-inch (2.5 cm) cubes

2 cups (520 g) low-sodium salsa (see recipe in Chapter 2)

4 cups (688 g) black beans, cooked or canned without salt

½ cup (120 ml) low-sodium chicken broth (see recipe in Chapter 2)

1 cup (150 g) chopped red bell peppers

1 cup (160 g) chopped onion

1 teaspoon cumin

2 tablespoons (15 g) chili powder

1 teaspoon oregano

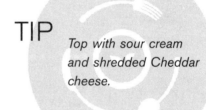

TIP

Top with sour cream and shredded Cheddar cheese.

Brown pork in skillet over medium-high heat. Drain. Combine pork and remaining ingredients in slow cooker. Cover and cook on low 8 to 10 hours.

Yield: 8 servings

Per serving: 196 g water; 221 calories (14% from fat, 37% from protein, 49% from carb); 21 g protein; 3 g total fat; 1 g saturated fat; 1 g monounsaturated fat; 1 g polyunsaturated fat; 28 g carb; 10 g fiber; 3 g sugar; 280 mg phosphorus; 61 mg calcium; 3 mg iron; 183 mg sodium; 788 mg potassium; 1316 IU vitamin A; 1 mg ATE vitamin E; 28 mg vitamin C; 36 mg cholesterol

Sausage Chili

Sausage adds an extra flavor dimension to this chili, which is otherwise a fairly traditional recipe.

1 pound (455 g) breakfast sausage (see recipe in Chapter 2)

1 pound (455 g) extra-lean ground beef

4 cups (1 kg) kidney beans, cooked or canned without salt

1 can (28 ounces, or 785 g) no-salt-added whole peeled tomatoes, cut up

1 cup (160 g) chopped onion

1 cup (150 g) chopped green bell pepper

1 cup (100 g) sliced celery

1 can (6 ounces, or 170 g) no-salt-added tomato paste

½ teaspoon minced garlic

2 teaspoons chili powder

In a skillet over medium-high heat, cook sausage and ground beef until browned; drain off excess fat. Transfer meat to slow cooker. Stir in the remaining ingredients. Cover and cook on low for 8 to 10 hours.

Yield: 10 servings

Per serving: 212 g water; 376 calories (53% from fat, 24% from protein, 23% from carb); 23 g protein; 22 g total fat; 8 g saturated fat; 10 g monounsaturated fat; 2 g polyunsaturated fat; 22 g carb; 8 g fiber; 3 g sugar; 256 mg phosphorus; 78 mg calcium; 4 mg iron; 82 mg sodium; 746 mg potassium; 344 IU vitamin A; 0 mg ATE vitamin E; 23 mg vitamin C; 66 mg cholesterol

Lamb and Bean Stew

We don't eat lamb very often, but this stew conjures up visions of France or some other great place to be.

8 ounces (225 g) dried navy beans

6 cups (1.4 L) water

(continued on page 298)

1 pound (455 g) lamb stew meat, cut into 1-inch
(2.5 cm) cubes

4 cups (950 ml) low-sodium chicken broth (see recipe
in Chapter 2)

1 cup (130 g) carrots, cut into 1-inch (2.5 cm) pieces

½ cup (50 g) celery, cut into 1-inch (2.5 cm) pieces

1 onion, cut into wedges

1 cup (235 ml) dry white wine

2 teaspoons minced garlic

3 bay leaves

1½ teaspoons rosemary, crushed

¼ teaspoon black pepper

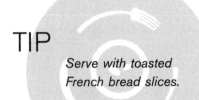

TIP

*Serve with toasted
French bread slices.*

Rinse and drain beans. In a 4-quart (3.8 L) stock pot, combine beans and the water. Bring to a boil; reduce heat and simmer for 10 minutes. Remove from heat. Cover and let stand for 1 hour. Drain beans in a colander; rinse beans. In a slow cooker, stir together beans, lamb, broth, carrots, celery, onion, wine, garlic, bay leaves, rosemary, and pepper. Cover and cook on low for 8 to 10 hours or on high for 4 to 5 hours. Remove and discard bay leaves before serving.

Yield: 6 servings

Per serving: 547 g water; 271 calories (19% from fat, 54% from protein, 27% from carb); 32 g protein; 5 g total fat; 2 g saturated fat; 2 g monounsaturated fat; 0 g polyunsaturated fat; 16 g carb; 5 g fiber; 3 g sugar; 269 mg phosphorus; 65 mg calcium; 4 mg iron; 159 mg sodium; 613 mg potassium; 3629 IU vitamin A; 0 mg ATE vitamin E; 4 mg vitamin C; 68 mg cholesterol

14

Hearty and Healthy Meatless Soups, Stews, and Chilis

O ver the years, we've tried to add more meatless meals to our diet. Soups and stews are one of the ways that we found offered us the filling meals we were looking for with enough substance and flavor that we didn't miss the meat. If you think you don't like vegetarian cooking, I'd suggest you start in this chapter, perhaps with one of the soups featuring beans or other legumes—or perhaps with one of the meatless chilis.

Tomato Rice Soup

Chunky tomatoes and tender rice make this soup a real hit.

2 cups (360 g) no-salt-added diced tomatoes

1 can (6 ounces, or 170 g) no-salt-added tomato paste

2 cups (475 ml) water

½ cup (50 g) chopped celery

1 cup (160 g) minced onion

1⅓ cups (245 g) rice

Put tomatoes, tomato paste, water, celery, and onion into slow cooker. Cook on high for 1 hour and then add rice. Cook for 4 hours more.

Yield: 4 servings

Per serving: 346 g water; 142 calories (3% from fat, 12% from protein, 84% from carb); 5 g protein; 1 g total fat; 0 g saturated fat; 0 g monounsaturated fat; 0 g polyunsaturated fat; 32 g carb; 4 g fiber; 10 g sugar; 95 mg phosphorus; 76 mg calcium; 3 mg iron; 73 mg sodium; 768 mg potassium; 847 IU vitamin A; 0 mg ATE vitamin E; 24 mg vitamin C; 0 mg cholesterol

Potato and Leek Soup

Warm and filling, this is a great cold-day soup. Put a loaf of bread in the bread machine on timed bake and come home to a wonderful dinner ready to sit down to.

6 large potatoes, cubed

2 leeks, washed and cut up

½ cup (80 g) chopped onion

½ cup (65 g) grated carrot

¼ cup (25 g) chopped celery

1 tablespoon (1.3 g) parsley

5 cups (1.2 L) vegetable broth (see recipe in Chapter 2)

¼ teaspoon pepper

⅓ cup (75 g) unsalted butter

13 ounces (370 ml) evaporated milk

Chopped chives

Put all ingredients into slow cooker or soup pot except milk and chives. Cook 10 to 12 hours on low or 4 to 6 hours on high. Stir in evaporated milk during last hour. To serve, sprinkle with chives.

Yield: 6 servings

Per serving: 594 g water; 549 calories (32% from fat, 10% from protein, 58% from carb); 14 g protein; 20 g total fat; 11 g saturated fat; 6 g monounsaturated fat; 2 g polyunsaturated fat; 82 g carb; 8 g fiber; 6 g sugar; 418 mg phosphorus; 256 mg calcium; 4 mg iron; 224 mg sodium; 2076 mg potassium; 2922 IU vitamin A; 85 mg ATE vitamin E; 42 mg vitamin C; 45 mg cholesterol

Potato Soup

This is a relatively simple soup but very satisfying.

6 large potatoes, peeled and cut into bite-size pieces

2 cups (320 g) chopped onions

1 cup (130 g) sliced carrot

½ cup (50 g) diced celery

5 cups (1.2 L) low-sodium vegetable broth (see recipe in Chapter 2)

½ teaspoon black pepper

1 tablespoon (1.3 g) parsley

¼ cup (55 g) unsalted butter

13 ounces (370 ml) evaporated milk

TIP

A few slices of cheese make this even better.

Put all ingredients except milk in slow cooker and cook on low for 10 to 12 hours or high for 3 to 4 hours. Stir in milk when potatoes are tender and continue cooking for about 1 hour more.

Yield: 6 servings

(continued on page 302)

Per serving: 616 g water; 474 calories (26% from fat, 13% from protein, 60% from carb); 16 g protein; 14 g total fat; 8 g saturated fat; 4 g monounsaturated fat; 1 g polyunsaturated fat; 73 g carb; 8 g fiber; 7 g sugar; 439 mg phosphorus; 287 mg calcium; 4 mg iron; 230 mg sodium; 2222 mg potassium; 4165 IU vitamin A; 65 mg ATE vitamin E; 39 mg vitamin C; 38 mg cholesterol

Italian Vegetable Soup

This is a vegetarian soup with Italian seasonings. It's not exactly minestrone but certainly not regular vegetable soup.

9 ounces (255 g) frozen green beans

8 ounces (225 g) frozen cauliflower

1 can (14 ounces, or 400 g) no-salt-added diced
　　tomatoes, undrained

1 teaspoon basil

1 teaspoon minced garlic

1 teaspoon oregano

½ cup (80 g) chopped onion

½ cup (50 g) sliced celery

¼ cup (50 g) barley

1 teaspoon black pepper

3 cups (700 ml) low-sodium vegetable broth (see recipe in Chapter 2)

1½ cups (355 ml) low-sodium vegetable juice

TIP *If desired, top each serving with pesto and Parmesan cheese.*

In slow cooker, combine all ingredients except broth and vegetable juice. In a medium bowl, combine broth and vegetable juice. Pour over vegetable mixture in cooker. Cover and cook on low for 6 to 8 hours or on high for 3 to 4 hours.

Yield: 6 servings

Per serving: 331 g water; 103 calories (10% from fat, 21% from protein, 68% from carb); 6 g protein; 1 g total fat; 0 g saturated fat; 0 g monounsaturated fat; 0 g polyunsaturated fat; 19 g carb; 5 g fiber; 6 g sugar; 114 mg phosphorus; 102 mg calcium; 2 mg iron; 130 mg sodium; 567 mg potassium; 1386 IU vitamin A; 1 mg ATE vitamin E; 48 mg vitamin C; 0 mg cholesterol

Mexican Bean Soup

This is a great Mexican-flavored soup featuring multiple kinds of beans.

1 cup (160 g) chopped onion

1 can (14 ounces, or 400 g) no-salt-added diced
   tomatoes

2 cups (342 g) pinto beans, cooked or canned
   without salt

2 cups (344 g) black beans, cooked, or canned
   without salt

2 cups (512 g) kidney beans, cooked or canned
   without salt

1 pound (455 g) frozen corn

1½ cups (390 g) low-sodium salsa (see recipe in
   Chapter 2)

2 tablespoons (15 g) Salt-Free Mexican Seasoning (see recipe in Chapter 2)

TIP *Serve topped with your choice of sour cream or shredded cheese (or both!).*

Combine all ingredients in slow cooker. Cover and cook on low 8 to 10 hours.

Yield: 8 servings

Per serving: 209 g water; 355 calories (4% from fat, 23% from protein, 73% from carb); 21 g protein; 2 g total fat; 0 g saturated fat; 0 g monounsaturated fat; 1 g polyunsaturated fat; 67 g carb; 18 g fiber; 6 g sugar; 400 mg phosphorus; 118 mg calcium; 6 mg iron; 123 mg sodium; 1394 mg potassium; 304 IU vitamin A; 0 mg ATE vitamin E; 14 mg vitamin C; 0 mg cholesterol

Creamy Bean Soup

This has become one of our favorite bean soup recipes. The milk just pushes it over the edge in creaminess.

6 cups (1.4 L) water

2 cups (386 g) dried pinto beans

¼ cup (40 g) chopped onion

¼ teaspoon marjoram

Dash black pepper

1 cup (235 ml) fat-free evaporated milk

1 tablespoon (8 g) flour

In a saucepan, bring water and beans to boiling; reduce heat and simmer, covered, 1½ hours. Pour beans and cooking liquid into a bowl; cover and chill. Drain beans, reserving the cooking liquid. Transfer beans to slow cooker. Stir in onion, marjoram, and dash pepper. Add enough of the reserved cooking liquid to cover, about 2 cups (475 ml). Cover and cook on low for 12 to 14 hours. Turn to high. Slowly blend milk into flour; stir into beans in cooker. Cover and cook until thickened and bubbly, 10 to 15 minutes. Mash beans slightly, if desired.

Yield: 6 servings

Per serving: 284 g water; 264 calories (3% from fat, 26% from protein, 71% from carb); 17 g protein; 1 g total fat; 0 g saturated fat; 0 g monounsaturated fat; 0 g polyunsaturated fat; 47 g carb; 10 g fiber; 6 g sugar; 351 mg phosphorus; 206 mg calcium; 3 mg iron; 64 mg sodium; 1052 mg potassium; 170 IU vitamin A; 50 mg ATE vitamin E; 5 mg vitamin C; 2 mg cholesterol

Split Pea Soup

This is a traditional split pea soup with a few additions. Does that make it non-traditional?

¾ cup (98 g) sliced carrots

½ cup (50 g) sliced celery

1 cup (160 g) chopped onion

1 parsnip, diced

1 pound (455 g) split peas, washed with stones removed

2 tablespoons (28 ml) olive oil

1 teaspoon thyme

4 cups (950 ml) low-sodium vegetable broth (see recipe in Chapter 2)

4 cups (950 ml) water

½ teaspoon pepper

2 teaspoons chopped fresh parsley

Combine all ingredients in slow cooker. Cover and cook on high 7 hours.

Yield: 6 servings

Per serving: 434 g water; 193 calories (27% from fat, 21% from protein, 52% from carb); 10 g protein; 6 g total fat; 1 g saturated fat; 4 g monounsaturated fat; 1 g polyunsaturated fat; 26 g carb; 8 g fiber; 6 g sugar; 158 mg phosphorus; 93 mg calcium; 2 mg iron; 184 mg sodium; 629 mg potassium; 2790 IU vitamin A; 2 mg ATE vitamin E; 8 mg vitamin C; 0 mg cholesterol

Pumpkin Soup

This soup is great either as a starter or the main part of the meal.

¼ cup (38 g) finely chopped green bell pepper

½ cup (80 g) finely chopped onion

1 cup (235 ml) low-sodium vegetable broth (see recipe in Chapter 2)

2 cups (490 g) puréed pumpkin

2 cups (475 ml) skim milk

¼ teaspoon thyme

¼ teaspoon nutmeg

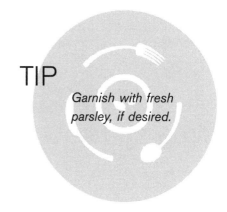

TIP

Garnish with fresh parsley, if desired.

Combine all ingredients in slow cooker and mix well.
Cover and cook on low 5 to 6 hours.

(continued on page 306)

Yield: 6 servings

Per serving: 204 g water; 75 calories (8% from fat, 26% from protein, 65% from carb); 5 g protein; 1 g total fat; 0 g saturated fat; 0 g monounsaturated fat; 0 g polyunsaturated fat; 13 g carb; 3 g fiber; 3 g sugar; 138 mg phosphorus; 155 mg calcium; 1 mg iron; 77 mg sodium; 383 mg potassium; 12903 IU vitamin A; 50 mg ATE vitamin E; 10 mg vitamin C; 2 mg cholesterol

Cauliflower Soup

This is a simple but cheesy soup that goes great with just bread for a light summer meal.

4 cups (400 g) diced cauliflower

2 cups (475 ml) water

8 ounces (225 g) fat-free cream cheese

½ cup (60 g) shredded Cheddar

½ cup (30 g) potato flakes

Combine cauliflower and water in a saucepan. Heat to boiling. Places cheeses in slow cooker. Stir in cauliflower and water. Mix well. Stir in potato flakes and cook on low for 2 to 3 hours.

Yield: 6 servings

Per serving: 184 g water; 168 calories (56% from fat, 20% from protein, 24% from carb); 9 g protein; 11 g total fat; 7 g saturated fat; 3 g monounsaturated fat; 1 g polyunsaturated fat; 10 g carb; 2 g fiber; 2 g sugar; 146 mg phosphorus; 139 mg calcium; 1 mg iron; 200 mg sodium; 247 mg potassium; 377 IU vitamin A; 97 mg ATE vitamin E; 41 mg vitamin C; 33 mg cholesterol

Creamy Broccoli and Mushroom Soup

This creamy vegetable soup is also good cold for those hot summer evenings.

8 ounces (225 g) mushrooms, sliced

2 pounds (900 g) broccoli

20 ounces (560 g) low-sodium cream of mushroom soup (see recipe in Chapter 2)

½ teaspoon thyme

2 cups (475 ml) fat-free evaporated milk

¼ teaspoon black pepper

Combine all ingredients in slow cooker. Cook on low 6 to 8 hours or on high 3½ to 4 hours.

Yield: 10 servings

Per serving: 192 g water; 106 calories (12% from fat, 28% from protein, 61% from carb); 8 g protein; 1 g total fat; 0 g saturated fat; 0 g monounsaturated fat; 0 g polyunsaturated fat; 17 g carb; 3 g fiber; 9 g sugar; 208 mg phosphorus; 200 mg calcium; 1 mg iron; 108 mg sodium; 742 mg potassium; 774 IU vitamin A; 62 mg ATE vitamin E; 82 mg vitamin C; 4 mg cholesterol

Broccoli Soup

Here's a simple broccoli soup, with just enough cheese to make it interesting.

2 pounds (900 g) broccoli

3 cups (700 ml) water

1 cup (235 ml) skim milk

½ cup (58 g) Cheddar cheese, cut into small cubes

Chop broccoli. Remove any tough stalks and discard. Place chopped broccoli and water (add more water to cover, if necessary) in slow cooker. Cover and cook on high 1 to 2 hours. Add skim milk. Cook for an additional 15 minutes. Stir in cheese and cook until cheese is melted into soup.

Yield: 5 servings

Per serving: 353 g water; 135 calories (31% from fat, 28% from protein, 40% from carb); 10 g protein; 5 g total fat; 3 g saturated fat; 1 g monounsaturated fat; 0 g polyunsaturated fat; 15 g carb; 5 g fiber; 3 g sugar; 242 mg phosphorus; 255 mg calcium; 1 mg iron; 175 mg sodium; 677 mg potassium; 1363 IU vitamin A; 64 mg ATE vitamin E; 162 mg vitamin C; 15 mg cholesterol

Vegetarian Minestrone

This minestrone is so good you won't even miss the meat.

6 cups (1.4 L) low-sodium vegetable broth (see recipe in Chapter 2)

¾ cup (98 g) chopped carrots

1½ cup (240 g) chopped onions

⅓ cup (33 g) chopped celery

½ teaspoon minced garlic

½ cup (60 g) cubed zucchini

1 cup (67 g) chopped kale

½ cup (100 g) pearl barley

2 cups (480 g) canned no-salt-added chickpeas, drained

1 tablespoon (1.3 g) parsley

½ teaspoon thyme

1 teaspoon oregano

1 can (28 ounces, or 785 g) no-salt-added crushed tomatoes

¼ teaspoon pepper

TIP

Sprinkle individual servings with shredded Parmesan cheese.

Combine all ingredients in slow cooker. Cover and cook on low 6 to 8 hours or until vegetables are tender.

Yield: 6 servings

Per serving: 469 g water; 238 calories (13% from fat, 22% from protein, 64% from carb); 14 g protein; 4 g total fat; 1 g saturated fat; 1 g monounsaturated fat; 1 g polyunsaturated fat; 40 g carb; 10 g fiber; 9 g sugar; 261 mg phosphorus; 185 mg calcium; 5 mg iron; 186 mg sodium; 896 mg potassium; 4708 IU vitamin A; 2 mg ATE vitamin E; 33 mg vitamin C; 0 mg cholesterol

Tomato Soup

This is the taste of fresh tomatoes in a bowl. I love to make this when the garden starts really producing tomatoes.

5 cups (1.2 L) diced tomatoes

1 tablespoon (16 g) no-salt-added tomato paste

4 cups (950 ml) low-sodium vegetable broth (see recipe in Chapter 2)

½ cup (80 g) minced onion

1 tablespoon (10 g) minced garlic

1 teaspoon basil

¼ teaspoon black pepper

Combine all ingredients in a slow cooker. Cook on low for 6 to 8 hours. Stir once while cooking.

Yield: 6 servings

Per serving: 287 g water; 62 calories (19% from fat, 28% from protein, 53% from carb); 5 g protein; 1 g total fat; 0 g saturated fat; 0 g monounsaturated fat; 0 g polyunsaturated fat; 9 g carb; 2 g fiber; 1 g sugar; 88 mg phosphorus; 64 mg calcium; 1 mg iron; 108 mg sodium; 473 mg potassium; 833 IU vitamin A; 2 mg ATE vitamin E; 34 mg vitamin C; 0 mg cholesterol

Summer Vegetable Soup

This is a great soup to experiment with. If you have fresh vegetables, by all means use them instead of frozen. If you like some vegetables better than others, use more. No matter what you substitute, you can't really go wrong.

4 cups (950 ml) low-sodium vegetable broth (see recipe in Chapter 2)

8 ounces (225 g) frozen corn

½ cup (65 g) chopped carrots

8 ounces (225 g) frozen green beans

(continued on page 310)

1 cup (120 g) sliced zucchini

2 cups (360 g) chopped tomatoes

½ cup (80 g) chopped onions

½ teaspoon minced garlic

½ teaspoon thyme

½ teaspoon basil

¼ teaspoon black pepper

1 cup (71 g) chopped broccoli

½ cup (65 g) frozen peas

Combine all ingredients except broccoli and peas in slow cooker. Cover and cook on low 7 hours or on high 3½ hours. Stir in broccoli. Cook an additional 45 minutes on high. Stir in peas. Cook an additional 15 minutes on high.

Yield: 8 servings

Per serving: 248 g water; 81 calories (12% from fat, 24% from protein, 65% from carb); 5 g protein; 1 g total fat; 0 g saturated fat; 0 g monounsaturated fat; 0 g polyunsaturated fat; 14 g carb; 4 g fiber; 3 g sugar; 101 mg phosphorus; 68 mg calcium; 1 mg iron; 120 mg sodium; 426 mg potassium; 2097 IU vitamin A; 1 mg ATE vitamin E; 30 mg vitamin C; 0 mg cholesterol

Vegetarian Vegetable Soup

If you are trying to cut back on the amount of red meat you eat, this soup is one way to do it and still have familiar food.

2 cups (260 g) sliced carrot

1 pound (455 g) frozen green beans

1 pound (455 g) frozen corn

1 can (28 ounces, or 785 g) no-salt-added diced tomatoes

1 cup (160 g) chopped onion

2 cups (475 ml) low-sodium vegetable broth (see recipe in Chapter 2)

1 tablespoon (15 ml) Worcestershire sauce

Combine all ingredients in slow cooker. Cover and cook on low 8 to 10 hours.

Yield: 8 servings

Per serving: 294 g water; 132 calories (14% from fat, 13% from protein, 73% from carb); 5 g protein; 2 g total fat; 1 g saturated fat; 1 g monounsaturated fat; 1 g polyunsaturated fat; 27 g carb; 6 g fiber; 7 g sugar; 124 mg phosphorus; 76 mg calcium; 2 mg iron; 101 mg sodium; 629 mg potassium; 6008 IU vitamin A; 0 mg ATE vitamin E; 30 mg vitamin C; 0 mg cholesterol

Vegetarian Stew

This tasty stew is chock full of good vegetables. And it's really easy to fix in the slow cooker.

1 cup (110 g) cubed potatoes

½ cup (65 g) sliced carrots

1 cup (160 g) chopped onion

½ cup (50 g) chopped celery

2 cups (360 g) no-salt-added stewed tomatoes

3 cups (700 ml) low-sodium vegetable broth (see recipe in Chapter 2)

1 teaspoon thyme

½ teaspoon parsley

½ cup (95 g) brown rice

1 pound (455 g) frozen green beans

1 pound (455 g) frozen corn

5¾ cups (1.4 L) low-sodium vegetable juice

Combine potatoes, carrots, onion, celery, tomatoes, vegetable broth, thyme, parsley, and rice in slow cooker. Cover and cook on high 2 hours. Stir in green beans, corn, and vegetable juice. Cover and cook on high 1 more hour and then reduce to low and cook 6 to 8 more hours.

Yield: 8 servings

Per serving: 471 g water; 184 calories (6% from fat, 15% from protein, 79% from carb); 8 g protein; 1 g total fat; 0 g saturated fat; 0 g monounsaturated fat; 0 g polyunsaturated fat; 40 g carb; 7 g fiber; 13 g sugar; 170 mg phosphorus; 108 mg calcium; 3 mg iron; 173 mg sodium; 1015 mg potassium; 4436 IU vitamin A; 1 mg ATE vitamin E; 67 mg vitamin C; 0 mg cholesterol

Hominy Stew

If you've never tried hominy (and I know there are some of you out there), this stew would be a good starting point. The peppers give it a vaguely Mexican flavor, but it's really just good.

1 can (28 ounces, or 785 g) no-salt-added diced tomatoes

4 ounces (115 g) canned chilies, chopped

4 cups (684 g) pinto beans, cooked or canned without salt

24 ounces (680 g) hominy, undrained

1 cup (160 g) chopped onion

2 cups (475 ml) water

2 tablespoons (15 g) Ranch Dressing Mix (see recipe in Chapter 2)

2 tablespoons (15 g) Salt-Free Mexican Seasoning (see recipe in Chapter 2)

TIP

Top with shredded Cheddar cheese.

Combine all ingredients in slow cooker. Cover and cook on low 8 to 10 hours.

Yield: 8 servings

Per serving: 204 g water; 658 calories (3% from fat, 17% from protein, 79% from carb); 29 g protein; 3 g total fat; 0 g saturated fat; 0 g monounsaturated fat; 1 g polyunsaturated fat; 134 g carb; 21 g fiber; 6 g sugar; 564 mg phosphorus; 155 mg calcium; 9 mg iron; 85 mg sodium; 1701 mg potassium; 134 IU vitamin A; 0 mg ATE vitamin E; 22 mg vitamin C; 0 mg cholesterol

Sweet Potato and Barley Stew

Here's a little different take on chili. The flavor is familiar, but the ingredients aren't. But don't let that stop you from trying it.

1 can (28 ounces, or 785 g) no-salt-added crushed tomatoes

1 medium sweet potato, peeled and cut into 1-inch (2.5 cm) cubes

2 cups (512 g) kidney beans, cooked or canned without salt

2 cups (475 ml) low-sodium chicken broth (see recipe in Chapter 2)

½ cup (80 g) chopped onion

¾ cup (113 g) chopped red bell pepper

½ cup (100 g) pearl barley

½ cup (120 ml) water

1 tablespoon (7.5 g) chili powder

1 tablespoon (15 ml) lime juice

1 teaspoon minced garlic

1 teaspoon ground cumin

½ teaspoon oregano

1 teaspoon black pepper

Lime wedges and/or chopped fresh cilantro (optional)

In a slow cooker, combine undrained tomatoes and remaining ingredients, except lime wedges and cilantro (if using). Cover and cook on low for 6 to 7 hours or on high for 3 to 4 hours. If desired, serve with lime wedges and/or top each serving with cilantro.

Yield: 6 servings

Per serving: 316 g water; 190 calories (5% from fat, 20% from protein, 75% from carb); 10 g protein; 1 g total fat; 0 g saturated fat; 0 g monounsaturated fat; 0 g polyunsaturated fat; 38 g carb; 11 g fiber; 6 g sugar; 182 mg phosphorus; 98 mg calcium; 4 mg iron; 91 mg sodium; 723 mg potassium; 5088 IU vitamin A; 0 mg ATE vitamin E; 43 mg vitamin C; 0 mg cholesterol

Curried Lima Soup

Curry powder and sour cream add interest to what would otherwise be a bland soup. But with them, it is full of flavor.

1½ cups (303 g) dried lima beans

4 cups (950 ml) water, divided

5 medium potatoes, finely chopped

(continued on page 314)

2 cups (460 g) fat-free sour cream

2 tablespoons (13 g) curry powder

In a medium saucepan, bring dried limas to a boil in 2 cups (475 ml) water. Boil, uncovered, for 2 minutes. Cover, turn off heat, and wait 2 hours. Drain water. Place beans in slow cooker. Add remaining 2 cups (475 ml) fresh water. Cover and cook 2 hours on high. During the last hour of cooking, add diced potatoes. Cook until potatoes are tender. Ten minutes before serving, add sour cream and curry powder.

Yield: 6 servings

Per serving: 504 g water; 378 calories (24% from fat, 12% from protein, 64% from carb); 11 g protein; 11 g total fat; 6 g saturated fat; 3 g monounsaturated fat; 1 g polyunsaturated fat; 62 g carb; 9 g fiber; 4 g sugar; 322 mg phosphorus; 142 mg calcium; 4 mg iron; 70 mg sodium; 1722 mg potassium; 417 IU vitamin A; 81 mg ATE vitamin E; 30 mg vitamin C; 31 mg cholesterol

Bean Soup with Cornmeal Dumplings

This soup has a southwestern flavor, perfectly set off by the cornmeal dumplings.

2 cups (512 g) kidney beans, cooked or canned without salt

2 cups (344 g) black beans, cooked or canned without salt

3 cups (700 ml) low-sodium chicken broth (see recipe in Chapter 2)

2 cups (360 ml) no-salt-added diced tomatoes

10 ounces (280 ml) frozen corn

1 cup (160 g) chopped onion

4 ounces (115 g) chopped green chilies

2 teaspoons chili powder

½ teaspoon minced garlic

2 tablespoons (15 g) Salt-Free Mexican Seasoning (see recipe in Chapter 2)

⅓ cup (42 g) flour

¼ cup (35 g) cornmeal

1 teaspoon baking powder

2 tablespoons (28 ml) egg substitute

2 tablespoons (28 ml) skim milk

1 tablespoon (15 ml) olive oil

Combine first 10 ingredients (through Mexican seasoning) in slow cooker. Cover and cook on low 8 to 10 hours. At the end of cooking time, turn cooker to high. Mix together flour, cornmeal, and baking powder. Combine egg, milk, and oil and stir into dry ingredients until just moistened. Drop dumplings by teaspoonful into soup. Cover and cook for 30 minutes.

Yield: 5 servings

Per serving: 430 g water; 362 calories (12% from fat, 20% from protein, 68% from carb); 19 g protein; 5 g total fat; 1 g saturated fat; 2 g monounsaturated fat; 1 g polyunsaturated fat; 65 g carb; 17 g fiber; 6 g sugar; 349 mg phosphorus; 173 mg calcium; 6 mg iron; 324 mg sodium; 1034 mg potassium; 614 IU vitamin A; 4 mg ATE vitamin E; 25 mg vitamin C; 0 mg cholesterol

Bean and Barley Soup

This bean and barley soup is so hearty and so good that even the people who think they have to have meat at every meal will love it.

1 tablespoon (15 ml) olive oil

1 cup (160 g) chopped onion

¾ teaspoon minced garlic

24 ounces (680 g) no-salt-added great northern beans, undrained

4 cups (950 ml) low-sodium vegetable broth (see recipe in Chapter 2)

4 cups (950 ml) water

1 cup (130 g) chopped carrots

1 cup (150 g) chopped green bell pepper

½ cup (50 g) chopped celery

½ cup (92 g) quick cooking barley

½ cup (30 g) chopped fresh parsley

2 bay leaves

½ teaspoon thyme

(continued on page 316)

½ teaspoon black pepper

1 can (14 ounces, or 400 g) no-salt-added diced tomatoes, undrained

Heat oil in a skillet over medium-high heat. Sauté onion and garlic until just soft. Combine onion mixture and remaining ingredients in slow cooker. Cook on low 8 to 10 hours. Discard bay leaves before serving.

Yield: 10 servings

Per serving: 321 g water; 164 calories (13% from fat, 21% from protein, 66% from carb); 9 g protein; 2 g total fat; 0 g saturated fat; 1 g monounsaturated fat; 1 g polyunsaturated fat; 28 g carb; 6 g fiber; 3 g sugar; 167 mg phosphorus; 101 mg calcium; 2 mg iron; 83 mg sodium; 549 mg potassium; 2538 IU vitamin A; 1 mg ATE vitamin E; 23 mg vitamin C; 0 mg cholesterol

Mexican Bean and Rice Soup

This is a great meatless chili-type soup. We like it with cornbread.

1 cup (160 g) chopped onion

½ cup (75 g) chopped green bell pepper

½ teaspoon minced garlic

2¼ cups (535 ml) low-sodium vegetable juice

2 cups (512 g) kidney beans, cooked or canned without salt

1½ cups (355 ml) water

½ cup (93 g) uncooked long-grain rice

1 teaspoon paprika

1 teaspoon chili powder

Combine all ingredients in slow cooker. Cover and cook on low 8 to 10 hours.

Yield: 6 servings

Per serving: 223 g water; 122 calories (3% from fat, 22% from protein, 75% from carb); 7 g protein; 0 g total fat; 0 g saturated fat; 0 g monounsaturated fat; 0 g polyunsaturated fat; 24 g carb; 7 g fiber; 4 g sugar; 117 mg phosphorus; 48 mg calcium; 2 mg iron; 60 mg sodium; 471 mg potassium; 1699 IU vitamin A; 0 mg ATE vitamin E; 37 mg vitamin C; 0 mg cholesterol

Black Bean Soup

A taste of the islands, this soup goes well with Bob Marley or Jimmy Buffett.

1 pound (455 g) dried black beans

2 cups (320 g) chopped onion

1 cup (150 g) chopped green bell pepper

1½ teaspoons minced garlic

1 tablespoon (7 g) cumin

2 teaspoons oregano

1 teaspoon thyme

½ teaspoon black pepper

3 cups (700 ml) water

2 tablespoons (28 ml) cider vinegar

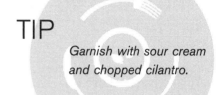

TIP

Garnish with sour cream and chopped cilantro.

Soak beans overnight in water to cover. Drain. Combine beans and remaining ingredients in slow cooker. Cover and cook on low 8-10 hours.

Yield: 8 servings

Per serving: 183 g water; 100 calories (5% from fat, 22% from protein, 73% from carb); 6 g protein; 1 g total fat; 0 g saturated fat; 0 g monounsaturated fat; 0 g polyunsaturated fat; 19 g carb; 6 g fiber; 2 g sugar; 101 mg phosphorus; 44 mg calcium; 2 mg iron; 7 mg sodium; 318 mg potassium; 105 IU vitamin A; 0 mg ATE vitamin E; 18 mg vitamin C; 0 mg cholesterol

Italian Bean Soup

A multi-bean soup with Italian flavor, this is great with garlic bread and a salad. You should be able to find a bean soup mixture in the dried bean section of most supermarkets.

1 pound (455 g) dried mixed beans

1 cup (160 g) chopped onion

(continued on page 318)

3 cups (700 ml) water

4 slices low-sodium bacon, cooked and crumbled

2 tablespoons (12 g) Italian seasoning

1 can (28 ounces, or 785 g) no-salt-added diced tomatoes

Cook beans according to package directions until almost done. Drain. Combine beans and remaining ingredients in slow cooker. Cover and cook on low 8 to 10 hours.

Yield: 6 servings

Per serving: 276 g water; 317 calories (9% from fat, 26% from protein, 66% from carb); 21 g protein; 3 g total fat; 1 g saturated fat; 1 g monounsaturated fat; 1 g polyunsaturated fat; 54 g carb; 14 g fiber; 6 g sugar; 291 mg phosphorus; 248 mg calcium; 10 mg iron; 74 mg sodium; 1693 mg potassium; 226 IU vitamin A; 1 mg ATE vitamin E; 15 mg vitamin C; 6 mg cholesterol

Pea Soup

It's called pea soup, but that shortchanges all the other good things that are in it. Suffice it to say that you'll end up with a bowl full of goodness.

2 tablespoons (28 ml) olive oil

1 cup (160 g) diced onion

1 bay leaf

1 teaspoon celery seed

1 cup (225 g) green split peas

¼ cup (50 g) pearl barley

½ cup (101 g) lima beans

10 cups (2.4 L) water

¼ teaspoon pepper

½ teaspoon basil

½ teaspoon thyme

½ teaspoon caraway seed

¼ cup (28 g) grated carrot

½ cup (50 g) diced celery

½ cup (30 g) fresh parsley

1 large potato, diced

Heat oil in a skillet over medium-high heat and sauté onion, bay leaf, and celery seed. Add to rest of ingredients in slow cooker and stir to combine. Cook on low about 4 to 6 hours. Remove bay leaf before serving.

Yield: 6 servings

Per serving: 488 g water; 257 calories (18% from fat, 18% from protein, 64% from carb); 12 g protein; 5 g total fat; 1 g saturated fat; 3 g monounsaturated fat; 1 g polyunsaturated fat; 42 g carb; 13 g fiber; 5 g sugar; 211 mg phosphorus; 70 mg calcium; 3 mg iron; 43 mg sodium; 810 mg potassium; 1450 IU vitamin A; 0 mg ATE vitamin E; 17 mg vitamin C; 0 mg cholesterol

Squash and Bean Soup

This may seem like an unusual combination when you first look at the ingredients, but it really works. The slow cooker allows all the different flavors to blend into one delicious whole.

1 cup (160 g) chopped onion

1 tablespoon (15 ml) olive oil

½ teaspoon ground cumin

¼ teaspoon cinnamon

½ teaspoon minced garlic

3 cups (420 g) butternut squash, peeled and cut into 1-inch (2.5 cm) cubes

1½ cups (355 ml) low-sodium vegetable broth (see recipe in Chapter 2)

2 cups (450 g) great northern beans, cooked or canned without salt

1 can (14 ounces, or 400 g) no-salt-added diced tomatoes, undrained

1 tablespoon chopped fresh cilantro

Combine all ingredients in slow cooker. Cover and cook on high 1 hour. Reduce heat to low and cook 2 to 3 hours.

(continued on page 320)

Yield: 6 servings

Per serving: 267 g water; 184 calories (15% from fat, 19% from protein, 66% from carb); 9 g protein; 3 g total fat; 1 g saturated fat; 2 g monounsaturated fat; 1 g polyunsaturated fat; 32 g carb; 7 g fiber; 4 g sugar; 182 mg phosphorus; 128 mg calcium; 3 mg iron; 52 mg sodium; 776 mg potassium; 7553 IU vitamin A; 1 mg ATE vitamin E; 24 mg vitamin C; 0 mg cholesterol

Baked Potato Soup

This great-tasting soup will remind you of a loaded baked potato, topped with bacon, cheese, and sour cream.

6 baking potatoes, peeled, cut in ½-inch (1.3 cm) cubes

1 cup (160 g) chopped onion

4 cups (950 ml) low-sodium chicken broth (see recipe in Chapter 2)

½ teaspoon minced garlic

¼ cup (55 g) unsalted butter

1 teaspoon black pepper

1 cup (235 ml) fat-free evaporated milk

½ cup (58 g) shredded Cheddar cheese

3 tablespoons (9 g) chopped fresh chives

½ cup (115 g) fat-free sour cream

6 slices low-sodium bacon, fried and crumbled

Combine first six ingredients (through pepper) in a slow cooker; cover and cook on high for 4 hours or low for 8 hours (potato should be tender). Mash mixture until potatoes are coarsely chopped and soup is slightly thickened. Stir in evaporated milk, cheese, and chives. Top each serving with sour cream and sprinkle with bacon and more cheese, if desired.

Yield: 6 servings

Per serving: 532 g water; 519 calories (30% from fat, 14% from protein, 56% from carb); 18 g protein; 18 g total fat; 10 g saturated fat; 5 g monounsaturated fat; 1 g polyunsaturated fat; 74 g carb; 9 g fiber; 9 g sugar; 441 mg phosphorus; 287 mg calcium; 4 mg iron; 303 mg sodium; 1876 mg potassium; 667 IU vitamin A; 163 mg ATE vitamin E; 76 mg vitamin C; 50 mg cholesterol

Easy Cheesy Potato Soup

You won't believe how rich this soup tastes until you try it. So what are you waiting for?

3 cups (700 ml) water

5 medium potatoes, diced finely

8 ounces (225 g) fat-free cream cheese, cubed

½ cup (80 g) chopped onion

1 teaspoon garlic powder

¼ teaspoon black pepper

½ teaspoon dill weed

½ cup (58 g) shredded Cheddar cheese

Combine all ingredients in slow cooker. Cover and cook on high 4 hours, stirring occasionally.

Yield: 6 servings

Per serving: 407 g water; 354 calories (27% from fat, 14% from protein, 59% from carb); 13 g protein; 11 g total fat; 7 g saturated fat; 3 g monounsaturated fat; 1 g polyunsaturated fat; 53 g carb; 6 g fiber; 4 g sugar; 306 mg phosphorus; 161 mg calcium; 3 mg iron; 203 mg sodium; 1503 mg potassium; 394 IU vitamin A; 97 mg ATE vitamin E; 28 mg vitamin C; 33 mg cholesterol

Potato Soup

This is a simple potato soup without a lot of frills and extras but still with great taste.

6 potatoes, peeled and diced

5 cups (1.2 L) low-sodium vegetable broth (see recipe in Chapter 2)

2 cups (360 g) diced onion

½ cup (50 g) diced celery

½ cup (65 g) diced carrots

¼ teaspoon pepper

(continued on page 322)

1½ cups (355 ml) evaporated milk

3 tablespoons (12 g) chopped fresh parsley

Combine all ingredients except milk and parsley in slow cooker. Cover and cook on high 7 to 8 hours or until vegetables are tender. Stir in milk and parsley.

Yield: 8 servings

Per serving: 452 g water; 296 calories (14% from fat, 16% from protein, 71% from carb); 12 g protein; 5 g total fat; 2 g saturated fat; 1 g monounsaturated fat; 1 g polyunsaturated fat; 54 g carb; 6 g fiber; 5 g sugar; 318 mg phosphorus; 201 mg calcium; 3 mg iron; 162 mg sodium; 1628 mg potassium; 1690 IU vitamin A; 2 mg ATE vitamin E; 30 mg vitamin C; 12 mg cholesterol

Southwestern Corn Soup

Here's a flavorful soup with the kick and the taste of the southwestern United States.

8 ounces (225 g) diced green chilies, undrained

1 cup (120 g) sliced zucchini

1 cup (160 g) thinly sliced onion

½ teaspoon minced garlic

1 teaspoon cumin

5 cups (1.2 L) low-sodium vegetable broth (see recipe in Chapter 2)

2 cups (480 g) no-salt-added canned chickpeas, rinsed and drained

10 ounces (280 g) frozen corn

1 teaspoon oregano

½ cup (30 g) chopped fresh cilantro

Combine all ingredients in slow cooker. Cook on low 4 hours.

Yield: 6 servings

Per serving: 349 g water; 177 calories (15% from fat, 24% from protein, 62% from carb); 11 g protein; 3 g total fat; 0 g saturated fat; 1 g monounsaturated fat; 1 g polyunsaturated fat; 29 g carb; 6 g fiber; 6 g sugar; 200 mg phosphorus; 109 mg calcium; 3 mg iron; 130 mg sodium; 526 mg potassium; 317 IU vitamin A; 2 mg ATE vitamin E; 9 mg vitamin C; 0 mg cholesterol

Pasta and Bean Soup

This is a hearty soup, similar to some Italian bean soups, but without the usual Italian seasonings.

1 cup (180 g) chopped tomatoes

½ cup (75 g) uncooked macaroni

½ cup (80 g) chopped onion

¼ cup (40 g) chopped green bell pepper

1 teaspoon basil

1 teaspoon Worcestershire sauce

½ teaspoon chopped garlic

1 can (15 ounces, or 420 g) no-salt-added kidney beans, drained

1 can (15 ounces, or 420 g) no-salt-added chickpeas, drained

2 cups (475 ml) low-sodium vegetable broth (see recipe in Chapter 2)

Combine all ingredients in slow cooker. Cook on low 5 to 6 hours.

Yield: 6 servings

Per serving: 224 g water; 216 calories (7% from fat, 24% from protein, 70% from carb); 13 g protein; 2 g total fat; 0 g saturated fat; 0 g monounsaturated fat; 1 g polyunsaturated fat; 38 g carb; 11 g fiber; 1 g sugar; 208 mg phosphorus; 87 mg calcium; 4 mg iron; 273 mg sodium; 562 mg potassium; 212 IU vitamin A; 1 mg ATE vitamin E; 18 mg vitamin C; 0 mg cholesterol

Tomato Lentil Soup

This soup is proof that vegetarian meals do not have to be short on flavor. Enjoy it with a slice of dark bread.

3 cups (700 ml) water

1 can (28 ounces, or 785 g) no-salt-added diced tomatoes, undrained

1 can (6 ounces, or 170 g) no-salt-added tomato paste

(continued on page 324)

½ cup (120 ml) dry red wine

½ teaspoon basil

½ teaspoon thyme

1 pound (455 g) lentils, rinsed and drained

1 cup (160 g) chopped onion

1 cup (130 g) sliced carrots

1 cup (100 g) sliced celery

1 teaspoon minced garlic

Combine water, tomatoes with juice, tomato paste, red wine, basil, and thyme in slow cooker. Add lentils, onion, carrots, celery, and garlic. Cover and cook on low 10 to 12 hours or on high 4 to 5 hours.

Yield: 8 servings

Per serving: 294 g water; 130 calories (4% from fat, 23% from protein, 74% from carb); 7 g protein; 1 g total fat; 0 g saturated fat; 0 g monounsaturated fat; 0 g polyunsaturated fat; 24 g carb; 7 g fiber; 8 g sugar; 157 mg phosphorus; 71 mg calcium; 4 mg iron; 60 mg sodium; 748 mg potassium; 3198 IU vitamin A; 0 mg ATE vitamin E; 18 mg vitamin C; 0 mg cholesterol

Wild Rice and Lentil Soup

Soups like this one make it easy to get the heart-healthy low-sodium, low-fat, and high-fiber combination.

½ cup (96 g) lentils, sorted, rinsed, and drained

3 cups (700 ml) water

½ cup (80 g) wild rice

2 cups (475 ml) low-sodium vegetable juice

10 ounces (280 g) frozen mixed vegetables

1 cup (235 ml) skim milk

½ cup (58 g) shredded Cheddar cheese

Cover lentils with water and soak overnight or for 6 to 8 hours. Drain and discard soaking water. Put all ingredients into slow cooker, including the 3 cups (700 ml) fresh water. Mix well. Cover and cook on low 5 to 8 hours or until the vegetables are done.

Yield: 8 servings

Per serving: 215 g water; 130 calories (21% from fat, 22% from protein, 58% from carb); 7 g protein; 3 g total fat; 2 g saturated fat; 1 g monounsaturated fat; 0 g polyunsaturated fat; 19 g carb; 4 g fiber; 4 g sugar; 171 mg phosphorus; 126 mg calcium; 1 mg iron; 120 mg sodium; 330 mg potassium; 2606 IU vitamin A; 40 mg ATE vitamin E; 18 mg vitamin C; 9 mg cholesterol

Barley and Mushroom Soup

This hearty meatless soup is full of flavor and filling enough to make a meal.

1 pound (455 g) mushrooms, sliced

1½ cups (240 g) chopped onions

½ teaspoon minced garlic

1 cup (100 g) chopped celery

1 cup (130 g) chopped carrots

5 cups (1.2 L) water, divided

½ cup (100 g) pearl barley

4 cups (950 ml) low-sodium vegetable broth (see recipe in Chapter 2)

4 teaspoons (20 ml) Worcestershire sauce

1½ teaspoons basil

1½ teaspoons parsley

1 teaspoon dill weed

1½ teaspoons oregano

½ teaspoon thyme

½ teaspoon garlic powder

(continued on page 326)

Combine all ingredients in slow cooker. Cook on low 7 to 8 hours or until vegetables are done.

Yield: 8 servings

Per serving: 372 g water; 98 calories (11% from fat, 25% from protein, 64% from carb); 6 g protein; 1 g total fat; 0 g saturated fat; 0 g monounsaturated fat; 0 g polyunsaturated fat; 16 g carb; 4 g fiber; 3 g sugar; 139 mg phosphorus; 74 mg calcium; 2 mg iron; 126 mg sodium; 503 mg potassium; 2812 IU vitamin A; 1 mg ATE vitamin E; 10 mg vitamin C; 0 mg cholesterol

Winter Vegetable Chili

An unusual meatless chili containing squash and carrots, this is great with cornbread or a loaf of Italian bread.

2 cups (280 g) cubed butternut squash

2 cups (260 g) sliced carrot

1 cup (160 g) chopped onion

1 can (28 ounces, or 785 g) no-salt-added diced tomatoes

4 ounces (115 g) chopped green chilies

1 cup (235 ml) low-sodium vegetable broth (see recipe in chapter 2)

2 tablespoons (15 g) chili powder

4 cups (688 g) black beans, cooked or canned without salt

Layer ingredients in slow cooker in order listed. Cover and cook on low 8 to 10 hours.

Yield: 6 servings

Per serving: 359 g water; 241 calories (6% from fat, 21% from protein, 73% from carb); 14 g protein; 2 g total fat; 0 g saturated fat; 0 g monounsaturated fat; 1 g polyunsaturated fat; 47 g carb; 15 g fiber; 8 g sugar; 246 mg phosphorus; 141 mg calcium; 5 mg iron; 174 mg sodium; 1100 mg potassium; 13062 IU vitamin A; 0 mg ATE vitamin E; 35 mg vitamin C; 0 mg cholesterol

Vegetable Chili

This simple meatless chili will surprise and please people with its assortment of vegetables and its great taste.

1 cup (160 g) chopped onion

20 ounces (560 g) frozen mixed vegetables

1 can (14 ounces, or 400 g) no-salt-added diced tomatoes, undrained

1 cup (245 g) no-salt-added tomato sauce

½ cup (120 ml) water

1 tablespoon (7.5 g) chili powder

Place onion in slow cooker. Place frozen vegetables in strainer; rinse with hot water to separate. Stir vegetables, undrained tomatoes, tomato sauce, water, and chili powder into onions. Cover and cook on low for 8 to 10 hours.

Yield: 4 servings

Per serving: 327 g water; 152 calories (5% from fat, 16% from protein, 80% from carb); 6 g protein; 1 g total fat; 0 g saturated fat; 0 g monounsaturated fat; 0 g polyunsaturated fat; 31 g carb; 9 g fiber; 11 g sugar; 127 mg phosphorus; 89 mg calcium; 3 mg iron; 90 mg sodium; 731 mg potassium; 6932 IU vitamin A; 0 mg ATE vitamin E; 25 mg vitamin C; 0 mg cholesterol

Black-Eyed Pea Chili

This one fits into our list of unusual chili recipes, but it is definitely worth trying. And after all, black-eyed peas aren't all that different from beans.

1 cup (160 g) finely chopped onion

1 cup (130 g) finely chopped carrots

1 cup (150 g) finely chopped red pepper

½ teaspoon minced garlic

4 teaspoons (10 g) chili powder

(continued on page 328)

1 teaspoon ground cumin

1 tablespoon (1 g) chopped cilantro

1 can (14 ounces, or 400 g) no-salt-added diced tomatoes

30 ounces (840 g) canned no-salt-added black-eyed peas, drained

4 ounces (115 g) diced green chilies

1 cup (235 ml) low-sodium vegetable broth (see recipe in Chapter 2)

TIP

Garnish individual servings with cheese and cilantro.

Combine all ingredients in slow cooker. Cover and cook on low 6 to 8 hours or high 4 hours.

Yield: 6 servings

Per serving: 279 g water; 242 calories (7% from fat, 23% from protein, 71% from carb); 15 g protein; 2 g total fat; 0 g saturated fat; 0 g monounsaturated fat; 1 g polyunsaturated fat; 45 g carb; 12 g fiber; 11 g sugar; 229 mg phosphorus; 96 mg calcium; 5 mg iron; 149 mg sodium; 913 mg potassium; 5101 IU vitamin A; 0 mg ATE vitamin E; 53 mg vitamin C; 0 mg cholesterol

Fresh Vegetable Chili

The flavor says chili, but the look is vegetable soup. And all in all, that's a winning combination.

1 tablespoon (15 ml) olive oil

1 cup (160 g) chopped onion

1 teaspoon minced garlic

½ cup (50 g) chopped celery

¾ cup (98 g) thinly sliced carrot

1 cup (150 g) chopped green bell pepper

1 cup (120 g) sliced zucchini

8 ounces (225 g) mushrooms, sliced

1¼ cups (285 ml) water

1 can (14 ounces, or 400 g) no-salt-added kidney beans, drained

1 can (14 ounces, or 400 g) no-salt-added diced tomatoes, undrained

1 teaspoon lemon juice

¼ teaspoon oregano

1 teaspoon ground cumin

1 teaspoon chili powder

1 teaspoon black pepper

Heat oil in a skillet over medium heat; sauté onions and garlic until tender. Add celery, carrot, green pepper, zucchini, and mushrooms to skillet and sauté 2 to 3 minutes. Transfer to slow cooker. Add remaining ingredients. Cover and cook on low 6 to 8 hours.

Yield: 10 servings

Per serving: 198 g water; 105 calories (14% from fat, 20% from protein, 65% from carb); 6 g protein; 2 g total fat; 0 g saturated fat; 1 g monounsaturated fat; 0 g polyunsaturated fat; 18 g carb; 6 g fiber; 5 g sugar; 115 mg phosphorus; 59 mg calcium; 2 mg iron; 49 mg sodium; 545 mg potassium; 7546 IU vitamin A; 0 mg ATE vitamin E; 23 mg vitamin C; 0 mg cholesterol

15

Simple, Nutrient-Rich Vegetables and Side Dishes

Are you one of those people like me who always seems to think about needing a vegetable for a meal just about the time everything else is ready? Do yourself a favor and start with the vegetable, putting it in the slow cooker first so you have it perfectly done by the time the rest of the meal is.

Corn Casserole

A creamy corn casserole is spiced up by the addition of a can of chopped green chili peppers.

20 ounces (560 g) frozen corn
8 ounces (225 g) fat-free cream cheese
4 ounces (115 g) chopped green chilies
¼ cup (55 g) unsalted butter

Combine all ingredients in slow cooker and cook until cheese and butter are melted and mixture is smooth, about 2 hours.

Yield: 6 servings

Per serving: 115 g water; 240 calories (55% from fat, 11% from protein, 34% from carb); 7 g protein; 15 g total fat; 9 g saturated fat; 4 g monounsaturated fat; 1 g polyunsaturated fat; 22 g carb; 3 g fiber; 4 g sugar; 145 mg phosphorus; 48 mg calcium; 1 mg iron; 148 mg sodium; 356 mg potassium; 826 IU vitamin A; 132 mg ATE vitamin E; 19 mg vitamin C; 42 mg cholesterol

Mexi-Corn

This Mexican flavored corn is great as a side dish, especially with Mexican meals, but also just with any plain piece of meat.

20 ounces (580 g) frozen corn, partially thawed
4 ounces (115 g) pimientos, chopped
¼ cup (38 g) finely chopped green bell pepper
¼ cup (60 ml) water
¼ teaspoon pepper
½ teaspoon paprika
½ teaspoon chili powder

(continued on page 332)

Combine all ingredients in slow cooker. Cover and cook on high 45 minutes, then on low 2 to 4 hours. Stir occasionally.

Yield: 8 servings

Per serving: 79 g water; 62 calories (5% from fat, 12% from protein, 83% from carb); 2 g protein; 0 g total fat; 0 g saturated fat; 0 g monounsaturated fat; 0 g polyunsaturated fat; 15 g carb; 2 g fiber; 3 g sugar; 45 mg phosphorus; 5 mg calcium; 1 mg iron; 8 mg sodium; 141 mg potassium; 521 IU vitamin A; 0 mg ATE vitamin E; 18 mg vitamin C; 0 mg cholesterol

Corn Pudding

This is a favorite side dish for family get-togethers, which is fine with me since it's so easy to make ahead of time.

2 pounds (900 g) frozen corn, thawed

½ cup (120 ml) egg substitute

1 cup (235 ml) skim milk

¼ teaspoon black pepper

2 tablespoons (26 g) sugar

3 tablespoons (24 g) flour

Spray slow cooker with nonstick cooking spray. Combine all ingredients well. Pour into prepared slow cooker. Cover and cook on high 3 hours.

Yield: 8 servings

Per serving: 128 g water; 140 calories (7% from fat, 17% from protein, 77% from carb); 7 g protein; 1 g total fat; 0 g saturated fat; 0 g monounsaturated fat; 0 g polyunsaturated fat; 29 g carb; 3 g fiber; 7 g sugar; 121 mg phosphorus; 58 mg calcium; 1 mg iron; 52 mg sodium; 278 mg potassium; 122 IU vitamin A; 19 mg ATE vitamin E; 4 mg vitamin C; 1 mg cholesterol

Asian Broccoli

This is a great Asian-flavored side dish.

2 pounds (900 g) broccoli, trimmed and chopped into
    bite-size piece

½ teaspoon minced garlic

½ cup (75 g) thinly sliced red bell pepper

¾ cup (120 g) sliced onion

¼ cup (60 ml) low-sodium soy sauce (see recipe in
    Chapter 2)

Dash black pepper

1 tablespoon (8 g) sesame seeds

TIP

Serve over brown rice.

Combine all ingredients except sesame seeds in slow cooker. Cook on low for 6 hours. Top with sesame seeds.

Yield: 8 servings

Per serving: 129 g water; 58 calories (14% from fat, 24% from protein, 62% from carb); 4 g protein; 1 g total fat; 0 g saturated fat; 0 g monounsaturated fat; 0 g polyunsaturated fat; 10 g carb; 4 g fiber; 3 g sugar; 98 mg phosphorus; 70 mg calcium; 1 mg iron; 64 mg sodium; 420 mg potassium; 998 IU vitamin A; 0 mg ATE vitamin E; 114 mg vitamin C; 0 mg cholesterol

Broccoli Casserole

Broccoli cooks in a cheesy sauce while a crispy topping forms in this popular side dish recipe.

20 ounces (560 g) frozen broccoli spears

1 can (10 ounces, or 280 g) low-sodium cream of celery soup

1¼ cups (150 g) grated Cheddar cheese, divided

¼ cup (25 g) minced scallions

12 saltines, crushed

(continued on page 334)

Spray slow cooker with nonstick cooking spray. In large bowl, combine broccoli, soup, 1 cup (115 g) of grated cheese, and scallions. Pour into prepared slow cooker. Sprinkle with crushed crackers and the remaining cheese. Cover and slip a wooden toothpick between lid and pot to vent. Cook on low 5 to 6 hours or on high 2 to 3 hours.

Yield: 6 servings

Per serving: 190 g water; 220 calories (47% from fat, 20% from protein, 33% from carb); 11 g protein; 12 g total fat; 6 g saturated fat; 3 g monounsaturated fat; 1 g polyunsaturated fat; 19 g carb; 3 g fiber; 2 g sugar; 231 mg phosphorus; 264 mg calcium; 2 mg iron; 607 mg sodium; 398 mg potassium; 1030 IU vitamin A; 91 mg ATE vitamin E; 85 mg vitamin C; 35 mg cholesterol

Creamed Spinach

Creamed spinach is a favorite of mine, and it goes great with a steak. This recipe, which is really more like a soufflé, makes the preparation really easy.

30 ounces (840 g) frozen spinach

2 cups (450 g) fat-free cottage cheese

1 cup (115 g) shredded Cheddar

¾ cup (175 ml) egg substitute

¼ cup (30 g) flour

½ cup (112 g) unsalted butter, melted

Mix together all ingredients and pour into slow cooker. Cook on high for 1 hour, then on low for 4 hours more.

Yield: 8 servings

Per serving: 170 g water; 277 calories (59% from fat, 26% from protein, 14% from carb); 19 g protein; 19 g total fat; 11 g saturated fat; 5 g monounsaturated fat; 1 g polyunsaturated fat; 10 g carb; 4 g fiber; 2 g sugar; 249 mg phosphorus; 333 mg calcium; 3 mg iron; 339 mg sodium; 471 mg potassium; 13450 IU vitamin A; 144 mg ATE vitamin E; 2 mg vitamin C; 50 mg cholesterol

Spinach Casserole

This makes a great creamy spinach dish, sort of halfway between a spinach dip and traditional creamed spinach.

20 ounces (560 g) frozen spinach, thawed and drained

2 cups (450 g) fat-free cottage cheese

½ cup (112 g) unsalted butter, cut into pieces

1½ cups (173 g) cubed Cheddar cheese

¾ cup (175 ml) egg substitute

¼ cup (31 g) flour

Spray slow cooker with nonstick cooking spray. Combine all ingredients in a bowl and pour into prepared slow cooker. Cover and cook on low for 4 to 5 hours.

Yield: 6 servings

Per serving: 188 g water; 398 calories (63% from fat, 25% from protein, 11% from carb); 26 g protein; 29 g total fat; 17 g saturated fat; 8 g monounsaturated fat; 2 g polyunsaturated fat; 12 g carb; 4 g fiber; 3 g sugar; 365 mg phosphorus; 450 mg calcium; 3 mg iron; 474 mg sodium; 496 mg potassium; 12345 IU vitamin A; 220 mg ATE vitamin E; 2 mg vitamin C; 79 mg cholesterol

Greek Green Beans and Tomatoes

Tomatoes and Greek spices give these beans a Mediterranean flavor.

1 pound (455 g) fresh green beans, cut into 1-inch (2.5 cm) lengths

½ teaspoon crushed garlic

1 cup (235 ml) no-salt-added diced tomatoes

1 cup (160 g) chopped onion

½ teaspoon dried oregano

1 teaspoon lemon juice

(continued on page 336)

1 tablespoon (15 ml) olive oil

Black pepper, to taste

Place ingredients in slow cooker. Stir. Cover and cook on low for 6 hours.

Yield: 4 servings

Per serving: 193 g water; 92 calories (32% from fat, 12% from protein, 56% from carb); 3 g protein; 4 g total fat; 1 g saturated fat; 2 g monounsaturated fat; 0 g polyunsaturated fat; 14 g carb; 5 g fiber; 5 g sugar; 66 mg phosphorus; 71 mg calcium; 2 mg iron; 16 mg sodium; 407 mg potassium; 858 IU vitamin A; 0 mg ATE vitamin E; 27 mg vitamin C; 0 mg cholesterol

Broccoli Rice Casserole

A hearty side dish of broccoli and rice in a creamy, cheesy sauce, this recipe only needs a piece of meat to make a complete meal.

1 pound (455 g) frozen broccoli, cooked and drained

10 ounces (280 g) low-sodium cream of mushroom soup (see recipe in Chapter 2)

⅓ cup (53 g) chopped onion

10 ounces (280 g) Swiss cheese, shredded

½ cup (120 ml) skim milk

1½ cups (248 g) cooked rice

Mix everything together, leaving enough cheese to sprinkle over the top. Place in slow cooker and top with reserved cheese. Cook on low for 2 hours.

Yield: 4 servings

Per serving: 270 g water; 437 calories (43% from fat, 25% from protein, 32% from carb); 27 g protein; 21 g total fat; 13 g saturated fat; 6 g monounsaturated fat; 1 g polyunsaturated fat; 35 g carb; 4 g fiber; 5 g sugar; 604 mg phosphorus; 797 mg calcium; 1 mg iron; 338 mg sodium; 798 mg potassium; 1355 IU vitamin A; 170 mg ATE vitamin E; 102 mg vitamin C; 68 mg cholesterol

Squash Casserole

Squash can be fairly plain. But this version is anything but, with carrots for color and lots of other good things for flavor.

4 cups (480 g) thinly sliced yellow squash

½ cup (80 g) chopped onion

1 cup (130 g) shredded carrot

1 can (10 ounces, or 280 g) low-sodium cream of chicken soup

1 cup (230 g) fat-free sour cream

¼ cup (31 g) flour

8 ounces (225 g) reduced-sodium stuffing mix, crumbled

½ cup (112 g) unsalted butter, melted

In large bowl, combine squash, onion, carrot, and soup. Mix sour cream and flour together; stir into vegetables. Toss stuffing crumbs with butter and place half in slow cooker. Add vegetable mixture and top with remaining stuffing crumbs. Cover and cook on low for 7 to 9 hours.

Yield: 6 servings

Per serving: 182 g water; 426 calories (51% from fat, 8% from protein, 41% from carb); 9 g protein; 25 g total fat; 14 g saturated fat; 7 g monounsaturated fat; 2 g polyunsaturated fat; 44 g carb; 3 g fiber; 7 g sugar; 157 mg phosphorus; 112 mg calcium; 3 mg iron; 668 mg sodium; 465 mg potassium; 4453 IU vitamin A; 188 mg ATE vitamin E; 15 mg vitamin C; 61 mg cholesterol

Vegetable Medley

This is a perfect summer side dish when fresh vegetables are abundant. Feel free to substitute based on taste and availability. It's excellent with ham or fish.

¾ cup (120 g) sliced onion

1 cup (100 g) celery, cut in 2-inch (5 cm) strips

1 cup (130 g) carrots, cut in 2-inch (5 cm) strips

(continued on page 338)

1 cup (100 g) green beans

½ cup (75 g) diced green bell pepper

1 large tomato, sliced

¼ cup (55 g) unsalted butter

⅛ teaspoon black pepper

1 tablespoon (13 g) sugar

3 tablespoons (25 g) tapioca

Mix ingredients and place in slow cooker. Cook on low for 3 to 4 hours.

Yield: 6 servings

Per serving: 107 g water; 126 calories (54% from fat, 4% from protein, 42% from carb); 1 g protein; 8 g total fat; 5 g saturated fat; 2 g monounsaturated fat; 0 g polyunsaturated fat; 14 g carb; 2 g fiber; 5 g sugar; 35 mg phosphorus; 31 mg calcium; 1 mg iron; 34 mg sodium; 260 mg potassium; 4226 IU vitamin A; 63 mg ATE vitamin E; 23 mg vitamin C; 20 mg cholesterol

Greek Eggplant

The flavor of the Mediterranean shines through this eggplant dish. Serve with grilled meat (kabobs are nice).

2 tablespoons (28 ml) olive oil

1 cup (160 g) chopped red onion

½ teaspoon crushed garlic

4 ounces (115 g) mushrooms, sliced

1 eggplant, unpeeled, cubed

½ cup (75 g) coarsely chopped green bell pepper

1 can (28 ounces, or 785 g) no-salt-added crushed tomatoes

2 tablespoons (3.4 g) fresh rosemary

2 tablespoons (8 g) chopped fresh parsley

Spray slow cooker with nonstick cooking spray. Heat olive oil in a skillet over medium heat and sauté onion, garlic, and mushrooms. Pour into prepared slow cooker. Add eggplant, green pepper, tomatoes, rosemary, and parsley to cooker. Cover and cook on low 5 to 6 hours.

Yield: 8 servings

Per serving: 187 g water; 75 calories (40% from fat, 10% from protein, 49% from carb); 2 g protein; 4 g total fat; 1 g saturated fat; 3 g monounsaturated fat; 0 g polyunsaturated fat; 10 g carb; 4 g fiber; 5 g sugar; 54 mg phosphorus; 45 mg calcium; 1 mg iron; 17 mg sodium; 418 mg potassium; 258 IU vitamin A; 0 mg ATE vitamin E; 21 mg vitamin C; 0 mg cholesterol

Caramelized Onions

The slow cooking makes slow work of caramelizing onions…but then, that's the point: long, slow cooking. And this way you don't need to watch them.

6 large sweet onions, such as Vidalia

¼ cup (55 g) unsalted butter

1¼ cups (285 ml) low-sodium chicken broth (see recipe in Chapter 2)

Peel onions. Remove stems and root ends. Place in slow cooker. Pour butter and broth over onions. Cook on low 12 hours.

Yield: 8 servings

Per serving: 143 g water; 100 calories (51% from fat, 6% from protein, 43% from carb); 2 g protein; 6 g total fat; 4 g saturated fat; 2 g monounsaturated fat; 0 g polyunsaturated fat; 11 g carb; 2 g fiber; 5 g sugar; 40 mg phosphorus; 31 mg calcium; 0 mg iron; 26 mg sodium; 188 mg potassium; 180 IU vitamin A; 48 mg ATE vitamin E; 9 mg vitamin C; 15 mg cholesterol

Stuffed Acorn Squash

This is a delightfully sweet squash dish, easily cooked in the slow cooker.

2 acorn squash

2 apples, peeled and chopped

½ cup (115 g) brown sugar

½ teaspoon cinnamon

¼ teaspoon nutmeg

2 teaspoons lemon juice

¼ cup (55 g) unsalted butter

Cut squash in half lengthwise; remove seeds. Divide chopped apple evenly among the squash halves. Sprinkle each half with one quarter of the brown sugar, cinnamon, nutmeg, and a few drops of lemon juice. Dot each with 1 tablespoon (14 g) of butter. Wrap each squash half securely in foil. Pour ¼ cup (60 ml) water into slow cooker. Stack the squash, cut side up, in cooker. Cover and cook on low for 5 hours. Unwrap; place squash on serving platter. Drain any syrup remaining in foil into small pitcher; serve with squash.

Yield: 4 servings

Per serving: 255 g water; 326 calories (31% from fat, 2% from protein, 67% from carb); 2 g protein; 12 g total fat; 7 g saturated fat; 3 g monounsaturated fat; 1 g polyunsaturated fat; 58 g carb; 4 g fiber; 33 g sugar; 95 mg phosphorus; 105 mg calcium; 2 mg iron; 19 mg sodium; 915 mg potassium; 1172 IU vitamin A; 95 mg ATE vitamin E; 30 mg vitamin C; 31 mg cholesterol

Glazed Root Vegetables

These cook up similar to roasted vegetables with the easy fixing afforded by the slow cooker.

2 parsnips, sliced

2 cups (260 g) sliced carrot

1 turnip, cut in 1-inch (2.5 cm) cubes

1 cup (235 ml) water

½ cup (100 g) sugar

3 tablespoons (42 g) unsalted butter

Boil vegetables in water for 10 minutes. Drain, reserving ½ cup (120 ml) of the liquid. Transfer vegetables to slow cooker. Pour reserved liquid over the top. Add sugar and butter. Cover and cook on low for 3 hours.

Yield: 6 servings

Per serving: 149 g water; 180 calories (29% from fat, 3% from protein, 68% from carb); 1 g protein; 6 g total fat; 4 g saturated fat; 2 g monounsaturated fat; 0 g polyunsaturated fat; 32 g carb; 4 g fiber; 23 g sugar; 62 mg phosphorus; 46 mg calcium; 1 mg iron; 183 mg sodium; 393 mg potassium; 7350 IU vitamin A; 48 mg ATE vitamin E; 16 mg vitamin C; 15 mg cholesterol

Vegetable Accompaniment

Yes, I know that's a strange name, but it's accurate. This is something we make as a one-dish accompaniment to whatever kind of meat we are having. And it goes well with anything.

4 potatoes, diced and peeled

1¼ cups (205 g) frozen corn

2 cups (360 g) seeded and diced tomatoes

1 cup (130 g) sliced carrots

½ cup (80 g) chopped onion

¼ teaspoon dill weed

¼ teaspoon black pepper

¼ teaspoon basil

¼ teaspoon rosemary

Combine all ingredients in slow cooker. Cover and cook on low 5 to 6 hours or until vegetables are tender.

(continued on page 342)

Yield: 8 servings

Per serving: 227 g water; 168 calories (3% from fat, 11% from protein, 87% from carb); 5 g protein; 1 g total fat; 0 g saturated fat; 0 g monounsaturated fat; 0 g polyunsaturated fat; 39 g carb; 5 g fiber; 4 g sugar; 145 mg phosphorus; 30 mg calcium; 2 mg iron; 27 mg sodium; 1028 mg potassium; 2940 IU vitamin A; 0 mg ATE vitamin E; 28 mg vitamin C; 0 mg cholesterol

Succotash

This makes big batch of what many may not call succotash since it contains tomatoes and potatoes. Whatever you call it, it's super-easy to fix and very tasty.

1 can (28 ounces, or 785 g) no-salt-added diced tomatoes, undrained

1 pound (455 g) frozen lima beans

1 pound (455 g) frozen corn

3 medium red potatoes, coarsely chopped

½ cup (120 ml) low-sodium chicken broth (see recipe in Chapter 2)

1 teaspoon crushed thyme

¼ teaspoon black pepper

In a 4- to 5-quart (3.8 to 4.8 L) slow cooker, combine undrained tomatoes, lima beans, corn, and potatoes. Add broth, thyme, and pepper. Cover and cook on low for 7 to 9 hours or on high for 3½ to 4½ hours.

Yield: 12 servings

Per serving: 135 g water; 111 calories (3% from fat, 16% from protein, 81% from carb); 5 g protein; 0 g total fat; 0 g saturated fat; 0 g monounsaturated fat; 0 g polyunsaturated fat; 24 g carb; 5 g fiber; 3 g sugar; 92 mg phosphorus; 40 mg calcium; 3 mg iron; 30 mg sodium; 423 mg potassium; 146 IU vitamin A; 0 mg ATE vitamin E; 12 mg vitamin C; 0 mg cholesterol

Glazed Carrots

Sweet carrots are made even sweeter with honey and apricot preserves. This one's sure to be popular with children as well as adults.

2 pounds (900 g) carrots, sliced

½ cup (80 g) chopped onion

¼ cup (60 ml) water

¼ cup (85 g) honey

¼ cup (80 g) apricot preserves

Place carrots and onions in slow cooker. Add water. Cover and cook on low 9 hours. Drain liquid from slow cooker. In a small bowl, mix honey and preserves together. Pour over carrots. Cover and cook on high 10 to 15 minutes.

Yield: 8 servings

Per serving: 121 g water; 110 calories (2% from fat, 4% from protein, 94% from carb); 1 g protein; 0 g total fat; 0 g saturated fat; 0 g monounsaturated fat; 0 g polyunsaturated fat; 27 g carb; 3 g fiber; 19 g sugar; 45 mg phosphorus; 43 mg calcium; 0 mg iron; 82 mg sodium; 391 mg potassium; 19064 IU vitamin A; 0 mg ATE vitamin E; 8 mg vitamin C; 0 mg cholesterol

Creamy Zucchini Casserole

This casserole is easy to put together but tastes great. Serve with chicken or fish.

3 cups (360 g) thinly sliced zucchini

1 cup (160 g) diced onion

1 cup (130 g) shredded carrot

10 ounces (280 g) low-sodium cream of mushroom soup (see recipe in Chapter 2)

10 ounces (280 g) low-sodium cream of chicken soup

(continued on page 344)

Spray slow cooker with nonstick cooking spray. Mix vegetables and soups together gently in slow cooker. Cover and cook on high 4 to 6 hours or until vegetables are as crunchy or as soft as you like.

Yield: 6 servings

Per serving: 184 g water; 78 cal (19% from fat, 12% from protein, 69% from carb); 2 g protein; 2 g total fat; 1 g saturated fat; 0 g monounsaturated fat; 1 g polyunsaturated fat; 14 g carb; 2 g fiber; 5 g sugar; 87 mg phosphorus; 35 mg calcium; 1 mg iron; 52 mg sodium; 623 mg potassium; 3718 IU vitamin A; 2 mg ATE vitamin E; 14 mg vitamin C; 3 mg Cholesterol

Mixed Squash Casserole

This squash casserole makes a great side dish for just about any kind of meal.

1½ cups (180 g) sliced zucchini

1½ cups (180 g) sliced yellow squash

1 cup (180 g) peeled and chopped tomatoes

¼ cup (25 g) sliced scallions

½ cup (75 g) chopped green bell pepper

¼ cup (60 ml) low-sodium chicken broth (see recipe in Chapter 2)

¼ cup (30 g) bread crumbs

In slow cooker, layer half the zucchini, squash, tomatoes, scallions, and green pepper. Repeat layers. Pour broth over vegetables. Sprinkle bread crumbs over top. Cover and cook on low 4 to 6 hours.

Yield: 8 servings

Per serving: 79 g water; 28 calories (11% from fat, 17% from protein, 72% from carb); 1 g protein; 0 g total fat; 0 g saturated fat; 0 g monounsaturated fat; 0 g polyunsaturated fat; 5 g carb; 1 g fiber; 1 g sugar; 31 mg phosphorus; 17 mg calcium; 0 mg iron; 10 mg sodium; 192 mg potassium; 271 IU vitamin A; 0 mg ATE vitamin E; 20 mg vitamin C; 0 mg cholesterol

Italian Zucchini

These zucchini cooked in an Italian seasoned tomato sauce can be used as a side dish for meat or pasta or can be used as a pasta sauce itself.

½ cup (80 g) chopped onion

½ cup (75 g) chopped green bell pepper

¼ cup (55 g) unsalted butter

1 can (6 ounces, or 170 g) no-salt-added tomato paste

4 ounces (115 g) mushrooms, sliced

2 tablespoons (12 g) Italian seasoning

1 cup (235 ml) water

2½ pounds (1.1 kg) zucchini, cut in ⅜-inch (0.9 cm) slices

4 ounces (115 g) shredded mozzarella cheese

In a saucepan, cook onion and green pepper in butter until tender but not brown. Transfer to a slow cooker. Stir in tomato paste, mushrooms, Italian seasoning, and water. Add zucchini, stirring gently to coat. Cover and cook on low for 8 hours. To serve, spoon into dishes; sprinkle with mozzarella.

Yield: 8 servings

Per serving: 189 g water; 145 calories (54% from fat, 17% from protein, 29% from carb); 7 g protein; 9 g total fat; 6 g saturated fat; 2 g monounsaturated fat; 1 g polyunsaturated fat; 11 g carb; 3 g fiber; 6 g sugar; 142 mg phosphorus; 118 mg calcium; 2 mg iron; 126 mg sodium; 688 mg potassium; 967 IU vitamin A; 72 mg ATE vitamin E; 38 mg vitamin C; 26 mg cholesterol

Sweet and Sour Red Cabbage

Sweet and sour red cabbage doesn't have to be high in sodium. The slow cooker makes cooking it easy, and it has plenty of room to make a double or triple batch so you can freeze some for later meals.

(continued on page 346)

4 cups (280 g) shredded red cabbage

1 cup (160 g) chopped onion

1 cup (150 g) peeled and chopped apple

½ cup (115 g) brown sugar

½ cup (120 ml) cider vinegar

Place vegetables in a slow cooker. Combine sugar and vinegar, pour over vegetables, and stir to mix. Cook on low for 7 to 8 hours.

Yield: 6 servings

Per serving: 112 g water; 111 calories (1% from fat, 4% from protein, 95% from carb); 1 g protein; 0 g total fat; 0 g saturated fat; 0 g monounsaturated fat; 0 g polyunsaturated fat; 27 g carb; 2 g fiber; 23 g sugar; 33 mg phosphorus; 51 mg calcium; 1 mg iron; 25 mg sodium; 278 mg potassium; 670 IU vitamin A; 0 mg ATE vitamin E; 37 mg vitamin C; 0 mg cholesterol

Apples and Kraut

Applesauce sweetens sauerkraut during the long slow cooking.

2 pounds (900 g) sauerkraut

2 cups (490 g) applesauce

1 cup (160 g) chopped onion

1 cup (225 g) brown sugar

2 tablespoons (13.4 g) caraway seeds

Combine ingredients in slow cooker and simmer for 3 or more hours.

Yield: 8 servings

Per serving: 174 g water; 187 calories (2% from fat, 3% from protein, 94% from carb); 2 g protein; 1 g total fat; 0 g saturated fat; 0 g monounsaturated fat; 0 g polyunsaturated fat; 47 g carb; 5 g fiber; 40 g sugar; 49 mg phosphorus; 76 mg calcium; 3 mg iron; 763 mg sodium; 379 mg potassium; 34 IU vitamin A; 0 mg ATE vitamin E; 20 mg vitamin C; 0 mg cholesterol

Orange Glazed Carrots

Carrots are cooked in the slow cooker and then finished with an orange glaze and pecans for a taste treat.

3 cups (390 g) thinly sliced carrots

2 cups (475 ml) water

3 tablespoons (42 g) unsalted butter

3 tablespoons (60 ml) orange marmalade

2 tablespoons (14 g) chopped pecans

Combine carrots and water in slow cooker. Cover and cook on high 2 to 3 hours or until carrots are done. Drain well and then stir in remaining ingredients. Cover and cook on high 20 to 30 minutes.

Yield: 5 servings

Per serving: 168 g water; 141 calories (55% from fat, 3% from protein, 42% from carb); 1 g protein; 9 g total fat; 5 g saturated fat; 3 g monounsaturated fat; 1 g polyunsaturated fat; 16 g carb; 2 g fiber; 11 g sugar; 37 mg phosphorus; 37 mg calcium; 0 mg iron; 63 mg sodium; 264 mg potassium; 13133 IU vitamin A; 57 mg ATE vitamin E; 5 mg vitamin C; 18 mg cholesterol

Slow Cooker Chili Rellenos

You could make a meal of these, but they are also great as a side dish with a grilled piece of meat that has been rubbed with Mexican seasonings.

4 ounces (115 g) whole green chilies

1 cup (115 g) grated Cheddar cheese

1 cup (115 g) grated Monterey Jack cheese

1 large tomato, sliced

4 eggs, separated

(continued on page 348)

¾ cup (175 ml) evaporated milk

2 tablespoons (16 g) flour

Spray sides and bottom of slow cooker with nonstick cooking spray. Remove seeds from chilies; cut into strips. Place half of chilies on bottom of slow cooker. Layer with Cheddar cheese, rest of chilies, Monterey Jack cheese, and tomato slices. Beat egg whites until stiff. Fold in slightly beaten yolks, milk, and flour. Pour over top of tomatoes in the pot. Cover and cook on high for 2 to 3 hours.

Yield: 4 servings

Per serving: 165 g water; 427 calories (63% from fat, 26% from protein, 11% from carb); 28 g protein; 30 g total fat; 17 g saturated fat; 9 g monounsaturated fat; 2 g polyunsaturated fat; 12 g carb; 1 g fiber; 2 g sugar; 536 mg phosphorus; 642 mg calcium; 2 mg iron; 545 mg sodium; 417 mg potassium; 1481 IU vitamin A; 226 mg ATE vitamin E; 30 mg vitamin C; 315 mg cholesterol

Stewed Tomatoes

Yes, you can buy salt-free stewed tomatoes. But if stores in your area don't happen to carry them or you just have extra tomatoes from the garden, you can also make your own and freeze them in resealable plastic bags for use at a later date.

4 large tomatoes

1 cup (160 g) chopped onion

¾ cup (75 g) chopped celery

½ cup (75 g) chopped green bell pepper

3 tablespoons (39 g) sugar

1 bay leaf

⅛ teaspoon black pepper

Core tomatoes; place in boiling water for about 15 to 20 seconds and then plunge into ice water to cool quickly; peel. Cut tomatoes in wedges. In slow cooker, combine tomatoes and remaining ingredients. Cover and cook on low 8 to 9 hours. Remove bay leaf. Serve as a side dish or freeze in portions for soups or other recipes.

Yield: 6 servings

Per serving: 141 g water; 61 calories (5% from fat, 8% from protein, 87% from carb); 1 g protein; 0 g total fat; 0 g saturated fat; 0 g monounsaturated fat; 0 g polyunsaturated fat; 14 g carb; 2 g fiber; 8 g sugar; 37 mg phosphorus; 18 mg calcium; 1 mg iron; 21 mg sodium; 315 mg potassium; 722 IU vitamin A; 0 mg ATE vitamin E; 38 mg vitamin C; 0 mg cholesterol

16

Heart-Healthy Potatoes, Rice, Grains, and Legumes

The starchy side dishes are another area where the slow cooker excels. If you have trouble boiling rice, leave it to slow cook to perfection. Looking for a great side dish like scalloped potatoes or macaroni and cheese? They're here too. You can even cook your holiday stuffing in the slow cooker, giving you another chance to use it to spread out the preparation of your holiday meal. There are also recipes for a variety of bean dishes, as well as other whole grains. In short, everyone should be able to find several things to like here.

Mashed Potatoes

The biggest advantage of these mashed potatoes, other than the added flavor of the cream cheese and sour cream, is that they can be made ahead of time. One less last minute thing to do for your holiday dinner.

6 tablespoons (84 g) unsalted butter, melted

2¼ cups (535 ml) skim milk

6¼ cups (375 g) potato flakes

6 cups (1.4 L) water

4 ounces (115 g) fat-free cream cheese, softened

1 cup (230 g) fat-free sour cream

Combine first four ingredients as directed on potato box. Whip cream cheese with electric mixer until creamy. Blend in sour cream. Fold potatoes into cheese and sour cream. Beat well. Place in slow cooker. Cover and cook on low 3 to 5 hours.

Yield: 10 servings

Per serving: 222 g water; 276 calories (39% from fat, 10% from protein, 51% from carb); 7 g protein; 12 g total fat; 8 g saturated fat; 3 g monounsaturated fat; 0 g polyunsaturated fat; 35 g carb; 2 g fiber; 1 g sugar; 162 mg phosphorus; 133 mg calcium; 1 mg iron; 120 mg sodium; 567 mg potassium; 496 IU vitamin A; 136 mg ATE vitamin E; 31 mg vitamin C; 35 mg cholesterol

Mashed Potatoes and Turnips

When I was growing up, we used to take plain boiled potatoes and turnips and mash them together with butter on top. So when I saw a slow cooker recipe for making real mashed potatoes with turnips added, I had to try it. I'm very glad I did.

3 pounds (1⅓ kg) baking potatoes, peeled and cut into 1-inch (2.5 cm) cubes

1½ pounds (680 g) turnips, peeled and cut into 1-inch (2.5 cm) cubes

5¼ cups (1.2 L) low-sodium chicken broth (see recipe in Chapter 2)

(continued on page 352)

¾ cup (175 ml) fat-free evaporated milk

¼ cup (55 g) unsalted butter

½ teaspoon black pepper

In a slow cooker, combine potatoes, turnips, and broth. Cover and cook on low for 6 to 7 hours or on high for 3 to 4 hours. Drain, reserving some of the cooking liquid. In a bowl, mash vegetables with a potato masher. In a small saucepan, combine milk and butter. Heat until milk is hot and butter melts. Add to potato mixture along with the pepper; mix well.

Yield: 12 servings

Per serving: 254 g water; 150 calories (24% from fat, 12% from protein, 64% from carb); 4 g protein; 4 g total fat; 2 g saturated fat; 1 g monounsaturated fat; 0 g polyunsaturated fat; 25 g carb; 4 g fiber; 5 g sugar; 123 mg phosphorus; 84 mg calcium; 1 mg iron; 93 mg sodium; 663 mg potassium; 184 IU vitamin A; 51 mg ATE vitamin E; 29 mg vitamin C; 11 mg cholesterol

Roasted Garlic Mashed Potatoes

Make your holiday mashed potatoes ahead of time and let the slow cooker take care of both cooking them and keeping them warm.

3 pounds (1⅓ kg) potatoes, peeled and cut into 2-inch (5 cm) pieces

2 tablespoons (20 g) roasted garlic

1 bay leaf

3½ cups (820 ml) low-sodium chicken broth (see recipe in Chapter 2)

1 cup (235 ml) skim milk

¼ cup (55 g) unsalted butter

½ teaspoon white pepper

2 tablespoons (6 g) chopped fresh chives

In a slow cooker, combine potatoes, garlic, and bay leaf. Pour broth over potatoes in cooker. Cover and cook on low for 6 to 8 hours or on high for 3 to 4 hours. Drain potatoes in a colander over a bowl to catch the juices. Remove and discard bay leaf. Return potatoes to slow cooker. Mash to desired consistency with a potato masher. In a small saucepan, heat milk and butter until steaming and butter is almost melted. Add milk mixture, white pepper, chives, and enough of the reserved cooking juices to the potato mixture to reach desired consistency.

Yield: 12 servings

Per serving: 177 g water; 127 calories (29% from fat, 11% from protein, 61% from carb); 3 g protein; 4 g total fat; 3 g saturated fat; 1 g monounsaturated fat; 0 g polyunsaturated fat; 20 g carb; 2 g fiber; 1 g sugar; 103 mg phosphorus; 47 mg calcium; 1 mg iron; 58 mg sodium; 580 mg potassium; 168 IU vitamin A; 44 mg ATE vitamin E; 10 mg vitamin C; 11 mg cholesterol

Herbed Potatoes

These new potatoes are cooked in the slow cooker and then tossed with fresh herbs to make them even better.

1½ pounds (680 g) new potatoes

¼ cup (60 ml) water

¼ cup (55 g) unsalted butter, melted

3 tablespoons (12 g) fresh parsley

1 tablespoon (15 ml) lemon juice

1 tablespoon (3 g) fresh chives

2 tablespoons (8 g) fresh dill weed

Wash potatoes and then peel a strip from around the center of each potato. Place the potatoes in a slow cooker; add water. Cover and cook on high for 2½ to 3 hours. Drain well. In saucepan, heat butter with parsley, lemon juice, chives, and dill. Pour mixture over potatoes; toss until thoroughly coated.

Yield: 6 servings

Per serving: 101 g water; 175 calories (39% from fat, 7% from protein, 54% from carb); 3 g protein; 8 g total fat; 5 g saturated fat; 2 g monounsaturated fat; 0 g polyunsaturated fat; 24 g carb; 3 g fiber; 1 g sugar; 83 mg phosphorus; 23 mg calcium; 1 mg iron; 14 mg sodium; 625 mg potassium; 442 IU vitamin A; 63 mg ATE vitamin E; 15 mg vitamin C; 20 mg cholesterol

Garlic Potatoes

These garlicky good potatoes are perfect with grilled meat or fish.

6 potatoes, peeled and cubed

2 teaspoons minced garlic

½ cup (80 g) chopped onion

2 tablespoons (28 ml) olive oil

Combine all ingredients in slow cooker. Cook on low 5 to 6 hours or until potatoes are soft.

Yield: 6 servings

Per serving: 311 g water; 305 calories (14% from fat, 9% from protein, 76% from carb); 7 g protein; 5 g total fat; 1 g saturated fat; 3 g monounsaturated fat; 1 g polyunsaturated fat; 60 g carb; 7 g fiber; 4 g sugar; 230 mg phosphorus; 42 mg calcium; 3 mg iron; 23 mg sodium; 1702 mg potassium; 26 IU vitamin A; 0 mg ATE vitamin E; 33 mg vitamin C; 0 mg cholesterol

Creamed Potatoes

Potatoes in a creamy cheese sauce will remind you of old-fashioned scalloped potatoes.

2 pounds (900 g) red potatoes, quartered

8 ounces (225 g) fat-free cream cheese, softened

10 ounces (280 g) cream of potato soup

2 tablespoons (15 g) ranch dressing mix (see recipe in Chapter 2)

Place potatoes in slow cooker. Beat together cream cheese, soup, and ranch dressing mix. Stir into potatoes. Cover and cook on low 8 hours or until potatoes are tender.

Yield: 8 servings

Per serving: 102 g water; 311 calories (16% from fat, 11% from protein, 73% from carb); 8 g protein; 6 g total fat; 4 g saturated fat; 2 g monounsaturated fat; 0 g polyunsaturated fat; 57 g carb; 9 g fiber; 2 g sugar; 169 mg phosphorus; 76 mg calcium; 9 mg iron; 390 mg sodium; 736 mg potassium; 228 IU vitamin A; 58 mg ATE vitamin E; 15 mg vitamin C; 18 mg cholesterol

Potatoes Au Gratin

Cheesy, creamy potatoes go well with just about any kind of meat (pork chops are my favorite) and are a snap to fix.

2 tablespoons (20 g) minced onion

½ teaspoon minced garlic

8 medium potatoes, sliced

8 ounces (225 g) fat-free cream cheese, cubed, divided

½ cup (58 g) shredded Cheddar cheese

Spray interior of slow cooker with nonstick cooking spray. In a small bowl, combine onion and garlic. Layer about one-fourth of the potatoes into the slow cooker. Sprinkle one-fourth of onion-garlic mixture over potatoes. Spoon about one-third of cream cheese cubes over top. Repeat layers, ending with the onion-garlic mixture. Cook on high 3 to 4 hours or until potatoes are tender. Stir potatoes to distribute the cream cheese. Sprinkle shredded cheese over top of the sliced potatoes. Cover and cook an additional 10 minutes or until the cheese is melted.

Yield: 8 servings

Per serving: 322 g water; 358 calories (20% from fat, 13% from protein, 67% from carb); 12 g protein; 8 g total fat; 5 g saturated fat; 2 g monounsaturated fat; 0 g polyunsaturated fat; 61 g carb; 6 g fiber; 4 g sugar; 310 mg phosphorus; 129 mg calcium; 3 mg iron; 157 mg sodium; 1739 mg potassium; 301 IU vitamin A; 73 mg ATE vitamin E; 32 mg vitamin C; 25 mg cholesterol

Slow Cooker Baked Potatoes

This is ideal for summertime since it will not heat up your kitchen. And you'll find that the potatoes bake evenly and turn out as good as oven-baked potatoes.

6 large potatoes

Wash and scrub potatoes. Prick potatoes with a fork and wrap in foil. Place in the slow cooker. Cover and cook on low 8 to 10 hours or on high 2½ to 4 hours.

(continued on page 356)

Yield: 6 servings

Per serving: 299 g water; 258 calories (2% from fat, 10% from protein, 88% from carb); 7 g protein; 1 g total fat; 0 g saturated fat; 0 g monounsaturated fat; 0 g polyunsaturated fat; 59 g carb; 6 g fiber; 4 g sugar; 225 mg phosphorus; 37 mg calcium; 3 mg iron; 22 mg sodium; 1679 mg potassium; 26 IU vitamin A; 0 mg ATE vitamin E; 32 mg vitamin C; 0 mg cholesterol

Scalloped Potatoes

Another one of those classic comfort foods. In this version, the preparation is simplified by using the slow cooker to create tender, creamy potatoes.

2 cups (475 ml) water

1 teaspoon cream of tartar

5 medium potatoes, thinly sliced

¼ cup (31 g) flour

⅛ teaspoon black pepper

1½ cups (355 ml) skim milk

½ cup (55 g) shredded Swiss cheese

½ cup (58 g) shredded Cheddar

Combine water and cream of tartar in large bowl. Stir. Add potatoes. Stir well. (This helps keep potatoes from darkening.) Drain. Turn potatoes into slow cooker. Stir flour and pepper together in saucepan. Whisk in milk gradually until no lumps remain. Heat and stir until boiling and thickened. Stir in cheeses and continue cooking until melted. Pour over potatoes in cooker. Cover and cook on low 6 to 8 hours.

Yield: 6 servings

Per serving: 336 g water; 331 calories (13% from fat, 18% from protein, 69% from carb); 15 g protein; 5 g total fat; 3 g saturated fat; 1 g monounsaturated fat; 0 g polyunsaturated fat; 57 g carb; 5 g fiber; 4 g sugar; 377 mg phosphorus; 299 mg calcium; 2 mg iron; 166 mg sodium; 1582 mg potassium; 277 IU vitamin A; 70 mg ATE vitamin E; 32 mg vitamin C; 17 mg cholesterol

Parmesan Potatoes

Potatoes and green beans cook in a Parmesan and sour cream sauce that adds incredible flavor.

6 medium red potatoes

¼ teaspoon black pepper

¼ teaspoon parsley flakes

½ teaspoon minced onion

½ cup (50 g) grated Parmesan cheese, divided

¼ cup (55 g) unsalted butter

1 pound (455 g) frozen green beans

1 pound (455 g) fat-free sour cream

Wash and scrub potatoes (do not peel). Boil in a large pan of water until tender and then drain. Cut potatoes into large sections. Place half of the potatoes in slow cooker. Sprinkle with half the pepper, parsley, and onion and 2 tablespoons (10 g) Parmesan. Cut half of the butter into pats and place on top of potatoes. Place green beans on top of potatoes. Put the rest of the potatoes on top and sprinkle again with remaining pepper, parsley, and onion and 2 tablespoons (10 g) Parmesan. Cut the remaining butter into pats and place over vegetables. Spread the sour cream evenly on top. Lightly sprinkle remaining Parmesan on top until it covers the sour cream. Heat in slow cooker on high for 1½ to 2 hours or until very hot, stirring after about 1 hour.

Yield: 6 servings

Per serving: 160 g water; 345 calories (49% from fat, 11% from protein, 40% from carb); 9 g protein; 19 g total fat; 12 g saturated fat; 5 g monounsaturated fat; 1 g polyunsaturated fat; 36 g carb; 7 g fiber; 2 g sugar; 223 mg phosphorus; 222 mg calcium; 5 mg iron; 176 mg sodium; 605 mg potassium; 1084 IU vitamin A; 149 mg ATE vitamin E; 21 mg vitamin C; 57 mg cholesterol

German Potato Salad

Since German potato salad is supposed to be warm anyway, cook the potatoes in the sauce in a slow cooker so the flavor soaks the whole way through.

2 large potatoes, sliced

½ cup (80 g) chopped onions

½ cup (50 g) sliced celery

¼ cup (38 g) diced green bell pepper

¼ cup (60 ml) vinegar

¼ cup (60 ml) oil

2 slices low-sodium bacon, cooked and crumbled

Chopped parsley

Combine all ingredients except bacon and parsley in slow cooker. Stir and cook for 5 to 6 hours on low. Garnish with bacon and parsley.

Yield: 3 servings

Per serving: 270 g water; 381 calories (48% from fat, 7% from protein, 44% from carb); 7 g protein; 21 g total fat; 3 g saturated fat; 6 g monounsaturated fat; 10 g polyunsaturated fat; 43 g carb; 5 g fiber; 4 g sugar; 194 mg phosphorus; 41 mg calcium; 2 mg iron; 71 mg sodium; 1269 mg potassium; 142 IU vitamin A; 1 mg ATE vitamin E; 34 mg vitamin C; 6 mg cholesterol

Baked Potato Slices

Onion soup mix gives an extra flavor boost to these potatoes, which are a great side dish with almost any kind of meat.

½ cup (112 g) unsalted butter

2 tablespoons (15 g) onion soup mix (see recipe in Chapter 2)

6 large potatoes

½ cup (120 ml) water

Combine butter and soup mix. Scrub potatoes and cut into ¼-inch (63 mm) slices. (Do not peel.) Alternate layers of potatoes and butter mixture in slow cooker. Pour water over top. Cook on low approximately 1½ to 2 hours.

Yield: 6 servings

Per serving: 322 g water; 397 calories (35% from fat, 7% from protein, 58% from carb); 7 g protein; 16 g total fat; 10 g saturated fat; 4 g monounsaturated fat; 1 g polyunsaturated fat; 59 g carb; 6 g fiber; 4 g sugar; 230 mg phosphorus; 44 mg calcium; 3 mg iron; 29 mg sodium; 1684 mg potassium; 499 IU vitamin A; 127 mg ATE vitamin E; 32 mg vitamin C; 41 mg cholesterol

Baked Sweet Potatoes

Baking sweet potatoes in the slow cooker means that you don't have to turn on the oven on those hot days. And they are just as good.

6 sweet potatoes

Scrub and prick sweet potatoes with fork. Wrap each in aluminum foil and arrange in slow cooker. Cover and cook on low 6 to 8 hours or on high 4 to 5 hours until each potato is soft.

Yield: 6 servings

Per serving: 121 g water; 115 calories (2% from fat, 7% from protein, 91% from carb); 2 g protein; 0 g total fat; 0 g saturated fat; 0 g monounsaturated fat; 0 g polyunsaturated fat; 27 g carb; 4 g fiber; 9 g sugar; 48 mg phosphorus; 41 mg calcium; 1 mg iron; 41 mg sodium; 347 mg potassium; 23767 IU vitamin A; 0 mg ATE vitamin E; 19 mg vitamin C; 0 mg cholesterol

Sweet Potatoes and Apples

Sweet potatoes and apples are one of those natural combinations. This version is flavored with maple syrup. It goes well with chicken or pork.

3 sweet potatoes, peeled and cubed

3 apples, peeled and sliced

¼ teaspoon pepper

1 teaspoon sage

1 teaspoon cinnamon

¼ cup (55 g) unsalted butter, melted

¼ cup (80 g) maple syrup

TIP

Sprinkle with toasted almonds or pecans when serving.

Place half the sweet potatoes in slow cooker. Layer half the apple slices on top. Mix together pepper, sage, and cinnamon; sprinkle half over apples. Mix together butter and maple syrup. Spoon half over the top. Repeat layers. Cover and cook on low 6 to 8 hours or until potatoes are soft, stirring occasionally.

Yield: 6 servings

Per serving: 122 g water; 192 calories (36% from fat, 3% from protein, 62% from carb); 1 g protein; 8 g total fat; 5 g saturated fat; 2 g monounsaturated fat; 0 g polyunsaturated fat; 31 g carb; 3 g fiber; 19 g sugar; 34 mg phosphorus; 41 mg calcium; 1 mg iron; 23 mg sodium; 264 mg potassium; 12156 IU vitamin A; 63 mg ATE vitamin E; 13 mg vitamin C; 20 mg cholesterol

Honey and Cinnamon Yams

These sweet and slightly spicy yams go especially well with pork.

4 cups (600 g) yams, cooked, peeled, and diced

1½ tablespoons (12 g) cornstarch

2 tablespoons (23 ml) cold water

1½ cups (510 g) honey

½ teaspoon cinnamon

1½ teaspoons lemon rind

¼ cup (60 ml) orange juice

2 teaspoons lemon juice

3 tablespoons (42 g) unsalted butter

Place yams in slow cooker. Combine remaining ingredients and pour over. Cook on low until done, about 4 to 6 hours.

Yield: 6 servings

Per serving: 96 g water; 427 calories (12% from fat, 2% from protein, 87% from carb); 2 g protein; 6 g total fat; 4 g saturated fat; 2 g monounsaturated fat; 0 g polyunsaturated fat; 98 g carb; 4 g fiber; 70 g sugar; 51 mg phosphorus; 24 mg calcium; 1 mg iron; 12 mg sodium; 677 mg potassium; 297 IU vitamin A; 48 mg ATE vitamin E; 16 mg vitamin C; 15 mg cholesterol

Stuffing

You can make this stuffing with dried herbs if that is all you have, but the fresh ones give it that little something extra.

3 tablespoons (42 g) unsalted butter

2 cups (320 g) chopped onion

1½ cups (150 g) chopped celery

¼ cup (15 g) chopped fresh parsley

1 tablespoon (1.7 g) chopped fresh rosemary

1 tablespoon (2.4 g) chopped fresh thyme

1 tablespoon (1.7 g) chopped fresh marjoram

1 tablespoon (2.5 g) chopped fresh sage

¼ teaspoon black pepper

8 cups (400 g) bread, cut in 1-inch (2.5 cm) cubes

1 cup (235 ml) low-sodium chicken broth (see recipe in Chapter 2)

(continued on page 362)

Melt butter in skillet over medium-high heat. Sauté onions and celery until transparent. Remove from heat and stir in parsley, rosemary, thyme, marjoram, sage, and pepper. Place bread cubes in large bowl. Add onion/herb mixture. Add enough broth to moisten. Mix well but gently. Spray slow cooker with nonstick cooking spray; pour stuffing into cooker. Cover and cook on high 1 hour. Reduce heat to low and continue cooking 3 to 4 hours.

Yield: 8 servings

Per serving: 104 g water; 182 calories (30% from fat, 12% from protein, 58% from carb); 6 g protein; 6 g total fat; 3 g saturated fat; 2 g monounsaturated fat; 1 g polyunsaturated fat; 27 g carb; 4 g fiber; 7 g sugar; 108 mg phosphorus; 82 mg calcium; 3 mg iron; 270 mg sodium; 238 mg potassium; 430 IU vitamin A; 36 mg ATE vitamin E; 7 mg vitamin C; 11 mg cholesterol

Herbed Rice

This is kind of like rice pilaf and extremely easy to make. The flavor goes well with chicken or pork.

3 cups (700 ml) low-sodium chicken broth (see recipe in Chapter 2)

1¼ cups (231 g) uncooked long-grain rice

1 teaspoon rosemary

¼ teaspoon marjoram

¼ cup (15 g) chopped fresh parsley

1 tablespoon (14 g) unsalted butter

½ cup (80 g) diced onion

Combine all ingredients in slow cooker. Cook on low 4 to 6 hours or until rice is fully cooked.

Yield: 6 servings

Per serving: 137 g water; 169 calories (13% from fat, 9% from protein, 78% from carb); 4 g protein; 2 g total fat; 1 g saturated fat; 1 g monounsaturated fat; 0 g polyunsaturated fat; 32 g carb; 1 g fiber; 1 g sugar; 64 mg phosphorus; 23 mg calcium; 2 mg iron; 74 mg sodium; 115 mg potassium; 275 IU vitamin A; 16 mg ATE vitamin E; 4 mg vitamin C; 5 mg cholesterol

Slow Cooker Rice

If you are one of those people who have trouble cooking rice, the slow cooker can make it perfectly for you every time.

1 cup (185 g) uncooked long-grain rice

2 cups (477 ml) water

½ tablespoon (7 g) unsalted butter

Combine all ingredients in slow cooker. Cover and cook on low 4 to 6 hours or on high 2 to 3 hours until rice is just fully cooked. Fluff with a fork. Serve.

Yield: 6 servings

Per serving: 83 g water; 121 calories (9% from fat, 7% from protein, 84% from carb); 2 g protein; 1 g total fat; 1 g saturated fat; 0 g monounsaturated fat; 0 g polyunsaturated fat; 25 g carb; 0 g fiber; 0 g sugar; 36 mg phosphorus; 11 mg calcium; 1 mg iron; 4 mg sodium; 37 mg potassium; 30 IU vitamin A; 8 mg ATE vitamin E; 0 mg vitamin C; 3 mg cholesterol

Beefy Rice Casserole

This is similar to some of the packaged rice mixes, but with better taste and a *lot* less sodium.

1 cup (185 g) uncooked long-grain rice

2 tablespoons (15 g) onion soup mix (see recipe in Chapter 2)

4 ounces (115 g) mushrooms, sliced

3 cups (700 ml) low-sodium beef broth (see recipe in Chapter 2)

2 tablespoons (28 g) unsalted butter

Mix everything together in slow cooker. Cook for 3 hours on low setting or until rice is tender.

Yield: 4 servings

(continued on page 364)

Per serving: 230 g water; 126 calories (45% from fat, 13% from protein, 42% from carb); 4 g protein; 6 g total fat; 4 g saturated fat; 2 g monounsaturated fat; 0 g polyunsaturated fat; 13 g carb; 1 g fiber; 1 g sugar; 66 mg phosphorus; 21 mg calcium; 1 mg iron; 114 mg sodium; 203 mg potassium; 177 IU vitamin A; 48 mg ATE vitamin E; 1 mg vitamin C; 15 mg cholesterol

Wild Rice

The slow cooker is a great way to cook all kinds of rice. This wild rice recipe will give you an easy and flavorful side dish.

½ cup (80 g) uncooked wild rice

½ cup (93 g) uncooked long-grain rice

8 ounces (225 g) mushrooms

½ cup (55 g) slivered almonds

¼ cup (38 g) chopped green bell pepper

¼ cup (60 g) chopped onion

½ teaspoon garlic powder

3 cups (700 ml) low-sodium chicken broth (see recipe in Chapter 2)

¼ cup (55 g) unsalted butter

Put all ingredients in the slow cooker. Cook on high 3 to 4 hours.

Yield: 3 servings

Per serving: 334 g water; 548 calories (47% from fat, 13% from protein, 40% from carb); 19 g protein; 30 g total fat; 11 g saturated fat; 13 g monounsaturated fat; 4 g polyunsaturated fat; 57 g carb; 6 g fiber; 4 g sugar; 417 mg phosphorus; 88 mg calcium; 4 mg iron; 89 mg sodium; 813 mg potassium; 526 IU vitamin A; 127 mg ATE vitamin E; 13 mg vitamin C; 41 mg cholesterol

Macaroni and Cheese

The slow cooker makes great macaroni and cheese, giving you that baked taste without having to turn on the oven. Buttermilk adds even more flavor to this recipe.

1 cup (235 ml) buttermilk

2 tablespoons (28 g) unsalted butter, melted

½ cup (120 ml) egg substitute

2 cups (230 g) grated Cheddar cheese, divided

8 ounces (225 g) macaroni, cooked and drained

Mix buttermilk, butter, egg substitute, and 1¼ cups (145 g) cheese well and then blend with macaroni and place in slow cooker. Top with remaining ¾ cup (80 g) cheese. Start cooking on high until hot and then turn to low and cook for about 4 hours.

Yield: 4 servings

Per serving: 142 g water; 457 calories (59% from fat, 22% from protein, 19% from carb); 26 g protein; 30 g total fat; 18 g saturated fat; 8 g monounsaturated fat; 2 g polyunsaturated fat; 21 g carb; 1 g fiber; 4 g sugar; 465 mg phosphorus; 569 mg calcium; 2 mg iron; 531 mg sodium; 287 mg potassium; 967 IU vitamin A; 222 mg ATE vitamin E; 1 mg vitamin C; 87 mg cholesterol

Curried Couscous

This side dish has it all: the flavor of fresh vegetables, the heat of curry powder and jalapeño, the sweetness of raisins, and the crunch of almonds. What's not to like?

1 medium onion, cut in thin wedges

2 cups (240 g) coarsely chopped yellow squash

1 can (28 ounces, or 785 g) no-salt-added diced tomatoes, undrained

4 ounces (115 g) chopped jalapeño chilies

2 cups (475 ml) water

2 tablespoons (12.6 g) curry powder

(continued on page 366)

11 ounces (310 g) couscous

1 cup (110 g) slivered almonds

½ cup (75 g) raisins

Fresh cilantro sprigs (optional)

In a slow cooker, combine onion, squash, undrained tomatoes, chilies, water, and curry powder. Cover and cook on low for 4 to 6 hours or on high for 2 to 3 hours. Stir in couscous. Turn off cooker. Cover and let stand for 5 minutes. Fluff couscous mixture with a fork. To serve, sprinkle each serving with almonds and raisins. If desired, garnish with cilantro sprigs.

Yield: 8 servings

Per serving: 204 g water; 361 calories (25% from fat, 13% from protein, 62% from carb); 12 g protein; 11 g total fat; 1 g saturated fat; 6 g monounsaturated fat; 3 g polyunsaturated fat; 59 g carb; 11 g fiber; 17 g sugar; 224 mg phosphorus; 116 mg calcium; 4 mg iron; 35 mg sodium; 850 mg potassium; 3943 IU vitamin A; 0 mg ATE vitamin E; 20 mg vitamin C; 0 mg cholesterol

Barley Risotto

OK, it's not really risotto, but the creamy texture of this side dish will remind you of risotto, and it's a lot easier to make.

2 cups (400 g) pearl barley

1¾ cups (410 ml) low-sodium chicken broth (see recipe in Chapter 2)

½ cup (65 g) shredded carrot

1 tablespoon (15 ml) lemon juice

1 teaspoon thyme

½ teaspoon minced garlic

½ teaspoon black pepper

½ cup (55 g) shredded Swiss cheese

1 cup (130 g) no-salt-added frozen peas

½ cup (120 ml) skim milk

2 tablespoons (28 g) unsalted butter

In a slow cooker, combine first seven ingredients (through pepper). Cover and cook on low for 5 to 5½ hours. Stir in Swiss cheese and remaining ingredients. Cover and let stand 10 minutes.

Yield: 6 servings

Per serving: 127 g water; 331 calories (23% from fat, 16% from protein, 61% from carb); 14 g protein; 9 g total fat; 5 g saturated fat; 2 g monounsaturated fat; 1 g polyunsaturated fat; 52 g carb; 12 g fiber; 3 g sugar; 285 mg phosphorus; 173 mg calcium; 3 mg iron; 87 mg sodium; 419 mg potassium; 2624 IU vitamin A; 67 mg ATE vitamin E; 5 mg vitamin C; 21 mg cholesterol

Barbecued Limas

Dried lima beans cook faster than many beans, so these are soaked but not precooked before going in the slow cooker.

1¼ cups (253 g) dried lima beans

¾ cup (120 g) onion, chopped in large pieces

½ teaspoon dry mustard

1 teaspoon cider vinegar

2 tablespoons (40 g) molasses

¼ cup (70 g) chili sauce (see recipe in Chapter 2)

Place beans in bowl and cover with water. Let beans soak overnight. Drain, reserving 1 cup (235 ml) liquid from beans. Combine all ingredients in slow cooker, including reserved soaking liquid. Cook on low 8 to 10 hours.

Yield: 6 servings

Per serving: 33 g water; 159 calories (2% from fat, 21% from protein, 78% from carb); 8 g protein; 0 g total fat; 0 g saturated fat; 0 g monounsaturated fat; 0 g polyunsaturated fat; 32 g carb; 7 g fiber; 9 g sugar; 151 mg phosphorus; 52 mg calcium; 3 mg iron; 18 mg sodium; 773 mg potassium; 168 IU vitamin A; 0 mg ATE vitamin E; 3 mg vitamin C; 0 mg cholesterol

Vegetarian Baked Beans

In this tasty bean recipe without meat, the beans are precooked to shorten the cooking time.

1 pound (455 g) navy beans

6 cups (1.4 L) water

¾ cup (120 g) chopped onion

¼ cup (60 g) low-sodium ketchup

½ cup (115 g) brown sugar

¾ cup (180 ml) water

1 teaspoon dry mustard

3 tablespoons (60 g) molasses

Soak beans in water overnight in large soup kettle. Cook beans in water until soft, about 1½ hours. Drain, discarding cooking liquid. Stir together beans and remaining ingredients in slow cooker. Mix well. Cover and cook on low 5 to 8 hours or until beans are well-flavored but not breaking down.

Yield: 8 servings

Per serving: 256 g water; 168 calories (2% from fat, 12% from protein, 86% from carb); 5 g protein; 0 g total fat; 0 g saturated fat; 0 g monounsaturated fat; 0 g polyunsaturated fat; 37 g carb; 6 g fiber; 20 g sugar; 94 mg phosphorus; 78 mg calcium; 2 mg iron; 16 mg sodium; 438 mg potassium; 71 IU vitamin A; 0 mg ATE vitamin E; 2 mg vitamin C; 0 mg cholesterol

Mexican Beans

These beans are similar to refried beans but with other good stuff added.

2 cups (342 g) canned no-salt-added pinto beans, drained

6 cups (1.4 L) water

1 teaspoon minced garlic

1 cup (180 g) tomato, peeled, seeded, and chopped

6 slices low-sodium bacon

½ cup (58 g) shredded Cheddar cheese

Combine beans, water, garlic, and tomato in slow cooker. Cover and cook on high 5 hours, stirring occasionally. When the beans become soft, drain off some liquid. While the beans cook, brown the bacon in a skillet. Drain, reserving drippings. Crumble bacon. Add half of bacon and 3 tablespoons (45 ml) drippings to beans. Stir and mash beans. To serve, sprinkle the remaining bacon and shredded cheese on top of beans.

Yield: 8 servings

Per serving: 204 g water; 237 calories (22% from fat, 25% from protein, 53% from carb); 15 g protein; 6 g total fat; 3 g saturated fat; 2 g monounsaturated fat; 1 g polyunsaturated fat; 31 g carb; 8 g fiber; 2 g sugar; 278 mg phosphorus; 122 mg calcium; 3 mg iron; 108 mg sodium; 762 mg potassium; 240 IU vitamin A; 22 mg ATE vitamin E; 6 mg vitamin C; 15 mg cholesterol

Island Black Beans

Rum, brown sugar, and spices give these beans a Caribbean flavor. Try them with pork or chicken.

2¼ cups (563 g) dried black beans

7 cups (1.6 L) water, divided

3 cups (700 ml) low-sodium chicken broth (see recipe in Chapter 2)

1 large onion, chopped

½ cup (120 ml) dark rum

2 tablespoons (30 g) packed brown sugar

1 tablespoon (8 g) grated fresh ginger

½ teaspoon minced garlic

2 teaspoons dry mustard

½ teaspoon cinnamon

½ teaspoon black pepper

¼ teaspoon ground cloves

(continued on page 370)

Rinse beans; drain. In a 4-quart (3.8 L) stock pot, combine beans and 6 cups (1.4 L) water. Bring to a boil; reduce heat. Simmer, uncovered, for 10 minutes. Cover and let stand for 1 hour. Drain and rinse beans. In a slow cooker, combine beans, remaining 1 cup (235 ml) water, broth, onion, rum, brown sugar, ginger, garlic, mustard, cinnamon, pepper, and cloves. Cover and cook on low for 11 to 12 hours or on high for 5 to 6 hours.

Yield: 6 servings

Per serving: 472 g water; 167 calories (5% from fat, 21% from protein, 73% from carb); 7 g protein; 1 g total fat; 0 g saturated fat; 0 g monounsaturated fat; 0 g polyunsaturated fat; 23 g carb; 6 g fiber; 6 g sugar; 115 mg phosphorus; 46 mg calcium; 2 mg iron; 82 mg sodium; 342 mg potassium; 8 IU vitamin A; 0 mg ATE vitamin E; 2 mg vitamin C; 0 mg cholesterol

Beans and Peppers

4 cups (950 ml) water

1½ cups (290 g) dried pinto beans

1 can (14 ounces, or 400 g) no-salt-added diced tomatoes, undrained

¾ cup (113 g) chopped green bell pepper

½ cup (80 g) chopped onion

1 tablespoon (15 g) brown sugar

½ teaspoon minced garlic

⅛ teaspoon pepper

3 slices low-sodium bacon, cooked, drained, and crumbled

In saucepan, bring water and beans to boiling; reduce heat and simmer, covered, 1½ hours. Pour into a bowl; cover and chill. Drain beans, reserving 1½ cups (355 ml) liquid. Transfer beans and reserved liquid to slow cooker. Stir in undrained tomatoes, green pepper, onion, brown sugar, garlic, and pepper. Cover and cook on low for 12 to 14 hours. Stir beans; top with crumbled bacon.

Yield: 6 servings

Per serving: 255 g water; 218 calories (10% from fat, 23% from protein, 67% from carb); 13 g protein; 2 g total fat; 1 g saturated fat; 1 g monounsaturated fat; 0 g polyunsaturated fat; 37 g carb; 9 g fiber; 6 g sugar; 241 mg phosphorus; 88 mg calcium; 3 mg iron; 51 mg sodium; 882 mg potassium; 150 IU vitamin A; 0 mg ATE vitamin E; 25 mg vitamin C; 4 mg cholesterol

Barbecue Lentils

These unusual lentils are a great side dish for grilled meat or to take to a picnic or tailgate party.

1½ cups (355 ml) water

1 cup (192 g) lentils

½ cup (80 g) chopped onion

1 can (14 ounces, or 400 g) no-salt-added diced tomatoes, undrained

1 tablespoon (20 g) chili sauce

2 tablespoons (30 g) brown sugar

½ teaspoon dry mustard

2 slices low-sodium bacon, cooked and crumbled

In saucepan bring water, lentils, and onion to a boil. Simmer, covered, 30 minutes. Transfer to slow cooker; stir in undrained tomatoes, chili sauce, brown sugar, and mustard. Cover and cook on low for 8 to 10 hours. Uncover; cook on high for 30 minutes. Stir; top with bacon.

Yield: 6 servings

Per serving: 159 g water; 88 calories (13% from fat, 20% from protein, 66% from carb); 5 g protein; 1 g total fat; 0 g saturated fat; 1 g monounsaturated fat; 0 g polyunsaturated fat; 15 g carb; 4 g fiber; 7 g sugar; 91 mg phosphorus; 37 mg calcium; 2 mg iron; 35 mg sodium; 298 mg potassium; 123 IU vitamin A; 0 mg ATE vitamin E; 8 mg vitamin C; 3 mg cholesterol

Refried Beans

This makes a big batch of refried beans. Using the slow cooker makes it easy to prepare. They freeze very nicely, so you can pack some away for the next time. The flavor is fairly traditional (despite the rather un-traditional coffee in the ingredients) and not too spicy at all.

1 pound (455 g) dried pinto beans

4 cups (950 ml) water

1 cup (235 ml) coffee

(continued on page 372)

1 teaspoon minced garlic

1 cup (160 g) diced onion

1 tablespoon (7 g) cumin

2 teaspoons chili powder

1½ teaspoons oregano

Rinse beans and place in a large bowl covered with water overnight. Drain and place in slow cooker along with remaining ingredients. Stir well, cover, and cook 8 to 10 hours or until beans are tender. Use a potato masher or large spoon to mash the beans until desired consistency.

Yield: 12 servings

Per serving: 115 g water; 141 calories (4% from fat, 24% from protein, 72% from carb); 8 g protein; 1 g total fat; 0 g saturated fat; 0 g monounsaturated fat; 0 g polyunsaturated fat; 26 g carb; 6 g fiber; 1 g sugar; 164 mg phosphorus; 57 mg calcium; 2 mg iron; 13 mg sodium; 580 mg potassium; 139 IU vitamin A; 0 mg ATE vitamin E; 4 mg vitamin C; 0 mg cholesterol

Baked Beans

This is a simple, but good, baked bean recipe. There are only a few ingredients, but the long, slow cooking makes the most of them.

2½ cups (538 g) dried navy beans

6 tablespoons (120 g) molasses

¼ cup (60 g) brown sugar

¼ pound (115 g) low-sodium bacon

¼ teaspoon pepper

Boil beans for 30 minutes to soften. Place beans in slow cooker. Add remaining ingredients. Cook for 10 hours on low, stirring every 3 hours or so.

Yield: 6 servings

Per serving: 56 g water; 304 calories (25% from fat, 17% from protein, 58% from carb); 13 g protein; 8 g total fat; 3 g saturated fat; 4 g monounsaturated fat; 1 g polyunsaturated fat; 45 g carb; 8 g fiber; 21 g sugar; 219 mg phosphorus; 105 mg calcium; 3 mg iron; 153 mg sodium; 742 mg potassium; 11 IU vitamin A; 2 mg ATE vitamin E; 0 mg vitamin C; 21 mg cholesterol

Southern Black-Eyed Peas

This is just what you need to bring you New Year's Day luck. And this recipe tastes great, so you won't mind eating them.

1 pound (455 g) dried black-eyed peas

4 cups (955 ml) water

¼ teaspoon pepper

1 cup (160 g) chopped onion

½ cup (50 g) chopped celery

½ pound (255 g) ham, cut in pieces

TIP

Serve over rice with cornbread.

Soak beans in water overnight. Drain and place in slow cooker. Add water and remaining ingredients. Cover and cook on high 1 to 2 hours and then turn to low and cook 8 to 9 hours.

Yield: 6 servings

Per serving: 265 g water; 175 calories (19% from fat, 33% from protein, 48% from carb); 15 g protein; 4 g total fat; 1 g saturated fat; 2 g monounsaturated fat; 1 g polyunsaturated fat; 21 g carb; 5 g fiber; 5 g sugar; 186 mg phosphorus; 34 mg calcium; 2 mg iron; 420 mg sodium; 479 mg potassium; 99 IU vitamin A; 0 mg ATE vitamin E; 4 mg vitamin C; 15 mg cholesterol

New England Baked Beans

These are traditional New England-style baked beans, flavored with ham and maple syrup.

1 pound (455 g) dried navy beans

½ cup (80 g) chopped onion

½ pound (225 g) ham

½ cup (115 g) packed brown sugar

½ cup (160 g) maple syrup

1 teaspoon salt

1 teaspoon dry mustard

Cover beans with water. Boil for 10 minutes and then let stand for 2 hours. Drain and put beans in slow cooker. Add all remaining ingredients along with 1 cup (235 ml) water; mix well. Cover and cook on low 10 to 12 hours. For thicker beans, uncover and turn to high during last hour.

Yield: 8 servings

Per serving: 71 g water; 236 calories (11% from fat, 18% from protein, 71% from carb); 11 g protein; 3 g total fat; 1 g saturated fat; 1 g monounsaturated fat; 1 g polyunsaturated fat; 43 g carb; 6 g fiber; 26 g sugar; 151 mg phosphorus; 69 mg calcium; 2 mg iron; 605 mg sodium; 425 mg potassium; 1 IU vitamin A; 0 mg ATE vitamin E; 1 mg vitamin C; 12 mg cholesterol

Pinto Beans

Here's a simple pinto bean recipe that is perfect as a side dish with any kind of grilled or barbecued meat.

1 pound (455 g) pinto beans, soaked overnight

4 cups (950 ml) cold water

1 cup (160 g) chopped onion

½ teaspoon minced garlic

1 teaspoon crushed red pepper (or 2 teaspoons chili powder)

4 slices low-sodium bacon

Put all ingredients in slow cooker. Cover and cook on high for 2 hours and then turn to low for 8 hours.

Yield: 8 servings

Per serving: 143 g water; 227 calories (9% from fat, 24% from protein, 66% from carb); 14 g protein; 2 g total fat; 1 g saturated fat; 1 g monounsaturated fat; 0 g polyunsaturated fat; 37 g carb; 9 g fiber; 2 g sugar; 261 mg phosphorus; 73 mg calcium; 3 mg iron; 41 mg sodium; 844 mg potassium; 14 IU vitamin A; 0 mg ATE vitamin E; 6 mg vitamin C; 4 mg cholesterol

Lima Beans

You could make a whole meal of this recipe. (I know this for a fact because I have). But it also makes a great side dish.

1 pound (455 g) dried lima beans

1½ cups (240 g) chopped onion

½ cup (50 g) chopped celery

2 large potatoes, peeled and diced

1 cup (130 g) sliced carrots

Wash beans; combine with remaining ingredients in slow cooker. Add water to cover vegetables and cook on low heat at least 10 hours.

Yield: 6 servings

Per serving: 217 g water; 192 calories (2% from fat, 16% from protein, 81% from carb); 8 g protein; 1 g total fat; 0 g saturated fat; 0 g monounsaturated fat; 0 g polyunsaturated fat; 40 g carb; 8 g fiber; 5 g sugar; 181 mg phosphorus; 53 mg calcium; 3 mg iron; 52 mg sodium; 1019 mg potassium; 3760 IU vitamin A; 0 mg ATE vitamin E; 19 mg vitamin C; 0 mg cholesterol

17

Whole Grain and Fiber-Rich Breads

Yes, you can bake bread in the slow cooker, both yeast breads for sandwiches or to accompany one of the soups or stews from an earlier chapter or sweet breads that are great for breakfast or dessert. One of the first slow cookers we bought had a special metal pan that you used for baking. I still have it and use it occasionally, even though the cooker it came with is long gone. I haven't seen one of those recently with the newer cookers, but there are ways to improvise. You can also use a metal coffee or nut can (but they are getting harder to find as more products are packed in paper or plastic containers) or any metal mold that holds the proper amount, such as gelatin molds, baking pans, etc. You want the pan to be about half full of the batter. To bake in your slow cooker, follow the steps below:

- Grease insert or can with solid shortening or a baking spray containing flour.
- Half fill the insert or can. This allows for rising.
- To allow heat to circulate around the insert, place a metal trivet or baking rack in the bottom of the cooker. If one isn't available, crumple up enough aluminum foil to raise the can about 1 inch (2.5 cm) from the bottom of the cooker.
- If the can does not have a lid, cover the can with a double thickness of paper towels.
- Place the lid on the cooker and bake according to recipe directions.
- Only lift lid to check for doneness. Lifting the lid too often will let necessary heat escape.

White Bread

This is plain and simple but a great base for toast or sandwiches.

2¾ teaspoons (7 g) yeast

1¼ cups (295 ml) warm water, divided

¼ cup plus 1 teaspoon (55 g) sugar, divided

¼ cup (60 ml) egg substitute

¼ cup (60 ml) canola oil

3½ cups (438 g) flour, divided

Dissolve the yeast in ¼ cup (60 ml) water with 1 teaspoon sugar. Let stand until bubbles form. Add egg substitute, oil, remaining 1 cup (235 ml) water, remaining ¼ cup (50 g) sugar, and 2 cups (250 g) flour until well mixed. Stir in remaining flour until dough is workable. Place dough in a 2-pound (900 g) coffee can sprayed with nonstick baking spray (one that contains flour). Place in slow cooker, cover, and cook on high for 2 to 3 hours. Remove and let stand for 5 minutes before removing from can.

Yield: 12 servings

Per serving: 33 g water; 199 calories (24% from fat, 10% from protein, 66% from carb); 5 g protein; 5 g total fat; 0 g saturated fat; 3 g monounsaturated fat; 2 g polyunsaturated fat; 33 g carb; 1 g fiber; 5 g sugar; 58 mg phosphorus; 10 mg calcium; 2 mg iron; 11 mg sodium; 75 mg potassium; 19 IU vitamin A; 0 mg ATE vitamin E; 0 mg vitamin C; 0 mg cholesterol

Honey Wheat Bread

This makes great sandwich bread, soft and full of flavor.

2 cups (475 ml) skim milk, warmed to 115°F (46°C)

2 tablespoons (28 ml) canola oil

¼ cup (85 g) honey

2¾ teaspoons (7 g) yeast

(continued on page 378)

3 cups (360 g) whole wheat flour

¾ cup (86 g) wheat bran

¼ cup (29 g) wheat germ

Preheat slow cooker on high for 30 minutes. Combine warm milk, oil, honey, yeast, and half the flour. With electric mixer, beat well for about 2 minutes. Add remaining flour; mix well. Place dough in well-greased baking pan; cover. Place in slow cooker, cover, and bake on high 3 hours.

Yield: 8 servings

Per serving: 62 g water; 270 calories (16% from fat, 15% from protein, 69% from carb); 11 g protein; 5 g total fat; 1 g saturated fat; 2 g monounsaturated fat; 2 g polyunsaturated fat; 51 g carb; 9 g fiber; 9 g sugar; 338 mg phosphorus; 110 mg calcium; 3 mg iron; 40 mg sodium; 425 mg potassium; 133 IU vitamin A; 38 mg ATE vitamin E; 1 mg vitamin C; 1 mg cholesterol

Whole Wheat Bread

This is tasty bread, great for sandwiches or morning toast.

2 cups (475 ml) skim milk, warmed to 115°F (46°C)

2 tablespoons (28 ml) canola oil

¼ cup (60 g) brown sugar

2¾ teaspoons (7 g) yeast

2½ cups (300 g) whole wheat flour

1¼ cups (171 g) bread flour

Mix together milk, oil, brown sugar, yeast, and half of each flour with electric mixer. Stir in the remaining flour. Place dough is greased bread or cake pan. Cover with greased foil. Place in cooker, cover, and cook on high 2½ to 3 hours. Let stand 10 minutes before removing from pan.

Yield: 8 servings

Per serving: 62 g water; 291 calories (14% from fat, 14% from protein, 71% from carb); 11 g protein; 5 g total fat; 1 g saturated fat; 2 g monounsaturated fat; 1 g polyunsaturated fat; 53 g carb; 5 g fiber; 7 g sugar; 239 mg phosphorus; 111 mg calcium; 3 mg iron; 42 mg sodium; 336 mg potassium; 129 IU vitamin A; 38 mg ATE vitamin E; 1 mg vitamin C; 1 mg cholesterol

Whole Grain Bread

This makes just about enough for a family meal. With just a little preparation time, you can have fresh bread even if you don't have a bread machine.

1 tablespoon (12 g) yeast

¼ cup (60 ml) warm water

1 cup (235 ml) skim milk, warmed to 115°F (46°C)

½ cup (40 g) rolled oats

2 tablespoons (28 ml) oil

2 tablespoons (40 g) honey

¼ cup (60 ml) egg substitute

¼ cup (29 g) wheat germ

2¾ cups (330 g) whole wheat flour

Spray a deep metal or glass bowl or 1-pound (455 g) coffee can with nonstick baking spray (one that contains flour). In bottom of slow cooker, place ½ cup (120 ml) water and a trivet or some crumpled foil. Turn on high to preheat. Dissolve yeast in warm water. Combine milk, oats, oil, honey, egg substitute, and wheat germ in a mixing bowl. Add yeast mixture. Mix in flour and knead until smooth and elastic, about 5 minutes. Turn dough into prepared bowl or can and cover loosely with foil. Place can or bowl in slow cooker on top of trivet or crumpled foil. Cover and bake on high for 3 hours.

Yield: 8 servings

Per serving: 47 g water; 243 calories (19% from fat, 16% from protein, 65% from carb); 10 g protein; 5 g total fat; 1 g saturated fat; 1 g monounsaturated fat; 3 g polyunsaturated fat; 42 g carb; 6 g fiber; 5 g sugar; 271 mg phosphorus; 68 mg calcium; 3 mg iron; 36 mg sodium; 333 mg potassium; 98 IU vitamin A; 19 mg ATE vitamin E; 1 mg vitamin C; 1 mg cholesterol

Granola Bread

This is a nice sweet bread that is good for breakfast or snacking.

2¾ cups (344 g) flour

¾ cup (150 g) sugar

4 teaspoons (18.4 g) baking powder

1 teaspoon cinnamon

½ cup (120 ml) egg substitute

1⅓ cups (315 ml) skim milk

¼ cup (60 ml) canola oil

½ teaspoon vanilla

1 cup (125 g) granola

¾ cup (131 g) chopped prunes

Stir together flour, sugar, baking powder, and cinnamon. In another bowl, combine egg substitute, milk, oil, and vanilla. Add to flour mixture; stir just until moistened. Fold in granola and chopped prunes. Turn into a well-greased 3-pound (1⅓ kg) shortening can. Cover loosely with foil to allow for expansion of dough. Place can in slow cooker. Cover and cook on high for 3½ hours. Remove can from cooker; cool 10 minutes in can.

Yield: 12 servings

Per serving: 48 g water; 259 calories (20% from fat, 9% from protein, 71% from carb); 6 g protein; 6 g total fat; 1 g saturated fat; 3 g monounsaturated fat; 2 g polyunsaturated fat; 46 g carb; 2 g fiber; 19 g sugar; 131 mg phosphorus; 147 mg calcium; 2 mg iron; 224 mg sodium; 186 mg potassium; 147 IU vitamin A; 17 mg ATE vitamin E; 1 mg vitamin C; 1 mg cholesterol

Oat Bran Bread

This is a really easy and delicious bread. It's good toasted, with cream cheese, or for sandwiches.

2 cups (250 g) flour

⅓ cup (67 g) sugar

1 teaspoon baking soda

1½ cups (120 g) rolled oats

1 cup (90 g) bran cereal, such as Kellogg's All-Bran

½ cup (75 g) raisins

½ cup (120 ml) egg substitute

1½ cups (355 ml) buttermilk

½ cup (170 g) molasses

Mix flour, sugar, baking soda, oats, bran cereal, and raisins in mixing bowl. Add egg substitute, buttermilk, and molasses and mix well. Divide into two 1-pound (445 g) coffee cans, a 2-quart (1.9 L) mold, or a 2-pound (900 g) can sprayed with nonstick baking spray (one that contains flour). Set in cooker and cover with 2 to 3 paper towels. With cover slightly ajar, cook on high 3 hours or until done. Let bread stand in can 10 minutes and then turn out on rack to cool.

Yield: 12 servings

Per serving: 44 g water; 232 calories (7% from fat, 11% from protein, 82% from carb); 7 g protein; 2 g total fat; 0 g saturated fat; 0 g monounsaturated fat; 1 g polyunsaturated fat; 50 g carb; 3 g fiber; 20 g sugar; 181 mg phosphorus; 102 mg calcium; 3 mg iron; 70 mg sodium; 448 mg potassium; 136 IU vitamin A; 29 mg ATE vitamin E; 1 mg vitamin C; 1 mg cholesterol

Tomato Herb Bread

This is a great bread to serve with soup or Italian food.

1 tablespoon plus 1 teaspoon (17 g) sugar, divided

⅓ cup (80 ml) water, warmed to 115°F (46°C)

2¾ teaspoons (7 g) yeast

4 cups (500 g) flour, divided

¼ cup (40 g) finely chopped onion

1 cup (245 g) no-salt-added tomato sauce

¼ cup (30 g) grated Cheddar cheese

(continued on page 382)

¼ teaspoon pepper

½ teaspoon oregano

Stir 1 teaspoon sugar into warm water in large warmed bowl. Sprinkle yeast over top. Let stand 10 minutes. Stir to dissolve yeast. Add 3 cups (375 g) flour and remaining ingredients. Beat with an electric mixer on low to moisten and then beat on high for 2 minutes. Add remaining 1 cup (125 g) flour. Turn into slow cooker sprayed with nonstick cooking spray. Smooth top. Cook on high for about 2½ hours. Loosen sides with knife. Turn out onto rack to cool.

Yield: 12 servings

Per serving: 32 g water; 179 calories (7% from fat, 13% from protein, 80% from carb); 6 g protein; 1 g total fat; 1 g saturated fat; 0 g monounsaturated fat; 0 g polyunsaturated fat; 35 g carb; 2 g fiber; 2 g sugar; 78 mg phosphorus; 31 mg calcium; 2 mg iron; 21 mg sodium; 142 mg potassium; 98 IU vitamin A; 7 mg ATE vitamin E; 3 mg vitamin C; 3 mg cholesterol

Carrot Bread

For those who like carrot cake but feel guilty eating it for breakfast (like me), this is the solution. It's a great, easy-to-make bread that tastes like carrot cake.

1 cup (125 g) flour

1 cup (200 g) sugar

1 teaspoon baking powder

1 teaspoon ground cinnamon

½ cup (120 ml) egg substitute

½ cup (120 ml) canola oil

2 cups (260 g) grated carrots

½ cup (55 g) chopped pecans

Combine the flour, sugar, baking powder, and cinnamon in a medium bowl. With an electric beater, beat the egg substitute until frothy. Toward the end, drizzle in the oil. With the beater on low, add the flour mixture a little at a time. Fold in the carrots and pecans. Pour into a 2-quart (1.9 L) mold sprayed with nonstick baking spray (one that contains flour). Place in the slow cooker; cover loosely with a plate. Cover the cooker and prop the lid a little to let excess steam escape. Bake on high for 2½ to 3½ hours.

Yield: 8 servings

Per serving: 43 g water; 353 calories (49% from fat, 5% from protein, 46% from carb); 4 g protein; 20 g total fat; 2 g saturated fat; 11 g monounsaturated fat; 6 g polyunsaturated fat; 42 g carb; 2 g fiber; 27 g sugar; 79 mg phosphorus; 64 mg calcium; 1 mg iron; 111 mg sodium; 201 mg potassium; 5441 IU vitamin A; 0 mg ATE vitamin E; 2 mg vitamin C; 0 mg cholesterol

Cranberry Orange Nut Bread

This flavorful breakfast bread with cranberry and orange is great with cream cheese.

2 cups (220 g) cranberries

½ cup (60 g) chopped walnuts

2 cups (250 g) flour

1 cup (200 g) sugar

1½ teaspoons baking powder

½ teaspoon baking soda

6 tablespoons (85 g) unsalted butter

¼ cup (60 ml) egg substitute

1 tablespoon (6 g) grated orange peel

½ cup (120 ml) orange juice

Spray a 2-quart (1.9 L) mold or coffee can with nonstick baking spray (one that contains flour). Preheat cooker on high. Grind cranberries and walnuts with coarse blade of food processor. In large mixing bowl, combine flour, sugar, baking powder, and baking soda. Cut in butter to form a coarse mixture. Make an indention in mixture and add egg substitute, orange peel, and orange juice. Beat only until lumps disappear. Add chopped cranberries and walnuts. Stir until evenly mixed. Pour batter into prepared pan. Place pan in cooker, cover, and bake for 3 hours. Cool loaf in pan for 15 minutes and then remove and cool completely.

Yield: 12 servings

(continued on page 384)

Per serving: 34 g water; 242 calories (34% from fat, 7% from protein, 59% from carb); 4 g protein; 9 g total fat; 4 g saturated fat; 2 g monounsaturated fat; 2 g polyunsaturated fat; 37 g carb; 2 g fiber; 18 g sugar; 73 mg phosphorus; 48 mg calcium; 1 mg iron; 72 mg sodium; 105 mg potassium; 219 IU vitamin A; 48 mg ATE vitamin E; 7 mg vitamin C; 15 mg cholesterol

Coconut Bread

This sweet bread can be eaten as a dessert or spread with cream cheese or jam for breakfast.

3 cups (375 g) flour

1 tablespoon (13.8 g) baking powder

1 cup (200 g) sugar

1 cup (85 g) flaked coconut

¼ cup (60 ml) egg substitute

1 cup (235 ml) skim milk

1 teaspoon vanilla extract

Spray two 1-pound (455 g) coffee cans or inserts with nonstick baking spray (one that contains flour). Mix flour, baking powder, and sugar; add coconut and mix thoroughly. Combine egg substitute, milk, and vanilla, and stir into dry ingredients. Mix well. Press batter into prepared pans. Set cans in slow cooker and cover cans with 3 paper towels. Cover and cook on high for 3 hours or until done. Cool on wire rack for 10 minutes before removing bread.

Yield: 8 servings

Per serving: 42 g water; 332 calories (10% from fat, 9% from protein, 81% from carb); 7 g protein; 4 g total fat; 3 g saturated fat; 0 g monounsaturated fat; 0 g polyunsaturated fat; 67 g carb; 2 g fiber; 25 g sugar; 142 mg phosphorus; 158 mg calcium; 3 mg iron; 218 mg sodium; 165 mg potassium; 91 IU vitamin A; 19 mg ATE vitamin E; 0 mg vitamin C; 1 mg cholesterol

Zucchini Bread

This is a good sweet bread for breakfast or snacking.

½ cup (120 ml) egg substitute

⅔ cup (160 ml) canola oil

¼ cup (50 g) sugar

1⅓ cups (160 g) peeled and grated zucchini

2 teaspoons vanilla

2 cups (250 g) flour

½ teaspoon baking powder

1 teaspoon cinnamon

½ teaspoon nutmeg

½ cup (55 g) chopped pecans

With mixer, beat egg substitute until light and foamy. Add oil, sugar, grated zucchini, and vanilla and mix well. Combine flour, baking powder, cinnamon, nutmeg, and pecans. Add to zucchini mixture. Mix well. Pour into greased 2-pound (900 g) coffee can or 2-quart (1.9 L) mold. Place in slow cooker. Cover top with 3 paper towels. Cover and bake on high 3 to 4 hours.

Yield: 8 servings

Per serving: 37 g water; 372 calories (59% from fat, 6% from protein, 35% from carb); 6 g protein; 25 g total fat; 2 g saturated fat; 14 g monounsaturated fat; 7 g polyunsaturated fat; 32 g carb; 2 g fiber; 7 g sugar; 86 mg phosphorus; 42 mg calcium; 2 mg iron; 61 mg sodium; 171 mg potassium; 103 IU vitamin A; 0 mg ATE vitamin E; 4 mg vitamin C; 0 mg cholesterol

Banana Bread

I always seem to have a few bananas that are past their peak. This is a good way to use them.

3 bananas, mashed

½ cup (112 g) unsalted butter, softened

(continued on page 386)

½ cup (120 ml) egg substitute

1 teaspoon vanilla

1 cup (200 g) sugar

1 cup (125 g) flour

1 teaspoon baking soda

Combine all ingredients in a mixing bowl. Beat with an electric mixer for 2 minutes. Pour into a 2-pound (900 g) coffee can sprayed with nonstick baking spray (one that contains flour). Cover with foil and place in slow cooker. Cover and cook on high for 2 to 2½ hours. Cool before removing from can.

Yield: 8 servings

Per serving: 39 g water; 296 calories (37% from fat, 5% from protein, 58% from carb); 4 g protein; 12 g total fat; 7 g saturated fat; 3 g monounsaturated fat; 1 g polyunsaturated fat; 44 g carb; 1 g fiber; 29 g sugar; 45 mg phosphorus; 16 mg calcium; 1 mg iron; 30 mg sodium; 174 mg potassium; 429 IU vitamin A; 95 mg ATE vitamin E; 2 mg vitamin C; 31 mg cholesterol

Lemon Bread

A sweet bread with just enough lemon flavor, this bread is good for breakfast or just as a snack. I like it with cream cheese.

½ cup (112 g) unsalted butter, softened

¾ cup (150 g) sugar

½ cup (120 ml) egg substitute

1½ teaspoons baking powder

1⅔ cups (208 g) flour

½ cup (120 ml) skim milk

½ cup (55 g) chopped pecans

1 tablespoon (6 g) grated lemon peel

Cream together butter and sugar. Add egg substitute and beat well; stir in milk. Stir baking powder into flour. Add to milk mixture. Stir in pecans and lemon peel. Spoon into 2-pound (900 g) coffee can sprayed with nonstick baking spray (one that contains flour). Cover with foil. Place in slow cooker and cook on high for 2 to 2½ hours.

Yield: 6 servings

Per serving: 44 g water; 450 calories (45% from fat, 7% from protein, 48% from carb); 8 g protein; 23 g total fat; 11 g saturated fat; 8 g monounsaturated fat; 3 g polyunsaturated fat; 55 g carb; 2 g fiber; 26 g sugar; 141 mg phosphorus; 126 mg calcium; 2 mg iron; 174 mg sodium; 188 mg potassium; 595 IU vitamin A; 139 mg ATE vitamin E; 2 mg vitamin C; 41 mg cholesterol

Cranberry Bread

I love this bread for breakfast, with nothing at all on it. It also makes a good companion to a salad with cranberries or other fruits.

1 cup (255 g) fat-free cottage cheese

½ cup (120 ml) egg substitute

1 cup (200 g) sugar

¾ cup (175 ml) skim milk

1 teaspoon vanilla

2¾ cups (345 g) Heart-Healthy Baking Mix (see recipe in Chapter 2)

½ cup (60 g) dried cranberries

Combine all ingredients. Spray slow cooker with nonstick cooking spray. Spread mixture in bottom of cooker. Cover and cook on high for 2 hours.

Yield: 8 servings

Per serving: 69 g water; 293 calories (3% from fat, 15% from protein, 83% from carb); 11 g protein; 1 g total fat; 2 g saturated fat; 1 g monounsaturated fat; 0 g polyunsaturated fat; 62 g carb; 2 g fiber; 26 g sugar; 183 mg phosphorus; 207 mg calcium; 2 mg iron; 340 mg sodium; 173 mg potassium; 228 IU vitamin A; 46 mg ATE vitamin E; 1 mg vitamin C; 11 mg cholesterol

Boston Brown Bread

This is the traditional accompaniment to Boston baked beans, but it's also good for breakfast with a little cream cheese.

½ cup (64 g) rye flour

½ cup (70 g) cornmeal

½ cup (60 g) whole wheat flour

3 tablespoons (39 g) sugar

1 teaspoon baking soda

½ cup (60 g) chopped walnuts

½ cup (75 g) raisins

1 cup (235 ml) buttermilk

⅓ cup (113 g) molasses

TIP *Rolling the cans on the counter and tapping on the sides will help to release the bread.*

Spray the inside of three clean 1-pound (445 g) vegetable cans with nonstick cooking spray. Combine dry ingredients. Stir in walnuts and raisins. Stir together buttermilk and molasses and then stir into dry mixture until well mixed. Spoon into cans. Cover each can with a piece of foil sprayed with nonstick cooking spray and fasten with a rubber band. Place in slow cooker. Pour boiling water into cooker to come halfway up the cans. Cover and cook on low for 4 hours.

Yield: 12 servings

Per serving: 23 g water; 157 calories (20% from fat, 9% from protein, 72% from carb); 4 g protein; 4 g total fat; 0 g saturated fat; 1 g monounsaturated fat; 2 g polyunsaturated fat; 29 g carb; 2 g fiber; 14 g sugar; 87 mg phosphorus; 52 mg calcium; 1 mg iron; 27 mg sodium; 287 mg potassium; 22 IU vitamin A; 1 mg ATE vitamin E; 0 mg vitamin C; 1 mg cholesterol

Cornbread

If you're trying to avoid last-minute preparation, make your cornbread in the slow cooker. It will bake while you prepare the rest of the meal.

1¼ cups (156 g) flour

¾ cup (105 g) cornmeal

¼ cup (50 g) sugar

4 teaspoons (18.4 g) baking powder

¼ cup (60 ml) egg substitute

1 cup (120 ml) skim milk

⅓ cup (80 ml) canola oil

Stir together flour, cornmeal, sugar, and baking powder. Combine remaining ingredients. Mix into dry ingredients until just moistened. Pour into a greased 2-quart (1.9 L) mold. Place on a rack (or on top of crumpled foil) in slow cooker. Cook on high for 2 to 3 hours.

Yield: 6 servings

Per serving: 51 g water; 338 calories (36% from fat, 8% from protein, 56% from carb); 7 g protein; 14 g total fat; 1 g saturated fat; 8 g monounsaturated fat; 4 g polyunsaturated fat; 47 g carb; 2 g fiber; 9 g sugar; 175 mg phosphorus; 249 mg calcium; 3 mg iron; 370 mg sodium; 168 mg potassium; 163 IU vitamin A; 25 mg ATE vitamin E; 0 mg vitamin C; 1 mg cholesterol

Italian Quick Bread

Good with soups or salads, this bread is an easy way to get that Italian flavor without the usual work of traditional breadsticks.

1½ cups (180 g) Heart-Healthy Baking Mix (see recipe in Chapter 2)

¼ cup (60 ml) egg substitute

½ cup (120 ml) skim milk

1 tablespoon (10 g) minced onion

(continued on page 390)

1 tablespoon (13 g) sugar

1 teaspoon Italian seasoning

½ teaspoon garlic powder

¼ cup (25 g) grated Parmesan cheese

Combine all ingredients except Parmesan. Spray slow cooker with nonstick cooking spray. Spread mixture in bottom of cooker. Sprinkle with cheese. Cover and cook on high for 1 hour.

Yield: 8 servings

Per serving: 24 g water; 116 calories (9% from fat, 18% from protein, 73% from carb); 5 g protein; 1 g total fat; 2 g saturated fat; 1 g monounsaturated fat; 0 g polyunsaturated fat; 22 g carb; 1 g fiber; 2 g sugar; 107 mg phosphorus; 145 mg calcium; 1 mg iron; 209 mg sodium; 98 mg potassium; 141 IU vitamin A; 29 mg ATE vitamin E; 1 mg vitamin C; 8 mg cholesterol

18

Easy, Calorie-Reduced Desserts and Sweets

There are a number of great desserts that can be made in the slow cooker. This includes everything from warm fruit sauces and crisps to real cakes. If you are baking a cake, read the instructions in the introduction to the previous chapter on baking breads. The method is the same.

Indian Pudding

This is a traditional New England dessert.

6 cups (1.4 L) milk, heated

1 cup (140 g) cornmeal

1 cup (340 g) dark molasses

¼ cup (50 g) sugar

¼ cup (55 g) unsalted butter

¼ teaspoon baking soda

½ cup (120 ml) egg substitute

TIP

Serve with a scoop of vanilla ice cream.

Mix half of hot milk with rest of ingredients in a saucepan over medium heat and heat to boiling. Add rest of milk. Transfer to slow cooker. Cook for 6 hours on low.

Yield: 6 servings

Per serving: 257 g water; 462 calories (18% from fat, 11% from protein, 72% from carb); 13 g protein; 9 g total fat; 5 g saturated fat; 2 g monounsaturated fat; 1 g polyunsaturated fat; 84 g carb; 1 g fiber; 53 g sugar; 320 mg phosphorus; 436 mg calcium; 4 mg iron; 164 mg sodium; 1317 mg potassium; 868 IU vitamin A; 213 mg ATE vitamin E; 0 mg vitamin C; 25 mg cholesterol

Bread Pudding

My wife says no one will ever make bread pudding like her grandmother, but this is pretty close. The slow cooker makes it easy to get a soft, delicious result.

½ cup (120 ml) egg substitute

2¼ cups (535 ml) milk

1 teaspoon vanilla

½ teaspoon cinnamon

2 cups (100 g) bread cubes

½ cup (115 g) brown sugar

½ cup (75 g) raisins

Combine all ingredients and pour into 1½-quart (1.4 L) baking dish. Place metal trivet or crumpled foil in bottom of slow cooker. Add ½ cup (120 ml) hot water to cooker. Set baking dish on trivet or foil. Cover and cook on high for about 2 hours.

Yield: 4 servings

Per serving: 156 g water; 303 calories (7% from fat, 14% from protein, 79% from carb); 11 g protein; 2 g total fat; 1 g saturated fat; 1 g monounsaturated fat; 1 g polyunsaturated fat; 62 g carb; 2 g fiber; 46 g sugar; 222 mg phosphorus; 238 mg calcium; 2 mg iron; 137 mg sodium; 590 mg potassium; 395 IU vitamin A; 84 mg ATE vitamin E; 1 mg vitamin C; 3 mg cholesterol

Caramel Bread Pudding

You could use this for breakfast, but to me it's more of a dessert recipe.

12 ounces (340 g) sweet bread, like challah or Hawaiian

4 cups (950 ml) skim milk

½ cup (100 g) sugar

¾ cup (175 ml) egg substitute

1 teaspoon vanilla

1 cup (225 g) caramel ice cream topping

Cube bread and place in slow cooker. Whisk together remaining ingredients except caramel topping. Pour over bread. Press bread down into mixture. Cover and refrigerate at least 4 hours. Cover and cook on low 7 to 8 hours. Drizzle topping over to serve.

Yield: 12 servings

Per serving: 106 g water; 220 calories (7% from fat, 15% from protein, 78% from carb); 8 g protein; 2 g total fat; 0 g saturated fat; 1 g monounsaturated fat; 1 g polyunsaturated fat; 44 g carb; 2 g fiber; 11 g sugar; 174 mg phosphorus; 166 mg calcium; 1 mg iron; 310 mg sodium; 283 mg potassium; 248 IU vitamin A; 57 mg ATE vitamin E; 1 mg vitamin C; 2 mg cholesterol

Strawberry Bread Pudding

This is a delightful variation on bread pudding, with strawberries lifting it above the ordinary. (My daughter would say that no bread pudding is ordinary, but that's a different discussion.)

5 cups (250 g) cubed French bread

2½ cups (570 ml) skim milk, scalded

2 egg yolks

1 cup (200 g) sugar

1 teaspoon vanilla

2 tablespoons (28 g) unsalted butter, melted

12 ounces (340 g) strawberries, at room temperature

TIP *You can vary the taste by using raspberries or blueberries or other breads like egg or Hawaiian bread.*

Place the bread cubes in the slow cooker. Whisk together the milk, egg yolks, sugar, vanilla, and butter. Stir in the berries and pour over the bread cubes. Gently press the bread down into the liquid (do not stir) and cook, covered, on low for 4 to 6 hours.

Yield: 6 servings

Per serving: 170 g water; 410 calories (16% from fat, 12% from protein, 71% from carb); 13 g protein; 8 g total fat; 4 g saturated fat; 2 g monounsaturated fat; 1 g polyunsaturated fat; 74 g carb; 2 g fiber; 38 g sugar; 222 mg phosphorus; 190 mg calcium; 3 mg iron; 440 mg sodium; 367 mg potassium; 445 IU vitamin A; 124 mg ATE vitamin E; 35 mg vitamin C; 82 mg cholesterol

Rice Pudding

Who can resist rice pudding, warm from the slow cooker. Not me, that's for sure.

2½ cups (413 g) cooked rice

3 tablespoons (42 g) unsalted butter

2 teaspoons vanilla

¾ cup (175 ml) egg substitute

1½ cup (355 ml) evaporated milk

⅔ cup (150 g) brown sugar

½ teaspoon nutmeg

1 cup (145 g) raisins

Spray slow cooker with nonstick cooking spray. Thoroughly combine all ingredients and pour into prepared slow cooker. Cover and cook on high 2 hours or low 4 to 6 hours. Stir after the first hour.

Yield: 6 servings

Per serving: 124 g water; 427 calories (25% from fat, 10% from protein, 65% from carb); 11 g protein; 12 g total fat; 7 g saturated fat; 3 g monounsaturated fat; 1 g polyunsaturated fat; 71 g carb; 1 g fiber; 40 g sugar; 230 mg phosphorus; 224 mg calcium; 2 mg iron; 136 mg sodium; 613 mg potassium; 541 IU vitamin A; 48 mg ATE vitamin E; 2 mg vitamin C; 34 mg cholesterol

Chocolate Pudding

This is really more of a cake than a pudding, but it's good no matter what you call it.

⅓ cup (67 g) sugar

2 tablespoons (28 g) unsalted butter

¼ cup (60 ml) egg substitute

1 ounce (28 g) unsweetened chocolate, melted and cooled

1¼ cups (156 g) flour

(continued on page 396)

1 teaspoon baking soda

½ cup (120 ml) buttermilk

½ teaspoon vanilla

Cream sugar and butter with an electric mixer. Add egg substitute and mix well. Beat in chocolate. Stir together flour and baking soda. Add to sugar mixture alternately with buttermilk and vanilla; beat well. Divide into two well-greased 1-pound (455 g) vegetable cans. Cover tightly with foil. Place in slow cooker. Pour ½ cup (120 ml) warm water around cans. Cover and cook on high 1½ hours. Remove cans from cooker; cool 10 minutes; unmold.

Yield: 8 servings

Per serving: 23 g water; 160 calories (29% from fat, 10% from protein, 61% from carb); 4 g protein; 5 g total fat; 3 g saturated fat; 1 g monounsaturated fat; 0 g polyunsaturated fat; 25 g carb; 1 g fiber; 9 g sugar; 59 mg phosphorus; 29 mg calcium; 2 mg iron; 32 mg sodium; 101 mg potassium; 121 IU vitamin A; 25 mg ATE vitamin E; 0 mg vitamin C; 8 mg cholesterol

Carrot Pudding

This tempting pudding, cooked in a fluted mold, is great for your holiday meal. But you don't have to wait for a holiday.

1¼ cups (156 g) flour

1 teaspoon baking powder

½ teaspoon baking soda

½ teaspoon cinnamon

½ teaspoon ground nutmeg

½ cup (120 ml) egg substitute

¾ cup (170 g) packed brown sugar

½ cup (112 g) unsalted butter

1 cup (130 g) sliced carrots

1 apple, peeled, cored, and cut in eighths

1 medium potato, peeled and cut in pieces

¾ cup (110 g) raisins

Stir together flour, baking powder, baking soda, cinnamon, and nutmeg. Place egg substitute, brown sugar, and butter in blender. Cover and blend until smooth. Add carrot to blender mixture; blend until chopped. Add apple; blend until chopped. Add potato; blend until finely chopped. Stir carrot mixture and raisins into dry ingredients; mix well. Turn into greased and floured 6-cup (1.4 L) mold; cover tightly with foil. Place in slow cooker. Cover and cook on high for 4 hours. Remove from cooker. Cool 10 minutes; unmold.

Yield: 8 servings

Per serving: 77 g water; 359 calories (30% from fat, 6% from protein, 64% from carb); 6 g protein; 12 g total fat; 7 g saturated fat; 3 g monounsaturated fat; 1 g polyunsaturated fat; 59 g carb; 3 g fiber; 32 g sugar; 111 mg phosphorus; 85 mg calcium; 2 mg iron; 116 mg sodium; 534 mg potassium; 3111 IU vitamin A; 95 mg ATE vitamin E; 7 mg vitamin C; 31 mg cholesterol

Tapioca

I'm a big tapioca fan, so finding out that you could cook it in the slow cooker was exciting news to me. This makes great, custard-flavored tapioca.

8 cups (1.9 L) skim milk

1¼ cups (250 g) sugar

1 cup (125 g) tapioca

1 cup (120 ml) egg substitute

1 teaspoon vanilla

Combine milk and sugar in slow cooker, stirring until sugar is dissolved as well as possible. Stir in tapioca. Cover and cook on high 3 hours. In a small mixing bowl, beat egg substitute slightly. Beat in vanilla and about 1 cup (235 ml) hot milk from slow cooker. When well mixed, stir egg mixture into slow cooker. Cover and cook on high 20 more minutes. Chill for several hours. Serve with whipped topping if you wish.

Yield: 10 servings

Per serving: 199 g water; 255 calories (5% from fat, 17% from protein, 78% from carb); 11 g protein; 1 g total fat; 0 g saturated fat; 0 g monounsaturated fat; 0 g polyunsaturated fat; 50 g carb; 0 g fiber; 26 g sugar; 252 mg phosphorus; 298 mg calcium; 1 mg iron; 161 mg sodium; 444 mg potassium; 490 IU vitamin A; 120 mg ATE vitamin E; 2 mg vitamin C; 4 mg cholesterol

Fruited Tapioca

This tapioca variation uses pineapple, but you could substitute other fruits as well.

2¼ cups (535 ml) water

2½ cups (570 ml) pineapple juice

½ cup (63 g) tapioca pudding mix

1 cup (200 g) sugar

15 ounces (420 g) crushed pineapple, undrained

Mix first four ingredients together in slow cooker. Cover and cook on high 3 hours. Stir in crushed pineapple. Chill for several hours.

Yield: 6 servings

Per serving: 241 g water; 267 calories (1% from fat, 1% from protein, 98% from carb); 1 g protein; 0 g total fat; 0 g saturated fat; 0 g monounsaturated fat; 0 g polyunsaturated fat; 68 g carb; 1 g fiber; 53 g sugar; 14 mg phosphorus; 29 mg calcium; 1 mg iron; 6 mg sodium; 213 mg potassium; 32 IU vitamin A; 0 mg ATE vitamin E; 16 mg vitamin C; 0 mg cholesterol

Slow Cooker Custard

This may seem like a bit of work at first glance, but it really only takes about 10 minutes. And the feeling of being transported back in time you'll get with the first taste makes it all worthwhile.

2 cups (475 ml) skim milk

¾ cup (175 ml) egg substitute

⅓ cup (67 g) sugar

1 teaspoon vanilla

¼ teaspoon cinnamon

½ teaspoon brown sugar

Heat milk in a small saucepan until a skin forms on top. Remove from heat and let cool slightly. Meanwhile, in a large mixing bowl combine egg substitute, sugar, and vanilla. Slowly stir cooled milk into egg-sugar mixture. Pour into a greased 1-quart (950 ml) baking dish which will fit into your slow cooker or into a baking insert designed for your slow cooker. Mix cinnamon and brown sugar in a small bowl. Sprinkle over custard mixture. Cover baking dish or insert with foil. Set container on a metal rack, trivet, or crumpled foil in slow cooker. Pour hot water around dish to a depth of 1 inch (2.5 cm). Cover and cook on high 2 to 3 hours or until custard is set. (When blade of a knife inserted in center of custard comes out clean, custard is set.) Serve warm from baking dish or insert.

Yield: 6 servings

Per serving: 100 g water; 107 calories (11% from fat, 27% from protein, 63% from carb); 7 g protein; 1 g total fat; 0 g saturated fat; 0 g monounsaturated fat; 1 g polyunsaturated fat; 16 g carb; 0 g fiber; 12 g sugar; 130 mg phosphorus; 136 mg calcium; 1 mg iron; 104 mg sodium; 256 mg potassium; 280 IU vitamin A; 50 mg ATE vitamin E; 1 mg vitamin C; 2 mg cholesterol

Pumpkin Pudding

Like pumpkin pie without the crust, this is sure to become a favorite.

1 can (15 ounces, or 420 g) unsweetened pumpkin

1½ cups (355 ml) fat-free evaporated milk

¼ cup (50 g) sugar

¼ cup (31 g) Heart-Healthy Baking Mix (see recipe in Chapter 2)

½ cup (120 ml) egg substitute

2 teaspoons pumpkin pie spice

1 teaspoon lemon peel

Combine all ingredients in slow cooker sprayed with nonstick cooking spray. Stir until lumps disappear. Cover and cook on low 3 hours. Serve warm or cold.

Yield: 8 servings

Per serving: 95 g water; 104 calories (7% from fat, 23% from protein, 70% from carb); 6 g protein; 1 g total fat; 0 g saturated fat; 0 g monounsaturated fat; 0 g polyunsaturated fat; 19 g carb; 2 g fiber; 13 g sugar; 130 mg phosphorus; 162 mg calcium; 1 mg iron; 103 mg sodium; 310 mg potassium; 8508 IU vitamin A; 53 mg ATE vitamin E; 3 mg vitamin C; 3 mg cholesterol

Apple Cake

This is à simple cake, but it's very moist and with great flavor.

1 cup (125 g) flour

¾ cup (150 g) sugar

2 teaspoons baking powder

1 teaspoon cinnamon

4 apples, chopped

¼ cup (60 ml) egg substitute

2 teaspoons vanilla

Combine flour, sugar, baking powder, and cinnamon. Add apples, stirring lightly to coat. Combine egg substitute and vanilla. Add to apple mixture. Stir until just moistened. Spoon into lightly greased slow cooker. Cover and bake on high 2½ to 3 hours. Serve warm.

Yield: 8 servings

Per serving: 64 g water; 172 calories (3% from fat, 6% from protein, 91% from carb); 3 g protein; 1 g total fat; 0 g saturated fat; 0 g monounsaturated fat; 0 g polyunsaturated fat; 40 g carb; 1 g fiber; 26 g sugar; 59 mg phosphorus; 81 mg calcium; 1 mg iron; 136 mg sodium; 104 mg potassium; 53 IU vitamin A; 0 mg ATE vitamin E; 3 mg vitamin C; 0 mg cholesterol

Carrot Cake

Carrot cake is my favorite, so you know I'd have to try a slow cooker recipe for it. And I do have to say it turned out marvelously.

½ cup (120 ml) canola oil

½ cup (120 ml) egg substitute

1 tablespoon (15 ml) hot water

½ cup (65 g) grated carrots

¾ cup plus 2 tablespoons (110 g) flour, divided

¾ cup (150 g) sugar

½ teaspoon baking powder

¼ teaspoon allspice

½ teaspoon cinnamon

¼ teaspoon cloves

½ cup (55 g) chopped pecans

½ cup (75 g) raisins

In large bowl, beat oil, egg substitute, and water for 1 minute. Add carrots. Mix well. In a separate bowl, stir together ¾ cup (94 g) flour, sugar, baking powder, allspice, cinnamon, and cloves. Add to carrot mixture. Toss nuts and raisins in bowl with 2 tablespoons (16 g) flour. Add to batter and mix well. Pour into greased and floured 3-pound (1⅓ kg) shortening can or slow cooker baking insert. Place can or baking insert in slow cooker. Cover insert with its lid or cover can with 3 paper towels, folded down over edge of slow cooker to absorb moisture. Cover paper towels with cooker lid. Cook on high 3 to 4 hours.

Yield: 8 servings

Per serving: 25 g water; 342 calories (50% from fat, 5% from protein, 45% from carb); 4 g protein; 20 g total fat; 2 g saturated fat; 11 g monounsaturated fat; 6 g polyunsaturated fat; 40 g carb; 2 g fiber; 26 g sugar; 72 mg phosphorus; 43 mg calcium; 1 mg iron; 65 mg sodium; 200 mg potassium; 1406 IU vitamin A; 0 mg ATE vitamin E; 1 mg vitamin C; 0 mg cholesterol

Slow Cooker Chocolate Cake

If you know someone who doesn't believe that you can make cakes and desserts in the slow cooker, this is the one to use to convince them. It's an incredibly rich cake, made directly in the slow cooker.

1¼ cups (285 g) brown sugar, divided

1 cup (125 g) flour

½ cup (45 g) unsweetened cocoa powder, divided

1½ teaspoons baking powder

½ cup (120 ml) skim milk

(continued on page 402)

2 tablespoons (28 g) unsalted butter, melted

½ teaspoon vanilla

1¾ cups (410 ml) boiling water

In a mixing bowl, mix together 1 cup (225 g) brown sugar, flour, ¼ cup (22 g) cocoa, and baking powder. Stir in milk, butter, and vanilla. Pour into slow cooker sprayed with nonstick cooking spray. In a separate bowl, mix together ¼ cup (60 g) brown sugar and ¼ cup (22 g) cocoa. Sprinkle over batter in the slow cooker. Do not stir. Pour boiling water over mixture. Do not stir. Cover and cook on high 1½ to 1¾ hours or until toothpick inserted into cake comes out clean.

Yield: 8 servings

Per serving: 69 g water; 284 calories (11% from fat, 4% from protein, 84% from carb); 3 g protein; 4 g total fat; 2 g saturated fat; 1 g monounsaturated fat; 0 g polyunsaturated fat; 63 g carb; 2 g fiber; 46 g sugar; 104 mg phosphorus; 125 mg calcium; 2 mg iron; 123 mg sodium; 295 mg potassium; 120 IU vitamin A; 33 mg ATE vitamin E; 0 mg vitamin C; 8 mg cholesterol

White Fruitcake

Yes, you can bake your fruitcake in the slow cooker. Some years ago, slow cookers came with a steaming pan that had a vented lid. I haven't seen any like this in some time, but you can also use something like a coffee can covered with foil that has vent holes punched in it.

½ cup (112 g) unsalted butter, softened

1 cup (200 g) sugar

4 eggs, separated

1½ cups (189 g) flour, plus more for coating fruit

1½ teaspoons (7 g) baking powder

1 cup (225 g) unsweetened crushed pineapple, well drained and juice reserved

⅔ cup (160 ml) pineapple juice, drained from crushed pineapple

1½ cups (220 g) golden raisins

4 ounces (115 g) mixed candied fruit

4 ounces (115 g) candied cherries, halved

1 cup (110 g) slivered almonds

½ teaspoon vanilla extract

½ teaspoon almond extract

Using an electric mixer, cream butter and sugar and then add egg yolks and beat well. Combine flour and baking powder and add alternately with pineapple juice to butter mixture. Sprinkle flour over raisins and candied fruit and toss to coat. Stir in raisins, candied fruit, crushed pineapple, vanilla, and almond extract, blending thoroughly. Beat egg whites until stiff but not dry; fold into batter. Pour into greased and floured cake pan and cover; place in slow cooker. Pour ½ cup (120 ml) water around cake pan in slow cooker. Cover and steam the fruitcake on high 3 to 5 hours. After baking, allow cake to rest in pan 10 to 15 minutes before removing. Let cool thoroughly before slicing. For mellowing, wrap in plastic wrap when cool.

Yield: 12 servings

Per serving: 52 g water; 369 calories (37% from fat, 8% from protein, 55% from carb); 8 g protein; 16 g total fat; 6 g saturated fat; 7 g monounsaturated fat; 2 g polyunsaturated fat; 52 g carb; 3 g fiber; 34 g sugar; 152 mg phosphorus; 90 mg calcium; 2 mg iron; 95 mg sodium; 322 mg potassium; 337 IU vitamin A; 89 mg ATE vitamin E; 4 mg vitamin C; 99 mg cholesterol

Cranberry Applesauce

It is very easy to make applesauce in the slow cooker. This version has cranberries added for even more flavor.

6 apples, peeled or unpeeled, cut into 1-inch (2.5 cm) cubes

½ cup (120 ml) apple juice

½ cup (55 g) fresh cranberries

¼ cup (50 g) sugar

¼ teaspoon cinnamon

Combine all ingredients in slow cooker. Cover and cook on low 3 to 4 hours or until apples are as soft as you like them. Serve warm or refrigerate and serve chilled.

Yield: 6 servings

(continued on page 404)

Per serving: 136 g water; 108 calories (2% from fat, 1% from protein, 97% from carb); 0 g protein; 0 g total fat; 0 g saturated fat; 0 g monounsaturated fat; 0 g polyunsaturated fat; 28 g carb; 2 g fiber; 24 g sugar; 17 mg phosphorus; 10 mg calcium; 0 mg iron; 2 mg sodium; 149 mg potassium; 54 IU vitamin A; 0 mg ATE vitamin E; 6 mg vitamin C; 0 mg cholesterol

Applesauce

Applesauce is easy to make in your slow cooker. Mash it to whatever level of chunkiness you desire.

3 pounds (1⅓ kg) apples, peeled, cored, and chopped

½ cup (115 g) brown sugar

½ cup (120 ml) water

¼ cup (60 ml) apple juice concentrate

3 tablespoons (45 ml) lemon juice

6-inch (15 cm) cinnamon stick, optional

Combine all ingredients in slow cooker. Cover and cook on low for 6 to 8 hours. Remove cinnamon stick, if used. Use a potato masher to mash to desired consistency.

Yield: 10 servings

Per serving: 137 g water; 117 calories (1% from fat, 1% from protein, 97% from carb); 0 g protein; 0 g total fat; 0 g saturated fat; 0 g monounsaturated fat; 0 g polyunsaturated fat; 31 g carb; 2 g fiber; 26 g sugar; 19 mg phosphorus; 18 mg calcium; 0 mg iron; 6 mg sodium; 190 mg potassium; 53 IU vitamin A; 0 mg ATE vitamin E; 12 mg vitamin C; 0 mg cholesterol

Spiced Applesauce

With the slow cooker, it's easy to make your own applesauce. And the flavor is better than anything you can get out of a jar.

4 pounds (1.8 kg) apples, pared, cored, and sliced

½ cup (100 g) sugar

½ teaspoon cinnamon

1 cup (235 ml) water

1 tablespoon (15 ml) lemon juice

Place apples in slow cooker. Combine sugar and cinnamon and mix with apples. Blend in water and lemon juice. Cover and cook on low 5 to 7 hours or on high 2½ to 3½ hours.

Yield: 8 servings

Per serving: 228 g water; 158 calories (2% from fat, 1% from protein, 97% from carb); 1 g protein; 0 g total fat; 0 g saturated fat; 0 g monounsaturated fat; 0 g polyunsaturated fat; 42 g carb; 3 g fiber; 36 g sugar; 25 mg phosphorus; 14 mg calcium; 0 mg iron; 1 mg sodium; 208 mg potassium; 87 IU vitamin A; 0 mg ATE vitamin E; 10 mg vitamin C; 0 mg cholesterol

Apple Butter

Apple butter is traditionally slow-cooked in huge tubs, but you can make it right in your slow cooker.

12 apples, preferable Jonathan or winesap

2 cups (475 ml) apple juice

5 cups (1 kg) sugar

2 tablespoons (14 g) cinnamon

1 tablespoon (6 g) allspice

1 tablespoon (6.6 g) cloves

(continued on page 406)

Wash, core, and quarter apples (no need to peel). Combine apples and apple juice in lightly oiled slow cooker. Cover and cook on low for 6 to 8 hours or high for 2 to 4 hours. When fruit is tender, put through a food mill to remove peel. Measure cooked fruit and return to slow cooker. For each pint of cooked fruit, add 1 cup (200 g) sugar, 1 teaspoon cinnamon, ½ teaspoon allspice, and ½ teaspoon cloves; stir well. Cover and cook on high for 6 to 8 hours, stirring about every 2 hours. Remove cover after 3 hours to allow fruit and juice to cook down.

Yield: 80 servings

Per serving: 22 g water; 62 calories (1% from fat, 0% from protein, 99% from carb); 0 g protein; 0 g total fat; 0 g saturated fat; 0 g monounsaturated fat; 0 g polyunsaturated fat; 16 g carb; 0 g fiber; 15 g sugar; 3 mg phosphorus; 5 mg calcium; 0 mg iron; 1 mg sodium; 28 mg potassium; 9 IU vitamin A; 0 mg ATE vitamin E; 1 mg vitamin C; 0 mg cholesterol

Stewed Apples

Dried apples are cooked in sweetened orange juice to produce a real treat.

9 ounces (225 g) dried apples

1 cup (235 ml) orange juice

1 cup (235 ml) water

½ cup (120 ml) maple syrup

1 tablespoon (15 ml) lemon juice

TIP *These are great warm, right out of the slow cooker, but the leftovers are also good cold.*

Place apples in slow cooker. Combine remaining ingredients and pour over apples. Cover and cook on low for 8 hours.

Yield: 6 servings

Per serving: 124 g water; 109 calories (2% from fat, 2% from protein, 97% from carb); 0 g protein; 0 g total fat; 0 g saturated fat; 0 g monounsaturated fat; 0 g polyunsaturated fat; 28 g carb; 1 g fiber; 20 g sugar; 10 mg phosphorus; 26 mg calcium; 0 mg iron; 4 mg sodium; 175 mg potassium; 49 IU vitamin A; 0 mg ATE vitamin E; 17 mg vitamin C; 0 mg cholesterol

Rum Raisin Bananas

It doesn't get any sweeter than this. These are perfect by themselves, but they're also good over vanilla ice cream.

3 tablespoons (45 ml) dark rum, divided

¼ cup (35 g) raisins

3 tablespoons (42 g) unsalted butter

¼ cup (60 g) brown sugar

4 bananas

¼ teaspoon nutmeg

¼ teaspoon cinnamon

Pour 2 tablespoons (30 ml) of the rum over the raisins in a bowl and set aside. Place the butter, brown sugar, and remaining 1 tablespoon (15 ml) rum in the slow cooker. Turn to high and cook until butter and sugar have melted. Peel the bananas and cut in half lengthwise. Place in the cooker. Cover and cook for 30 minutes, turning halfway through the time. Pour the reserved rum and raisins over the bananas and cook 10 minutes longer. Combine nutmeg and cinnamon and sprinkle over bananas before serving.

Yield: 4 servings

Per serving: 95 g water; 284 calories (29% from fat, 2% from protein, 68% from carb); 2 g protein; 9 g total fat; 6 g saturated fat; 2 g monounsaturated fat; 0 g polyunsaturated fat; 47 g carb; 3 g fiber; 33 g sugar; 42 mg phosphorus; 27 mg calcium; 1 mg iron; 9 mg sodium; 532 mg potassium; 338 IU vitamin A; 71 mg ATE vitamin E; 10 mg vitamin C; 23 mg cholesterol

Apple Cobbler

Apples and granola bake together to a slow cooker perfection.

2 cups (220 g) peeled and sliced apples

2 cups (250 g) granola

(continued on page 408)

1 teaspoon cinnamon

¼ cup (85 g) honey

2 tablespoons (28 g) unsalted butter, melted

Spray inside of 3- to 4-quart (2.9 to 3.8 L) slow cooker with nonstick cooking spray. Combine apples, granola, and cinnamon in slow cooker and mix well. Stir together honey and butter and drizzle over apple mixture. Mix gently. Cover and cook on low 5 to 7 hours or until apples are tender.

Yield: 4 servings

Per serving: 55 g water; 302 calories (22% from fat, 5% from protein, 73% from carb); 4 g protein; 8 g total fat; 4 g saturated fat; 2 g monounsaturated fat; 1 g polyunsaturated fat; 58 g carb; 3 g fiber; 37 g sugar; 122 mg phosphorus; 28 mg calcium; 1 mg iron; 197 mg sodium; 180 mg potassium; 200 IU vitamin A; 48 mg ATE vitamin E; 2 mg vitamin C; 15 mg cholesterol

TIP

Serve this slow cooker cobbler with fruit yogurt, if desired.

Hot Spiced Fruit

This is great for Thanksgiving or during the winter. It's best served the next day to allow spices to blend with fruit. You can also add apricots, Queen Anne cherries, or any other fruit you like.

1 pound (455 g) peaches canned in water, undrained

1 pound (455 g) pears canned in water, undrained

1 pound (455 g) pineapple canned in water, undrained

1 cup (250 g) stewed prunes

½ cup (160 g) orange marmalade

2 tablespoons (28 g) unsalted butter

1 stick cinnamon

⅛ teaspoon nutmeg

⅛ teaspoon ground cloves

Drain liquid from all fruit, reserving 1½ cups (355 ml) to make syrup. Combine marmalade, butter, cinnamon stick, nutmeg, cloves, and reserved liquid in a saucepan. Bring to boil, then simmer 3 to 4 minutes. Cut fruit into chunks and gently add to saucepan. Transfer to slow cooker and cook on low at least 4 hours.

Yield: 12 servings

Per serving: 116 g water; 130 calories (13% from fat, 2% from protein, 85% from carb); 1 g protein; 2 g total fat; 1 g saturated fat; 1 g monounsaturated fat; 0 g polyunsaturated fat; 30 g carb; 3 g fiber; 26 g sugar; 21 mg phosphorus; 21 mg calcium; 0 mg iron; 10 mg sodium; 205 mg potassium; 305 IU vitamin A; 16 mg ATE vitamin E; 7 mg vitamin C; 5 mg cholesterol

Brandied Fruit

This makes a marvelous topping for ice cream or pound cake. Or you could just attack it with a spoon.

20 ounces (560 g) pineapple chunks, undrained

4 plums, pitted and cut into pieces

2 apples, cored and cubed

2 pears, cored and cubed

½ cup (65 g) dried apricots

⅓ cup (75 g) brown sugar

¼ cup (55 g) unsalted butter, melted

¼ cup (60 ml) brandy

2 tablespoons (19 g) pearl tapioca, crushed

Combine fruit in slow cooker. In a small bowl, combine remaining ingredients. Pour over fruit and stir. Cover and cook on low for 3½ to 4 hours.

(continued on page 410)

Yield: 12 servings

Per serving: 114 g water; 129 calories (29% from fat, 2% from protein, 69% from carb); 1 g protein; 4 g total fat; 2 g saturated fat; 1 g monounsaturated fat; 0 g polyunsaturated fat; 22 g carb; 2 g fiber; 17 g sugar; 15 mg phosphorus; 20 mg calcium; 0 mg iron; 4 mg sodium; 182 mg potassium; 398 IU vitamin A; 32 mg ATE vitamin E; 8 mg vitamin C; 10 mg cholesterol

Baked Apples

My mother used to make baked apples in the fall when they were plentiful, but it was never as easy as this. Just stick them in the slow cooker and forget them.

2 tablespoons (18 g) raisins

½ cup (100 g) sugar

6 apples, cored but left whole and unpeeled

1 teaspoon cinnamon

2 tablespoons (28 g) unsalted butter

¼ cup (60 ml) water

Mix raisins and sugar together in a small bowl. Stand apples on bottom of slow cooker. Spoon raisin-sugar mixture into centers of apples, dividing evenly among apples. Sprinkle stuffed apples with cinnamon. Dot with butter. Pour the water along the edge of the cooker. Cover and cook on low 3 to 5 hours or on high 2½ to 3½ hours until apples are tender but not collapsing.

Yield: 6 servings

Per serving: 122 g water; 237 calories (15% from fat, 1% from protein, 85% from carb); 1 g protein; 4 g total fat; 2 g saturated fat; 1 g monounsaturated fat; 0 g polyunsaturated fat; 53 g carb; 2 g fiber; 49 g sugar; 19 mg phosphorus; 15 mg calcium; 0 mg iron; 1 mg sodium; 145 mg potassium; 168 IU vitamin A; 32 mg ATE vitamin E; 5 mg vitamin C; 10 mg cholesterol

Peach Cobbler

Warm and sweet, this is an old-fashioned kind of dessert. You can use either fresh or canned peaches.

4 cups fresh (680 g), or canned (888 g) sliced peaches

¼ cup (20 g) rolled oats

⅓ cup (42 g) Heart-Healthy Baking Mix (see recipe in Chapter 2)

½ cup (100 g) sugar

½ cup (115 g) brown sugar

¼ teaspoon cinnamon

½ cup (120 ml) water, or reserved peach juice if using canned peaches

TIP

Serve warm with vanilla ice cream or frozen yogurt.

Spray inside of slow cooker with nonstick cooking spray. Place peaches in slow cooker. In a bowl, mix together oats, baking mix, sugar, brown sugar, and cinnamon. When blended, stir in water or juice until well mixed. Spoon batter into cooker and stir into peaches, just until blended. Cover and cook on low 4 to 5 hours.

Yield: 6 servings

Per serving: 167 g water; 245 calories (1% from fat, 4% from protein, 95% from carb); 2 g protein; 0 g total fat; 0 g saturated fat; 0 g monounsaturated fat; 0 g polyunsaturated fat; 62 g carb; 3 g fiber; 52 g sugar; 65 mg phosphorus; 53 mg calcium; 1 mg iron; 55 mg sodium; 297 mg potassium; 653 IU vitamin A; 5 mg ATE vitamin E; 6 mg vitamin C; 2 mg cholesterol

Apple Crisp

The recipe for apple crisp is made even easier by using canned pie filling. But it tastes just as good as if you made it all by hand.

4 cups (1 kg) apple pie filling

¾ cup (60 g) quick cooking oats

½ cup (115 g) brown sugar

½ cup (63 g) flour

¼ cup (55 g) unsalted butter, at room temperature

Place pie filling in slow cooker. Combine remaining ingredients until crumbly. Sprinkle over apple filling. Cover and cook on low 2 to 3 hours.

Yield: 8 servings

Per serving: 87 g water; 229 calories (26% from fat, 4% from protein, 70% from carb); 2 g protein; 7 g total fat; 4 g saturated fat; 2 g monounsaturated fat; 1 g polyunsaturated fat; 41 g carb; 3 g fiber; 29 g sugar; 54 mg phosphorus; 23 mg calcium; 1 mg iron; 10 mg sodium; 154 mg potassium; 229 IU vitamin A; 48 mg ATE vitamin E; 0 mg vitamin C; 15 mg cholesterol

19

Effortless and Delicious Drinks

All the stuff I said about appetizers way back in the introduction to Chapter 3 applies here as well. The slow cooker allows you to make hot drinks ahead of time and keep them warm until you are ready to serve them. This is a big advantage if you are having a party or dinner, but you might also imagine having the perfect hot drink waiting when you return from caroling or sledding. This chapter contains recipes for cider and other fruit-based drinks, drinks containing rum or wine, and everyone's favorite, chocolate.

Hot Cocoa

Hot cocoa just like the good old days, but without having to stand over the stove stirring.

½ cup (100 g) sugar

½ cup (45 g) unsweetened cocoa powder

2 cups (475 ml) boiling water

3½ cups (448 g) nonfat dry milk powder

6 cups (1.4 L) water

1 teaspoon vanilla

TIP *Top with marshmallows and sprinkle with cinnamon.*

Combine sugar and cocoa powder in slow cooker. Add 2 cups (475 ml) boiling water. Stir well to dissolve. Add dry milk powder, 6 cups (1.4 L) water, and vanilla. Stir well to dissolve. Cover and cook on low 4 hours, or on high 1 to 1½ hours. Before serving, beat with rotary beater to make frothy. Ladle into mugs.

Yield: 9 servings

Per serving: 212 g water; 150 calories (5% from fat, 26% from protein, 70% from carb); 10 g protein; 1 g total fat; 1 g saturated fat; 0 g monounsaturated fat; 0 g polyunsaturated fat; 28 g carb; 2 g fiber; 25 g sugar; 296 mg phosphorus; 338 mg calcium; 1 mg iron; 153 mg sodium; 527 mg potassium; 625 IU vitamin A; 187 mg ATE vitamin E; 1 mg vitamin C; 5 mg cholesterol

Mocha

This is chocolate and coffee, with a little cinnamon flavor, topped by whipped cream. This is every bit as good—and a whole lot cheaper—than what you'll get at your local coffee shop.

2 cups (475 ml) brewed coffee

6 heaping tablespoons (45 g) instant hot chocolate mix

1 cinnamon stick, broken into large pieces

1 cup (235 ml) whipping cream

1 tablespoon (8 g) powdered sugar

Put coffee, hot chocolate mix, and cinnamon sticks into slow cooker. Stir. Cover and cook on high 1 to 2 hours or until very hot. Discard cinnamon pieces. Just before serving, pour the whipping cream into a chilled mixer bowl. Beat cream on high speed until soft peaks form. Fold sugar into whipped cream. Beat again on high speed until stiff peaks form. Ladle hot chocolate coffee into small cups. Top each with a dollop of whipped cream.

Yield: 6 servings

Per serving: 91 g water; 153 calories (39% from fat, 4% from protein, 57% from carb); 2 g protein; 7 g total fat; 4 g saturated fat; 2 g monounsaturated fat; 0 g polyunsaturated fat; 22 g carb; 1 g fiber; 19 g sugar; 32 mg phosphorus; 115 mg calcium; 0 mg iron; 38 mg sodium; 136 mg potassium; 203 IU vitamin A; 55 mg ATE vitamin E; 6 mg vitamin C; 22 mg cholesterol

Hot White Chocolate

For something a little different, make hot chocolate using white chocolate.

3 cups (700 ml) skim milk

3 cups (700 ml) fat-free evaporated milk

1½ cups (255 g) white chocolate chips

2 teaspoons vanilla

Combine all ingredients in slow cooker. Cook on low for 3 to 4 hours or on high for 1 to 2 hours.

Yield: 8 servings

Per serving: 160 g water; 288 calories (33% from fat, 18% from protein, 49% from carb); 13 g protein; 11 g total fat; 6 g saturated fat; 3 g monounsaturated fat; 0 g polyunsaturated fat; 35 g carb; 0 g fiber; 30 g sugar; 347 mg phosphorus; 474 mg calcium; 0 mg iron; 194 mg sodium; 579 mg potassium; 575 IU vitamin A; 172 mg ATE vitamin E; 2 mg vitamin C; 10 mg cholesterol

Hot Apple Cider

This is apple cider with a little bit of spice and a nice citrus touch this is popular with kids and adults alike.

7 cups (1.6 L) apple cider

2 cups (475 ml) orange juice

½ cup (120 ml) honey

6 whole cloves

1 apple, peeled

1 orange, sliced

Combine first 3 ingredients in a Dutch oven or large kettle. Insert cloves into apple. Add apple and orange slices to juice mixture. Bring to a boil. Reduce heat and simmer 5 minutes. Transfer to slow cooker. Cook on low for 2 hours. Keep warm in the cooker for serving.

Yield: 14 servings

Per serving: 162 g water; 121 calories (2% from fat, 2% from protein, 96% from carb); 1 g protein; 0 g total fat; 0 g saturated fat; 0 g monounsaturated fat; 0 g polyunsaturated fat; 31 g carb; 1 g fiber; 26 g sugar; 16 mg phosphorus; 19 mg calcium; 1 mg iron; 5 mg sodium; 253 mg potassium; 62 IU vitamin A; 0 mg ATE vitamin E; 20 mg vitamin C; 0 mg cholesterol

Spiced Cider

Cinnamon candies help to provide the spice for this apple cider.

½ gallon (1.9 L) apple cider, divided

¼ cup (56 g) red hots candies

¼ cups brown sugar

1 teaspoon cloves

1 teaspoon allspice

Combine 2 cups (475 ml) cider, red hots, and brown sugar and microwave on medium for 7 to 8 minutes. Add cloves and allspice. Mix with remainder of cider. Heat in slow cooker until flavor is well developed, at least one hour.

Yield: 8 servings

Per serving: 218 g water; 144 calories (2% from fat, 0% from protein, 97% from carb); 0 g protein; 0 g total fat; 0 g saturated fat; 0 g monounsaturated fat; 0 g polyunsaturated fat; 36 g carb; 0 g fiber; 34 g sugar; 19 mg phosphorus; 27 mg calcium; 1 mg iron; 11 mg sodium; 325 mg potassium; 5 IU vitamin A; 0 mg ATE vitamin E; 3 mg vitamin C; 0 mg cholesterol

Wassail

This is another hot drink based on cider but with more orange juice and a little different combination of spices.

1 cup (200 g) sugar

½ teaspoon ground ginger

1½ cinnamon sticks

½ teaspoon allspice

1 cup (235 ml) water

4 cups (950 ml) orange juice

2½ quarts (2.4 L) apple cider or juice

1½ cups (355 ml) lemon juice

Mix the first four ingredients in a saucepan. Stir in water and simmer until sugar dissolves, stirring constantly. Add orange juice, apple cider, and lemon juice to sugar mixture. Transfer to slow cooker and cook on low for 2 hours. Serve warm or cool. Refrigerate to serve chilled.

Yield: 12 servings

Per serving: 301 g water; 206 calories (2% from fat, 2% from protein, 96% from carb); 1 g protein; 0 g total fat; 0 g saturated fat; 0 g monounsaturated fat; 0 g polyunsaturated fat; 52 g carb; 1 g fiber; 40 g sugar; 26 mg phosphorus; 26 mg calcium; 1 mg iron; 8 mg sodium; 441 mg potassium; 73 IU vitamin A; 0 mg ATE vitamin E; 42 mg vitamin C; 0 mg cholesterol

Cider Tea Punch

This spicy apple and tea combination is a perfect warmer for those cold winter nights.

½ gallon (1.9 L) apple cider

½ gallon (1.9 L) tea

1 lemon, sliced

1 orange, sliced

3 cinnamon sticks

1 tablespoon (6 g) whole cloves

1 tablespoon (6 g) whole allspice berries

¼ cup (60 g) brown sugar

Combine all ingredients in slow cooker. Heat on low for 2 hours.

Yield: 16 servings

Per serving: 123 g water; 430 calories (1% from fat, 1% from protein, 98% from carb); 1 g protein; 1 g total fat; 0 g saturated fat; 0 g monounsaturated fat; 0 g polyunsaturated fat; 109 g carb; 1 g fiber; 18 g sugar; 25 mg phosphorus; 25 mg calcium; 1 mg iron; 11 mg sodium; 391 mg potassium; 32 IU vitamin A; 0 mg ATE vitamin E; 101 mg vitamin C; 0 mg cholesterol

Maple Cider

Maple syrup adds a little different kind of sweetness to this spiced cider.

½ gallon (1.9 L) apple cider

4 cinnamon sticks

2 teaspoons whole cloves

2 teaspoons whole allspice berries

2 tablespoons (36 g) orange juice concentrate

2 tablespoons (40 g) maple syrup

Combine ingredients in slow cooker. Cover and heat on low for 2 hours. Serve warm.

Yield: 10 servings

Per serving: 178 g water; 112 calories (3% from fat, 1% from protein, 96% from carb); 0 g protein; 0 g total fat; 0 g saturated fat; 0 g monounsaturated fat; 0 g polyunsaturated fat; 28 g carb; 0 g fiber; 25 g sugar; 17 mg phosphorus; 23 mg calcium; 1 mg iron; 8 mg sodium; 277 mg potassium; 20 IU vitamin A; 0 mg ATE vitamin E; 7 mg vitamin C; 0 mg cholesterol

Cranberry Orange Cider

Fruity cider, with a hint of cinnamon if desired.

4 cups (950 ml) apple cider

2 cups (475 ml) cranberry juice

1 cup (235 ml) orange juice

1½ cups (355 ml) apricot nectar

4 cinnamon sticks, optional

Combine all ingredients thoroughly in slow cooker. Cover and cook on low 4 to 10 hours. Serve warm from the cooker.

Yield: 10 servings

Per serving: 181 g water; 104 calories (2% from fat, 1% from protein, 97% from carb); 0 g protein; 0 g total fat; 0 g saturated fat; 0 g monounsaturated fat; 0 g polyunsaturated fat; 26 g carb; 0 g fiber; 11 g sugar; 13 mg phosphorus; 14 mg calcium; 1 mg iron; 6 mg sodium; 211 mg potassium; 473 IU vitamin A; 0 mg ATE vitamin E; 33 mg vitamin C; 0 mg cholesterol

Citrus Cider

This is a warm fruity punch, good for both children and adults.

1 cup (200 g) sugar

2 cinnamon sticks

1 teaspoon nutmeg

2 cups (475 ml) apple cider

3 cups (700 ml) orange juice

1 orange

Combine all ingredients except the orange in slow cooker. Cover and cook on low 4 to 10 hours or on high 2 to 3 hours. Float thin slices of orange in cooker before serving.

Yield: 12 servings

Per serving: 105 g water; 120 calories (2% from fat, 2% from protein, 96% from carb); 1 g protein; 0 g total fat; 0 g saturated fat; 0 g monounsaturated fat; 0 g polyunsaturated fat; 30 g carb; 1 g fiber; 23 g sugar; 12 mg phosphorus; 16 mg calcium; 0 mg iron; 2 mg sodium; 196 mg potassium; 84 IU vitamin A; 0 mg ATE vitamin E; 29 mg vitamin C; 0 mg cholesterol

Spiced Raspberry Punch

Raspberries, cranberries, and orange blend together in a fruity punch.

4 cups (950 ml) cranberry juice

3 cups (700 ml) water

¾ cup (213 g) frozen orange juice concentrate, thawed

10 ounces (280 g) frozen raspberries, thawed

2 oranges, sliced

6 cinnamon sticks

12 whole allspice berries

Combine all ingredients in slow cooker. Heat on high 1 hour or until hot. Turn to low while serving.

Yield: 10 servings

Per serving: 223 g water; 114 calories (2% from fat, 4% from protein, 94% from carb); 1 g protein; 0 g total fat; 0 g saturated fat; 0 g monounsaturated fat; 0 g polyunsaturated fat; 28 g carb; 3 g fiber; 11 g sugar; 24 mg phosphorus; 34 mg calcium; 0 mg iron; 6 mg sodium; 239 mg potassium; 167 IU vitamin A; 0 mg ATE vitamin E; 60 mg vitamin C; 0 mg cholesterol

Thanksgiving Punch

We've made this several times for holiday meals. The pineapple juice cuts the tartness of the cranberry, and the spices are just enough.

2 pounds (900 g) cranberry sauce, mashed

4 cups (950 ml) water

4 cups (950 ml) pineapple juice

¼ cup (60 g) brown sugar

¼ teaspoon nutmeg

¼ teaspoon cloves

¼ teaspoon allspice

12 cinnamon sticks

Combine all ingredients in slow cooker except cinnamon sticks. Cover and heat on low 4 hours. Serve in mugs with cinnamon stick stirrers.

Yield: 12 servings

Per serving: 118 g water; 176 calories (1% from fat, 1% from protein, 98% from carb); 0 g protein; 0 g total fat; 0 g saturated fat; 0 g monounsaturated fat; 0 g polyunsaturated fat; 45 g carb; 1 g fiber; 41 g sugar; 12 mg phosphorus; 18 mg calcium; 1 mg iron; 26 mg sodium; 145 mg potassium; 36 IU vitamin A; 0 mg ATE vitamin E; 10 mg vitamin C; 0 mg cholesterol

Cranberry Punch

This is sort of warm cranberry sangria, I suppose, or just cranberry punch.

8 whole cardamom pods

2 cinnamon sticks

12 whole cloves

4 cups (950 ml) dry red wine

1½ cups (426 g) frozen cranberry concentrate, thawed

2½ cups (570 ml) water

½ cup (170 g) honey

1 orange, sliced into 8 thin crescents

To make a spice packet, pinch open cardamom pods to release seeds and place them on a piece of cheesecloth or paper coffee filter. Add cinnamon sticks and cloves. Tie with a string to make a bag. Pour wine, cranberry concentrate, water, and honey into slow cooker. Heat on low. Submerge spice packet in the liquid and heat but do not boil. Let punch steep on low for up to 4 hours. To serve, remove and discard spice bag. Float an orange slice in each cup. Serve warm.

Yield: 8 servings

Per serving: 220 g water; 261 calories (0% from fat, 1% from protein, 99% from carb); 0 g protein; 0 g total fat; 0 g saturated fat; 0 g monounsaturated fat; 0 g polyunsaturated fat; 45 g carb; 1 g fiber; 38 g sugar; 33 mg phosphorus; 27 mg calcium; 1 mg iron; 9 mg sodium; 224 mg potassium; 66 IU vitamin A; 0 mg ATE vitamin E; 32 mg vitamin C; 0 mg cholesterol

Mulled Non-Wine

Here's a delightful hot punch for those who prefer non-alcoholic beverages.

1 orange

4-inch (10 cm) cinnamon stick, broken

12 whole cloves

12 whole allspice berries

4 cups (750 ml) cranberry juice

2 cups (475 ml) pomegranate juice

2 cups (475 ml) cherry juice blend

¼ cup (60 g) brown sugar

Use a vegetable peeler to remove peel in wide strips from the orange, being careful to avoid the bitter white part underneath. For spice bag, cut a 6-inch (15 cm) square from a double thickness of cotton cheesecloth. Place orange peel, broken cinnamon sticks, cloves, and allspice in the center of the cheesecloth square. Bring up corners of the cheesecloth; tie closed with clean kitchen string. In a slow cooker, combine cranberry juice, pomegranate juice, cherry juice, and brown sugar. Add spice bag to cooker. Cover and cook on low for 5 to 6 hours or on high for 2½ to 3 hours. Remove and discard spice bag.

Yield: 10 servings

Per serving: 190 g water; 128 calories (2% from fat, 2% from protein, 96% from carb); 1 g protein; 0 g total fat; 0 g saturated fat; 0 g monounsaturated fat; 0 g polyunsaturated fat; 32 g carb; 1 g fiber; 12 g sugar; 17 mg phosphorus; 31 mg calcium; 0 mg iron; 6 mg sodium; 249 mg potassium; 215 IU vitamin A; 0 mg ATE vitamin E; 51 mg vitamin C; 0 mg cholesterol

Hot Apple Cranberry Drink

Hot spiced apple cranberry juice mixture is perfect for a cold day.

6 cups (1.4 L) apple juice

6 cups (1.4 L) cranberry juice

2 cinnamon sticks

Dash of nutmeg

Combine ingredients in slow cooker and heat on low until warmed through, about an hour.

Yield: 12 servings

Per serving: 197 g water; 116 calories (1% from fat, 1% from protein, 99% from carb); 0 g protein; 0 g total fat; 0 g saturated fat; 0 g monounsaturated fat; 0 g polyunsaturated fat; 29 g carb; 0 g fiber; 12 g sugar; 9 mg phosphorus; 12 mg calcium; 0 mg iron; 11 mg sodium; 159 mg potassium; 11 IU vitamin A; 0 mg ATE vitamin E; 12 mg vitamin C; 0 mg cholesterol

Spiced Tea

This lets you mix up a big batch of spiced tea powder and then make it in whatever quantities you want in the slow cooker.

1 cup (32 g) instant tea

2 cups (416 g) instant orange drink mix

1 cup (200 g) sugar

2 tablespoons (28 g) lemonade mix

1 tablespoon (6.6 g) ground cloves

1 tablespoon (7 g) ground cinnamon

Combine all ingredients and store in an airtight container. Add ¼ cup (50 g) of mix for each quart (960 ml) of water to slow cooker. Heat on low until warm, stirring occasionally to make sure powder is dissolved.

Yield: 48 servings

Per serving: 0 g water; 62 calories (1% from fat, 0% from protein, 99% from carb); 0 g protein; 0 g total fat; 0 g saturated fat; 0 g monounsaturated fat; 0 g polyunsaturated fat; 16 g carb; 0 g fiber; 12 g sugar; 15 mg phosphorus; 34 mg calcium; 0 mg iron; 1 mg sodium; 26 mg potassium; 168 IU vitamin A; 0 mg ATE vitamin E; 24 mg vitamin C; 0 mg cholesterol

Tropical Tea

Here's a citrus-flavored tea to warm you up and make you think of the islands on a cold night.

6 cups (1.4 L) boiling water

6 tea bags

⅓ cup (67 g) sugar

2 tablespoons (40 g) honey

1½ cups (355 ml) orange juice

1½ cups (355 ml) pineapple juice

1 orange, sliced

Pour boiling water over tea bags. Cover; let stand 5 minutes. Add remaining ingredients. Heat in slow cooker on low 2 to 3 hours.

Yield: 9 servings

Per serving: 249 g water; 93 calories (2% from fat, 3% from protein, 95% from carb); 1 g protein; 0 g total fat; 0 g saturated fat; 0 g monounsaturated fat; 0 g polyunsaturated fat; 23 g carb; 1 g fiber; 17 g sugar; 11 mg phosphorus; 23 mg calcium; 0 mg iron; 6 mg sodium; 174 mg potassium; 80 IU vitamin A; 0 mg ATE vitamin E; 29 mg vitamin C; 0 mg cholesterol

Russian Tea

Russian tea is a spiced and fruited tea that is a perfect recipe for the slow cooker.

1 gallon (3.8 L) water

2 teaspoons ground cinnamon

3 cloves

3 tea bags

1½ cups (300 g) sugar

¾ cup (213 g) frozen orange juice, thawed

¾ cup (213 g) frozen lemonade, thawed

Combine water, cinnamon, cloves, and tea bags in saucepan. Boil 2 to 3 minutes. Remove tea bags and add juices. Remove cloves. Transfer to slow cooker and cook on low for one hour to blend flavors.

Yield: 16 servings

Per serving: 251 g water; 98 calories (1% from fat, 1% from protein, 99% from carb); 0 g protein; 0 g total fat; 0 g saturated fat; 0 g monounsaturated fat; 0 g polyunsaturated fat; 25 g carb; 0 g fiber; 19 g sugar; 2 mg phosphorus; 13 mg calcium; 0 mg iron; 8 mg sodium; 31 mg potassium; 10 IU vitamin A; 0 mg ATE vitamin E; 5 mg vitamin C; 0 mg cholesterol

Wassail Rum Punch

This recipe is a variation of one that has been popular since the days of colonial America. Maybe it's the rum that gives it its popularity.

1 gallon (3.8 L) apple juice

4 apples

4 oranges

1 cup (145 g) raisins

1 tablespoon (15 ml) rum extract

½ cup (120 ml) rum

2 tablespoons (12 g) allspice

4 cups (950 ml) brewed tea

Sugar, to taste

Cinnamon sticks

The night before you'd like to serve the punch, slice the oranges and cut apples into quarters. Place into a large bowl with raisins and then add the rum extract, rum, and allspice. Blend together. Cover; let stand in the refrigerator overnight. The next day, place fruit-rum mixture in slow cooker at least 1 hour before serving. Add in the tea and sugar to taste. Then add the cinnamon sticks. Serve piping hot.

Yield: 24 servings

Per serving: 189 g water; 249 calories (1% from fat, 2% from protein, 97% from carb); 1 g protein; 0 g total fat; 0 g saturated fat; 0 g monounsaturated fat; 0 g polyunsaturated fat; 60 g carb; 2 g fiber; 27 g sugar; 30 mg phosphorus; 31 mg calcium; 1 mg iron; 14 mg sodium; 398 mg potassium; 80 IU vitamin A; 0 mg ATE vitamin E; 49 mg vitamin C; 0 mg cholesterol

Hot Buttered Rum

This is a traditional grog for warming up a cold night.

½ cup (112 g) unsalted butter

3 cinnamon sticks

6 whole cloves

½ teaspoon nutmeg

8 cups (1.9 L) hot water

2 cups (475 ml) rum

Put all ingredients in slow cooker. Stir well. Cover and cook on high for 2 hours and then turn to low for 3 to 10 hours. Serve from slow cooker in warm mugs.

Yield: 15 servings

Per serving: 147 g water; 123 calories (99% from fat, 0% from protein, 0% from carb); 0 g protein; 6 g total fat; 4 g saturated fat; 2 g monounsaturated fat; 0 g polyunsaturated fat; 0 g carb; 0 g fiber; 0 g sugar; 3 mg phosphorus; 6 mg calcium; 0 mg iron; 5 mg sodium; 4 mg potassium; 189 IU vitamin A; 51 mg ATE vitamin E; 0 mg vitamin C; 16 mg cholesterol

Hot Rum and Fruit Punch

If you like cold fruity rum drinks, it's a pretty good bet you'll like this warm one too.

8 cups (1.9 L) apple cider

2 cups (475 ml) cranberry juice

1¼ cups (250 g) sugar

1 cinnamon stick

1 teaspoon whole allspice berries

1 orange, studded with whole cloves

1 cup (235 ml) rum

(continued on page 428)

Put all ingredients into slow cooker. Cover and cook on high 1 hour, then on low 4 to 8 hours. Serve warm from cooker.

Yield: 12 servings

Per serving: 207 g water; 232 calories (1% from fat, 1% from protein, 98% from carb); 0 g protein; 0 g total fat; 0 g saturated fat; 0 g monounsaturated fat; 0 g polyunsaturated fat; 48 g carb; 1 g fiber; 40 g sugar; 15 mg phosphorus; 21 mg calcium; 1 mg iron; 7 mg sodium; 233 mg potassium; 41 IU vitamin A; 0 mg ATE vitamin E; 14 mg vitamin C; 0 mg cholesterol

Spiced Apple Wine

We've got spiced cider and spiced wine, so why not spiced cider wine? It just makes sense.

5 cups (1.2 L) apple cider

3 cups (700 ml) dry red wine

¼ cup (60 g) brown sugar

½ teaspoon whole cloves

¼ teaspoon whole allspice berries

1 cinnamon stick

Combine all ingredients in slow cooker. Cover and cook on low 3 to 4 hours. Remove cloves, allspice, and cinnamon before serving.

Yield: 9 servings

Per serving: 189 g water; 155 calories (2% from fat, 1% from protein, 98% from carb); 0 g protein; 0 g total fat; 0 g saturated fat; 0 g monounsaturated fat; 0 g polyunsaturated fat; 24 g carb; 0 g fiber; 21 g sugar; 29 mg phosphorus; 22 mg calcium; 1 mg iron; 10 mg sodium; 287 mg potassium; 2 IU vitamin A; 0 mg ATE vitamin E; 1 mg vitamin C; 0 mg cholesterol

Mulled Wine

This is a fairly traditional mulled wine, of the kind that has been around since colonial days.

½ teaspoon whole cloves

½ teaspoon whole allspice berries

8 cups (1.9 L) dry red wine

2 cinnamon sticks

1 teaspoon nutmeg

Orange slices, optional

Cinnamon sticks, optional

TIP *Garnish individual servings with orange slices or cinnamon sticks.*

Place cloves and allspice in cheesecloth bag or tea ball. Combine spice bag, wine, 2 cinnamon sticks, and nutmeg in slow cooker. Cook on high 1 hour. Reduce heat and simmer 2 to 3 hours.

Yield: 10 servings

Per serving: 163 g water; 162 calories (5% from fat, 3% from protein, 93% from carb); 0 g protein; 0 g total fat; 0 g saturated fat; 0 g monounsaturated fat; 0 g polyunsaturated fat; 5 g carb; 0 g fiber; 1 g sugar; 44 mg phosphorus; 17 mg calcium; 1 mg iron; 8 mg sodium; 242 mg potassium; 1 IU vitamin A; 0 mg ATE vitamin E; 0 mg vitamin C; 0 mg cholesterol

20

Cooking Terms, Weights and Measurements, and Gadgets

Cooking Terms

Are you confused about a term I used in one of the recipes? Take a look at the list here and see if there might be an explanation. I've tried to include anything that I thought might raise a question.

Al dente

"To the tooth," in Italian — The pasta is cooked just enough to maintain a firm, chewy texture.

Bake

To cook in the oven — Food is cooked slowly with gentle heat, concentrating the flavor.

Baste

To brush or spoon liquid, fat, or juices over meat during roasting to add flavor and to prevent it from drying out

Beat

To smooth a mixture by briskly whipping or stirring it with a spoon, fork, wire whisk, rotary beater, or electric mixer

Blend

To mix or fold two or more ingredients together to obtain equal distribution throughout the mixture

Boil

To cook food in heated water or other liquid that is bubbling vigorously

Braise

A cooking technique that requires browning meat in oil or other fat and then cooking slowly in liquid — The effect of braising is to tenderize the meat.

Bread

To coat the food with crumbs (usually with soft or dry breadcrumbs), sometimes seasoned

Broil

To cook food directly under the heat source

Broth or Stock

A flavorful liquid made by gently cooking meat, seafood, or vegetables (and/or their by-products, such as bones and trimming), often with herbs and vegetables, in liquid, usually water

Brown

A quick sautéing, pan/oven broiling, or grilling done either at the beginning or end of meal preparation, often to enhance flavor, texture, or eye appeal

Brush

Using a pastry brush to coat a food such as meat or bread with melted butter, glaze, or other liquid

Chop

To cut into irregular pieces

Coat

To evenly cover food with flour, crumbs, or a batter

Combine

To blend two or more ingredients into a single mixture

Core

To remove the inedible center of fruits such as pineapples

Cream

To beat butter, with or without sugar, until light and fluffy — This process traps in air bubbles, which create height in cookies and cakes when they're baked.

Cut In

To work butter into dry ingredients

Dash

A measure approximately equal to $\frac{1}{16}$ teaspoon

Deep Fry

To completely submerge the food in hot oil — A quick way to cook some food and, as a result, this method often seems to seal in the flavors of food better than any other technique.

Dice

To cut into cubes

Direct Heat

Heat waves radiate from a source and travel directly to the item being heated with no conductor between them — Examples are grilling, broiling, and toasting.

Dough

Used primarily for cookies and breads — Dough is a mixture of fat (such as butter), flour, liquid, and other ingredients that maintains its shape when placed on a flat surface, although it will change shape once baked through the leavening process.

Dredge

To coat lightly and evenly with sugar or flour

Dumpling

A batter or soft dough that is formed into small mounds that are then steamed, poached, or simmered

Dust

To sprinkle food lightly with spices, sugar, or flour for a light coating

Fold

To cut and mix lightly with a spoon to keep as much air in the mixture as possible

Fritter

Sweet or savory foods coated with or mixed into batter, then deep-fried

Fry

To cook food in hot oil, usually until a crisp brown crust forms

Glaze

A liquid that gives an item a shiny surface — Examples are fruit jams that have been heated, or chocolate that has been thinned.

Grease

To coat a pan or skillet with a thin layer of oil

Grill

To cook over the heat source (traditionally over wood or charcoal) in the open air

Grind

To mechanically cut a food into small pieces

Hull

To remove the leafy parts of soft fruits such as strawberries or blackberries

Knead

To work dough with the heels of your hands in a pressing and folding motion until it becomes smooth and elastic

Marinate

To combine food with aromatic ingredients to add flavor

Mince

To chop food into tiny irregular pieces

Mix

To beat or stir two or more foods together until they are thoroughly combined

Pan-fry

To cook in a hot pan with small amount of hot oil, butter, or other fat, turning the food over once or twice

Poach

Simmering in a liquid

Pot Roast

A large piece of meat, usually browned in fat, cooked in a covered pan

Purée

Food that has been mashed or processed in a blender or food processor

Reduce

To cook liquids down so that some of the water they contain evaporates

Roast

To cook uncovered in the oven

Sauté

To cook with a small amount of hot oil, butter, or other fat, tossing the food around over high heat

Sear

To brown a food quickly on all sides using high heat to seal in the juices

Shred

To cut into fine strips

Simmer

To cook slowly in a liquid over low heat

Skim

To remove the surface layer (of impurities, scum, or fat) from liquids such as stocks and jams while cooking — This is usually done with a flat slotted spoon.

Smoke

To expose foods to wood smoke to enhance their flavor and help preserve and/or evenly cook them

Steam

To cook in steam by suspending foods over boiling water in a steamer or covered pot

Stew

To cook food in liquid for a long time until tender, usually in a covered pot

Stir

To mix ingredients with a utensil

Stir-fry

To cook quickly over high heat with a small amount of oil by constantly stirring — This technique often employs a wok.

Toss

To mix ingredients lightly by lifting and dropping them using two utensils

Whip

To beat an item to incorporate air, augment volume, and add substance

Zest

The thin, brightly colored outer part of the rind of citrus fruits — It contains volatile oils, used as a flavoring.

Weights and Measurements

First of all, here's a quick refresher on measurements.

3 teaspoons = 1 tablespoon

2 tablespoons = 1 fluid ounce

4 tablespoons = 2 fluid ounces = ¼ cup

5⅓ tablespoons = 16 teaspoons = ⅓ cup

8 tablespoons = 4 fluid ounces = ½ cup

16 tablespoons = 8 fluid ounces = 1 cup

2 cups = 1 pint

4 cups = 2 pints = 1 quart

16 cups = 8 pints = 4 quarts = 1 gallon

Metric Conversions

One of the questions that my newsletter readers have raised is whether I could also publish recipes with metric measurements. This would certainly be a good idea, since most of the world uses the metric system. Unfortunately, the software I use doesn't have a way to automatically convert from US to metric measurements. There are some measurements that I can give you an easy conversion for, such as Fahrenheit to Celsius oven temperatures. Other things are not so easy. The information below is intended to be helpful to those readers who use the metric system of weights and measures.

Measurements of Liquid Volume

The following measures are approximate, but close enough for most, if not all, of the recipes in this book.

1 quart = 950 milliliters

1 cup = 235 milliliters

¾ cup = 175 milliliters

½ cup = 120 milliliters

⅓ cup = 80 milliliters

¼ cup = 60 milliliters

1 fluid ounce = 28 milliliters

1 tablespoon = 15 milliliters

1 teaspoon = 5 milliliters

Measurements of Weight

Much of the world measures dry ingredients by weight, rather than volume, as is done in the United States. There is no easy conversion for this, since each item has a different weight. However, the following conversions may be useful.

1 ounce = 28 grams

1 pound = 455 grams (about half a kilogram)

Oven Temperatures

Finally, we come to one that is relatively straightforward, the Fahrenheit to Celsius conversion.

100°F = 39°C

150°F = 66°C

200°F = 93°C

225°F = 110°C

250°F = 120°C, or gas mark ½

275°F = 140°C, or gas mark 1

300°F = 150°C, or gas mark 2

325°F = 165°C, or gas mark 3

350°F = 180°C, or gas mark 4

375°F = 190°C, or gas mark 5

400°F = 205°C, or gas mark 6

425°F = 220°C, or gas mark 7

450°F = 230°C, or gas mark 8

475°F = 240°C, or gas mark 9

500°F = 260°C, or gas mark 10

Gadgets I Use

The following are some of the tools that I use in cooking. Some are used very often and some very seldom, but they all help make things a little easier or quicker. Why are some things here and others not? No reason, except that most of these are things I considered a little less standard than a stove, oven, grill, and mixer.

Blender

Okay, so everyone has a blender. And it's a handy little tool for blending and puréeing things. I don't really think I need to say any more about that.

Bread Machine

When I went on a low-sodium diet, I discovered that one of the biggest single changes that you can make to reduce your sodium intake is to make your own bread. Most commercial bread has well over 100 mg per slice. Many rolls and specialty breads are in the 300–400 mg range. A bread machine can reduce the amount of effort required to make your own bread to a manageable level. It takes at most 10 minutes to load it and turn it on. You can even set it on a timer to have your house filled with the aroma of fresh bread when you come home. Even if you're not watching your sodium, there is nothing like the smell of bread baking and the taste right out of the "oven."

Canning Kettle

If you are planning on making batches of things like pickles and salsa in volume so you don't have to go through the process every couple of weeks, then you are going to need a way to preserve things. Most items can be frozen, of course, if that is your preference. But some things just seem to me to work better in jars. What you need is a kettle big enough to make sure the jars can be covered by water when being processed in a boiling water bath. There are also racks to sit the jars in and special tongs to make lifting them in and out of the water easier. I've had a porcelain-covered kettle I used for canning for many years, and it also doubled as a stockpot before I got the one described below. It's better for canning than for soup because the relatively thin walls allow the water to heat faster (and the soup to burn).

Deep Fryer

Obviously, if you are watching your fat intake, this should not be one of your most often-used appliances. I don't use it nearly as often as I used to, but it still occupies a place in the appliance garage in the corner of the kitchen counter. It's big enough to cook a batch of fries or fish for three to four people at a time.

Food Processor

I'm a real latecomer to the food processor world. It always seemed like a nice thing to have, but something I could easily do without. We bought one to help shred meat and other things for my wife's mother, who was having some difficulty swallowing large chunks of food. I use it now all the time to grind bread into crumbs or chop the peppers and onions that seem to go into at least three meals a week. It's a low-end model that doesn't have the power to grind meat and some of the heavier tasks, but I've discovered it's a real time saver for a number of things.

Contact Grill

The George Foreman models are the most popular example of this item. My son's girlfriend gave me this for Christmas a few years ago. (And he didn't have the good sense to hang onto her...but that's a different story.) I use it fairly often. When we built our house, we included a cooktop with a built-in grill, and for years we used that regularly. I still use it for some things—I much prefer the way it does burgers or steak when it's too cold to grill them outside, for example—but it's difficult to clean and doesn't do nearly as nice a job as the Foreman at things like grilled veggies and fish. And the design allows the fat to drain away, giving you a healthier, lower-fat meal.

Grinder

Many years ago we bought an all-in-one appliance that included a stand mixer, blender (the one we still use), food chopper, and a grinder attachment. The grinder was never a big deal that got any use until I started experimenting with sausage recipes. Since then, I've discovered that grinding your own meat can save you both money and fat. Buying a beef or pork roast on sale, trimming it of most of the fat, and grinding it yourself can give you hamburger or sausage meat that is well over 90 percent lean and still less expensive than the fattier stuff you buy at the store. So now the grinder gets fairly regular use.

Hand Chopper

My daughter got this gem while she was in school in North Carolina. It was from one of those guys with the podium and the auctioneer's delivery and the extra free gifts if you buy it within the next 10 minutes. Neither of us has ever seen one like it since. The food processor has taken over some of its work, but it still does a great job chopping things like onions as fine as you could want without liquefying them.

Pasta Maker

I bought this toy after seeing it on a Sunday-morning TV infomercial. It's a genuine "As Seen on TV" special, but try not to hold that against it. Unlike the pasta cutters that merely slice rolled dough into flat noodles, this one mixes the whole mess and then extrudes it through dies with various shaped holes in them. The recipes say you can use any kind of flour, but I've found that buying the semolina flour that is traditionally used for pasta gives you dough that's easier to work with, as well as better texture and flavor. The characterization of it as a "toy" is pretty accurate. There aren't really any nutritional advantages over store-bought pasta. If you buy the semolina, the cost is probably about the same as some of the more expensive imported pasta. But it's fun to play with, it makes a great conversation piece, and the pasta tastes good.

Salad Shooter

We seem to end up with a lot of these gadgets, don't we? This is another one that's been around for a while, but it's still my favorite implement for shredding potatoes for hash browns or cabbage for coleslaw.

Sausage Stuffer

This is really an addition to the grinder. I found it at an online appliance repair website. It is really just a series of different-sized tubes that fit on the end of the grinder to stuff your ground meat into casings. I do this occasionally to make link sausage, but most of the time I just make patties or bulk sausage.

Slicer

This was a close-out floor model that I bought years ago. Before going on the low-sodium diet, I used to buy deli meat in bulk and slice it myself. Now I most often use it to slice a roast or smoked piece of meat for sandwiches.

Slow Cooker

Whatever the brand, no kitchen should be without one.

Smoker

This was another pre-diet purchase that has been used even more since. I started with one that originally used charcoal. Then I bought an add-on electric heat source for it that works a lot better in cold weather. Last year, the family gave me a fancy electric smoker that seals like an oven and has a thermostat to hold the temperature. Not only do I like the way it does ribs and other traditional smoked foods, but we also use it fairly regularly to smoke a beef or pork roast or turkey breast to use for sandwiches.

Springform Pan

This is a round, straight-sided pan. The sides are formed into a hoop that can be unclasped and detached from its base.

Steamer (Rice Cooker)

I use this primarily for cooking rice, but it does a great job steaming vegetables too. It does make excellent rice, perfect every time. So I guess the bottom line is that those of you who have trouble making rice like me (probably because, like me, you can't follow the instructions not to peek) should consider getting one of these or one of the Japanese-style rice cookers.

Stockpot

The key here is to spend the extra money to get a heavy-gauge one (another thing I eventually learned from personal experience.). The lighter-weight ones not only will dent and not sit level on the stove, but they will burn just about everything you put in them. Mine also has a heavy glass lid that seals the moisture in well.

Turbocooker

This was another infomercial sale. It is a large, dome-lidded fry pan with racks that fit inside it. You can buy them at many stores too, but mine is the "Plus" model that has two steamer racks and a timer. It really will cook a whole dinner quickly, "steam frying" the main course and steaming one or two more items. The only bad news is most of the recipes involve additions and changes every few minutes, so even if you only take a half hour to make dinner, you spend that whole time at the stove.

Waffle Maker

We don't use this often, but it makes a nice change of pace for breakfast or dinner.

Wok

This is a round-bottomed pan popular in Asian cooking.

After being diagnosed with congestive heart failure, Dick logue threw himself into the process of creating healthy versions of his favorite recipes. A cook since the age of twelve, he grows his own vegetables, bakes his own bread, and cans a variety of foods. He currently has a website www.lowsodiumcooking.com and weekly online newsletter. He is the author of *500 Low Sodium Recipes, 500 Low-Cholesterol Recipes, 500 High-fiber Recipes, and 500 Low-Glycemic-Index Recipes.*

INDEX